THE GREAT OKEECHOBEE HURRICANE

of

1928

The Story of the Second Deadliest Hurricane
in American History and the Deadliest
Hurricane in Bahamian History

WAYNE NEELY

iUniverse

THE GREAT OKEECHOBEE HURRICANE OF 1928 THE STORY OF THE SECOND DEADLIEST HURRICANE IN AMERICAN HISTORY AND THE DEADLIEST HURRICANE IN BAHAMIAN HISTORY

Some images courtesy of NOAA/NWS/NCEP/National Hurricane Center

iUniverse books may be ordered through booksellers or by contacting:

iUniverse
1663 Liberty Drive
Bloomington, IN 47403
www.iuniverse.com
1-800-Authors (1-800-288-4677)

Satellite image of Hurricane Andrew at peak intensity in August 23rd and 24th 1992 over the Bahamas. Hurricane Andrew was a small, powerful and destructive hurricane that made landfall over the Bahamas, Florida and Louisiana and Mississippi. Image courtesy of NOAA-The National Hurricane Center.

ISBN: 978-1-4917-5446-7 (sc)
ISBN: 978-1-4917-5445-0 (e)

Library of Congress Control Number: 2014921370

Printed in the United States of America.

iUniverse rev. date: 12/09/2014

DEDICATION

This book is dedicated first and foremost to all of the victims of the *Great Okeechobee Hurricane of 1928*. It is my hope that their stories will live on for future generations to read about and to appreciate why this storm was regarded as one of the 'Greatest and Deadliest Hurricanes of the North Atlantic!'

To my sister Alexandria who went home to be with the Lord at only 8 days of age.

To Mr. Les Brown, who at a conference held here in the Bahamas through his own unique way and method reminded me: 1) "Pass it on"; 2) "It is important how you use your down time"; 3) "Someone's opinion of you doesn't have to become a reality"; and 4) "In the time of adversity, expand!" To the late Dr. Myles Munroe, who always reminded me: 1) "Die empty!" 2) "Pursue your purpose!" 3) "Sight is the function of the eyes and vision is the function of the heart,"; and 4) "Maximize your potential." I listened to them, and this book is the end result...In memory of Dr. Myles Munroe, you may be gone but your legacy lives on...RIP

Thank you, Mr. Les Brown and Dr. Myles Munroe, for your invaluable contribution to my life.

Dr. Martin Luther King, Jr., once said, "Faith is taking the first step even when you don't see the whole staircase."

Mahatma Gandhi once said, "You must be the change you want to see in the world!" and "There are 2 types of people in this world, those that take the credit and those that actually do the work. Take my advice and follow the latter, as there is a lot less competition there."

Vivian Greene once said, "Life is not about waiting for the storm to pass...It's about learning to dance in the rain."

Nelson Mandela once said, "Education is the most powerful weapon which you can use to change the world."

CONTENTS

FOREWORD

The phrase "natural catastrophe" is an oxymoron; violent phenomena such as earthquakes and hurricanes being very much an integral part of the natural world. We like the phrase perhaps because it deflects attention from the true source of calamity: us. We build cities on the flanks of volcanoes and in known flood plains, relying on our collective amnesia to create an illusion of safety. It is thus that virtually every "natural disaster" has at its root its own particular tale of human failing. Each tale tells a rich and fascinating part of our history – a history we seem doomed to repeat.

Few Americans today know that the Great Okeechobee Hurricane of 1928 was the second deadliest natural disaster in U.S. history, and therein lies a story behind the story. Most of the dead were black migrant workers from the Bahamas, so little regarded in the Florida of the 1920s that they were not even counted in censuses, making an accurate death toll impossible. Florida's government was not much concerned about the welfare of migrant workers and was slow to respond to the catastrophe. The hurricane occurred at a time when the state was trying to recreate the tremendous real estate boom of earlier in the decade, a boom that was shattered partially as a result of the Miami Hurricane of 1926. The last thing it wanted was negative publicity about hurricanes. Even so, the haste with which this tragic event was forgotten is astonishing.

Wayne Neely is the ideal person to restore this great historical event to its rightful place in our consciousness. A professional weather forecaster and author, he grew up in the Bahamas hearing many hurricane stories and experienced his first while still in primary school. He is the author of nine books about hurricanes. The captivating story you are about to read sets the 1928 hurricane in the cultural, political and scientific context of

1920's America. Much as is the case with climate scientists today, weather forecasters of that era were under pressure from politicians and businesses not to 'scare the public'; this may help explain why highly trained Weather Bureau forecasters kept predicting that the storm would turn away from its inexorable march toward Florida's east coast. By the time they knew for sure that disaster was inevitable, it truly was. In the horrible aftermath, these same forces pressured the Red Cross to downplay the death toll so as not to frighten away real estate investors.

Mr. Neely skillfully tells the whole story of the 1928 hurricane disaster. It is the story of the clash of a sublime natural phenomenon with a human society that seems permanently unable to cope with it. And it is the age-old story of the victory of short-sighted moneyed interests over common sense and science, in which the losers are disproportionately the poor and neglected. It is a story of a storm, of 1920s America, and, alas, of our future.

Kerry Emanuel

American Professor in the Department of Earth, Atmospheric, and Planetary Science-Massachusetts Institute of Technology (MIT)

Kerry Emanuel (born April 21, 1955) is an American professor of meteorology, currently working at the Massachusetts Institute of Technology (MIT) in Cambridge. In particular, he has specialized in atmospheric convection and the mechanisms acting to intensify hurricanes. In May of 2006, he was named one of the *"Time Magazine's* 100 most influential people who Shape Our World." In 2007, he was elected as a member of the U.S. National Academy of Sciences.

He hypothesized in 1994 about a super powerful type of hurricane (hypercane) which could be formed if the average sea surface temperature increased another 15°C more than it's ever been. In the Bulletin of the American Meteorological Society, he put forward the conclusion that global warming is likely to increase the intensity but decrease the frequency of hurricanes and cyclone activity. In 2013, with other leading experts, he was co-author of an open letter to policy makers, which stated that "continued opposition to nuclear power threatens humanity's ability to avoid dangerous climate change."

Kerry Emanuel is Professor of Atmospheric Science in the Department of Earth, Atmospheric, and Planetary Science at MIT. He is the author of: 1) *Divine Wind: The History and Science of Hurricanes*, 2) *Atmospheric Convection* and 3) *What We Know About Climate Change.*

PREFACE

"*On the sixteenth of September, in the year of nineteen twenty-eight, God started riding early, and He rode to very late. He rode out on the ocean, chained the lightning to His wheel, stepped on the land at West Palm Beach, and the wicked hearts did yield. In the storm, oh, in the storm, Lord, somebody got drowned. Got drowned, Lord, in the storm!*"[1]

The chances are good that you have never heard of the Great Lake Okeechobee Hurricane of 1928, or if you have that it has long since been forgotten. Numerous books and papers have been written on the Great Galveston Hurricane of 1900, Hurricane Katrina, Hurricane Andrew and many other notable storms. The Titanic's sinking has been portrayed on film. Sadly, the Okeechobee's storm, the second largest peace-time calamity in loss of life, has been neglected. Now, for possibly the first time, you may learn about all aspects of this storm and from the survivors' own personal accounts of what it was like to experience such a cataclysm.

One word properly describes this hurricane, and that is "hell." A raging inferno of rolling, swirling waters, of shrieking, demonic winds, of lashing rain and of darkness, black and absolute. There were no atheists that night on the shores of Okeechobee. Then, for those still living, came the second phase of hell; the phase of desolation and despair; of searching in the flooded woods and marshes, in elder clumps and saw grass for the horrible remains of family members, friends and neighbours; of loading them into trucks by unending scores; and finally of burning them in heaps of dozens when they could no longer be transported. It is hard to know

---

[1]   Kleinberg, E. (2003) *Black Cloud-The Deadly Hurricane of 1928*, Carroll & Graf Publishers, pg. 95.

which hell was worse. Those who have experienced this storm firsthand have endeavored to erase the recollections from their memories.

This storm occurred in 1928. Racism was not only deeply entrenched-it was the norm and that played a significant role in the impact of the storm. To put it quite frankly, blacks were second class citizens in their own country, and it was even worse for the foreign migrant workers. In the heart of the black community, and among some of the oldest neighbourhoods in the city of West Palm Beach, at the intersection of Tamarind Avenue and 25th Street, sits an extensive 1-1/2 acre lot containing the remains of some 674 unidentified men, women, and children; victims of the Great Okeechobee Hurricane. At the Port Mayaca cemetery in Martin County, another stone marker was placed over a mass grave of about 1,600 victims. Near the Belle Glade Public Library in downtown Belle Glade, a beautiful memorial stands as a remembrance of the deadly storm and its devastation. They were farmers and migrant farm labourers of western Palm Beach County. Mostly blacks from the Bahamas, they were segregated even in death and were interred without coffins, as coffins were reserved for whites only.

Some 80 years later, community leaders such as, Robert and Dorothy Hazard and others came together and worked to have the site beautified and registered as a National Historic Landmark, ensuring the site and the dignity of those who died in Florida's most deadly hurricane is preserved. The September 16, 1928, Great Okeechobee Hurricane is the second deadliest storm in United States history. In total, the hurricane killed over 4,118 people and caused around $100 million (over $1.34 billion 2014 US dollars) in damages over the course of its path.[2]

The Earth's climate is a key protagonist in the story of humanity: our survival as a species has depended on cycles of freeze and thaw, days of storms or days of sunshine and the ability of our ancestors to adapt to changes in the weather and terrain. The warming and cooling of the planet's oceans and land are vital to its ability to support life. Humans and wildlife migrate from continent to continent and inhabit parts of the globe, seeking food and shelter, all at the mercy of the weather. As this book shows, life and weather go hand-in-hand, and one of my challenges as a meteorologist

---

[2]   http://en.wikipedia.org/wiki/1928_Okeechobee_hurricane.

is to anticipate these changes and pass it on to the public so they can be forewarned about some impending disaster or weather phenomena and make any necessary changes to protect their life and property. Choosing to press on or retreat in time, before the arrival of a severe storm such as a hurricane, can be a life-or-death decision. Hurricanes not only bring with them their strong winds, torrential rainfall or storm surge, but also the negative impacts of these storms on man's ever expanding society.

The changing weather of our planet—which has experienced hurricanes throughout its history-has of course, physically shaped the landscape, as well as the life it supports, and the superb descriptions and images in this book are a testament to this fact. Hurricanes presents the evidence of continuing cycles of wind, rain, cloud, and other atmospheric parameters in select regions of the world. Our planet's unique variety of climates is both surprising and spectacular. Of course, dramatic one-off events, such as storms, floods, and hurricanes, also bring chaos and devastation in their wake, leaving their own mark on the landscape, as well as on the history of a place. Long ago, hurricanes were thought of as a sign from a powerful deity; the hurricane is, in fact, a dramatic phenomenon brought about by the complex interplay of the difference in the heating of the Earth's atmosphere. While we do know that our climate is changing, the powerful images and descriptions of hurricanes here in this book offer a comprehensive picture of not only how far we have come in our understanding of hurricanes, but also how far we still have to go.

In September 1979, I was a student in a primary school located in the quiet community of South Andros, here in the Bahamas, when I experienced my first hurricane, called Hurricane David. I remember seeing the damage it did to my grandmother's house and the massive amount of trees uprooted in this storm. I can definitely say that it was this moment in history that I was first bitten by the 'hurricane bug' and was one of the deciding factors that help pushed me in the direction to pursue a career in meteorology. While in college, I studied the nature and dynamics of tropical cyclones and their global impact. I soon learned of the Bahamas and the United States' vulnerability to devastating hurricanes and that they were sitting ducks for a major hurricane disaster, and in fact, even today they still are susceptible to future hurricanes. But news about hurricanes always seemed to focus on Florida. Its extensive exposed coastline, uniquely flat land, shallow coastal waters, and the large Lake Okeechobee make it extremely prone to hurricane surge. Much of its existing land was originally swamp. Perhaps that's the way we should have left it—pristine, remote, full of wildlife, and very susceptible to hurricanes. Today, it is fair to say that it is too late for that now, with the major developments taking place in the state of Florida over the recent years.

Most of the land in Florida is within sixty miles of the ocean, making it and everything built on it extremely vulnerable to the ravages of hurricanes. Florida's exploding population is a major concern for hurricane planners. Every day 600 people move into the state of Florida alone, and 220,000 per year move into the coastal areas of Florida, and sadly, the majority of these new Florida residents have little or no hurricane experience. Nearly all of the state's residents live in or near coastal zones, which exacerbates the hurricane threat. Gusting winds coming from the ocean don't get much of a chance to slow down over Florida's flat, smooth, swampy landscape before impacting residents and their property. In fact, Florida's coastline is the most densely populated area of the state.

Unfortunately, hurricane waves have pounded every portion of Florida's coast. Florida's hurricanes have long been a significant factor in the overall vitality of the state. At times, hurricanes have literally changed the course of Florida's growth, development and history. The first changes likely occurred when Florida's indigenous peoples learned to adapt their living conditions to the threat of hurricanes. Many of Florida's economic woes have been associated with big hurricanes. In modern times, Florida's agricultural and tourist industries have sometimes faltered with the passage of major hurricanes. In 1992, Hurricane Andrew ravaged South Florida, temporarily crippled the state's home insurance industry by inflicting over $26.5 billion in damages, causing many insurers to pull out of Florida.

There was one hurricane and a tropical storm to impact the Bahamas in 1928. This was an extremely inactive year for hurricanes making landfall in the Caribbean and South Florida, but an active one for the Bahamas. Don't be surprised by this high total of two storms impacting the Bahamas in one year because the Bahamas is one of the most active areas hit by hurricanes and tropical storms in the North Atlantic. The Bahamas on average gets brushed or hit by a hurricane once every three years, and gets hit by a major hurricane once every 12 years. There are three Bahamian islands ranked in the top 10 impacts from tropical systems of all cities, islands and countries in the North Atlantic Basin, and they are Andros, Abaco and Grand Bahama. Third on the list is Grand Bahama, and it is affected once every 1.61 years, and since 1871 it was "brushed" or hit by a tropical storm or hurricane 88 times. The average years between direct hurricane hits are once every 4.06 years. Sixth on the list is Abaco, which is affected once every 1.78 years, and since 1871 it was brushed or hit by a tropical storm or hurricane 80 times. The average years between direct hurricane hits are once every 3.64 years. Seventh on the list is Andros. Andros is affected once every 1.82 years, and since 1871 it was brushed or hit by a tropical storm or hurricane 78 times. The average years between direct hurricane hits are once every 4.90 years.[3]

The first on the list of the most active areas to get hit or brushed by a tropical storm or hurricane is Cape Hatteras, North Carolina, which is affected once every 1.37 years, and since 1871 it was brushed or hit by a tropical storm or hurricane 104 times. The average years between direct hits are once every 4.30 years. Second is Morehead City, North Carolina, fourth is Grand Cayman, fifth is Wilmington, North Carolina, eighth is Bermuda, ninth is Sable Island, Nova Scotia, and tenth is Boca Raton, Florida. Palm Beach, Florida is number twenty-two on the list, which is affected once every 2.12 years and since 1871 was brushed or hit by a tropical storm or hurricane 67 times. The average years between direct hurricane hits are once every 5.68 years. Interestingly, New Providence, here in the Bahamas, is ranked 44th on the list and is affected every 2.41 years. It was brushed or hit by a tropical storm or hurricane 59 times since 1871. The average years between direct hurricane hits are once every 5.68 years. In the history of hurricane record keeping, one of the most active hurricane seasons (second only to the 2005 hurricane season which saw 27 named storms and one unnamed storm) on record in the Bahamas and throughout the region was the 1933 hurricane season (which produced 21 named storms that year), which saw four powerful hurricanes and a tropical storm affecting the Bahamas.[4]

---

[3] www.hurricanecity.com data base on the hurricanes of the North Atlantic. Information courtesy of Jim Williams- used with permission.

[4] www.hurricanecity.com data base on the hurricanes of the North Atlantic. Information courtesy of Jim Williams- used with permission.

On September 17, 1928, one of the most powerful storms of the twentieth century came unannounced into the lives of people of the Greater and Lesser Antilles, Puerto Ricans, Bahamians and Floridians, leaving utter devastation in its wake. The Great Okeechobee Hurricane, or Saint (San) Felipe Segundo (Spanish for 'second') Hurricane of 1928, as it came to be known, changed everything, from the landscape and its inhabitants' lives, to the Weather Bureau and US Army Corps of Engineers' practices, to the measure and kinds of relief Floridians would receive during this great storm and the resulting pace of regional economic recovery. Over the years, Florida, the Bahamas and the rest of the Caribbean have experienced many great storms. Some have been not very deadly or destructive, while others have left horrendous damage and a significant amount of deaths, but all have tested the spirit, strength, and resolve of the people they affected. Some have passed namelessly and uneventfully into meteorological history, while others on the other hand made their presence felt in a significant way.

Each storm has brought its own distinctive wrath, though at times only in a limited region, like the Lake Okeechobee region in 1928, which felt the full effects of the storm. We can indeed say that Floridians over the years have proved that they can adapt and recover from any and everything that Mother Nature can throw at them. The importance of our appreciation of the power of these storms was made very clear during the devastating 1928 hurricane season. The Great Okeechobee Hurricane of 1928, or Saint Felipe (Phillip) Segundo Hurricane, was one of the most destructive and powerful storms to strike South Florida. This system developed in the far eastern Atlantic, and then made its way into the Caribbean, and then over South Florida, inflicting massive casualties during its lifetime. Among the many South Florida residents and migrant workers whose lives were rocked by the Great Okeechobee Hurricane, little in these pages will surprise or amaze you more than the great impact this storm had on the state of Florida. Because of its incredible intensity and destruction, this storm remains a milestone in Florida's national hurricane archives. In the aftermath of this storm, those involved in the recovery effort faced enormous challenges, as you will see later.

This book does not attempt to report every single aspect of this storm, but instead offers a chronological account of the more significant aspects of this storm. It is compiled from a wide variety of sources, but relies heavily on the National Weather Service, the Bahamas National Archives and the National Hurricane Center records, Florida State Archives, other Caribbean countries storm statistics and numerous works by other weather historians. Newspaper and magazine reports, historical publications, letters, and personal interviews were also essential sources used to compile the information contained in this book. Photographs that document the impact of this great storm are historical treasures, and those taken during and after this storm are extremely rare. The images reproduced in this book were collected from museums, newspapers, libraries, government agencies and archives, relief organizations, businesses, and family albums. Furthermore, many individuals so graciously contributed to the completion of this work. Hopefully, by taking a look at this great storm of the past, we can gain some insight into the nature and recurrence of our hurricane risks of the future. Perhaps we can therefore better prepare for the next great hurricane that strikes the Bahamas, or Florida or anywhere else within this region for that matter. This compelling history successfully weaves science, historical accounts, and social analyses to create a comprehensive picture of one of the most powerful and devastating hurricanes to hit Florida to date.

Hurricanes have been described in various ways by the great thinkers of our time, from William Shakespeare, Christopher Columbus, Ralph Waldo Emerson, Benjamin Franklin, and even Alexander Hamilton. In many, if not all, instances, hurricanes have been painted at best as beneficent, nurturing and kind, and at worst as benign. That is not the hurricane you will meet on these pages. The hurricane here is closer to the one that the late, great writer Maya Angelou had in mind when she said, "Nature has no mercy at all. Nature says, 'I'm going to snow. If you have on a bikini and no snowshoes, that's tough. I am going to snow anyway.'"[5]

In this book, hurricanes strike ferociously and vigorously, and they blow violently in the form of strong, merciless winds, massive storm surges or torrential rainfall. The hurricanes in this book are furious, uncontrollable and quite often deadly. This walk through history lends context to the constantly active forces that are hurricanes, and then you will witness the fury of hurricanes firsthand, through compelling stories of utter devastating effects from hurricanes in general, and more specifically

---

[5] www.poemhunter.com/maya-angelou/quotations/page-4

from the Great Okeechobee Hurricane of 1928. Cameras record many things well, but they record few things as dramatically as they do with regards to this deadly hurricane.

What you will see on the pages that follow really happened, not only in our time, but also in the time of our immediate forbearers. Through stunning photography and awe-inspiring personal recollections of this storm, I will revisit the Great Okeechobee Hurricane of 1928 and answer the age old question of what caused this hurricane to be so deadly and destructive. Interspersed throughout this book are special sections that will help you understand the factors at play when hurricanes unleash their fury. If you've ever wondered what conditions bring about a hurricane, where and why they form, or how much energy is contained in a hurricane, you'll find what you seek in these chapters, illustrated by the most thrilling pictures of this hurricane gone wild that you will ever see. The fury of a hurricane is a terrible beauty to behold, and it's a fascinating topic of study and contemplation. This book allows you to see, learn and think. Furthermore, it allows you to thrill at the wonders—and the fury—of hurricanes.

Over the last 24 years of my life as a professional Bahamian meteorologist, hurricanes and their impact on my country of the Bahamas and the region as a whole have led me to write nine books on hurricanes. These books have allowed me to procure some of the best meteorologists in the business to write the foreword for me, from Bryan Norcross (Ph.D.), Hurricane Specialist at the Weather Channel; the late Herbert Saffir, co-creator of the Saffir-Simpson Hurricane Wind Scale; Phil Klotzbach (Ph.D.), from Colorado State University; Professor William Gray, from Colorado State University; Steve Lyons (Ph.D.), former Hurricane Specialist at the Weather Channel and now Meteorologist in Charge of the San Angelo NWS Office in Texas; Chris Landsea (Ph.D.), Science and Operations Officer at the National Hurricane Center; and in this book Kerry Emanuel (Ph.D.), Professor of Meteorology at Massachusetts Institute of Technology (MIT). This was done not only to add credibility to these books, but also to show the importance of hurricanes and their great impact on the lives of people of all walks of life here in the Bahamas and around the region. The weather affects everyone, and it is our constant companion whether we like it or not and can be as tranquil, as turbulent, as phenomenal, and sometimes as unpredictable as life itself.

INTRODUCTION

" The tempest arose and worried me so that I knew not where to turn; eyes never beheld the seas so high, angry, and covered with foam... Never did the sky look more terrible. The people were so worn out, that they longed for death to end their terrible suffering."[6] Columbus' description of the tempest is an experience that people in the Bahamas and Florida have faced many times over during the previous centuries. The belief in earlier times was that the extensive stream of winds rushing with great velocity was due to the anger of Tempestate, the Roman Goddess of Storms or Huracán, the Taíno Indians god of storms. Similarly, the word 'gale' originates from the Norse word 'galinn', which is the furious storm brought about by witches. The name 'hurricane' is derived from the Taíno and Mayan Indians' word 'Huracán', the god of thunderstorms and hurricanes.

Merciless, inconvenient, terrifying, powerful, dangerous, unforgiving, and deadly are some of the many terms used to describe the wrath of hurricanes. Although only a few natural disasters in U.S. history can compare to Katrina's catastrophe or Sandy's costly damage, those cataclysms are just two in an endless string of global tropical cyclone-related rampages. History, myth, folklore, and even literature are littered with hurricanes that have changed the course of history. In an instant, hurricanes can irreversibly alter the shape of our planet and the lives of millions of people. And yet, unlike volcanic eruptions and earthquakes, which can ravage with no prior warnings whatsoever, hurricanes are visible and evolving, emerging from a string of clues that offer the tantalizing promise of predictability—a promise, alas, that across the ages goes unheeded or unrealized, often with catastrophic and deadly results.

---

[6]   *Christopher Columbus Log Book*.

Hurricanes develop whenever the heat of the sun stirs air in motion to create a difference in air pressure and temperature—blowing out from areas of high pressure, where the air is cool, and sinking into areas of low pressure, where it is warm and rising, and it is in these low pressure locales that we find hurricanes developing here in the tropics. Near the equator, the sun's heat energy is at its most powerful. Here, its heat energy generates a gigantic wind machine that draws in winds from the north and south, controlling not only hurricanes, but also weather throughout the tropics. In the summer, the tropical sun beats down so strongly on the ocean surface that vast amounts of water turn to steam. Huge clouds then build up—each of which could become a cumulonimbus cloud. This cloud is a dense, towering, vertical cloud associated with thunderstorms and atmospheric instability, forming from water vapour and carried by powerful upward air currents high into the atmosphere. For a while, they remain separate and unthreatening, but given the spin of these disorganized storms, they become more structured and develop into a hurricane.

A hurricane is an extremely violent cyclonic cyclone, shaped somewhat like a funnel, that finds its origins in the tropical regions of the North Atlantic Ocean, with sustained winds in excess of 74 mph, and in the northern hemisphere, it moves anti-clockwise at speeds of average 6 to 15 mph. The center (averaging about 14 miles in diameter) is called the eye, and hurricane-force winds can extend well over 100 miles from the center. Usually the hurricane season extends from June 1st through November 30th, but both the Bahamas and Florida have experienced a hurricane in just about every month of the year. From space, hurricanes look stunningly beautiful, but the images mask a sequence of events when it comes to their strong, gusty winds, massive storm surges or their torrential rainfall that they inflict on us residents of the North Atlantic.

Florida, jutting like a thumb into the sea between the sub-tropical Atlantic and the Gulf of Mexico, is the most exposed of all states within the United States to hurricanes. Since hurricanes approach from the Atlantic to the east, the Caribbean from the south, and the Gulf of Mexico to the west, since it extends further southward than any state, Florida experiences numerous hurricanes which on average are more intense. Because of their frequency and severity, they are a most important factor in the Florida economy. Florida is considered synonymous with sunshine and is frequently called the Sunshine State, but mention of the state also brings to mind summer or fall tropical storms and hurricanes. These storms generally move in a westerly to northwesterly direction through the Caribbean and Atlantic toward Florida's east coast, and generally northward in the Gulf of Mexico or southern Caribbean Sea during the latter part of the season. Many Spanish galleons loaded with gold, silver, and other treasures have met a swift and untimely demise at the hand of a hurricane or tropical storm. As a result, treasure hunting is an active and frequently profitable business today in Florida.

In September 1928, the Great Lake Okeechobee Hurricane, began life near the Cape Verde Islands and developed into a massive Category 5 hurricane. Winds were as high as 160 mph, but it was the torrential rainfall and the lake and sea surges that did the most damage. The hurricane moved very slowly through the Caribbean and South Florida, causing widespread flooding, a massive death toll and the destruction of many settlements along its path. The economic effects in the Caribbean and South Florida were catastrophic. In total, an estimated $100 (1928 USD) million dollars (over $1.34 billion in 2014 US dollars) worth of damage occurred, severely hindering the development of these countries. In Martinique, approximately 85%-95% of banana crops were destroyed, 70%-80% of tree crops suffered severe damage, and 40% of sugar cane was completely ruined.

In Puerto Rico, some sugar mills ("Centrales") that had cost millions of dollars to build were reduced to rubble. Reports say that 24,728 homes were completely destroyed and 192,444 were partially destroyed. Most of the sugar cane fields were flooded, thus losing the year's crops. Half of the coffee plants and half of the shade trees that covered these were destroyed; almost all of the coffee harvested was lost. The coffee industry would take years to recover, since coffee needs shade trees to grow. The tobacco farms also had great losses. After this hurricane, Puerto Rico never regained its position as a major coffee exporter. Coastal damage in Florida near the point of landfall was catastrophic. Inland, the hurricane wreaked much more widespread destruction along the more heavily populated region around Lake Okeechobee, flooding and washing away most of the farms and homes.

The devastating Great Okeechobee Hurricane of 1928, which affected the Caribbean and South Florida, reminded us all of the devastating power of Earth's mightiest storms, called hurricanes. These are storms that are formed between the Tropics of Cancer and Capricorn in the Atlantic and Pacific Oceans, as well as the Indian Ocean. They have different names, depending on the location of where they are formed. In the Atlantic, they are called hurricanes; in the north-west Pacific, typhoons; in the Indian Ocean, they are known as tropical cyclones; while north of Australia, they are sometimes referred to as Willy Willies.

In September 1928, about 50,000 persons lived in South Florida. The land and real estate boom was already beginning to fade, although many subdivisions and new communities were still being built. The devastating Great Miami Hurricane of September 1926 had already sounded a loud alarm to the new residents about the vulnerability of their new homes to tropical cyclones. However, most of the damage from that storm was in Dade and Broward counties. Even so, a bellwether of what was to come occurred with the Great Miami Hurricane of 1926, as flood waters from Lake Okeechobee were swept by that storm into Moore Haven, the county seat of Glades County, killing over 100 persons.

The City of Palm Beach, founded only 34 years earlier by Henry Flagler, was incorporated in 1911 and had become a playground for the rich and famous, while West Palm Beach grew up on the opposite side of Lake Worth as a place where the support staff lived. The Atlantic breezes were balmy, and the climate was warm. On the opposite side of the county, a quite different situation was emerging. The rich, black muck soil near Lake Okeechobee was already being utilized for its tremendous agricultural productivity. The newly incorporated town of Belle Glade was growing steadily, fueled by the rapidly expanding agriculture in fields nearby. A rural, agrarian society dependent on migrant labour was plowing and harvesting along the shores of the lake behind a hastily built muck levee.

To recover potentially valuable farmland, the government started an ambitious project to drain the Everglades in 1910. As a result, workers built a series of canals to drain the water from the lake eastward and southward, thereby lowering the water level and drying out parts of the Everglades. An earthen dike spanning 5 to 8 feet high was built around the lake's south end to control the floods that came about after heavy rains. To cultivate the new farmland, farmers brought in much needed thousands of migrant workers, many from the Bahamas, which had similar climate and similar soil composition as that of South Florida. Several new towns developed on the shores of the lake. Belle Glade, on the southeastern shore, was incorporated in April 1928, and while it was home to thousands of sharecroppers and migrant workers, it had only 209 registered voters.

During most of the Everglades' reclamation, South Florida was spared a major storm. However, the Great Miami Hurricane of 1926 exposed the great susceptibility of the new lakeside towns to flooding from Lake Okeechobee. Passing just south of the lake, the storm's strong winds piled Okeechobee's water up against its southwestern banks, breaching the dike and flooding the town of Moore Haven, drowning hundreds of people. Two years later, a far worse disaster was visited on the southern shores of Okeechobee.

Only two years after the Great Miami Hurricane, what would become the second Category 4 hurricane to strike South Florida in as many years formed just off the coast of Africa in early September. It moved across the Atlantic and totally destroyed the island of Guadeloupe on September 12th, then moved through the Virgin Islands and made a direct hit on the island of Puerto Rico on the 13th, which was on the feast day of Saint Felipe (Phillip). Considering the ample warnings given, only about 312 persons were killed by this storm in Puerto Rico. It is known as the Saint Felipe II Hurricane because of the feast day on which it struck this island. To some extent, the devastation in Puerto Rico provided some advance warnings to the residents of Florida's east coast. It moved through the islands of the Bahamas on September 14th-15th, and on Sunday evening around 6:15pm, September 16th, the hurricane made landfall in the United States in Palm Beach County, between Jupiter and Boca Raton.

The second deadliest storm to strike the United States, the Great Okeechobee Hurricane of 1928, caused more than 2,500 deaths in Florida, and it is the deadliest storm of recent times. Hurricane Katrina claimed the lives of approximately 1,836 people. The hurricane occurred before the practice of assigning official code names to tropical storms was instituted, and thus it is commonly referred to under a variety of descriptive names. Typical names for the storm include 'Great Okeechobee Hurricane of 1928', 'the Saint Felipe II Hurricane', and especially in some older documents, 'the Great Florida Storm' or 'the 1928 Storm.' Its forerunner, Saint Felipe I Hurricane, was the second tropical cyclone of the 1876 North Atlantic hurricane season. Saint Felipe affected Puerto Rico for ten hours, killing nineteen people. Although there were only 19 deaths reported, historians suspected the Spanish Government withheld the actual damage and death toll data for Puerto Rico. At least two drowning deaths occurred in Onslow County, North Carolina.

The hurricane came straight over the West Palm Beach area, but its damage was not limited to that city. The pattern of destruction suggests it was a very large storm. It left damage along 130 miles of coastline from Vero Beach to Miami. Damage in coastal Palm Beach County was severe, especially in the Jupiter area, where the eye wall of the hurricane persisted longer than at any other location because of where the storm crossed the coast. A storm surge around 10 feet with waves likely as high as 20 feet crashed into the barrier islands, including Palm Beach. The greatest loss of life was around Lake Okeechobee. As the Category 4 hurricane moved inland, the strong winds piled the water up at the south end of the lake, ultimately topping the levee and rushing out onto the fertile land. Thousands of people, mostly non-white migrant farm workers, drowned as water several feet deep spread over an area approximately 6 miles wide and 75 miles long around the south end of the lake. Of course, the effect of the flood was devastating, and the loss of life, both human and animal, was apocalyptic. The horrible floods in the towns of Pahokee, Canal Point, Chosen, Belle Glade, and South Bay resulted in the drowning of many people, probably three quarters or more of whom were non-white field workers. The flood waters lasted for several weeks, and survivors were found wandering as late as September 22nd.

The primitive houses, many of which had been erected in the last two or three years, were instantly crushed, and the debris formed a rolling wall whose advance destroyed everything in its path. Those who escaped this onslaught sought refuge in trees, where many were killed by poisonous water moccasins also fleeing from the rising water. Several people were swept miles into the Everglades; a few managed to find their way back to civilization, but many never made it. Virtually everyone who had elected to ride out the storm on the lake islands, as did a group of migrant workers who, ignoring warnings that strong winds would return, ventured out during the lull accompanying the passage of the eye. Some 274 women and children survived aboard two barges that miraculously rode out the storm. Others managed to clamber onto the roof of the Belle Glade Hotel, the only building in that town to come through relatively intact.

Florida is a state in the southeastern region of the United States, bordered to the west by the Gulf of Mexico, to the north by Alabama and Georgia, to the east by the Atlantic Ocean, and to the south by the Straits of Florida. Florida is the 22nd most extensive, the 4th most populous, and the 8th most densely populated state of the United States. The state capital is Tallahassee, the largest city is Jacksonville, and the largest metropolitan area is the Miami metropolitan area. Much of Florida is a peninsula between the Gulf of Mexico, the Atlantic Ocean, and the Straits of Florida. Its geography is notable for a coastline, omnipresent water and the annual threat of dangerous hurricanes. Florida has the longest coastline in the contiguous United States and is the only state that borders both the Gulf of Mexico and the Atlantic Ocean. Much of the state is at or near sea level and is characterized by sedimentary soil. The climate varies from subtropical in the north to tropical in the south.

Florida's extensive ocean shoreline extends over 1,350 miles, and among the states, it is second only to Alaska's in length. Facing both the Atlantic Ocean and the Gulf of Mexico, its irregular coast is made up of barrier islands, sandy cusps, and keys broken and segmented by inlets, estuaries, rivers, and bays. Even though Florida covers more than 65,000 square miles, no part of the state is more than seventy miles from the Atlantic or Gulf coasts' waters. Its low-lying terrain, in some areas only a few feet above sea level, extends miles inland from the coast. Its many rivers, lakes, and glades are prone to flooding from heavy rains. Along with its position in a near-tropical sea, these physical features contribute to Florida's great vulnerability to the recurring effects of hurricanes and tropical storms.

It has become a ritual of every summer season. From half a world away, we tune into the local or international news stations and watch by satellite for embryonic tropical storms. We plot their growth, give them personal names, and track their every movement across the sea. With each new hurricane season, we wonder if this will be the year of a major, devastating storm. For some Floridians, fears about such a storm have become nightmarish realities in recent years. In 1928, the Great Okeechobee Hurricane blasted the southern end of the state and left an epic disaster in its wake. Often times, our attention remains focused on the recent hurricane events like Andrew or Katrina, but Florida has had a long and brutal hurricane history. Countless hurricanes have over washed its Atlantic and Gulf coast shores and scarred its interior counties. Through the centuries, thousands of Floridians have lost their lives in the desperate struggle against the waves and winds of hurricanes.

Weather is one of the common denominators of our lives. It helps shape our culture, character, conduct, health and everyday lives. It frequents the pages of our history and can change its course. It colours our conversations, folklore, and literature; it rains on our parades, awes us with its power and beauty, frightens us, and sometimes it even kills us. In many ways, weather and climate have played a significant role in the history and development of Florida. Early settlers were plagued by severe summer storms and mosquito borne fevers. But by the late nineteenth century, a new wave of developers advertised the beneficial effects of Florida's warm and balmy tropical climate and built extensive railroads and resorts to host droves of annual tourists. Agricultural interests also found wealth in Florida's long, favorable growing seasons. Hunters and naturalists enjoyed a bounty of wildlife unlike the range of wildlife found in any other state. Florida prospered because of its latitude and its great natural beauty. Today, millions are drawn to its almost winterless weather and the relaxed lifestyle that comes along with it. Its mild climate and seemingly endless beaches are two of the most inviting physical resources. Unfortunately, these same features make it a frequent target for dangerous hurricanes.

In the aftermath of the two great and very destructive storms that ravaged Florida in 1926, the people of South Florida gained a new respect for the awesome forces of these storms. After a quiet season in 1927, the first of two hurricanes in 1928 was taken very seriously. Even though it was a modest Category 2 storm that eventually landed up the coast from Miami-Fort Lauderdale area, great apprehension gripped the coastal residents of South Florida when the first storm warnings were issued in August. Many scrambled to board northbound trains or otherwise escape the area in advance of the storm. Fortunately, the damage from this first storm was modest. Some houses were unroofed, and frail ones were destroyed. Highways were flooded and in some areas completely washed away. Many bridges were undermined, requiring replacement. Many citrus trees were uprooted, and new plants had to be replanted in the wake of this storm. Only two deaths were reported in Florida, both in the vicinity of the Indian River. However, overall the damages to the state of Florida were relatively minor compared with other storms during this era. Unfortunately, this 'apparent' good luck would not last for long because on September 16th and 17th, the Great Okeechobee Hurricane would strike the state of Florida, causing catastrophic damage to the Lake Okeechobee region.

Before the system of assigning names to hurricanes was initiated during the early 1950s, some tropical storms and hurricanes were often named with reference to the year of their occurrence and the area they devastated, thus the name—The Great Okeechobee Hurricane of 1928. The word 'Great' simply meant that the storm had sustained winds or 136 mph or more. For those who lived through the storm, it remains the weather event of their lifetimes. The Great Okeechobee Hurricane, or Saint Felipe Segundo Hurricane, was a deadly hurricane that struck the Leeward Islands, Puerto Rico, the Bahamas, and Florida in September of 1928. It was the second recorded hurricane to reach Category 5 status on the Saffir-Simpson Hurricane Scale in the Atlantic basin, after the 1924 Cuba hurricane; as of 2014, it remained the only recorded hurricane to strike Puerto Rico at Category 5 strength, and it is one of the ten most intense hurricanes to make landfall in the United States.

The Great Okeechobee Hurricane of 1928—in the telling of Florida's extensive hurricane history, no other hurricane disaster can compare to its death toll of at least 2,500 persons in Florida. At the time of the catastrophe, many in South Florida said the actual deaths were over 2,300; some said it may have been as high as 3,500. Whichever figure is correct, it ranks among the United States' worst natural disasters. In fact, only the Great Galveston Hurricane of 1900 (over 8,000 persons), the Johnstown flood of 1889 (2,200 persons), and the two hurricanes of 1893 (2,000 persons each) are likely to have caused similar amounts of deaths on American soil. It arrived on the coast near Palm Beach on the night of September 16, 1928, just two years after the Great Miami Hurricane of 1926 devastated South Florida, and like its predecessor, it cast its most sinister blow on those persons who lived on the southern edges of Lake Okeechobee. Most of the storm victims were mostly black Bahamian migrant workers, who came to the region to be employed as farm labourers.

The Great Okeechobee Hurricane was a Category 4 hurricane that tracked across Lake Okeechobee's northern shore, causing the shallow waters to reach heights of more than 15 feet. The surge was forced southward, causing terrible flooding in the lowlands at the lake's south end, a region occupied primarily by black migrant workers. Thousands of these migrant workers died as the flood waters rushed over the area. After the storm, the Red Cross counted 1,836 dead, but still more bodies were discovered in later years. So in 2005, the National Hurricane Center in Florida revised the figure upwards to 'at least 2,500.' To prevent future similar disasters, dikes were built around the lake by the U.S. Army Corps of Engineers. This hurricane is ranked as the second deadliest hurricane to strike the United States and sixth most intense hurricane to strike the United States.

It is a huge lake; so big that standing at its shore is like staring at the wide and expansive Atlantic Ocean. For centuries, no white man saw it; even to this day, it is hidden not by mystery, but by a massive dike built after this hurricane in 1928. Native Americans called it "big water." Even today, locals still refer to it simply as "the lake." This lake, as they called it, remains one of the largest breadbasket farming areas of the United States. Along its southeastern shore is situated a number of farm towns, and one of the main ones is the town of Belle Glade. Along its main street, in front of its library, stands a compelling sculpture, which is motionless and silent but tells of a dramatic time in the Okeechobees' history. It portrays a man, a woman, and a boy running to escape a wall of water. The woman carries an infant in her arms. As they look over their shoulders, they raise their arms in a feeble attempt to ward off an unseen wall of water. Below the statue, a concrete relief shows houses, people, vegetation, animals swirling helplessly in water. What is absent in this sculpture is the deafening sound of the mighty rush of wind, the pounding torrential rains and the loud screams from the storm victims.

The majority of persons who died in this storm were black migrant workers, mainly from the Bahamas, US and other Caribbean islands. This hurricane may have also accounted for the most deaths of black people in a single day in U.S. history. One has to wonder if the hurricane had drowned 3,000 white elite businessmen in downtown West Palm Beach or disrupted a black-tie event on the high end of West Palm Beach instead of killing mostly black migrant workers from the Bahamas and rest of the Caribbean in the vegetable fields of Florida's interior, might it have received more attention over the years?

Palm Beach County is an area of two clear and distinct class contrasts of people. It is one of the largest counties in the eastern United States and is home to one of the world's greatest enclaves of wealth and society. Its glittering oceans, bright sunshine and balmy temperatures attract tourists from around the world. On the other hand, a half-hour drive several miles to the west opens you up to another world, one comprised of dirt roads, tractors, and never-ending agricultural farms. Even to this day, the people who work there do some of the country's toughest and most backbreaking work and live in some of its poorest towns.

In the mid to late 1920s, the North Atlantic was under the influence of La Niña atmospheric conditions, which is the opposite of El Niño. This resulted in increased hurricane activity during this period over the North Atlantic. El Niño and La Niña are opposite phases of what is known as the 'El Niño-Southern Oscillation (ENSO)' cycle. The ENSO cycle is a scientific term that describes the fluctuations in temperature between the ocean and atmosphere in the east-central Equatorial Pacific (approximately between the International Date Line and 120 degrees west). La Niña is sometimes referred to as the 'cold phase' of ENSO, and El Niño as the 'warm phase' of ENSO.

These deviations from normal surface temperatures can have large-scale impacts, not only on ocean processes, but also on global weather and climate. La Niña means 'the Little Girl' in Spanish. La Niña is also sometimes called 'El Viejo,' anti-El Niño, or simply "a cold event." La Niña episodes represent periods of below-average sea surface temperatures across the east-central Equatorial Pacific. Global climate La Niña impacts tend to be opposite those of El Niño impacts. In the tropics, ocean temperature variations in La Niña also tend to be opposite those of El Niño. During a La Niña year, winter temperatures are warmer than normal in the Southeast and cooler than normal in the Northwest. With these conditions brought about by La Niña, and with all other weather parameters being equal, there are typically more hurricanes during the La Niña phase; the opposite is true for El Niño. El Niño means 'the Little Boy,' or 'Christ Child' in Spanish. El Niño was originally recognized by fishermen off the coast of South America in the 1600s, with the appearance of unusually warm waters in the Pacific Ocean. The name was chosen based on the time of year (around Christmas time, during the month of December) during which these warm waters events tended to occur.

CHAPTER ONE

The History behind the word 'Hurricane' and other Tropical Cyclone Names

What is a hurricane? Simply put, it is a large, violent storm that originates in a tropical region and features extremely high winds-by definition, in excess of 74 miles per hour that blow anti-clockwise about the center in the northern hemisphere. It also brings drenching rains and has the ability to spin off tornadoes. Hurricanes are storms that form between the tropics of Cancer and Capricorn in the Atlantic, Pacific and Indian Oceans.

They have different names, depending on where they are formed and located throughout the world. In the Atlantic they are called hurricanes, in the north-west Pacific typhoons, in the Indian Ocean they are known as tropical cyclones, while north of Australia they are sometimes called Willy Willies. However, by any name, they are impressive to behold. To form, hurricanes need sea surface temperatures of 26.5°C or greater, abundant moisture and light winds in the upper atmosphere. Around 80 tropical storms form each year, with most of them occurring in the south or south-east of Asia. The North Atlantic region accounts for only a mere 12 percent of the worldwide total of tropical cyclones. These storms are enormous creatures of nature, often between 100 and 500 miles in diameter. They may last from a few days to a week or more, and their tracks are notoriously unpredictable.

A tropical cyclone is a powerful storm system characterized by a low pressure center and numerous severe thunderstorms that produce strong winds and flooding rainfall. A tropical cyclone feeds on the heat released (latent heat) when moist air rises and the water vapor it contains condenses. They are fueled by a different heat mechanism than other cyclonic windstorms such as nor'easters, European windstorms, and polar lows, leading to their classification as "warm core" storm systems. A fully developed hurricane is a vast heat engine. It has the power of 400 of the largest nuclear bombs, and enough energy to match the United States' electricity consumption for six months. The power comes from clusters of thunderstorms corralled together by winds into huge rings hundreds of miles across within the tropics.

The term 'tropical' simply refers to both the geographic origin of these systems, which forms almost exclusively in tropical regions of the Earth, and their formation in maritime tropical air masses. The term "cyclone" refers to a family of such storms' cyclonic nature, with anti-clockwise rotation in the northern hemisphere and clockwise rotation in the southern hemisphere. Depending on their location and strength, tropical cyclones are referred to by other names, such as hurricanes, typhoons, tropical storms, cyclonic storms, tropical depressions and simply cyclones, which all have low atmospheric pressure at their center. A hurricane consists of a mass of organized thunderstorms that spiral in towards the extreme low pressure of the storm's eye or center. The most intense thunderstorms will have the heaviest rainfall, and the highest winds occurring outside the eye, in the region known as the eyewall. In the eye itself, the air is warm, winds are light, and skies are generally clear and rain-free but can also be cloudy to overcast. When a hurricane reaches land, it begins to run out of energy. Yet it is here that it causes most destruction. Long before the main storm arrives, coasts are battered by huge waves stirred up by the winds. Winds circulates anti-clockwise, and so these waves are largest on the right side of the hurricane at the front—the right front quadrant.

Captain George Nares, a nineteenth century Scottish naval officer and polar explorer, was always on the lookout for hurricanes. "June-too soon," he wrote. "July-stand by; August-look out you must; September-remember; October-all over." Whatever you think about the dynamics of hurricanes-two things can be said about them, and that is they are very unpredictable and extremely destructive. The forces of nature, such as deadly hurricanes, have shaped the lives of people from the earliest times.

Indeed, the first 'meteorologists' were priests and shamans of ancient communities. Whatever lifestyles these ancient people followed, they all developed beliefs about the world around them. These beliefs helped them to explain how the world began, what happens in the future, or what happened after a person died.

The world of spirits was very important. Those people, who became noted for their skills at interpreting signs in the world around them, became spiritual leaders in their communities. All religions and different races of people recognized the power of the weather elements, and most scriptures contain tales about or prophecies foretelling great natural disasters sometimes visited upon a community because of the sins of its citizens. Ancient peoples often reacted to the weather in a fearful, superstitious manner. They believed that mythological gods controlled the weather elements, such as winds, rain and sun, which governed their existence. When weather conditions were favorable, there would be plenty of game to hunt, fish to catch, and bountiful harvests. But their livelihood was at the mercy of the wild weather because fierce hurricanes could damage villages of flimsy huts, destroy crops and generate vast floodwaters that could sweep away livestock.

In times of hurricanes, food shortages and starvation were constant threats, as crops failed and game animals became scarce when their food supplies dried up due to a hurricane. These ancient tribes, as you will see later, believed that their weather fortunes were inextricably linked with the moods and actions of their gods. For this reason, they spent a great deal of time and effort appeasing these mythological weather gods. Many of these ancient tribes tried to remain on favorable terms with their deities through a mixture of prayers, rituals, dances and sometimes even human sacrifices. In some cultures, such as the Aztecs of Central America, they would offer up human sacrifices to appease their rain-god Tláloc. In addition, Quetzalcoatl, the all-powerful and mighty deity in the ancient Aztec society whose name means 'Precious Feathered Serpent,' played a critical role; he was the creator of life and controlled devastating hurricanes. The Egyptians celebrated Ra, the Sun god. Thor was the Norse god of thunder and lightning, a god to please so that calm waters would grace their seafaring expeditions. The Greeks had many weather gods; however, it was Zeus who was the most powerful of them all.

The actual origin of the word 'hurricane' and other tropical cyclone names were based on the many religions, cultures, myths, and races of people. In modern cultures, 'myth' has come to mean a story or an idea that is not true. The word 'myth' comes directly from the Greek word 'mythos'(μύθος), whose many meanings include, 'word', 'saying', 'story', and 'fiction.' Today, the word 'myth' is used any and everywhere, and people now speak of myths about how to catch or cure the common cold. But the age-old myths about hurricanes in this book were an important part of these people's religions, cultures, and everyday lives. Often times, they were both deeply spiritual and culturally entertaining and significant. For many of these ancient races, their mythology was their history, and there was often little, if any, distinction between the two. Some myths were actually based on historical events, such as devastating hurricanes or even wars, but myths often offer us a treasure trove of dramatic tales. The active beings in myths are generally gods and goddesses, heroes and heroines, or animals. Most myths are set in a timeless past before recorded and critical history began. A myth is a sacred narrative in the sense that it holds religious or spiritual significance for those who tell it, and it contributes to and expresses systems of thoughts and values. It is a traditional story, typically involving supernatural beings or forces or creatures, which embodies and provides an explanation, aetiology (origin myths), or justification for something such as the early history of a society, a religious belief or ritual, or a natural phenomenon.

The United Nation's sub-body, the World Meteorological Organization estimates that in an average year, about 80 of these tropical cyclones kills up to 15,000 people worldwide and cause an estimate of several billion dollars' worth of property damage alone. Meteorologists have estimated that between 1600 to today, hurricanes have caused well over 200,000 deaths in this region alone and over 8 million deaths worldwide. Hurricanes, typhoons and cyclones are all the same kind of violent storms originating over warm tropical ocean waters and are called by different names all over the world. From the Timor Sea to as far as northwestern Australia, they are called cyclones or by the Australian colloquial term of 'Willy-Willies', from an old Aboriginal word (derived from whirlwind). In the Bay of Bengal and the Indian Ocean, they are simply called Cyclones (an English name based on a Greek word meaning "coil" as in "coil of a snake" because the winds that spiral within them resemble the coils of a snake) and are not named even to this day.

They are called 'hurricanes' (derived from a Carib, Mayan or Taínos/Arawak Indian word) in the Gulf of Mexico, Central and North America, the Caribbean and Eastern North Pacific Oceans (east of the International Dateline). A Hurricane is the name given to these intense storms of tropical origin, with sustained winds exceeding 64 knots (74 miles per hour). In the Indian Ocean all the way to Mauritius and along the Arabian Coasts they are known as 'Asifa-t.' In Mexico and Central America, hurricanes are also known as El Cordonazo, and in Haiti they are known as Tainos. While they are called Typhoons [originating from the Chinese word 'Ty-Fung' (going back to as far as the Song (960-1278) and Yuan (1260-1341) dynasties) translated to mean 'Big or Great Wind'...], in the Western North Pacific and in the Philippines and the South China Sea (west of the International Dateline) they are known as 'Baguios' or 'Chubasco'(or simply a Typhoon). The word Baguio was derived from the Philippine city of Baguio, which was inundated in July, 1911, with over 46 inches of rain in a 24-hour period. Also, in the scientific literature of the 1600s, including the book 'Geographia Naturalis' by geographer Bernhardus Varenius, the term whirlwind was used, but this term never achieved regional or worldwide acceptance as a name for a hurricane.

In Japan, they are known as 'Repus,' or by the more revered name of a Typhoon. The word "taifū" (台風) in Japanese means Typhoon; the first character meaning "pedestal" or "stand"; the second character meaning wind. The Japanese term for "divine wind" is Kamikaze (神風). The Kamikaze, were a pair or series of typhoons that were said to have saved Japan from two Mongol invasion fleets under Kublai Khan, who attacked Japan in 1274 and again in 1281. The latter is said to have been the largest attempted naval invasion in history, whose scale was only recently eclipsed in modern times by the D-Day invasion by the allied forces into Normandy in 1944. This was the term that was given to the typhoon winds that came up and blew the Mongol invasion fleet off course and destroyed it as it was poised to attack Japan.

On October 29, 1274, the first invasion began. Some 40,000 men, including about 25,000 Mongolians, 8,000 Korean troops, and 7,000 Chinese seamen, set sail from Korea in about 900 ships to attack Japan.

With fewer troops and inferior weapons, the Japanese were far outmatched and overwhelmed and were sure to be defeated. But at nightfall, just as they were attacking the Japanese coastal forces, the Korean sailors sensed an approaching typhoon and begged their reluctant Mongol commanders to put the invasion force back at sea or else it would be trapped on the coast and its ships destroyed at anchor by this typhoon. The next morning, the Japanese were surprised and delighted to see the Mongol fleet struggling to regain the open ocean in the midst of a great typhoon. The ships, sadly, were no match for this great storm, and many foundered or were simply dashed to bits and pieces on the rocky coast. Nearly 13,000 men perished in this storm, mostly by drowning. This Mongol fleet had been decimated by a powerful typhoon as it was poised to attack Japan.

With the second storm, even as Kublai Khan was mounting his second Japanese offensive, he was waging a bitter war of conquest against southern China, whose people had resisted him for 40 years. But finally, in 1279, the last of the southern providences, Canton, fell to the Mongol forces, and China was united under one ruler for the first time in three hundred years. Buoyed by success, Kublai again tried to bully Japan into submission by sending his emissaries to the Japanese, asking them to surrender to his forces. But this time the Japanese executed his emissaries, enraging him even further and thereby paving the way for a second invasion. Knowing this was inevitable; the Japanese went to work building coastal fortifications, including a massive dike around Hakozaki Bay, which encompasses the site of the first invasion.

The second Mongol invasion of Japan assumed staggering proportions. One armada consisted of 40,000 Mongols, Koreans, and Chinese, who were to set sail from Korea, while a second, larger force of some 100,000 men were to set out from various ports in south China. The invasion plan called for the two armadas to join forces in the spring before the summer typhoon season, but unfortunately the southern force was late, delaying the invasion until late June 1281. The Japanese defenders held back the invading forces for six weeks until on the fifteenth and sixteenth of August, history then repeated itself when a gigantic typhoon decimated the Mongol fleet poised to attack Japan again.

As a direct result of these famous storms, the Japanese came to think of the typhoon as a 'divine wind' or 'kamikaze' sent by their gods to deliver their land from the evil invaders. Because they needed another intervention to drive away the Allied forces in WWII, they gave this name to their Japanese suicide pilots as nationalist propaganda. In the Japanese Shinto religion, many forces of nature are worshipped as gods, known as 'kami', and are represented as human figures. The Japanese god of thunder is often depicted as a strong man beating his drum. The Japanese called it Kamikaze, and the Mongols never ever returned to attack Japan again because of their personal experiences with these two great storms. In popular Japanese myths at the time, the god Raijin was the god who turned the storms against the Mongols. Other variations say that the god Fūjin or Ryūjin caused the destructive kamikaze. This use of *kamikaze* has come to be the common meaning of the word in English.[7]

Whatever name they are known by in different regions of the world, they refer to the same weather phenomena a 'tropical cyclone.' They are all the same severe tropical storms that share the same fundamental characteristics, aside from the fact that they rotate clockwise in the southern hemisphere and counterclockwise in the northern hemisphere. However, by World Meteorological Organization International Agreement, the term tropical cyclone is the general term given to all hurricane-type storms that originate over tropical waters. The term cyclone, used by meteorologists, refers to an area of low pressure in which winds move counterclockwise in the northern hemisphere around the low pressure center and are usually associated with bad weather, heavy rainfall and strong wind speeds. Whereas, a tropical cyclone was the name first given to these intense circular storms by Englishman Captain Henry Piddington (1797-1848), who was keenly interested in storms affecting India and spent many years collecting information on ships caught in severe storms in the Indian Ocean. He would later become the President of the Marine Courts of Inquiry in Calcutta, India. He used the term tropical cyclone to refer to a tropical storm that blew the freighter 'Charles Heddles' in circles for nearly a week in Mauritius in February of 1845. In his book '*Sailor's Hornbook for the Laws of Storms in All Parts of the World*,' published in 1855, he called these storms cyclones, from the Greek word for coil of a snake. He called

---

[7] Emanuel, K.(2005) *Divine Wind-The History and Science of Hurricanes*, Oxford University Press, pgs. 3-5.

these storms tropical cyclones because it expressed sufficiently what he described as the 'tendency to move in a circular motion.'

The word cyclone is from the Greek word 'κύκλος', meaning 'circle' or Kyklos meaning 'coils of the snake', describing the rotating movement of the storm. An Egyptian word 'Cykline' meaning to 'to spin' has also been cited as a possible origin. In Greek mythology, Typhoeus or Typhōn was the son of Tartarus and Gaia. He was a monster with many heads, a man's body, and a coiled snake's tail. The king of the gods and god of the sky and weather, Zeus, fought a great battle with Typhoeus and finally buried him under Mount Etna. According to legend, he was the source of the powerful storm winds that caused widespread devastation, the loss of many lives and numerous shipwrecks. The Greek word 'typhōn' meaning 'whirlwind', comes from this legend, another possible source for the origin of the English word 'typhoon.' The term is most often used for cyclones occurring in the Western Pacific Ocean and Indian Ocean. In addition, the word is an alteration of the Arabic word, tūfān, meaning hurricane, and the Greek word, typhōn, meaning violent storm and an Egyptian word 'Cykline' meaning to 'to spin.'

The history of the word 'typhoon' presents a perfect example of the long journey that many words made in coming to the English Language vocabulary. It travelled from Greece to Arabia to India and also arose independently in China before assuming its current form in our language. The Greek word typhōn, used both as the name of the father of the winds and a common noun meaning 'whirlwind, typhoon,' was borrowed into Arabic during the Middle Ages, when Arabic learning both preserved and expanded the classical heritage and passed it on to Europe and other parts of the world. In the Arabic version of the Greek word, it was passed into languages spoken in India, where Arabic-speaking Muslim invaders had settled in the eleventh century. Thus, the descendant of the Arabic word, passing into English through an Indian language and appearing in English in forms such as touffon and tūfān, originally referred specifically to a severe storm in India.

The modern form of typhoon was also influenced by a borrowing from the Cantonese variety of Chinese, namely the word 'Ty-Fung', and respelled to make it look more like Greek. 'Ty-Fung', meaning literally 'great wind', was coincidentally similar to the Arabic borrowing and is first recorded in English guise as tuffoon in 1699. The Cantonese tai-fung and the Mandarin ta-feng are derived from the word jufeng. It is also believed to have originated from the Chinese word 'jufeng.' 'Ju' can mean either 'a wind coming from four directions' or 'scary'; 'feng' is the generic word for wind. Arguably, the first scientific description of a tropical cyclone and the first appearance of the word jufeng in the literature are contained in a Chinese book called '*Nan Yue Zhi* (Book of the Southern Yue Region)', written around A.D. 470. In that book, it is stated that "Many Jufeng occur around Xi'n County. Ju is a wind (or storm) that comes in all four directions. Another meaning for Jufeng is that it is a scary wind. It frequently occurs in the sixth and seventh month (of the Chinese lunar calendar; roughly July and August of the Gregorian calendar). Before it comes, it is said that chickens and dogs are silent for three days. Major ones may last up to seven days, and minor ones last one or two days. These are called heifeng (meaning black storms/winds) in foreign countries."[8]

European travellers to China in the sixteenth century took note of a word sounding like typhoon being used to denote severe coastal windstorms. On the other hand, typhoon was used in European texts and literature around 1500, long before systematic contact with China was established. It is possible that the European use of this word was derived from Typhon, the draconian Earth demon of Greek Legend. The various forms of the word from these different countries coalesced and finally became typhoon, a spelling that officially first appeared in 1819 in Percy Bysshe Shelley's play 'Prometheus Unbound.' This play was concerned with the torments of the Greek mythological figure Prometheus and his suffering at the hands of Zeus. By the early eighteenth century, typhon and typhoon were in common use in European literature, as in the famous poem 'Summer' by Scottish poet James Thomson (1700-1748):

"*Beneath the radiant line that grits the globe,*
The circling Typhon, whirled from point to point.
Exhausting all the rage of all the sky,

---

[8]   Emanuel, K.(2005) *Divine Wind-The History and Science of Hurricanes*, Oxford University Press, pgs. 18-21.

And dire Ecnephia, reign."[9]

In Yoruba mythology, Oya, the female warrior, was the goddess of fire, wind and thunder. When she became angry, she created tornadoes and hurricanes. Additionally, to ward off violent and tropical downpours, Yoruba priests in southwestern Nigeria held ceremonies around images of the thunder and lightning god Sango to protect them from the powerful winds of hurricanes. When these storms are over Senegal in West Africa near the Cape Verde Islands, the Senegalese pray to the sea god that give and take away life for protection from these storms. The elders of this nation chant supplications and toss a concoction of wine, grain, milk and water into the waves; priest cut a cow's neck and let it bleed into the surf, then throw its limbs into the water. They do all of this in hopes of appeasing the fickle, exacting sea and obtaining a quiet summer without storms.

In ancient Egyptian legend, Set was regarded as the god of storms. He was associated with natural calamities like hurricanes, thunderstorms, lightning, earthquakes and eclipses. In Iroquois mythology, Ga-oh was the wind giant whose house was guarded by several animals, each representing a specific type of wind. The Bear was the north wind, who brought winter hurricanes, and he was also capable of crushing the world with his storms or destroying it with his cold air. In Babylonian mythology, Marduk, the god of gods, defeated the bad tempered dragon goddess Tiamat with the help of a hurricane. When the other gods learned about Tiamat's plans to destroy them, they turned to Marduk for help. Armed with a bow and an arrow, strong winds and a powerful hurricane, Marduk captured Tiamat and let the hurricane winds fill her jaws and stomach. Then he shot an arrow into her belly and killed her and then became the lord of all the gods.

The Meso-American and Caribbean Indians worshipped many gods. They had similar religions based on the worship of mainly agricultural and natural elements gods, even though the gods' names and the symbols for them were a bit different. People asked their gods for good weather, lack of hurricanes, abundant crops and good health or for welfare. The main Inca god was the creator god Viracocha. His assistants were the gods of

---

[9]   Emanuel, K. (2005) *Divine Wind-The History and Science of Hurricanes*, Oxford University Press, pg. 21.

the Earth and the sea. As farming occupied such an important place in the region, the 'Earth mother' or 'Earth goddess' was particularly important. The Aztecs, Mayas, Taínos and other Indians adopted many gods from other civilizations. As with the Mayans, Aztecs and Taínos, each god was connected with some aspects of nature or natural forces, and in each of these religions, hurricanes or the fear of them and the respect for them played a vital part of their worship. The destructive power of storms like hurricanes inspires both fear and fascination, and it is no surprise that humans throughout time have tried to control these storms. Ancient tribes were known to make offerings to the weather gods to appease them. People in ancient times believed that these violent storms were brought on by angry weather gods. In some cultures, the word for hurricane means 'storm god', 'evil spirit', 'devil' or 'god of thunder and lightning.'

The word 'hurricane' comes to us via the early Spanish explorers of the New World, who were told by the Indians of this region of an evil god capable of inflicting strong winds and great destruction on their lives and possessions. The natives of the Caribbean and Central America had a healthy respect for hurricanes and an uncanny understanding of nature. In the legends of the Mayan civilizations of Central America and the Taínos of the Caribbean, these gods played an important role in their Creation. According to their beliefs and myths, the wicked gods Huracán, Hurrikán, Hunraken, and Jurakan annually victimized and savagely ravaged their homes, inflicting them with destructive winds, torrential rainfall and deadly floods. These natives were terrified whenever these gods made an appearance. They would beat drums, blew conch shells, shouted curses, engage in bizarre rituals and did everything possible to thwart these gods and drive them away. Sometimes they felt they were successful in frightening them off, and at other times their fury could not be withstood and they suffered the consequences from an angry weather god. Some of these natives depicted these fearsome deities on primitive carvings as a hideous creature with swirling arms, ready to release his winds and claim its prey.

There are several theories about the origin of the word 'hurricane'; some people believe it originated from the Caribbean Taíno-Arawak speaking Indians. It is believed that these Indians named their storm god 'Huracán', and over time it eventually evolved into the English word 'hurricane.'

Others believed that it originated from the fierce group of cannibalistic Indians called the Caribs, but according to some historians this seems like the least likely source of this word. Native people throughout the Caribbean Basin linked hurricanes to supernatural forces and had a word for these storms, which often had similar spellings, but they all signified death and destruction by some evil spirit, and the early European colonial explorers to the New World picked up the native names. Actually, one early historian noted that the local Caribbean Indians, in preparation for these storms, often tied themselves to trees to keep from being blown away from the winds of these storms. According to one early seventeenth-century English account, Indians on St. Christopher viewed 'Hurry-Cano' as a "tempestuous spirit." These ancient Indians of this region personalized the hurricane, believing that it was bearing down on them as punishment by the gods for something they had done-or not done. These days, there is more science and less superstition to these powerful storms of nature called hurricanes. Yet we humanize hurricanes with familiar names, and the big ones become folkloric and iconic characters, their rampages woven into the histories of the Caribbean, North and Central American coastal towns and cities.

Another popular theory about the hurricane's origin is that it came from the Mayan Indians of Mexico, who had an ancient word for these storms, called 'Hurrikán' (or 'Huracán'). Hurrikán was the Mayan god of the storm. He was present at all three attempts to create humanity, in which he did most of the actual work of creating human beings under the direction of Kukulkán (known by the Aztec name Quetzalcoatl) and Tepeu. Unlike the other Creators, Hurrikán was not heavily personified by the Mayans and was generally considered to be more like the winds and the storms themselves. In the Mayan language, his name means "one-legged." The word hurricane is derived from Hurrikán's name. Hurrikán is similar to the Aztec god Tlaloc.

In Mayan mythology, 'Hurrikán' ("one legged") was a wind, storm and fire god and one of the creator deities who participated in all three attempts of creating humanity. 'Hurrikán' was the Mayan god of big wind, and his image was chiseled into the walls of the Mayan temples. He was one of the three most powerful forces in the pantheon of deities, along with Cabrakán (earthquakes) and Chirakán (volcanoes). He also caused the Great Flood after the first humans angered the gods. He supposedly lived in the windy mists above the floodwaters and repeated "Earth" until land came up from the seas. In appearance, he has one leg, the other being transformed into a serpent, a zoomorphic snout or long-nose, and a smoking object such as a cigar, torch holder or axe head, which pierces a mirror on his forehead.

Actually, the first human historical record of hurricanes can be found in the ancient Mayan hieroglyphics. A powerful and deadly hurricane struck the Northern Yucatán in 1464, wiping out most of the Mayan Indian population of that area. According to Mayan mythology, the Mayan rain and wind god Chac sent rain for the crops. But he also sent hurricanes, which destroyed crops and flooded villages. The Mayans hoped that if they made offerings to Chac (including human sacrifices), the rains would continue to fall, but the hurricanes would cease. Every year, the Mayans threw a young woman into the sea as a sacrifice to appease the god Hurrikán, and a warrior was also sacrificed to lead the girl to Hurrikán's underwater kingdom. Also, one of the sacrifices in honour of this god was to drown children in wells. In some Maya regions, Chac, the god of rain and wind, was so important that the facades of their buildings were covered with the masks of Chac. In actual fact, at its peak it was one of the most densely populated and culturally dynamic societies in the world, but still they always built their homes far away from the hurricane-prone coast.

By customarily building their major settlements away from the hurricane-prone coastline, the Mayan Indians practiced a method of disaster mitigation that, if rigorously applied today, would reduce the potential for devastation along coastal areas. The only Mayan port city discovered to date is the small-to-medium sized city of Tulum, on the east coast of the Yucatán Peninsula south of Cancun. Tulum remained occupied when the Spaniards first arrived in the sixteenth century, and its citizens were more prepared for the storms than for the Spaniards. As the many visitors to these ruins can see, the ceremonial buildings and grounds of the city were so skillfully constructed that many remain today and withstand many hurricanes. The Indians of Guatemala called the god of stormy weather 'Hunrakán.' Of course, the Indians did not observe in what period of the year these hurricanes could strike their country; they believed that the devil or the evil spirits sent them whenever they pleased.

Their gods were the uncontrollable forces of nature on which their lives were wholly dependent, the sun, the stars, the rains and the storms.

The Taínos were generally considered to be part of the Taíno-Arawak Indians, who travelled from the Orinoco-Amazon region of South America to Venezuela and then into the Caribbean Islands of the Dominican Republic, Haiti, the Bahamas, Jamaica, Puerto Rico, and as far west as Cuba. Christopher Columbus called these inhabitants of the western hemisphere 'Indians' because he mistakenly thought he had reached the islands on the eastern side of the Indian Ocean. The word 'Taíno' comes directly from Christopher Columbus because they were the indigenous set of people he encountered on his first voyage to the Caribbean, and they called themselves 'Taíno', meaning 'good' or 'noble', to differentiate themselves from their fierce enemies-the Carib Indians. This name applied to all the Island Taínos, including those in the Lesser Antilles. These so-called Indians were divided into innumerable small ethnic groups, each with its own combination of linguistic, cultural, and biological traits.

Locally, the Taínos referred to themselves by the name of their location. For example, those in Puerto Rico referred to themselves as Boricua, which means 'people from the island of the valiant noble lords.' Their island was called Borike'n, meaning 'great land of the valiant noble lord.' Those occupying the Bahamas called themselves 'Lucayo' or 'Lucayans', meaning 'small islands.' Another important consequence of their navigation skills and their canoes was the fact that the Taínos had contact with other indigenous groups of the Americas, including the Mayas of Mexico and Guatemala. What is the evidence to suggest that the Taínos had contact with the Mayan culture? There are many similarities between the Mayan god 'Hurrikán' and Taíno god 'Huracán', also similarities in their ballgames and similarities in their social structure and social stratification. Furthermore, the Meso-Indians of Mexico also flattened the heads of their infants in a similar fashion to the Island based Taínos and their relatives.

In the 1930s, the Smithsonian Institute excavated a Chosen, Florida burial mound. On one distinct level of the Chosen mound, the graves of small-boned, short people with elongated heads were found, reminiscent of the Maya and very different from the tall, large-boned Calusas race in Florida. The Maya, a trading society, had trade routes that ran from Venezuela and Bacatá (Bogotá) to the Bahamas. Emeralds that could only come from the Chivor mines in Columbia were found in Mexico. On an expedition to conquer the Incas, Francisco Pizzaro intercepted an oceanic raft from Peru heading north to Costa Rico. A trade link or influence connecting Lake Okeechobee and the Meso-American Mayas was a real and intriguing possibility. One canoe dredged up in Boca Raton area in 1957—made out of a cypress tree trunk—was forty-six feet long. It was an ocean canoe, one that would take thirty people and trade goods to the Bahamas or Cuba. During the Spanish colonial period, it was not unusual for Calusa traders to make the two-day canoe trip across the Florida Straits to barter with their brethren in Cuba.

The Taíno Indians believed in two supreme gods, one male and the other female. They also believed that man had a soul and that after death he would go to a paradise called 'Coyaba', where the natural weather elements such as droughts and hurricanes would be forgotten in an eternity of feasting and dancing. In the Taíno Indians culture, they believed in a female zemí (spirit) named Guabancex, who controlled hurricanes, among other things-but when angered, she sent out her herald Guataba to order all the other zemis to lend her their winds, and with this great power she made the winds and the waters move and cast houses to the ground and uprooted trees. Representations of Guabancex portrayed her head as the eye of the storm, with twisting arms symbolizing the swirling winds. The international symbol that we use today for hurricanes was derived from this zemi. The various likenesses of this god invariably consist of a head of an indeterminate gender with no torso, two distinctive arms spiraling out from its sides. Most of these images exhibit cyclonic (counterclockwise) spirals. The Cuban ethnologist Fernando Ortiz believes that they were inspired by the tropical hurricanes that have always plagued the Caribbean. If so, the Taínos discovered the cyclonic or vortical nature of hurricanes many hundreds of years before the descendants of European settlers did. How they may have made this deduction remains a mystery to this day.

The spiral rain bands so well known to us from satellites and radars were not officially 'discovered' until the meteorological radar was developed during World War II, and they are far too big to be discerned by eye from the ground. It is speculated that these ancient people surveyed the damage done by the hurricane, and based on the direction by which the trees fell, concluded that the damage could only have been done by rotating winds.

Or perhaps they witnessed tornadoes or waterspouts, which are much smaller phenomena whose rotation is readily apparent, and came to believe that all destructive winds are rotary. They also believed that sickness or misfortunes such as devastating hurricanes were the works of malignant or highly displeased zemis, and good fortune was a sign that the zemis were pleased. To keep the zemis pleased, great public festivals were held to propitiate the tribal zemis, or simply in their honour. On these occasions, everyone would be well-dressed in elaborate outfits, and the cacique would lead a parade beating a wooden drum. Gifts of the finest cassava were offered to the zemis in hopes that the zemis would protect them against the four chief scourges of the Taínos' existence: fire, sickness, the Caribs, and most importantly devastating hurricanes.

The language of the Taínos was not a written one, and written works from them are very scarce. Some documentation of their lifestyles may be found in the writings of Spanish priests, such as Bartholomew de Las Casas in Puerto Rico and the Dominican Republic during the early 16th century. Some of the Taíno origin words were borrowed by the Spanish and subsequently found their way into the English Language and are modern day reminders of this once proud and vigorous race of people. These words include: avocado, potato, buccaneer, cay, manatee, maize, guava, barbacoa (barbecue), cacique (chief), jamaca (hammock), Tabacú (tobacco), caniba (cannibal), canoa (canoe), Iguana (lizard), and huracán or huruká (hurricane).

Interestingly, two of the islands in the Bahamas, Inagua and Mayaguana both derived their names from the Lucayan word 'Iguana.' Bimini (meaning "two small islands" in English), another island here in the Bahamas, also got its name from these Indians; however, most of the other islands here in the Bahamas and the rest of the Caribbean were also given Indian names, but they have been changed over the many years and centuries by various groups of people who settled or passed through the Bahamas or other Caribbean islands. For example, in the Bahamas the Lucayans called the island of Exuma-Yuma, San Salvador was called Guanahani, Long Island was called Samana, Cat Island was called Guanima, Abaco was called Lucayoneque, Eleuthera was called Cigateo, Rum Cay was called Manigua and Crooked Island was called Saomere. Christopher Columbus, when he came to the Bahamas and landed on

Guanahani, renamed it San Salvador, Manigua, he renamed it Santa Maria de la Concepcion, Yuma, he renamed it Fernandina, Saomete, he renamed it Isabella, and the Ragged Island chain he renamed Islas de Arenas.[10] However, for the early Spanish explorers, the islands of the Bahamas were of no particular economic value, so therefore they established only temporary settlements, mainly to transport the peaceful Indians to be used as their slaves in East Hispaniola and Cuba to mine the valuable deposits of gold and silver and to dive for pearls.

Jurakán is the phonetic name given by the Spanish settlers to the god of chaos and disorder that the Taíno Indians in Puerto Rico (and also the Carib and Arawak Indians elsewhere in the Caribbean) believed controlled the weather, particularly hurricanes. From this we derive the Spanish word huracán, and eventually the English word hurricane. As the spelling and pronunciation varied across various indigenous groups, there were many alternative names along the way. For example, many West Indian historians and indigenous Indians called them by the various names, including Juracán, furacan, furican, haurachan, herycano, hurachano, hurricano, and so on. The term makes an early appearance in William Shakespeare's King Lear (Act 3, Scene 2). Being the easternmost of the Greater Antilles, Puerto Rico is often in the path of many of the North Atlantic tropical storms and hurricanes that tend to come ashore on the east coast of the island. The Taínos believed that Juracán lived at the top of a rainforest peak called El Yunque (literally, the anvil, but truly derived from the name of the Taíno god of order and creation, Yuquiyú), from where he stirred the winds and caused the waves to smash against the shore.

In the Taíno culture, it was said that when the hurricane was upon them, these people would shut themselves up in their leaky huts and shouted and banged drums and blew shell trumpets to keep the evil spirits of the hurricane from killing them or destroying their homes and crops. According to Taíno legend, the goddess Atabei first created the Earth, the sky, and all the celestial bodies. The metaphor of the sacred waters was included because the Taínos attributed religious and mythical qualities to water. For example, the goddess Atabei was associated with water. She was also the goddess of water. Yocahú, the supreme deity, was also associated

---

[10]   Barratt, P. (2006) *Bahamas Saga-The Epic Story of the Bahama Islands*, Author House, pg. 51.

with water. Both of these deities are called Bagua, which is water, the source of life. This image of water as a sacred entity was central to their beliefs. They were at the mercy of water for their farming. Without rain, they would not be able to farm their conucos.

These Indians prayed to the twin gods of rain and fair weather so that they would be pleased and prayed to these gods to keep the evil hurricane away from their farms and homes. To continue her (Atabei) work, she bore two sons, Yucaju and Guacar. Yucaju created the sun and moon to give light and then made plants and animals to populate the Earth. Seeing the beautiful fruits of Yucaju's work, Guacar became jealous and began to tear up the Earth with powerful winds, renaming himself Jurakan, the god of destruction. Yucaju then created Locuo, a being intermediate between a god and a man, to live in peaceful harmony with the world. Locuo, in turn, created the first man and woman, Guaguyona and Yaya. All three continued to suffer from the powerful winds and floods inflicted by the evil god Jurakán. It was said that the god Jurakán was perpetually angry and ruled the power of the hurricane. He became known as the god of strong winds, hence the name today of hurricane. He was feared and revered, and when the hurricanes blew, the Taínos thought they had displeased Jurakán. Jurakán would later become Huracán in Spanish and Hurricane in English.

The origin of the name "Bahamas" is unclear in the history of these islands. Some historians believe it may have been derived from the Spanish word baja mar, meaning lands of the 'shallow seas', or the Lucayan Indian word for the island of Grand Bahama, ba-ha-ma meaning 'large upper middle land.'[11] The seafaring Taíno people moved into the uninhabited Southeastern Bahamas from the islands of Hispaniola and Cuba sometime around 1000-800 A.D. These people came to be known as the Lucayans. According to various historians, there were estimated reports of well over 20,000 to 30,000+ Lucayans living in the Bahamas at the time of world famous Spanish explorer Christopher Columbus's arrival in 1492. Christopher Columbus' first landfall in the New World was on an island called San Salvador, which is generally accepted to be present-day San Salvador (also known as Watlings Island) in the Southeastern Bahamas.

---

[11] Saunders, A. (2006) *History of Bimini Volume 2*, New World Press, pgs. 5-9.

The Lucayans called this island Guanahaní, but Columbus renamed it San Salvador (Spanish for "Holy Saviour").[12] However, Columbus discovery of this island of San Salvador is a very controversial and debatable topic among historians, scientists and lay-people alike. Even to this day, some of them still suggest that Columbus made his landfall in some other islands in the Bahamas, such as Rum Cay, Samana Cay, Cat Island, and some even suggested he landed as far south as the Turks and Caicos Islands. However, it still remains a matter of great debate and mystery within the archeological and scientific community. Regrettably, that question may never be solved, as Columbus' original log book has been lost for centuries, and the only evidence is in the edited abstracts made by Father Bartholomew Las Casas.

In the Bahamas, Columbus made first contact with the Lucayans and exchanged goods with them. The Lucayans-a word that meant 'meal-eaters' in their own language, from their dependence upon cassava flour made from the bitter manioc root as their staple starch food. They were sub-Taínos of the Bahamas and believed that all of their islands were once part of the mainland of America but had been cut off by the howling winds and waves of the hurricanes, and they referred to these storms as huruká. The Lucayans (the Bahamas being known then as the Lucayan Islands) were sub-Taínos who lived in the Bahamas at the time of Christopher Columbus landfall on October 12, 1492. Sometime between 1000-800 A.D., the Taínos of Hispaniola, pressured by over-population and trading concerns, migrated into the southeastern islands of the Bahamas. The Taínos of Cuba moved into the northwestern Bahamas shortly afterwards. They are widely thought to be the first Amerindians encountered by the Spanish.

Early historical accounts describe them as a peaceful set of people, and they referred to themselves as 'Lucayos,' 'Lukku Kairi' or 'Lukku-Cairi', meaning 'small islands' or 'island people' because they referred to themselves by the name of their location. The Lucayans spoke the Ciboney dialect of the Taíno language. This assumption was made from the only piece of speech that was recorded phonetically and has been passed down to us. Las Casas informs us that the Taíno Indians of the

---

[12]   Saunders, A. (2006) *History of Bimini Volume 2*, New World Press, pgs. 6-9.

Greater Antilles and Lucayans were unable to understand one another, 'here'(in Hispaniola), he wrote "they do not call gold 'caona' as in the main part of the island, nor 'nozay' as on the islet of Guanahani(San Salvador) but tuob."[13] This brief hint of language difference tends to reinforce the theory that the Bahamian Islands were first settled by people coming from eastern Cuba of the sub-Taíno culture.

Before Columbus arrived in the Bahamas, there were about 20,000 to 30,000+ Lucayans living there, but because of slavery, diseases such as smallpox and yellow fever (to which they had no immunity), and other hardships brought on by the arrival of the Europeans, by 1517 they were virtually non-existent. As a matter of fact, when Spanish Conquistador Ponce de Leon visited those islands in 1513 in search of the magical 'Fountain of Youth,' he found no trace of these Lucayan Indians, with the exception of one elderly Indian woman. These Indians of the Caribbean and Central America lived in one of the most hurricane prone areas of the Earth; as a result, most of them built their temples, huts, pyramids and houses well away from the hurricane prone coastline because of the great fear and respect that they had for hurricanes.

Many early colonists in the Caribbean took solace by displaying a Cord of Saint Francis of Assisi, a short length of rope with three knots with three turns apiece, in their boats, churches and homes as a protective talisman during the hurricane season. Various legends and lore soon developed regarding Saint Francis and his connection with nature, including tropical weather and hurricanes. According to tradition, if these residents untied the first knot of the cord, winds would pick up, but only moderately. Winds of 'half a gale' resulted from untying the second knot. If all three knots were untied, winds of hurricane strength were produced. Today, some descendants of African slaves in the West Indies still tie knots in the leaves of certain trees and hang them in their homes to ward off hurricanes.

Similar accounts also emerged from encounters with the Carib Indians. In old historical accounts, these Indians were referred to by various names, such as, 'Caribs,' 'Charaibes,' 'Charibees' and 'Caribbees', and they were a mysterious set of people who migrated from the Amazon jungles of South

---

[13]   Barratt, P. (2006) *Bahamas Saga-The Epic Story of the Bahama Islands*, Author House, pg. 51.

America.[14] They were a tribe of warlike and cannibalistic Indians who migrated northwards into the Caribbean in their canoes, overcoming and dominating an earlier race of peaceful people called the Arawaks. While Columbus explored all parts of the West Indies, his successors colonized only those parts inhabited by the Arawak or Taíno Indians, avoiding the Carib inhabited islands because they lacked gold, but most importantly because the Carib Indians were too difficult to subjugate. Ironically, the region became known as the Caribbean, named after these fierce Indians.

Their practice of eating their enemies so captured the imagination of the Europeans that the Caribbean Sea was also named after these Indians. The English word 'cannibal' is derived from the term 'Caniba', used by the Arawaks to refer to the Caribs eating the flesh of their enemies. Their raids were made over long distances in large canoes and had as one of their main objectives to take the Arawak women as their captives, wives and slaves. While on the other hand, the captured Arawak men were tortured and killed and then barbecued and eaten during an elaborate ceremony because it was believed that if they did this, they would obtain their enemies' personal power and control their spirits. The French traveller Charles de Rochefort wrote that when these Caribs Indians heard the thunder clap, they would "make all the haste they can to their little houses and sit down on low stools about the fire, covering their faces and resting their heads on their hands and knees, and in that posture they fall a weeping and say...Maboya is very angry with them: and they say the same when there happens a Hurricane."[15]

The Caribs were terrified of spilling fresh water into the sea because they believed that it aroused the anger of hurricanes. They had no small stone gods but believed in good and powerful bad spirits called 'Maboya', which caused all the misfortunes of their lives. They even wore carved amulets and employed medicine men to drive the evil Maboya away. When a great and powerful storm began to rise out of the sea, the Caribs blew frantically into the air to chase it away and chewed manioc bread and spat it into the wind for the same purpose. When that was no use, they gave way to panic and crouched in their communal houses, moaning with their

---

14   Saunders, A. (2006) *History of Bimini Volume 2*, New World Press, pg. 14.
15   Mulcahy, M. (2006) *Hurricanes and Society in the British Greater Caribbean, 1624-1783*, The John Hopkins University Press, pg. 35.

arms held over their heads. They felt that they were reasonably safe there because they fortified their houses with corner posts dug deep into the ground. They also believed that beyond the Maboya were great spirits, the male sun and the female moon. They believed that the spirits of the stars controlled the weather. They also believed in a bird named Savacou, which was sent out by the angry Maboya to call up the hurricane, and after this task was finished, this bird would then be transformed into a star.

According to noted English Historian John Oldmixon of the late 1600's and early 1700's, he reported that the Carib Indians excelled in forecasting hurricanes. Writing about a hurricane that occurred in 1740 on the island of St. Christopher he said:- "Hurricanes are still frequent here, and it was some time since the custom of both the English and French inhabitants in this and the other Charibbees-Islands, to send about the month of June, to the native Charibbees of Dominica and St. Vincent, to know whether there would be any hurricanes that year; and about 10 or 12 Days before the hurricane came they constantly sent them word, and it was rarely failed." According to Carib Indians 'Signs or Prognosticks,' a hurricane comes "on the day of the full change, or quarters of the moon. If it will come on the full moon, you being in the change, then observe these signs. That day you will see the skies very turbulent, the sun more red than at other times, a great calm, and the hills clear of clouds or fogs over them, which in the high-lands are seldom so. In the hollows of the Earth or wells, there will be great noise, as if you were in a great storm; the stars at night will look very big with Burs about them, the north-west sky smelling stronger than at other times, as it usually does in violent storms; and sometimes that day for an hour or two, the winds blows very hard westerly, out of its usual course. On the full moon you have the same signs, but a great Bur about the moon, and many about the moon, and many about the sun. The like signs must be taken notice of on the quarter-days of the moon."[16]

According to several elderly Carib Indians, hurricanes had become more frequent in the recent years following the arrival of the Europeans to the Caribbean, which they viewed as punishment for their interactions

---

[16]   *An Early Colonial Historian: John Oldmixon and the British Empire in America-Journal of American Studies Vol.3 (August, 1973)*, Cambridge University Press, pgs. 113-123.

with them. In fact, as early as the 1630s, English colonists reported that Carib Indians knew when storms would strike by the number of rings that appeared around the moon: three rings meant the storm would arrive in three days, two rings meant two days and one ring meant the storm would arrive in one day. Of course, the connection between such signs and the onset of hurricanes was indeed a very unreliable way to predict the onset of hurricanes. The Carib Indians, while raiding islands in the Caribbean, would kill off the Arawak men and take the Arawak women as wives and mothers to their children. Actually, when the Europeans came to the Caribbean, they surprisingly found that many Carib women spoke the Taíno language because of the large number of female Taíno captives among them. So, it is speculated that a word like 'hurricane' was passed into the Carib speech, and this was how these fierce people learned about the terror of these savage storms. Native Indians of the West Indies often engaged in ritual purifications and sacrifices and offered songs and dances to help ward off hurricanes.

An Aztec myth tells that when the gods created the world, it was dark and cold. The youngest of the gods sacrificed himself to create a sun. But it was like him, weak, dim and feeble. Only when more powerful gods offered themselves did the sun blaze into life and shine brightly on them. However, there was one disadvantage, and that was that these gods needed constant fuel, human lives and the Aztecs obliged. They offered tens of thousands of human sacrifices a year just to make sure that the sun rose each morning and to prevent natural disasters such as devastating hurricanes from destroying their communities and villages. Tlaloc was an important deity in Aztec religion, a god of rain, fertility, and water. He was a beneficent god who gave life and sustenance, but he was also feared for his ability to send hurricanes, hail, thunder and lightning and for being the lord of the powerful element of water. In Aztec iconography, he is usually depicted with goggle eyes and fangs. He was associated with caves, springs and mountains. He is known for having demanded child sacrifices.

The Aztec god Tezcatlipoca (meaning Lord of the Hurricane) was believed to have special powers over the hurricane winds, as did the Palenque god Tahil (Obsidian Mirror) and the Quiché Maya sky god Huracán. The Aztec god Tezcatlipoca was feared for his capricious nature and the Aztecs called him Yaotl (meaning 'Adversary'). Tonatiuh was the

Aztec Sun god, and the Aztecs saw the sun as a divinity that controlled the weather, including hurricanes and consequently, all human life forms. The Aztecs of Mexico, in particular, built vast temples to the sun god Tonatiuh and made bloody sacrifices of both human and animal to persuade him to shine brightly on them and in particular not send any destructive hurricanes their way and to allow prosperity for their crops. When they built these temples, they were constructed according to the Earth's alignment with the sun, but most importantly they were always constructed with hurricanes in mind and away from the hurricane-prone coastline.

The Aztec people considered Tonatiuh the leader of Tollán, their heaven. He was also known as the fifth sun because the Aztecs believed that he was the sun that took over when the fourth sun was expelled from the sky. Mesoamerican creation narratives proposed that before the current world age began, there were a number of previous creations. The Aztecs' account of the five suns or world ages revealed that in each of the five creations, the Earth's inhabitants found a more satisfactory staple food than eaten by their predecessors. In the era of the first sun, which was governed by Black Tezcatlipoca, the world was inhabited by a race of giants who lived on acorns. The second sun, whose presiding god was a serpent god called Quetzatzalcóatl, was believed to be the creator of life and in control of the vital rain-bearing winds, and he saw the emergence of a race of primitive humans who lived on the seeds of the mesquite tree.

After the third age, which was ruled by Tláloc, in which people lived on plants that grew on water, such as the water lily, people returned to a diet of wild seeds in the fourth age of Chalchiúhtlicue. It was only in the fifth and current age, an age subject to the sun god Tonatiuh that the people of Mesoamerica learned how to plant and harvest maize. According to their cosmology, each sun was a god with its own cosmic era. The Aztecs believed they were still in Tonatiuh's era, and according to their creation mythology, this god demanded human sacrifices as a tribute, and without it he would refuse to move through the sky, hold back on the rainfall for their crops and would send destructive hurricanes their way. It is said that some 20,000 people were sacrificed each year to Tonatiuh and other gods, though this number, however, is thought to be highly inflated either by the Aztecs, who wanted to inspire fear in their enemies, or the Spaniards, who wanted to speak-ill of the Aztecs. The Aztecs were fascinated by the sun, so they worshiped and carefully observed it and had a solar calendar second only in accuracy to the Mayans.

It was Captain Fernando de Oviedo who gave these storms their modern name when he wrote, "So when the devil wishes to terrify them, he promises them the 'Huracan,' which means tempest."[17] The Portuguese word for them is Huracao, which is believed to have originated from the original Taíno word Huracán. The Native American Indians had a word for these powerful storms, which they called 'Hurucane', meaning 'evil spirit of the wind.' When a hurricane approached the Florida coast, the medicine men of the North American Indians worked frantic incantations to drive the evil hurricane away. There's a folklore that the Seminole Indians can mystically sense a storm well ahead of time by watching the sawgrass bloom. These Indians of Florida were actually the first to flee from a storm, citing the blooming of the Florida Everglades sawgrass. They believed that only 'an atmospheric condition' such as a major hurricane would cause the pollen to bloom on the sawgrass several days before a hurricane's arrival, giving the native Indians an advanced warning of the impending storm. Black educator Mary McLeod Bethune repeated a story that these Indians were seen leaving several days before the storm, saying, "Follow Indian, Indian no fool, going to dry land, big water coming." One has to wonder if the Seminoles, like other Indians of the region, had a 'sixth sense' when it came to hurricanes.

Many other sub-culture Indians had similar words for these powerful storms, which they all feared and respected greatly. The Quiche people of southern Guatemala believed in the god Huraken, for their god of thunder and lightning. For example, the Galibi Indians of Dutch and French Guiana called these hurricanes Yuracan and Hyroacan or simply the devil. Other Guiana Indians called them Yarukka, and other similar Indian names were Hyrorokan, aracan, urican, huiranvucan, Yurakon, Yuruk or Yoroko. As hurricanes were becoming more frequent in the Caribbean, many of the colonists and natives of this region had various words and spellings, all sounding phonetically similar for these powerful storms. The English called them 'Hurricanes', 'Haurachana', 'Uracan', 'Herocano', 'Harrycane', 'Tempest', and 'Hyrracano.' The Spanish called them 'Huracán'and 'Furicane', and the Portuguese called them 'Huracao', and 'Furicane.' The French had for a long time adapted the Indian word called 'Ouragan', and the Dutch referred to them as 'Orkan.' These various spellings were used until the word 'hurricane' was finally settled on in the English Language. Among the Caribbean, Central and North American peoples, the word 'hurricane' seems to have always been associated with evil spirits and violence.

After his first voyage to the New World, Columbus returned to Isabella in Hispaniola with seventeen ships. Columbus' settlers built houses, storerooms, a Roman Catholic Church, and a large house for Columbus. He brought more than a thousand men, including sailors, soldiers, carpenters, stonemasons, and other workers. Priests and nobles came as well. The Spaniards brought pigs, horses, wheat, sugarcane, and guns. Rats and microbes came with them as well. The settlement took up more than two hectares. At the time, some estimated the Taíno Indian population in Hispaniola to be as high as one million persons. They lived on fish and staples such as pineapple, which they introduced to the Spaniards. The food that they provided was important to the Spaniards. Describing these Indians, Columbus said that there were no finer people in the world. In March 1494, Columbus' men began to search, with Taíno Indians, in the mountains of Hispaniola for gold, and small amounts were found. In June 1495, a large storm that the Taíno Indians called a hurricane hit the island. The Indians retreated to the mountains, while the Spaniards remained in the colony. Several ships were sunk, including the flagship, the 'Marie-Galante.'

Christopher Columbus, on his first voyage, managed to avoid encountering any hurricanes but it wasn't until some of his later voyages that he encountered several hurricanes that disrupted these voyages to the New World. Based on his first voyage before encountering any hurricanes, Columbus concluded that the weather in the New World was benign: "In all the Indies, I have always found May-like weather," he commented. Although sailing through hurricane-prone waters during the most dangerous months, he did not have any serious hurricane encounters on his early voyage. However, on his final voyages, Christopher Columbus himself weathered at least three of these dangerous storms. The town of La Isabella was struck by two of the earliest North Atlantic hurricanes observed by Europeans in 1494 and 1495. Columbus provided the earliest account of a hurricane in a letter written to Queen Isabella in 1494. In this letter, he wrote, "The tempest arose and worried me so that I knew not where to turn; Eyes never behold the seas so high, angry and covered by foam. We were forced to keep out in this bloody ocean, seething like a pot of hot fire. Never did the sky look more terrible; for one whole day and night it blazed like a furnace. The flashes came with such fury and frightfulness that we all thought the ships would be blasted. All this time the water never ceased to fall from the sky...The people were so worn out, that they longed for death to end their terrible suffering."[18]

The extensive shallow banks and coral reefs in the vicinity of most Caribbean islands present hazards to navigation that were immediately appreciated by the Spanish explorers. These dangers were compounded by violent tropical storms and hurricanes that appeared without sufficient warning and by the unseaworthy character of vessels that had spent months cruising in shipworm-infested waters. Despite the explorers' exercising what must have seemed like due caution, there is an extensive list of shipwrecks. Columbus himself lost nine ships: Santa María, which was wrecked near Haiti on Christmas Eve on his first voyage; Niña and three other vessels at La Isabella in 1495; and the entire fleet of his fourth voyage-Vizcaina and Gallega off the coast of Central America in 1503, and Capitana and Santiago in Puerto Santa Gloria, Jamaica, 1504. However, as early as June of 1494, the small town of Isabella, founded by Columbus on Hispaniola, became the first European settlement destroyed by a hurricane. The Spaniards who accompanied Columbus on his four voyages to the New World took back to Europe with them a new concept of what a severe storm could be, and naturally, a new word of Indian origin. It seems that the Indian word was pronounced 'Furacán' or 'Furacánes' during the early years of discovery and colonization of America. Peter Martyr, one of the earliest historians of the New World, said that they were called by the natives 'Furacanes,' although the plural is obviously Spanish. The Rev. P. du Tertre, (1667) in his great work during the middle of the seventeenth century, wrote first 'ouragan', and later 'houragan.'

---

[18] http://www.fascinatingearth.com/node/311

After 1474, some changes in the Spanish language were made. For instance, words beginning with 'h' were pronounced using the 'f' consonant.' The kingdoms of Aragon and Castile were united in 1474, before the discovery of America, and after that time some changes in the Spanish language were made. One of them involved words beginning with the letter 'h.' In Aragon, they pronounced such words as 'f'. As Menéndez Pidal said, "Aragon was the land of the 'f', but the old Castilian lost the sound or pronunciation," so that Spanish Scholar Nebrija (Nebrija wrote a grammar of the Castilian language and is credited as the first published grammar of any Romance language) wrote, instead of the lost 'f', an aspirated 'h.' Menéndez wrote concerning the pronunciation of the word 'hurricane' and its language used by Fernando Colón, son of Christopher Columbus, "Vacillation between 'f' and 'h' is very marked predominance of the 'h.' And so, the 'h' became in Spanish a silent letter, as it still is today."

Father Bartholomew de Las Casas, referring to one of these storms, wrote: "At this time the four vessels brought by Juan Aguado were destroyed in the port (of Isabella) by a great tempest, called by the Indians in their language 'Furacán.' Now we call them hurricanes, something that almost all of us have experienced at sea or on land..."[19] Las Casas, outraged by the brutal treatment of the Indians on Hispaniola, declared that the wrath of the hurricane that struck Hispaniola was the judgment of God on the city and the men who had committed such sins against humanity. All other European languages coined a word for the tropical cyclone, based on the Spanish 'Huracán.' Gonzalo Fernandez de Oviedo (Oviedo y Valdes, 1851, Book VI, Ch. III) is more explicit in his writings concerning the origin of the word 'hurricane.' He says: "Hurricane, in the language of this island, properly means an excessively severe storm or tempest; because, in fact, it is only a very great wind and a very great and excessive rainfall, both together or either these two things by themselves." Oviedo further noted

---

[19] Millas, C.J. (1968) *Hurricanes of The Caribbean and Adjacent Regions 1492-1800*, Edward Brothers Inc/ Academy of Arts and Sciences of the Americas Miami, Florida. Pg. xi.

that the winds of the 'Huracán' were so "fierce that they topple houses and uproot many large trees."[20]

Even in the English Language, the word 'hurricane' evolved through several variations. For example, William Shakespeare mentioned it in his play 'King Lear', where he wrote "Blow, winds, and crack your cheeks! Rage! Blow! You catracts and hurricanes, spout till you have drench'd out steeples, drown'd the cocks!" Girolamo Benzoni, in 1565 in his Book History of the New World, mentioned his encounter with a hurricane in Hispaniola, which at the time he referred to as 'Furacanum.' "In those days a wondrous and terrible disaster occurred in this country. At sunrise such a horrible, strong wind began that the inhabitants of the island thought they had never seen or heard anything like it before. The raging storm wind (which the Spaniards called Furacanum) came with great violence, as if it wanted to spit heaven and Earth apart from one another, and hurl everything to the ground...The people were as a whole so despairing because of their great fear that they run here and there, as if they were senseless and mad, and did not know what they did...The strong and frightful wind threw some entire houses and capitals including the people from the capital, tore them apart in the air and threw them down to the ground in pieces. This awful weather did such noticeable damage in such a short time that not three ships stood secure in the sea harbour or came through the storm undamaged. For the anchors, even if they were yet strong, were broken apart through the strong force of the wind and all the masts, despite their being new, were crumpled. The ships were blown around by the wind, so that all the people in them were drowned. For the most part the Indians had crawled away and hidden themselves in holes in order to escape such disaster."[21]

As stated earlier, Christopher Columbus did not learn on his first voyage, the voyage of discovery, of the existence of such terrible 'tempests' or 'storms.' He had the exceptional good fortune of not being struck by any of them during this voyage. The Indians, while enjoying pleasant weather, had no reason to speak about these storms to a group of strangers who

---

[20] Millas, C.J. (1968) *Hurricanes of The Caribbean and Adjacent Regions 1492-1800*, Edward Brothers Inc/ Academy of Arts and Sciences of the Americas Miami, Florida. Pg. xi.

[21] Benzon, G. (1837) *History of the New World Vol. 21*, Hakluyt Society.

spoke a language that they could not understand. Naturally, Columbus did not say one word about these awful storms in his much celebrated letter "The letter of Columbus on the Discovery of America." However, on his second voyage things were quite different.

After arriving on November 3, 1493, at an island in the Lesser Antilles that he named Dominica, Columbus sailed northward and later westward, to Isabella Hispaniola, the first city in the New World, at the end of January 1494. Then in June of that year, 1494, Isabella was struck by a hurricane, the first time that European men had seen such a terrible storm. Surely, for the first time they heard the Taíno Indians, very much excited, extending their arms raised upward into the air and shouting, "Furacán! Furacán!" when the storm commenced. We can indeed say that it was that moment in history when the word 'hurricane' suddenly appeared to the Europeans. Columbus was not at that time in Isabella because he was sailing near the Isle of Pines, Cuba. So, his companions of the ships 'Marigalante' and 'Gallega' were the first white men to hear these words, which were of Indian origin and about a phenomenon of the New World. Knowledge of 'Furacanes,' both the word and the terrifying storms it described, remained limited to Spanish speakers until 1555, when Richard Eden translated Columbus' ship report and other Spanish accounts of the New World, making it the first time it appeared in the English vocabulary.

In October of 1495, probably in the second half of the month, another hurricane struck Isabella, which was much stronger than the first. It finally gave Columbus, who was there at the time, the opportunity of knowing what a hurricane was and of its destructive abilities. It also gave him the opportunity of hearing the Indians shouting the same word with fear and anxiety on their faces, on the account of these terrible storms of the tropics, which they believed were caused by evil spirits. Christopher Columbus would later declare that "nothing but the service of God and the extension of the monarchy would induce him to expose himself to such danger from these storms ever again."[22] 'The Niña' was the only vessel that was the smallest, oldest and the most fragile at the time, but amazingly it withstood that hurricane. The other two ships of Columbus, 'The San Juan' and 'The Cordera,' were in the harbour and were lost or badly damaged by

---

[22] Tannehill, I.(1950) *Hurricanes-Their Nature and History*, Princeton University Press, pg. 141.

this hurricane. Columbus gave orders to have one repaired and another ship known as 'India' constructed out of the wreck of the ones that had been destroyed, making it the first ship to be built in the Caribbean by Europeans.

In 1502, during his fourth voyage, Columbus warned the Governor Don Nicolas de Orvando of Santo Domingo of an approaching hurricane, but he was ignored; as a result, a Spanish treasure fleet set sailed and lost 21 of 30 ships with 500 men. Columbus had a serious disagreement with the bureaucrats appointed by Spain to govern the fledgling colonies in the Caribbean to extract gold, pearl and other precious commodities from the native Indians. Among the more unfriendly of these exploiters was Don Nicolas de Orvando, the Governor of Hispaniola, with whom Columbus had been forbidden to have any contact by the request of his Spanish sovereigns. But as Columbus approached Santa Domingo, he recognized the early signs of an approaching hurricane, such as large ocean swells and a veil of cirrostratus clouds overhead. Concerned for the safety of his men and ships, he sent a message to Governor Orvando, begging him to be allowed to seek refuge in Santa Domingo Harbour. Columbus had observed that the Governor was preparing a large fleet of ships to set sail for Spain, carrying large quantities of gold and slaves, and warned him to delay the trip until the hurricane had passed. Refusing both the request and the advice, Orvando read Columbus' note out loud to the crew and residents, who roared with laughter at Columbus' advice. Unfortunately, the laughter was very short-lived, and Orvando's ships left port only to their own demise when 21 of the 30 ships were lost in a hurricane between Hispaniola and Puerto Rico. An additional four of them were badly damaged, but fortunately they were able to return to port, where they, too, eventually sunk. Only one ship, the *Aguja*, made it to Spain, and that one, no doubt to Orvando's intense distress, was carrying what little remained of Columbus' own gold.

Meanwhile, Columbus, anticipating strong winds from the north from this hurricane, positioned his fleet in a harbour on the south side of Hispaniola. On June 13, the storm hit with ferocious northeast winds. Even with the protection of the mountainous terrain to the windward side, the fleet struggled. In Columbus' own words, "The storm was terrible and on that night the ships were parted from me. Each one of them was reduced to an extremity, expecting nothing save death; each one of them was certain the others were lost."[23] The anchors held only on Columbus' ship; the others were dragged out to sea, where their crews fought for their lives. Nevertheless, the fleet survived with only minimal damage. Almost 18 months later, Columbus returned to Santo Domingo, only to discover that it had been largely destroyed by the hurricane.

When the Europeans first attempted to create settlements in the Caribbean and the Americas, they quickly learned about these storms. As time passed and these settlers learned more about their new homeland, they experienced these storms on such a regular basis that they became accustomed to them. Eventually, they began calling them equinoctial storms, as the storms would normally hit in the weeks around the period of the fall equinox, which in the northern hemisphere occurs in late September.

English explorers and privateers soon contributed their own accounts of encounters with these storms. In 1513, Juan Ponce de León completed the first recorded cruise along the Florida coast and came ashore near present-day St. Augustine to claim Florida for Spain. Famous for his unsuccessful search for the magical 'Fountain of Youth,' he might have discovered Florida earlier had it not been for the ravages of hurricanes. In August of 1508, he was struck by two hurricanes within two weeks. The first drove his ship onto the rocks near the Port of Yuna, Hispaniola, and the second left his ship aground on the southwest coast of Puerto Rico. Soon after Hernando Cortés found treasures of gold and silver in the newly discovered lands of the West, expeditions to retrieve the riches of the New World for Spain began in earnest. In 1525, Cortés lost the first ship he sent to Mexico in a severe hurricane, along with its crew of over seventy persons. Famous English explorer Sir John Hawkins wrote his own encounters with these storms. Sir John Hawkins wrote that he left Cartagena in late July 1568 "Hoping to have escaped the time of their stormes...which they call Furicanos."[24] Hawkins did not leave soon enough, and he and his ships

---

[23] National Geographic Magazine, November 1986-*A Columbus Casebook-A Supplement to "Where Columbus Found the New World."*

[24] Mulcahy, M. (2006) *Hurricanes and Society in the British Greater Caribbean, 1624-1783*, The John Hopkins University Press, pgs. 14-15.

were bashed by an "extreme storme", as he referred to it, lasting several days.

English Explorer Sir Francis Drake encountered several major hurricanes while sailing the dangerous seas of the Americas and the Atlantic Ocean, and in most cases these encounters changed the course of West Indian and American history. Sir Francis Drake, who travelled the seas of the globe in quest of glory and valuable loot, nearly lost his ships in the fleet on the Outer Banks of Carolina. One of his most famous encounters was with a major hurricane that occurred while he was anchored near the ill-fated Roanoke colony in present day North Carolina in June of 1586. His ships were anchored just off the banks while he checked on the progress of Sir Walter Raleigh's colonists on Roanoke Island. The hurricane lasted for three days, scattering Drake's fleet and nearly destroying many of his ships. There was no greater thorn in the side of the Spaniards than Francis Drake. His exploits were legendary, making him a hero to the English but a simple pirate to the Spaniards, and for good reasons because he often robbed them of their valuable treasures. To the Spanish, he was known as El Draque, "the Dragon"; "Draque" is the Spanish pronunciation of "Drake." As a talented sea captain and navigator, he attacked their fleets and took their ships and treasures. He raided their settlements in America and played a major role in the defeat of the greatest fleet ever assembled, the "Spanish Armada."

No other English seaman brought home more wealth or had a bigger impact on English history than Drake. At the age of 28, he was trapped in a Mexican port by Spanish war ships. He had gone there for repairs after an encounter with one of his first major hurricanes at sea. Drake escaped but some of the sailors left behind were so badly treated by the Spanish that he swore revenge. He returned to the area in 1572 with two ships and 73 men. Over the next fifteen months, he raided Spanish towns and their all-important Silver train across the isthmus from Panama. Other English accounts reported ships damaged or lost in storms characterized by extreme wind and rain, some of which were definitely hurricanes. The English (including Drake and Hawkins) had a great respect for hurricanes, to such an extent that as the hurricane season was understood to be approaching, more and more pirates went home or laid up their ships in some sheltered harbour until the last hurricane had passed and was replaced by the cool air of old man winter.

Probably those that first discovered the period of the year in which hurricanes developed were Spanish priests, officers of the navy or army, or civilians that had lived for a long time in the Caribbean. By the end of the sixteenth century, they should have already known the approximate period that these hurricanes occurred. The Roman Catholic Church knew early on that the hurricane season extended at least from August to October because the hierarchy ordered that all of the churches in the Caribbean say a special prayer to protect them from these deadly hurricanes. The prayer that had to be said was: 'Ad repellendas tempestates,' translated to mean 'for the repelling of the hurricanes or tempests.' It was also ordered that the prayer should be said in Puerto Rico during August and September and in Cuba in September and October. This indicates that it was known that hurricanes were more frequent in those islands during the months mentioned. Eventually, West Indian colonists, through first-hand experiences with these storms, gradually learned that hurricanes struck the Caribbean within a well-defined season. Initially, those early colonists believed that hurricanes could strike at any time of the year, but by the middle of the seventeenth century most of them recognized that there was a distinct hurricane season. This was because the hurricanes simply occurred too frequent within a particular time period for them to remain strange and unusual in their eyes. Numerous letters and reports written by colonists specifically discussed the period between July and October as the 'time of hurricanes.'

The geography of hurricanes challenged the concept of these storms as 'national judgments or divine favor' by which God spoke to a specific group of people or country. Individual storms routinely struck various islands colonized by different European powers. For example, in 1707 a hurricane devastated the English Leeward Islands, the Dutch Islands of Saba and St. Eustatius, and the French Island of Guadeloupe. In 1674, a Dutch attack on the French Islands was thwarted by a hurricane, which also caused significant damage in the English Leeward Islands and in Barbados. The presence of hurricanes made colonists question their ability to transform the hostile environment of the Caribbean and by extension their ability to establish successful and stable societies here. But hurricanes raised other questions as well: What caused them? What forces gave rise to such powerful and dangerous storms? For some-probably a significant majority during the first several decades of the seventeenth century-they believed that these storms came directly from the hands of God. They interpreted hurricanes as 'wondrous events' or 'divine judgments' for human sins. Others linked hurricanes to various natural processes, including shifting wind patterns. The explosion of various natural processes, including shifting wind patterns, the explosion of various chemicals in the atmosphere, and the celestial movement of the planets and stars.

CHAPTER TWO

The Naming of Hurricanes

North Atlantic Tropical Cyclone Names

2014	2015	2016	2017	2018	2019
Arthur	Ana	Alex	Arlene	Alberto	Andrea
Bertha	Bill	Bonnie	Bret	Beryl	Barry
Cristobal	Claudette	Colin	Cindy	Chris	Chantal
Dolly	Danny	Danielle	Don	Debby	Dorian
Edouard	Erika	Earl	Emily	Ernesto	Erin
Fay	Fred	Fiona	Franklin	Florence	Fernand
Gustav	Grace	Gaston	Gert	Gordon	Gabrielle
Hanna	Henri	Hermine	Harvey	Helene	Humberto
Ike	Ida	Ian	Irma	Isaac	Imelda
Josephine	Joaquin	Julia	Jose	Joyce	Jerry
Kyle	Kate	Karl	Katia	Kirk	Karen
Laura	Larry	Lisa	Lee	Leslie	Lorenzo
Marco	Mindy	Matthew	Maria	Michael	Melissa
Nana	Nicholas	Nicole	Nate	Nadine	Nestor
Omar	Odette	Otto	Ophelia	Oscar	Olga
Paulette	Peter	Paula	Philippe	Patty	Pablo
Rene	Rose	Richard	Rina	Rafael	Rebekah
Sally	Sam	Shary	Sean	Sara	Sebastien
Teddy	Teresa	Tobias	Tammy	Tony	Tanya
Vicky	Victor	Virginie	Vince	Valerie	Van
Wilfred	Wanda	Walter	Whitney	William	Wendy

Information Courtesy of NOAA-National Hurricane Center.

For as long as people have been tracking and reporting hurricanes, also known as tropical cyclones, they've been struggling to find ways to identify them. Until well into the 20th century, newspapers and forecasters in the Caribbean and the Americas devised names for storms that referenced their time period, geographic location or intensity or some other distinguishing factor. It's a funny thing, this naming of storms. We don't name tornadoes, blizzards, or frontal systems. It would seem silly, but we do name our hurricanes. On the opposite corners of our stormy planet, meteorologists name their cyclones too (although with sometimes more meaningful or symbolic names).

Hurricanes are the only weather disasters that have been given their own iconic names, such as Hurricanes Sandy, Andrew, Gilbert, Katrina, Camille or Mitch. No two hurricanes are the same, but like people, they share similar characteristics; yet, still they have their own unique stories to tell. The naming of storms or hurricanes has undergone various stages of development and transformation. Initially, the word 'Hurricane' accompanied by the year of occurrence was used. For example, 'the Great Hurricane of 1780', which killed over 22,000 persons in Martinique, Barbados and St. Eustatius. Another example was 'the Great Storm of 1703', whose incredible damage of the British Isles was expertly detailed by Robinson Crusoe's author, Daniel Defoe. The naming scheme was later substituted by a numbering system (e.g. Hurricane #1, #2, #3 of 1833 etc...); however, this became too cumbersome and confusing, especially when disseminating information about two or more storms within the same geographical area or location.

For the major hurricanes of this region, they were often named after the particular country or city they devastated. This was especially true for severe hurricanes, which made their landing somewhere in the Caribbean or the Americas. Three notable examples were: first, 'the Great Dominican Republic Hurricane of 1930', which killed over 8,000 persons in the Dominican Republic. The 1930 Dominican Republic Hurricane, also known as 'Hurricane San Zenon', is the fifth deadliest North Atlantic hurricane on record. The second of only two known tropical cyclones in the very quiet 1930 North Atlantic hurricane season, the hurricane was first observed on August 29 to the east of the Lesser Antilles. The cyclone was a small but intense Category 4 hurricane.

Next was 'the Pointe-à-Pitre Hurricane of 1776', which devastated the country of Guadeloupe and killed over 6,000 persons and devastated its largest city and economic capital of Pointe-à-Pitre. The 1776 Pointe-à-Pitre hurricane was at one point the deadliest North Atlantic on record. Although its intensity and complete track is unknown, it is known that the storm struck Guadeloupe on September 6, 1776, near Pointe-à-Pitre, which is currently the largest city on the island. At least 6,000 fatalities occurred on Guadeloupe, which was a higher death toll than any other known hurricane before it to hit that country. The storm struck a large convoy of French and Dutch merchant ships, sinking or running aground 60% of the vessels. The ships were transporting goods to Europe.

Finally, 'the Great Nassau Hurricane of 1926', which devastated the city of Nassau in the Bahamas during the 1926 North Atlantic hurricane season. The Great Nassau Hurricane of 1926, also known as 'the Bahamas-Florida Hurricane of July 1926' and 'Hurricane San Liborio,' was a destructive Category 4 hurricane that affected the Bahamas at peak intensity. Although it weakened considerably before its Florida landfall, it was reported as one of the most severe storms to affect Nassau in the Bahamas in several years until the Great Lake Okeechobee Hurricane of 1928, which occurred just two years later. Approximately 268 persons died in this storm in the Bahamas.

In some cases, they were even named after the holiday on which they occurred, for example, 'the Great Labour Day Hurricane of 1935.' The Great Labour Day Hurricane of 1935 was the strongest tropical cyclone during the 1935 North Atlantic hurricane season. This compact and intense hurricane caused extensive damage in the Bahamas and the upper Florida Keys. To this day, the Great Labour Day Hurricane of 1935 is the strongest and most intense hurricane on record to ever have struck the United States in terms of barometric pressure. The Great Labour Day Hurricane of 1935 was one of the strongest recorded hurricane landfalls worldwide. It was the only hurricane known to have made landfall in the United States with a minimum central pressure below 900 Mbar; only two others have struck the United States with winds of Category 5 strength on the Saffir-Simpson Scale. It remains the third-strongest North Atlantic hurricane on record, and it was only surpassed by Hurricane Gilbert (888Mbar) in 1988 and Hurricane Wilma (882Mbar) in 2005. In total, at least 408 people were killed by this hurricane.

In some cases they were named after the ship which experienced that particular storm. Two notable examples were: - 'the Racer's Storm of 1837' and 'the Sea Venture Hurricane of 1609.' The 1837 Racer's Storm was a very powerful and destructive hurricane in the 19th century, causing 105 deaths and heavy damage to many cities on its 2,000+ mile path. The Racer's Storm was the 10th known tropical storm in the 1837 North Atlantic hurricane season. The Racer's Storm was named after the British war ship HMS Racer, which encountered the storm in the extreme northwest Caribbean on September 28th. Another example was 'the Sea Venture Hurricane of 1609.' On July 28th of 1609, a fleet of seven tall ships, with two pinnaces in tow carrying 150 settlers and supplies from Plymouth, England, to Virginia to relieve the starving Jamestown colonists, was struck by a hurricane while en route there. They had been sent by the Virginia Company of London to fortify the Jamestown settlement. Sir George Somers' mission was to resupply the six hundred or so pioneers who a year before had settled in the infant British colonial settlement of King James' Town, sited in one of the estuaries south of the Potomac River.

The ship *'Sea Venture'* was grounded at Bermuda, which for some time was called Somers Island after the ship's captain, Admiral Sir George Somers. After being struck by this hurricane, the *Sea Venture* sprung a leak and everyone on board worked frantically to save this ship and their lives by trying to pump the water out of the hull of the ship. They tried to stem the flow of water coming into the ship by stuffing salt beef and anything else they could find to fit into the leaks of the ship. After this proved futile, most of the crew simply gave up hope, falling asleep where they could, exhausted and aching from their relentless but futile efforts. But just as they were about to give up and face the grim reality that they would be lost to the unforgiving Atlantic Ocean, they spotted the island of Bermuda. Somers skillfully navigated the floundering Sea Venture onto a reef about half a mile to the leeward side of Bermuda. They used the ship's long boat to ferry the crew and passengers ashore.

The passengers of the shipwrecked *Sea Venture* became Bermuda's first inhabitants, and their stories helped inspire William Shakespeare's writing of his final play 'The Tempest', making it perhaps the most famous hurricane in early American history. "And another storm brewing," William Shakespeare wrote in 'The Tempest.' "I hear it sing in the wind."[25] Most of those venturing to the New World had no knowledge of the word or the actual storm. The lead ship, the three-hundred-ton *Sea Venture*, was the largest in the fleet and carried Sir Thomas Gates, the newly appointed

---

[25]   http://www.william-shakespeare.info/shakespeare-play-the-tempest.html.

governor of the colony, and Sir Georges Somers, admiral of the Virginia Company. It is interesting to note that Shakespeare did not name his play 'The Hurricane.' He actually did know the word "hurricano" because it appears in two earlier plays, King Lear and Troilus and Cressida. Maybe he recognized that such a title would be confusing and unfamiliar to most of his audience, so he chose a more familiar word 'The Tempest', instead. Though the island was uninhabited, Spaniards had visited Bermuda earlier and set ashore wild pigs. The shipwrecked passengers fed on those wild pigs, fish, berries and other plentiful game on the island. Although they yearned to stay on that island paradise, they managed to make two vessels *'Patience'* and *'Deliverance'* out of what was left of the Sea Venture, and ten months later they set sail for Jamestown. However, some persons remained on the island and became the first colonists of that island, including Admiral Sir George Somers, who initially left with the other Jamestown passengers but eventually returned and died on that island. To this day, Bermuda still celebrates 'Somers' Day' as a public holiday.

In some instances, hurricanes were named after important persons within this region; one such storm was the 'Willoughby Gale of 1666.' The word 'gale' during these colonial times was often interchanged with the word 'hurricane', but they often meant the same thing-a hurricane, and not the official term we now use today for the definition of a 'meteorological gale.' This storm was named after the British Governor of Barbados, Lord Francis Willoughby, who lost his life aboard the flagship *'Hope'* along with over 2,000 of his troops in his fleet in this hurricane. He was appointed Governor of Barbados by Charles II in May of 1650 and attempted to negotiate the strained politics of that island, which also experienced a division between the Royalists and Parliamentarians. His last act on behalf of the English Crown came in July 1666, when having learned of the recent French seizure of St. Kitts, he formed a relief force of two Royal Navy Frigates, twelve other large vessels (including commandeered merchant ships), a fire ship, and a ketch, bearing over 2,000 men.

Lord Willoughby had planned to proceed north to Nevis, Montserrat, and Antigua to gather further reinforcements before descending on the French. Leaving Barbados on July 28th, his fleet waited for the French just off the coast of Martinique and Guadeloupe, where he sent a frigate to assault the harbour and ended up capturing two French merchant vessels on August 4th. This success could not be exploited, however, as that night most of his force was destroyed by a strong hurricane, including the flagship *Hope*, from which Willoughby drowned during the storm. This hurricane occurred in 1666 and was a very intense storm which struck the islands of St. Kitts, Guadeloupe, and Martinique. The fleet was actually caught by surprise by this hurricane after leaving Barbados en-route to St. Kitts and Nevis to aid the colonists there to help battle against the French attacks. After the storm, only two vessels from this fleet were ever heard from again, and the French captured some of these survivors. All of the vessels and boats on the coast of Guadeloupe were dashed to pieces. For a period in the late seventeenth century, some colonists referred to especially powerful and deadly hurricanes as "Willoughby Gales."

Personal names were also used elsewhere in this region, for example, 'Saxby's Gale' which occurred in Canada in 1869 and was named after a naval officer who was thought to have predicted it. The Saxby Gale was the name given to a tropical cyclone that struck eastern Canada's Bay of Fundy region on the night of October 4–5, 1869. The storm was named for Lieutenant Stephen Martin Saxby, a naval instructor and amateur astronomer who, based on his astronomical studies, had predicted extremely high tides in the North Atlantic Ocean on October 5, 1869, which would produce storm surges in the event of a storm. The hurricane caused extensive destruction to port facilities and communities along the Bay of Fundy coast in both New Brunswick and Nova Scotia, as well as Maine, particularly Calais, St. Andrews, St. George, St. John, Moncton, Sackville, Amherst, Windsor and Truro. Much of the devastation was attributed to a 2-metre storm surge created by the storm, which coincided with a perigean spring tide; the Bay of Fundy having one of the highest tidal ranges in the world. The Saxby Gale storm surge produced a water level that gave Burntcoat Head, Nova Scotia, the honor of having the highest tidal range ever recorded. It is also thought to have formed the long gravel beach that connects Partridge Island, Nova Scotia, to the mainland.

The storm (which pre-dated the practice of naming hurricanes) was given the name 'Saxby' in honor of Lieutenant Stephen Martin Saxby, Royal Navy, who was a naval instructor and amateur astronomer. Lt. Saxby had written a letter of warning, published December 25, 1868, in London's 'The Standard' newspaper, in which he notes the astronomical forces predicted for October 5, 1869, which would produce extremely high tides in the North Atlantic Ocean during the height of hurricane season. Lt. Saxby followed this warning with a reminder published on September 16, 1869, to 'The Standard', in which he also warns of a major 'atmospheric disturbance' that would coincide with the high water level at an undetermined location. Many newspapers took up Saxby's warning in the coming days.

In a monthly weather column published October 1, 1869, in Halifax's 'The Evening Express,' amateur meteorologist Frederick Allison relayed Lt. Saxby's warning for a devastating storm the following week. Despite the warning, many readers throughout the United Kingdom, Canada, Newfoundland and the United States dismissed Saxby since there were frequent gales and hurricanes during the month of October. The fact that the high tides occurred throughout the North Atlantic basin was unremarkable and astronomically predictable, except for their coinciding with the hurricane that struck the Gulf of Maine and Bay of Fundy to produce the devastating storm surge. Lt. Saxby's predictions were considered quite lunatic at the time. Some believed that his predictions were founded upon astrology, which was not the case.

Another example was 'the Daniel Defoe Hurricane of 1703', which occurred in November of 1703 and moved from the Atlantic across to southern England. It was made famous by an obscure political pamphleteer, Daniel Defoe. It was six years before he wrote the world famous book *'Robinson Crusoe.'* At the time the hurricane struck, he needed money, so the storm gave him the idea of collecting eye-witness accounts of the storm and publishing them in a pamphlet. He printed and sold this pamphlet under the very strange and exceptionally long title of *'The storm or collection of the Most Remarkable Casualties and Disasters which happened in the late Dreadful Tempest both by Sea and Land.'* In total, around 8,000 sailors lost their lives, untold numbers perished in the floods on shore, and 14,000 homes, 400 windmills and 16,000 sheep were destroyed. Some of the windmills burned down because they turned so fast in the fierce winds that friction generated enough heat to set them on fire. The damage in London alone was estimated to have cost £2 million (at 18th century prices).

An additional example was 'the Benjamin Franklin Hurricane of October 1743,' which affected the Northeastern United States and New

England, brought gusty winds and rainy conditions as far as Philadelphia, and produced extensive flooding in Boston. This was the first hurricane to be measured accurately by scientific instruments. John Winthrop, a professor of natural philosophy at Harvard College, measured the pressure and tides during the storm passage. This storm wasn't particularly powerful, but it was memorable because it garnered the interest of future patriot and one of the founders of the United States, Benjamin Franklin, who believed the storm was coming in from Boston. He was wrong because it was actually going to Boston. From this information, he surmised that the storm was travelling in a clockwise manner from the southwest to northeast. Putting two and two together, Franklin concluded that the low pressure system was causing the storm to move in this manner.

One aspect of the Earth's general circulation is that storms are not stationary; they move, and in somewhat predictable ways. Until the mid-eighteenth century, it had been generally assumed that storms were born, played out, and died in a single location and that they did not move across the Earth's surface. Benjamin Franklin had planned to study a lunar eclipse one evening in September 1743, but the remnants of this hurricane ruined his evening. This was a big disappointment to him because he had been looking forward to the lunar eclipse that this storm had obscured. His curiosity aroused, Franklin gathered additional details about the storm by reading the Boston newspapers and learned that the storm had moved up the Atlantic seaboard and against the surface winds. He learned that this hurricane struck Boston a day later, sending flood tides sweeping over the docks, destroying boats, and submerging waterfront streets. In the succeeding months, he collected additional reports from travellers and newspapers from Georgia to Nova Scotia and satisfied himself that at least in this part of the world, storms have a tendency to take a northeasterly path up the Atlantic Coast. Thus science took the first step toward a basic understanding of hurricanes and their movements.

Benjamin Franklin is also popularly known for his off-the-wall weather experiment years later, where during a thunderstorm, in 1752, he carried out a dangerous experiment to demonstrate that a thunderstorm generates electricity. He flew a kite, with metal objects attached to its string, high in the sky into a thunderstorm cloud (Cumulonimbus). The metal items produced sparks, proving that electricity had passed along the wet string.

After discovering that bolts of lightning were in fact electricity, with this knowledge Franklin developed the lightning rod to allow the lightning bolt to travel along the rod and safely into the ground. This discovery by Franklin is still used even to this day all over the world. A year later, after Benjamin Franklin's famous kite flight, Swedish physicist G.W. Richmann conducted a similar experiment following Franklin's instructions to the letter, and as fate would have it, he was struck by lightning, which killed him instantly. Sailing home from France on the fifth of September, 1789, after his great years as a U.S. Ambassador, Benjamin Franklin experienced a storm that may have been the same storm that devastated Dominica. He was eighty years old and suffering from "the Stone" but was busy observing the temperatures of the sea water, which would eventually lead to his discovery of the Gulf Stream.

Finally, there was the 'Alexander Hamilton Hurricane of 1772,' which he experienced growing up as a boy living in the Caribbean on the island of St. Kitts in the Leeward Islands. This was an extremely powerful and deadly hurricane. He later on in life became the confidential aide to George Washington, and his greatness rests on his Federalist influence on the American Constitution as much as on his financial genius as the first United States Secretary of the Treasury. Today he is featured on the United States ten dollar bill and he is one of two non-presidents featured on currently issued United States bills. The other is Benjamin Franklin, who is found on the United States $100 bill. A westward moving hurricane hit Puerto Rico on August 28. It continued through the Caribbean, hitting Hispaniola on August 30 and later on Jamaica. It moved northwestward through the Gulf of Mexico and hit just west of Mobile, Alabama, on September 4th. Many ships were destroyed in the Mobile area, and its death toll was very severe. In Pensacola, it destroyed most of the wharves. The most devastation occurred in the vicinity of Mobile and the Pasca Oocola River. All shipping at the Mouth of the Mississippi was driven into the marshes; this included the ship 'El Principe de Orange', from which only 6 persons survived.

This storm was famously described by Alexander Hamilton, who was living on the island of St. Croix at the time and wrote a letter about it to his father in St. Kitts. The letter was so dramatic and moving that it was published in newspapers locally on the island and first in New York, and then in other states (please see my book- *'Rediscovering Hurricanes'* for a complete copy of this letter), and the locals on St. Kitts raised enough money to have him brought to America to receive a formal education to make good use of his intellectual abilities. This was because this letter created such a sensation that some planters of St. Kitts, in the midst of the hurricane devastation, took up a collection to send him to America for better schooling because they saw in him great potential. By 1774, he was a student at King's College, now Columbia University, in New York. On St. Kitts, the damage was considerable, and once again many houses were flattened, and there were several fatalities and many more injuries. Total damage from this storm alone was estimated at £500,000 on St. Kitts. The second storm struck just three days later, causing even more significant damage to the few remaining houses on this island already battered and weakened by the previous storm in 1772.

Several claimants have been put forth as the originators of the modern tropical cyclone 'naming' system. However, it was forecaster Clement Lindley Wragge, an Australian meteorologist who in 1887 began giving women's names, names from history and mythology and male names, especially names of politicians who offended him, to these storms before the end of the 19th century. He was a colourful and controversial meteorologist in charge of the Brisbane, Australia, Government weather office. He initially named the storms after mythological figures but later named them after politicians he didn't like. For example, Wragge named some of these storms using biblical names, such as Ram, Raken, Talmon, and Uphaz, or the ancient names of Xerxes and Hannibal. Wragge even nicknamed one storm Eline, a name that he thought was reminiscent of "dusty maidens with liquid eyes and bewitching manners." Most ingeniously, he gained a measure of personal revenge by naming some of the nastiest storms with politicians' names, such as Drake, Barton, and Deakin. By properly naming a hurricane, he was able to publicly describe a politician (perhaps a politician who was not too generous with the weather bureau appropriations) as "causing great distress" or "wandering aimlessly about the Pacific." By naming these storms after these hated politicians, he could get a degree of revenge on them without suffering any repercussions from them. During his last days in office, he fought with the Australian

Government over the right to issue national forecasts, and he lost and was fired in 1902.

For a while, hurricanes in the West Indies were often named after the particular Saint's Day on which the hurricane occurred. As Christianity took hold in the West Indies, the naming system of storms here in the Caribbean was based on the Catholic tradition of naming these storms with the 'Saint' of the day (e.g. San Ciprian on September 26th). This system for naming them was haphazard and not really a system at all. Powerful hurricanes hitting especially the Spanish speaking islands of the Caribbean got Catholic Saints' names. According to Historian Alejandro Tapia, the first hurricane to be named with the Saint of the day was the 'Hurricane of San Bartolomé' which devastated Puerto Rico and the Dominican Republic on August 24th and 25th of 1568. The earlier tropical cyclones were simply designated by historians' years later after their passages.

One example of a great storm named after a Saint of the day was 'Hurricane Saint Felipe I', which struck Puerto Rico on September 13, 1876. Another example was 'Hurricane Saint Felipe II', which occurred, strangely enough, on the very same date 52 years later on September 13, 1928. Another hurricane, which was named the 'Hurricane of Saint Elena', struck Puerto Rico on August 18, 1851, and caused massive casualties. Then there was the 'Hurricane of Santa Ana' (in English, Saint Anne), which struck Puerto Rico and Guadeloupe on July 26, 1825, the date of the feast in honor of the Mother of the Blessed Virgin, which killed over 1,300 persons. In addition, there was the 'Hurricane of Saint Ciriaco', which killed 3,369 persons in Puerto Rico on August 8, 1899, (feast day of Saint Cyriacus) and remains one of the longest duration tropical storms (28 days) to hit the Caribbean or anywhere in the world.

The tradition of naming storms after the Saint of the day officially ended with Hurricane Betsy in 1956, which is still remembered as the 'Hurricane of Santa Clara.' However, years later with the passage of Hurricane Donna in 1960, the storm was recognized as the 'Hurricane of San Lorenzo.' At this time, only the major hurricanes were given names, so most storms, especially the minor storms before 1950 in the North Atlantic, never received any kind of special designation. This is why this hurricane in 1929 was never named but was simply referred to as 'the

Great Bahamas Hurricane of 1929.' The word 'Great' simply meant that the hurricane was a powerful storm and that it had sustained winds of 136 mph or greater and a minimum central pressure of 28.00 inches or less.

Later, latitude-longitude positions were used. At first, they listed these storms by the latitude and longitude positions where they were first reported. This was cumbersome, slow, open to errors and confusing. For example, a name like 'Hurricane 12.8°N latitude and 54.7°W longitude' was very difficult to remember, and it would be easy to confuse this storm with another that was seen two months later but almost at the same location. In addition, this posed another significant problem in the 1940's, when meteorologists began airborne studies of tropical cyclones and ships and aircrafts communicated mainly in Morse code. This was fine for the letters of the alphabet, but it was awkward at dealing with numbers because it was slow and caused confusion among its users.

In this region, these early storms were often referred to as gales, severe gales, equinoctial storms, or line storms. The latter two names referred to the time of the year and the location from which these storms were born (referring to the Equatorial line). Gauging the strength and fury of a seventeenth or eighteenth-century storm was quite a difficult task because at the time these colonists had no means of measuring the wind speeds of a hurricane. Contemporaries recognized a hierarchy of winds ranging from 'a stark calm' to 'a small Gale' to 'a Top-Sail Gale' to 'a fret of wind' and 'a Tempest.' These terms were later replaced by the word 'hurricane', but such terms offered little help in interpreting the power of hurricanes or differentiating lesser tropical storms from hurricanes. Furthermore, increased development of the built environment over time meant that the potential for damage, even from minor storms, increased as well, making damage estimates a questionable foundation for judging the power of storms.

Experience has shown that using distinctive names in communications is quicker and less subject to error than the cumbersome latitude-longitude identification methods. The idea was that the names should be short, familiar to users, easy to remember, and that their use would facilitate communications with millions of people of different ethnic races threatened by the storm. This was because a hurricane can last for a week or more and there can be more than one storm at a given time, so weather forecasters starting naming these storms so that there would be absolutely no confusion when talking about a particular storm. Names are easier to use and facilitate better communications among individuals and meteorologists with language barriers within the same geographical region, such as within the Caribbean, Central America and North America.

The first U.S. named hurricane (unofficially named) was Hurricane George, which was the fifth storm in 1947 season. George had top winds of 155 mph as it came ashore around mid-day on September 17th, between Pompano Beach and Delray Beach. The second hurricane unofficially named was Hurricane Bess (named for the outspoken First Lady of the USA, Bess Truman, in 1949). The third storm was nicknamed by the news media 'Hurricane Harry', after the then President of the United States Harry Truman. United States Navy and Air Force meteorologists working in the Pacific Ocean began naming tropical cyclones during World War II, when they often had to track multiple storms. They gave each storm a distinctive name in order to distinguish the cyclones more quickly than listing their positions when issuing warnings.

Towards the end of World War II, two separate United States fleets in the Pacific lacking sufficient weather information about these storms were twice badly damaged when they sailed directly into them, resulting in massive causalities. Three ships were sunk, twenty-one were badly damaged, 146 planes were blown overboard, and 763 men were lost. One of the results that came out of these tragedies was the fact that all U.S. Army and Navy planes were then ordered to start tracking and studying these deadly storms so as to prevent similar disasters like those ones from occurring again. During World War II, this naming practice became widespread in weather map discussions among forecasters, especially Air Force and Navy meteorologists, who plotted the movements of these storms over the wide expanses of the Pacific Ocean. Using the convention of applying 'she' to inanimate objects such as vehicles, these military meteorologists, beginning in 1945 in the Northwest Pacific, started naming these storms after their wives and girlfriends. However, this practice didn't last too long, for whatever reason, but my guess is that those women rejected or took offense to being named after something that was responsible for so much damage and destruction. Another theory was that this practice was started by a radio operator who sang, "Every little breeze seems to whisper Louise" when issuing a hurricane warning. From that point on, that particular hurricane and future hurricanes were referred to as Louise and the use of female names for hurricanes became standard practice.

An early example of the use of a woman's name for a storm was in the best-selling pocketbook novel *Storm*, by George R. Stewart, published by Random House in 1941, which has since been made into a major motion picture by Walt Disney, further promoting the idea of naming storms. It involved a young meteorologist working in the San Francisco Weather Bureau Office tracking a storm, which he called 'Maria,' from its birth as a disturbance in the North Pacific to its death over North America many days later. The focus of the book is a storm named Maria, but pronounced 'Ma-Rye-Ah.' Yes, the song in the famous Broadway show 'Paint Your Wagon' named "They Call the Wind Maria" was inspired by this fictional storm. He gave it a name because he said that he could easily say 'Hurricane Maria' rather than 'the low pressure center which at 6pm yesterday was located at latitude one-seventy four degrees east and longitude forty-three degrees north', which he considered too long and cumbersome. As Stewart detailed in his novel, "Not since at any price would the Junior Meteorologist have revealed to the Chief that he was bestowing names-and girls' names-upon those great moving low-pressure areas." He unofficially gave the storms in his book women names such as Lucy, Katherine and Ruth, after some girls he knew because he said that they each had a unique personality. It is not known whether George Stewart was indeed the inspiration for the trend toward naming hurricanes, which came along later in the decade, but it seems likely.[26]

In 1950, military alphabet names (e.g. Able, Baker, Charley, Dog, Easy, Fox etc...) were adopted by the World Meteorological Organization (WMO), and the first named Atlantic hurricane was Able in 1950. The Joint Army/Navy (JAN) Phonetic Alphabet was developed in 1941 and was used by all branches of the United States military until the promulgation of the NATO phonetic alphabet in 1956, which replaced it. Before the JAN phonetic alphabet, each branch of the armed forces used its own phonetic alphabet, leading to difficulties in inter-branch communications. This naming method was not very popular and caused a lot of confusion

---

[26]   Stewart, George R. (1941) <u>*Storm*</u>, University of Nebraska Press.

because officials soon realized that this naming convention would cause more problems in the history books if more than one powerful Hurricane Able made landfall and caused extensive damage and death to warrant retirement. This was because hurricanes that have a severe impact on the lives or the economy of a country or region are remembered for generations after the devastation they caused, and some go into weather history, so distinguishing one storm name from another is essential for the history books.

The modern naming convention came about in response to the need for unambiguous radio communications with ships and aircrafts. As air and sea transportation started to increase and meteorological observations improved in number and quality, several typhoons, hurricanes or cyclones might have to be tracked at any given time. To help in their identification, in 1953 the systematic use of only regular women names were used in alphabetical order, and this lasted until 1978. The 1953's Alice was the first real human-named storm. At the time, they named them after women because these meteorologists reasoned that people might pay more attention to a storm if they envisioned it as a tangible entity, a character, rather than just a bundle of wind. But the use of only women names eventually was rejected as sexist, and forecasters finally went with both male and female names. Beginning in 1960, four semi-permanent sets of names were established, to be re-cycled after four years. This list was expanded to ten sets in 1971, but before making it through the list even once, these sets were replaced by the now familiar 6 sets of men and women names.

This naming practice started in the Eastern Pacific in 1959 and in 1960 for the remainder of the North Pacific. It is interesting to note that in the Northwest Pacific Basin, the names, by and large, are not personal names. While there are a few men and women names, the majority of the Northwest Pacific tropical cyclone names generally reflect Pacific culture, and the names consists of flowers, animals, birds, trees, or even foods, while some are just descriptive adjectives. In addition, the names are not allotted in alphabetical order but are arranged by the contributing nation, with the countries being alphabetized. For example, the Cambodians have contributed Naki (a flower), Krovanh (a tree) and Damrey (an elephant). China has submitted names such as Yutu (a mythological rabbit), Longwang (the dragon king and god of rain in Chinese mythology), and Dainmu (the mother of lightning and the goddess in charge of thunder). Micronesian typhoon names include Sinlaku (a legendary Kosrae goddess) and Ewiniar (the Chuuk Storm god). Hurricanes in the central Pacific have name lists for only four years and use Hawaiian names.

In the North Atlantic Basin in 1979, gender equality finally reached the naming process of hurricanes when thousands of sexism complaints written to the WMO and feminists groups in the USA and worldwide urged the WMO to add men's names; hence, both men and women names were used alternately, and this practice is still in use today. That year would also herald the practice of drawing up a list of names in advance of the hurricane season, and today an alphabetical list of 21 names is used. Hurricane Bob was the first North Atlantic storm named after a man in the 1979 hurricane season; however, it was not retired (it would eventually be retired in the 1991 hurricane season). Hurricane David was the second storm named after a man and it was the first male storm to be retired in the North Atlantic Region. This was due to the great death toll and substantial damage it inflicted to the countries of Dominica, the Dominican Republic and the Bahamas during the last week of August and the first week of September in 1979.

Since 1979, the naming list now includes names from non-English speaking countries within this region, such as Dutch, French and Spanish names, which also have a large presence here in the Caribbean. This is done to reflect the diversity of the different ethnic languages of the various countries in this region, so the names of Spanish, French, Dutch, and English persons are used in the naming process. The names of storms are now selected by a select committee from member countries of the World Meteorological Organization that falls within that particular region of the world, and we here in the Caribbean come under Region IV for classification purposes. This committee meets once a year after the hurricane season has passed and before the beginning of the new hurricane season to decide on which names to be retired and to replace those names with a new set of names when and where necessary.

The practice of giving different names to storms in different hurricane basins has also led to a few rare circumstances of name-changing storms. For example, in October of 1988, after Atlantic Hurricane Joan devastated Central America, it proceeded to move into the Pacific and became Pacific tropical storm Miriam. Hurricane Joan was a powerful hurricane that caused death and destruction in over a dozen countries in the Caribbean and Central America. Another example was Hurricane Hattie, which was a powerful Category 5 hurricane that pounded Central America on Halloween during the 1961 North Atlantic hurricane season. It caused $370 million in damages and killed around 275 persons. Hattie is the only hurricane on record to have earned three names (Hattie, Simone, Inga) while crossing into different basins twice. Hattie swept across the Caribbean and came ashore in the town of Belize City, British Honduras (now called Belize), on October 31st. It was a strong Category 4 hurricane at landfall, having weakened from a Category 5 hurricane just offshore. After making landfall, its remnants crossed over into the Pacific and attained tropical storm status again under the name Simone. In a remarkable turn of events, after Simone itself made landfall, its remnants crossed back over to the Gulf of Mexico, where the storm became Tropical Storm Inga before dissipating. However, it is debatable whether Inga in fact formed from the remnants of Simone at all.

It is interesting to note here that the letters Q, U, X, Y, and Z are not included in the hurricane list because of the scarcity of names beginning with those letters. However, in other regions of the world, some of these letters are used; for example, only "Q" and "U" are omitted in the Northeastern Pacific Basin. When a storm causes tremendous damage and death, the name is taken out of circulation and retired for reasons of sensitivity. It is then replaced with a name of the same letter and of the same gender, and if possible, the same language as the name being retired (e.g. neither Hurricane Irene in 2011 nor Hurricane Katrina in 2005 will ever be used again). The list includes one tropical storm, Allison of 2001, which caused billions in damage from its heavy rains.

The name used the most, at least with the same spelling, is Arlene (seven times), while Frances and Florence have been used seven and six times, respectively. However, considering different spellings of the same name, Debbie/Debby has been used seven times, and Anna/Ana has been used eight times. The first name to be called into use five times was Edith, but that name hasn't been used since 1971. After the 1996 season, Lilly has the distinction of being the first 'L' name to be used three times, while Marco is the first 'M' name to be used more than once. The name

Kendra was assigned to a system in the 1966 hurricane season, but in post-season analysis it was decided it had not been a bona fide tropical storm. This storm marked the birth of reclassification of storms in the post-hurricane season (Hurricane Andrew was a storm that was reclassified from a Category four hurricane to a Category five hurricane in the off season).

In only five years (2005, 1995, 2010, 2011,2012) have names beginning with the letter 'O' and beyond been used, but there have been several other years in which more than 14 storms have been tracked, such as: 1887-19 storms, 1933-21 storms, 1936-16 storms, 1969-18 storms, 1995-19 storms, 2005-28 storms, 2010-19 storms, 2011-19 storms and 2012-19 storms. The 2010 Atlantic hurricane season has been extremely active, being the most active season since 2005. It must be noted that the 2010, 2011 and 2012 seasons ties the record with the 1995 North Atlantic hurricane season and the 1887 North Atlantic hurricane season for the third most named storms (19). Furthermore, 2010 also ties the record with the 1969 North Atlantic hurricane season and 1887 for the second most hurricanes (12). The 2012 Atlantic hurricane season was the third most active season, tied with 1887, 1995, 2010, and 2011. It was an above average season in which 19 tropical cyclones formed. All nineteen depressions attained tropical storm status, and ten of these became hurricanes. Two hurricanes further intensified into major hurricanes. The first three of these years were well before the naming of storms began, but 1969 requires an explanation. This was early in the era of complete satellite coverage, and forecasters were still studying the evolution of non-tropical systems (sub-tropical) into warm-core, tropical-type storms. Several systems that year were not named as tropical because they began at higher latitudes and were initially cold-cored.

Formal classification of subtropical (hybrid type) cyclones and public advisories on them began in 1972, and a few years later a review was made of satellite imagery from the late 60's and early 70's, and several of these systems were included as tropical storms. In fact, two of the storms added in 1969 were hurricanes, so 1969 now stands as having 12 hurricanes. Today, subtropical storms are named using the same list as tropical storms and hurricanes. This makes sense because subtropical cyclones often take on tropical characteristics. Imagine how confusing it would be if the system got a new name just because it underwent internal changes. There is no subtropical classification equivalent to a hurricane. The assumption is that once a storm got that strong, it would have acquired tropical characteristics and therefore be called a hurricane, or it would have merged with an extratropical system in the North Atlantic and lost its name altogether. For example, on October 24, 1979, a subtropical storm briefly reached hurricane strength as it neared Newfoundland, Canada. It quickly combined with another low-pressure system, but it was never named.

Whenever a hurricane has had a major impact, any country affected by the storm can request that the name of the hurricane be 'retired' by agreement of the World Meteorological Organization (WMO). Prior to 1969, officially, retiring a storm name actually meant that it cannot be reused for at least 10 years, to facilitate historic references, legal actions, insurance claim activities, etc...and to avoid public confusion with another storm of the same name. But today these storms are retired indefinitely, and if that happens, it is replaced with a storm's name with the same gender because the retired storm often becomes a household name in the regions or countries it affected. When that list of names is exhausted, the Greek Alphabet (Alpha, Beta, Gamma, Delta, Epsilon, Zeta, Eta, Theta, Iota, Kappa and Lambda) is used. It must be noted that so far this list has only been used once in either the Pacific or the Atlantic Basins, which was in the North Atlantic hurricane season of 2005. It is important to note here that there were a few subtropical storms that used the Greek Alphabet in the 1970's, but they were really not truly tropical in nature.

If a storm forms in the off-season, it will take the next name on the list based on the current calendar date. For example, if a tropical cyclone formed on December 29th, it would take the name from the previous season's list of names. If a storm formed in February, it would be named from the subsequent season's list of names. Theoretically, a hurricane or tropical storm of any strength can have its name retired; retirement is based entirely on the level of damage and death caused by a storm. However, up until 1972 (Hurricane Agnes), there was no Category 1 hurricane that had its name retired, and no named tropical storm had its name retired until 2001 (Tropical Storm Allison). Allison is the only tropical storm to have its name retired without ever having reached hurricane strength. This is at least partially due to the fact that weaker storms tend to cause less damage, and the few weak storms that have had their names retired caused most of their destruction through heavy rainfall rather than winds.

While no request for retirement has ever been turned down, some storms such as Hurricane Gordon in 1994 caused a great deal of death and destruction but nonetheless was not retired, as the main country affected-Haiti-did not request retirement. Hurricane Gordon in 1994 killed 1,122 persons in Haiti, and 23 deaths in other nations. Damage in the United States was estimated at $400 million, and damages in Haiti and Cuba were severe. Despite the tremendous damage caused, the name 'Gordon' was not retired and was reused in both the 2000 and 2006 North Atlantic hurricane seasons. Since 1950, 77 storms have had their names retired. Of these, two (Carol and Edna) were reused after the storm for which they were retired but were later retroactively retired, and two others (Hilda and Janet) were included on later lists of storm names but were not reused before being retroactively retired. Before 1979, when the first permanent six-year storm names list began, some storm names were simply not used anymore. For example, in 1966, 'Fern' was substituted for 'Frieda,' and no reason was cited.

In the North Atlantic Basin, in most cases, a tropical cyclone retains its name throughout its life. However, a tropical cyclone may be renamed in several situations. First, when a tropical storm crosses from the Atlantic into the Pacific, or vice versa, before 2001 it was the policy of National Hurricane Center (NHC) to rename a tropical storm that crossed from the Atlantic into the Pacific, or vice versa. Examples included Hurricane Cesar-Douglas in 1996 and Hurricane Joan-Miriam in 1988. In 2001, when Iris moved across Central America, NHC mentioned that Iris would retain its name if it regenerated in the Pacific. However, the Pacific tropical depression developed from the remnants of Iris was called Fifteen-E instead. The depression later became Tropical Storm Manuel. NHC explained that Iris had dissipated as a tropical cyclone prior to entering the eastern North Pacific Basin; the new depression was properly named Fifteen-E, rather than Iris. In 2003, when Larry was about to move across Mexico, NHC attempted to provide greater clarity: "Should Larry remain a tropical cyclone during its passage over Mexico into the Pacific, it would retain its name. However, a new name would be given if the surface circulation dissipates and then regenerates in the Pacific."[27] Up to now, it is extremely rare for a tropical cyclone to retain its name during the passage from the Atlantic to the Pacific, or vice versa.

Second, storms are renamed in situations where there are uncertainties of the continuation of storms. When the remnants of a tropical cyclone redevelop, the redeveloping system will be treated as a new tropical cyclone if there are uncertainties of the continuation, even though the original system may contribute to the forming of the new system. One example is the remnants of Tropical Depression #10 reforming into Tropical Depression #12 from the 2005 season, which went on to become the powerful and deadly Hurricane Katrina. Another example was a storm that had the most names, as stated earlier; in 1961, there was one tropical storm that had three lives and three names. Tropical Storm Hattie developed off the Caribbean Coast of Nicaragua on October 28, 1961, and drifted north and west before crossing Central America at Guatemala. It re-emerged into the Pacific Ocean on November 1st and was re-christened Simone. Two days later, it recurved back towards the coastline of Central America and crossed over into the Atlantic via Mexico, re-emerging into the Gulf of Mexico as Inga.

---

[27] www.nhc.noaa.gov/archice/2003/dis/al172003.discus.016.shtml.

CHAPTER THREE

The Boom and Bust period in Florida during the 1920s

I n the 1920s, South Florida was a shining gem, attracting investors and snowbirds who wanted a piece of the cities of gold lying in the warm sun. They injected their vast financial resources into the region with such intemperance that opportunistic salesmen made fortunes buying and selling the same property over and over. Those sellers and buyers and dreamers created a frenzy that would fling them even deeper into the Great Depression that was about to end the partying. The 1920s were a prosperous time for much of the nation, including Florida. Florida's new railroads, built by Henry Flagler, opened up large areas to development, spurring Florida's land boom of the 1920s.

Investors of all kinds, mostly from outside Florida, raced to buy and sell rapidly appreciating land in newly developing communities such as Miami and Palm Beach. Led by entrepreneurs Carl Fisher and George Merrick, Miami was transformed by land speculation and ambitious building projects into an emerging metropolis. A growing awareness in the northern colder states of the attractive South Florida winter climate, along with local promotion of speculative investing, spurred the boom. A majority of the people who bought land in Florida were able to do so without even stepping foot in the state, by hiring intermediaries. By 1924, the main issues in state elections were how to attract more industry and the need to build and maintain good roads for tourists. During the time frame, the population of the entire state of Florida grew from less than one million in 1920 to 1,263,540 in 1925.

By 1925, the market ran out of buyers to pay the high prices, and soon the boom became a bust. The Great Miami Hurricane of 1926, which nearly destroyed the city and further depressed the real estate market, sent it into a downward spiral. In 1928 another hurricane struck South Florida. The Great Okeechobee Hurricane of 1928 made landfall near Palm Beach, severely damaging the local infrastructure. In townships near Lake Okeechobee, the storm breached a dike separating the water from land, creating a storm surge that killed over 2,500 persons and destroying many of the towns in the vicinity of the lake, such as Belle Glade and Pahokee.

The history of Florida began when it was established as a military and agricultural colony of Spain. It also developed a tourism industry when it was still a frontier and has had numerous real estate booms and busts in the 501 years since its discovery. However, the period in the 1920s was one of the more notable ones for the state of Florida. Florida was discovered by Ponce de Leon in 1513, when he landed in the vicinity of present day St. Augustine. Ponce de Leon named the new land "Pascua de Florida" (feast of flowers) because he first spotted it on April 2, 1513, Palm Sunday. St. Augustine was founded in 1565 by Pedro Menendez de Aviles as a colony of Spain and was the northernmost Spanish outpost designed to protect the trade routes of the Spanish treasure fleets carrying gold, silver, gems, cocoa, spices, and other exotic goods back to Spain.

The construction of the Castillo de San Marcos, a coquina fortress, began in 1672 on the site of nine earlier wooden forts, as a defensive move to counter the new English colony of Charles Towne (1670), in the Carolinas. Pensacola was permanently colonized in 1698. The Spanish had established three main ranching areas in the Gainesville, Palatka, and Tallahassee areas during their colonial period. The first Florida land boom occurred between 1782 and 1784, when British Loyalists families fled the American Patriots after the Revolutionary War and settled in St. Augustine and along the upper St. Johns River. During this period of time, the English living in Florida increased by 280%.

Florida became a territory of the United States in 1821 and the 27th state on March 3, 1845. A new territory meant new opportunities and a land boom in Florida. St. Augustine and Pensacola were the two largest cities in the new territory, and the territorial governor appointed a commission to select a site for a new capital midway between the two cities. Tallahassee was established as the territorial capital in 1824. The Florida panhandle has a 2,300 square mile area of elevated hammock, pine forest and savanna, which was ideal for agricultural development. The land boom that began in 1821 was clustered around the antebellum towns of Madison, Marianna, Monticello, and Quincy, with plantation development focused on cotton. Apalachicola became the third largest cotton exporting port on the Gulf of Mexico.

The first Florida steamboat appeared on the Apalachicola River in 1827. Union troops never reached the Florida Capitol or plantation belt during the Civil War (1861 to 1865), and the cotton crop of 1865 was sold at a premium. Eventually, Florida's restructured plantation system failed due to failing crops, declining prices, cash shortages, and the attack of the boll weevil. Northerners bought many former cotton plantations as private quail hunting preserves.

As agricultural development boomed in north Florida, after 1821, at its southernmost tip, Key West grew into Florida's largest town by 1850. After the United States bought the Louisiana Territory from France, new ports were developed along the Gulf Coast and the hazardous Florida Straits became one of the busiest shipping routes in the world. The Florida Straits have dangerous currents, unpredictable weather, as well as the treacherous Florida coral reefs extending along the Keys, posing yet another danger to ships. In addition, in the mid-1800s Cuba and the Keys were home to an estimated 10,000 pirates, including Black Caesar and Blackbeard. Ships attempting to escape the pirates often ran aground and sank in shallow waters. Bahamian salvagers, or wreckers in the local vernacular, often seized the cargo and dismantled parts of the wrecked ships. Key West was made home port to the U.S. Navy West India Squadron in an effort to end piracy in the area. Key West, with its natural harbour and strategic location, was established as a salvage port and eventually a military base and was one of the richest towns in the United States on a per capita basis at the time. The development of the steamboat and its 1827 arrival in Florida helped open up the interior for commerce and tourism.

In 1864, a writer for the *New York Herald* wrote, "I am confident no sane man who knows what Florida is would give a thousand dollars to gain possession of all the territory beyond the St. Johns. No decent man would think of living in that state outside two or three points on the St. Johns and the Gulf."[28] In the next 15 years, not much happened in Florida. Florida's 1880 population was 269,000 people, who lived mostly in Jacksonville, Key West, Pensacola, Tallahassee, and Tampa.

In 1880, the state of Florida had to pay $1,000,000 in interest on $14,000,000 in bonds and did not have the funds to do so. The bonds were nearly worthless, and Florida's credit non-existent. The state treasurer kept what little money there was in a New York bank. Florida was nearing bankruptcy and faced the loss of credit to keep the State's business running. Florida had one asset, 20,000,000 acres of "swamp and overflowed" land granted to it by the Federal Government under the Swamp and Overflowed Lands Act of 1850. This acreage was controlled by the Trustees of the Internal Improvement Fund. The future of Florida looked very bleak.[29]

Enter Philadelphia businessman and financier Hamilton Disston, who was active in the progressive Republican Party. He was fascinated by real estate and learned of substantial land being offered in Florida at very low prices. Disston was able to acquire 4,000,000 acres for $0.25 per acre, or $1,000,000. He had $100,000 to $200,000 in cash and singed a promissory note for the balance and closed on June 1, 1881. Hamilton Disston saved Florida from bankruptcy and purchased 6,250 square miles of land, or one-ninth of the state. Instantly, the state of Florida's credit was restored and outside capital (mostly from Henry Flagler and Henry Plant) flowed into Florida. The so-called Bourbon Democrats (mostly planters and businessmen) were pleased that the debt had been repaid without raising taxes.

The bulk of Disston's holdings ranged south from what is now Kissimmee to, and surrounding, Lake Okeechobee. Disston also owned about 150,000 acres in what is now Pinellas County, of which about 12,000 acres was to be developed into Disston City in 1884 (Gulfport, as of 1910), his planned resort city on Boca Ciega Bay and his first Florida headquarters. A Waldorf Hotel was built near the wharf and Disston Boulevard, now 49th Street, which extended northward. Disston held discussions with Peter Demens (the former Pyotr Dementyvev from Russia)

[28] Robinson, J. (2009) *Historic Osceola County: An Illustrated History*, Historical Publishing Network, pg. 40.
[29] www.learningace.com/doc/1643684/.../floridarealestatehistory

about extending his Orange Belt Railroad to Disston City. Disston offered 60,000 acres and his influence in Tallahassee to Demens to extend his new railroad to Disston City. Demens wanted an additional 50,000 acres; Disston declined. Demens completed the link between the lower St. Johns River and Lake Apopka, and then extended the Orange Belt Railroad 120 miles to the Pinellas Peninsula. On June 8, 1888, the first train arrived at its terminal in southern Pinellas County with one passenger. The area had no official name, no streets, and no sidewalks. Demens named the location St. Petersburg after Saint Petersburg, Russia, where he had spent much of his youth. St. Petersburg boomed, and Disston City declined.

Disston established his field headquarters in Kissimmee and began a massive drainage operation in the Kissimmee River basin. Disston next established the 20,000 acre St. Cloud Sugar Plantation. Disston was betting that water transportation, the steamboat, was the key to Florida's future. Disston, through the Disston Land Company and other related ventures, drained swampland and opened new areas to agricultural development. Philadelphia banks loaned him funds, and he floated bond issues to provide more investment capital. Florida and Disston were riding a boom. New towns such as Kissimmee City, Narcoosee, Runnymede, and Southport were built on former swampland, and other towns such as Ancolote, Fort Myers, and Tarpon Springs were also developed during the 1880s boom. It was estimated that by 1893, the Disston Land Company had conveyed about 1,200,000 acres of reclaimed land and lowered the level of Lake Okeechobee by about four-and-one-half feet. The Trustees of the Internal Improvement Fund chartered 564 railroads, of which 251 were built in whole or part during this boom period from 1881 to 1893.

Along came developers Henry Flagler and Henry Plant, who greatly impacted the development of Florida in a significant way. Henry Morrison Flagler (January 2, 1830 – May 20, 1913) was an American industrialist and a founder of Standard Oil. He was also a key figure in the development of the Atlantic coast of Florida and founder of what became the Florida East Coast Railway. He is known as the father of Miami, Florida, and founded the city of Palm Beach. Henry Bradley Plant (October 27, 1819 - June 23, 1899) was involved with many transportation projects, mostly railroads, in the U.S. state of Florida. Eventually he owned the Plant System of railroads, which became part of the Atlantic Coast Line Railroad. Plant

City, located near Tampa, was named after him. Florida grew rapidly as a resort destination as Henry Flagler (Florida East Coast Railway) and Henry Plant (Plant System) on the west coast extended their rails ever southward and the private railcars followed.

As the railroads moved further south, resort hotels were built in frontier towns for winter tourists. Flagler built new multi-million dollar resort hotels at each new railhead: the opulent Carrere & Hastings-designed Spanish Renaissance style Ponce de Leon Hotel, 1888 (now Flagler College); the Cordova, 1888 (now Casa Monica Hotel); and the Alcazar Hotel, 1889; Triad in St. Augustine; the wood frame Royal Poinciana Hotel, 1894 (Palm Beach); and the wood frame Royal Palm Hotel, 1896 (Miami). Henry Flagler also founded West Palm Beach in 1894 as a community to house the construction crews working across Lake Worth on Palm Beach Island, and eventually the servants working in Palm Beach's two grand hotels (Royal Poinciana and The Breakers (1896)). Along with these massive developments came the need for workers and the need of the state to feed this inflow of people into the state of Florida. The Bahamian migrant workers came to Florida in droves to fulfill both of these needs.

Florida entered a period of frenzied real estate activity and speculative excess on a grandiose scale in the 1920s. Intense building began in Miami in the early 1920s and quickly led to increased real estate activity. Speculators began to buy land and sell it for small profits within a few months. Then the winter tourists began to invest. Profits increased as turnover time decreased. Windfall profits began to escalate to unsustainable levels and were merely a pyramiding of paper profits. Real estate values began to inflate rapidly. Word of Florida's real estate activity spread across the county, and people poured into the state, eager for easy and quick profits.

The big 1926 and 1928 hurricanes devastated Florida with high winds and surging floodwaters. The huge task of rebuilding and the financial losses inflicted by these hurricanes were enormous and caused thousands of Florida's residents to abandon their new-found homes and return to their northern cities. The population of Florida plummeted on a downward spiral. Real estate values also plummeted as former residents sold properties for whatever the real estate market would yield.

The Florida land boom of the 1920s was Florida's first real estate bubble, which burst in 1925, leaving behind entire new cities and the remains of failed development projects such as Aladdin City in south Miami-Dade County and Isola di Lolando in north Biscayne Bay. The preceding land boom shaped Florida's future for decades to come and created entirely new cities out of the Everglades land that remain today. The story includes many parallels to the modern real estate boom, including the forces of outside speculators, easy credit access for buyers, and rapidly appreciating property values.

By the 1920s, its economic prosperity had set the conditions for a real estate bubble in Florida. Miami had an image as a tropical paradise, and outside investors across the United States began taking an interest in Miami real estate. Due in part to the publicity talents of audacious developers such as Carl G. Fisher of Miami Beach, famous for purchasing a huge lighted billboard in New York's Time Square proclaiming "It's June In Miami", property prices rose rapidly on speculation and a land and development boom ensued. Brokers and dealers speculated wildly in all classes of commodities as well, ordering supplies vastly in excess of what were actually needed, and even sending shipments to only a general destination, with the end result being that railroad freight cars became stranded in the state, choking the movement of rail traffic.

By January 1925, investors were beginning to read negative press about Florida investments. Forbes magazine warned that Florida land prices were based solely upon the expectation of finding a customer, not upon any reality of land value. New York bankers and the IRS both began to scrutinize the Florida real estate boom as a giant sham operation. Speculators intent on flipping properties at huge profits began to have a difficult time finding new buyers. To make matters worse, in October 1925, the "Big Three" railroad companies operating in Florida—the Seaboard Air Line Railway, the Florida East Coast Railway, and the Atlantic Coast Line Railroad—called an embargo due to the rail traffic gridlock, permitting only foodstuffs, fuel, perishables, and essential commodities to enter or move within the state.

Then, on January 10, 1926, the *Prinz Valdemar*, a 241-foot, steel-hulled schooner, sank in the mouth of the turning basin of Miami Harbour and blocked access to the harbour. The old Danish warship had been on its way to becoming a floating hotel. Because the railroads were still embargoing non-essential shipments, it now became completely impossible to bring building supplies into the Miami area, and the city's image as a tropical paradise began to crumble. In his book *Miami Millions*, Kenneth Ballinger wrote that the *Prinz Valdemar* capsize incident saved a lot of people a lot of money by revealing cracks in the Miami façade. "In the enforced lull which accompanied the efforts to unstopper the Miami Harbour," he wrote, "many a shipper in the North and many a builder in the South got a better grasp of what was actually taking place here." New buyers failed to arrive, and the property price escalation that fueled the land boom stopped. The days of Miami properties being bought and sold at auction as many as ten times in one day were over.[30]

Although the railroads lifted the embargo in May 1926, the boom nevertheless fizzled out. Disaster then followed in the shape of the Great Miami Hurricane of 1926, which drove many developers into bankruptcy. Furthermore, the 1928 Great Lake Okeechobee Hurricane and the Wall Street Crash of 1929 continued the catastrophic downward economic trend, and the Florida land boom was officially over as the Great Depression began. The Great Depression and the devastating arrival of the Mediterranean fruit fly a year later destroyed both the tourist and citrus industries upon which Florida greatly depended and drove the final nail in their coffin with regards to Florida's economic growth. In a few years, the tropical paradise called Florida had been transformed into an unwelcoming, humid remote area with few or no economic prospects. Florida's economy would not recover until World War II.

On September 16, 1928, a powerful storm struck Palm Beach County. It was equal to a Category 4 hurricane on the Saffir-Simpson Hurricane Wind Scale. The deadly hurricane reached shore with winds between 130 to 150 miles per hour. It dropped more than 18 inches of rain in less than 24 hours. This hurricane damaged or destroyed almost everything in its path. The strong winds and heavy rainfall caused Lake Okeechobee to overflow. Belle Glade, Pahokee, South Bay, and other surrounding communities were flooded. Flooding and high winds killed more than 2,500 people in the Glades. Yet the survivors overcame the disaster and rebuilt their towns. Because of this disaster, the Herbert Hoover Dike was built around Lake Okeechobee to prevent flooding in the future.

---

[30]   Kenneth Ballinger: *Miami Millions*, Miami: (self-published), 1936, pg. 139.

The residents of this area endured the Great Miami Hurricane of 1926 in Florida, but they did not expect another storm of the same magnitude or greater in the space of just two short years.

Most of the victims of the 1928 hurricane died near Lake Okeechobee, and they were brought and buried by the truckload to West Palm Beach. At Woodlawn Cemetery, 69 bodies were buried, 61 of them white; a marble headstone was added later. The rest of the African American bodies were placed in a mass grave at Tamarind Avenue and 25th Street. For about ten years, Robert Hazard and his non-profit, 'Storm of '28 Coalition,' fought to gain recognition for the black victims. The City of West Palm Beach placed a marker in 2003 to the black victims who died in this storm, on the 75th anniversary of the "Storm of '28."

By August 1925, the Florida East Coast Railway was overwhelmed by the demands of passengers and freight, which interfered with its ability to maintain its equipment properly. The railroad placed an embargo on non-perishable goods, and by winter, at least 7,000 freight cars sat in Jacksonville, waiting to head south. As news of real estate scams by con artists reached the North, panicked investors there cancelled their long-distance real estate contracts. In the early fall, Florida Governor John W. Martin led a delegation to New York to fight the flow of bad publicity. They held a seminar, "The truth about Florida," at the Waldorf-Astoria Hotel, owned by T. Coleman du Pont, an investor in Addison Mizner's development of Boca Raton in southern Palm Beach County. One week later, du Pont and several other board members left Mizner Development Corporation.

Although imagined values started the fall of Florida's boom, very visible events brought more tragedy to Palm Beach County. First, on September 18, 1926, a powerful hurricane from Miami moved across the west side of Lake Okeechobee, killing more than 390 people and taking its toll on the farms of the Glades communities, as well as those along the east coast. Because of the destruction caused by the Great Miami Hurricane of 1926, potential buyers were afraid to purchase Florida land and developers went broke. On March 15, 1927, The *New York Times* reported: "Three banks in Palm Beach County failed to open their doors this morning (in West Palm Beach, Lake Worth, and Delray), bringing the number closed in the county in the last week to six and causing runs on the two largest banks still open in West Palm Beach."[31]

By the next day, rumors had already spread in West Palm Beach that the U.S. Government had gone broke, too. About 400 owners of savings accounts at the West Palm Beach Post Office, mostly from the black community, withdrew their funds of up to $2,500 each, the maximum of post office accounts. The *New York Times* called it the first run in post office history. Yet the worst was still to come.

On September 16, 1928, a Category 4 hurricane, with winds reaching 150 miles per hour, destroyed over 8,000 homes and hundreds of commercial buildings in Palm Beach County. Although coastal areas sustained extensive property damage, it was flooding from Lake Okeechobee and high winds that killed more than 2,500 people, most of them migrant farmers and labourers from Belle Glade, Pahokee, and South Bay, the majority of which were Bahamian migrant workers.

By the time the New York Stock Exchange crashed in October 1929, sending the nation into the Great Depression, southeast Florida was already in a depression of its own. From 1929 to 1930, the recorded value of all real estate in West Palm Beach dropped 53 percent to $41.6 million; by 1935 it was down to $18.2 million, little more than its pre-boom value. However, on the bright side, the boom period left behind a developing infrastructure of highways, transportation, hotels, commercial buildings, and homes. Several new hotels had opened before the Great Miami Hurricane of 1926 and the Great Okeechobee Hurricane of 1928 struck. Even before the stock market crash of 1929, several declared bankruptcy, searched for new investors, or changed names and management. Others were sold, including the Whitehall Hotel in June 1929, for a mere $2,600 plus its $3 million of debt.

Long after the death of Henry Flagler in 1913, the Whitehall Hotel received a ten-story upgrade that opened as the Whitehall Hotel on New Year's Eve 1927. The *Post* described its atmosphere as an "apartment hotel" and more formal than the Royal Poinciana Hotel, with dining and dancing in its beautiful Jardin Royal by the lake. When Flagler's heirs converted Whitehall to the Flagler Museum, most of the additions were demolished.

---

[31]   http://www.pbchistoryonline.org/page/the-bust

Although still operating, the Seaboard Air Line Railway declared bankruptcy in 1930. The same year, a new depot was built for the Florida East Coast Railway, which followed Seaboard into bankruptcy in 1931. Both companies were managed by court-appointed receivers for many years. Despite all these problems, the private sector in Palm Beach continued to build new houses. Zell Davis, who served as state's attorney from 1968 to 1972, first lived on 21st Street in Riviera Beach, near his Bahamian relatives. While others sank into poverty in the late 1920s, Davis' family prospered as bootleggers during the Prohibition era. Davis moved to a large house on 35th Street in West Palm Beach in 1931 when he was five, and throughout his lifetime he always remained aware of his good fortune during the pre and post-Depression years.

The Town of Jupiter felt the bust sooner than other parts of Palm Beach County. In 1925, the town made plans to establish zoning of residential and commercial areas and add plazas, a yacht club, and a civic center. The following year, street lights were installed, and a water system to accommodate a population of 500. But by 1927, the town needed a short-term loan to pay for the lights and residents requested that some be left unlit to reduce expenses. When many property owners did not pay their taxes, the town at first seized the land, and then repealed the tax ordinance for the year.

After World War I, an unprecedented building boom began in Palm Beach County. The Roaring '20s was a time when a person's wealth and success were measured by what he or she had owned. However, by the mid-1920s, people lost everything as the Land Boom went bust. Henry Flagler's death in 1913 did not diminish the popularity of the winter playground for the wealthy that he had created in Palm Beach, nor did it slow the growth it precipitated in southeast Florida. An ever-growing flow of visitors and residents produced a need for businesses, entertainment facilities, and an expanded infrastructure of schools, houses of worship, services, and transportation routes. The resulting small building boom in Florida in the early teens and early to mid-twenties paused during the United States involvement in World War I from 1917 to 1918, when the government restricted the use of building materials. Following the end of World War I, growth in Palm Beach County exploded. The 1920s Land Boom was a period of extremes in wealth, development, and weather. By the end of the decade, it all came crashing down just as quickly as it had begun.

CHAPTER FOUR

The reasons for the movement of Bahamian Labour to Florida in the early to mid-1900s

The movement of Bahamian people to Florida may be studied through the lens of various disciplines: sociology, ethnography, economics, politics, or public policy. Generally, however, migrants move to areas of economic growth and opportunity; these are described as the "pull factors" that encourage migration. The "push factors" that typically force people to leave their homes and families and migrate are poverty, lack of opportunity, land shortages, and poor living or working conditions.

The study of migration and population growth in the Bahamas begins with their discovery by Christopher Columbus in 1492. Amidst a tropical setting, Lucayan Indians, Spaniards, Englishmen and Blacks, each in their own turn, has left a mark on these islands just east of Florida and north of Cuba. The Spaniards stayed just long enough to exploit the most exportable commodity—the Lucayan Indians. Then, for a century or more these islands were a no man's land until the seafaring Bermudians called Eleutheran Adventurers established a settlement on the island of Eleuthera in the winter of 1647-48. The Eleutheran Adventurers were a group of English Puritans and religious independents who left Bermuda to settle on the island of Eleuthera, in the Bahamas. This group represents the first concerted European effort to colonize the Bahamas—no effort was made while the islands were under Spanish rule—but their claim to the islands would not survive the political turmoil of the Restoration in England.

The newcomers suffered many hardships: an early period of piracy and frequent reprisals from the Spanish and the French. By using the ingenious techniques of the amphibian, however, they managed to hold on until the end of the American Revolution when the arrival of many Loyalists and their slaves imposed a cotton-growing economy on the traditional seagoing way of life. Most of the islands, other than the previously settled Eleuthera and New Providence, were then effectively occupied for the first time. All the while, the capital city of Nassau, on New Providence, was strengthening its position, not only in title, but as an actual head of the colony. By the end of slavery in 1838, the general pattern of present-day life had been formed, and only the details within the geographical and chronological framework were to change afterwards.

Most agricultural ventures that followed cotton—pineapples, sisal, tomatoes—rarely prospered for long. The difficulty in easily reaching a market was and still is probably the greatest handicap. The sea, though, was harvested with much more success. Shipwrecks, sponges, fish, turtles, and salt have all been important resources. Its most recent gift—the water itself—when combined with the mild climate, offers an unsurpassed natural habit for a growing tourist trade, by far the former colony's largest industry today.

Wars and related disturbances have always plagued the islands. Their strategic location, more than anything else, has made them from past to present readily susceptible to outside stimulus. Aside from an unstable early history, the islands of the Bahamas have been used as a base for running the blockade of the Southern Confederacy from 1861 to 1865, as well as Prohibition in the 1920s. A significant period of population growth began with the era of Prohibition in the United States following World War I. The Bahamas had not received as stimulating an impetus to its economy since the Civil War. Rum-running reacted on the nervous system of the islands like a shot of adrenalin, and the heart began to beat furiously.

For a brief span, high seas adventure held the attention of many Bahamians. Prohibition in America during the 1920s created something of a mini-boom in the island's economy when the rumrunners moved in. Prohibition also encouraged many Americans to visit Nassau. Persons of wealth began to take up residence there for the reason that the government levied no income tax. Two of the largest hotels in Nassau were built in the 1920s, the Nassau Harbour was deepened, and real estate value began to rise. The post-World War I boom saw the Out-Islanders beginning to flock to Nassau, and to a lesser extent to Florida, to find means of employment. Whereas less than one-quarter of the population lived on New Providence in 1921, the percentage rose to one-third ten years later. But the new prosperity was short-lived. They have also been used as "unsinkable flattops" by patrol planes in World War II and as a source of field workers for farms in the United States.

In the 1920s, farming, fishing, sponging and public works were tried, but the high demand for agricultural workers in Florida came to the rescue of a large number of these Bahamian workers, who migrated to the state of Florida to find means of employment, many choosing not to return home. For example, in 1924, approximately nine percent of the island of Andros' population had been steadily engaged in seasonal farm work in the United States. Migration has been a fundamental feature of the Bahamian labour history in the 20th century. Most migration has been the result of economic motivation, and by that I mean the internal movement of people from the Out or Family Islands to Nassau in search of work and better living standards or the migration of Bahamian labourers abroad. At the beginning of the 20th century, Bahamians moved to Panama to help build the Panama Canal, or to Florida in the 1920s to help build the city of Miami and to work in the agriculture sector.[32]

The number of black people, especially those from the Caribbean, who migrated to the United States increased dramatically during the first three decades of the twentieth century, peaking in 1924 at 12,250 per year and falling off during the Depression. The foreign-born black population increased from 20,000 in 1900 to almost 100,000 by 1930. In the period from 1880 to 1930, labour migration of Bahamians, unlike that of other British West Indians, was primarily confined to the nearby state of Florida.[33] This chapter examines the economic structure of the Bahamas, which, with the decline of major agricultural export staples, promoted this outward migration, particularly to Miami, in the early years of the twentieth century. It discusses the implications of oscillating and permanent migration for the sending area. This discussion involves

---

[32]   http://www.inmotionaame.org/migrations
[33]   http://www.inmotionaame.org/migrations

a consideration of the effects of labour migration on the Family Island's agriculture and the impact of remittances on economic development in the Bahamas.

In the British Caribbean, the years 1880-1920 were marked by large-scale net emigration to foreign countries as labour responded to the opportunities for employment generated primarily by the expansion of American capital investment. Although the Bahamas supplied labour for the construction of the Panama Canal and other American enterprises in Central America and the Caribbean, the main destination for Bahamian labour was the state of Florida, across the Gulf Stream. This population movement constituted migration in reverse.

There were two main waves of labour migration to Florida from the Bahamas in the period under examination. The first of these was the migration to Key West, Florida, which lasted from the 1870s into the first decade of the twentieth century. This outward movement was succeeded by (and overlapped with) the "Miami Craze", which lasted from 1905 to 1924, when immigration restrictions virtually closed the American labour market to Bahamian labour.

As early as the 1820s and 1830s, Bahamian wreckers (primarily from Abaco) had migrated to Key West, where they were largely responsible for its emergence as a wrecking center. In 1849, the *Bahama Herald* reported that approximately two-thirds of the white inhabitants of Abaco were leaving or had already left to take up their abode at Key West, to become fishermen or wreckers. A factor in the early out-migration of white Abaconians to Key West was racial prejudice. Governor Charles Bayley observed in 1860 that natives of Abaco, who then formed at least two-thirds of the population of Key West, had migrated because they were "disgusted at the civil and religious equality of the negroes."[34]

The establishment of Key West as a center for sponging operations in the 1870s also attracted Bahamian immigrants. J.H. Webb, the Superintendent of Census in the colony, observed in 1881 that one of the factors that explained the slow rate of population growth in New Providence as compared with the rest of the colony in the period from 1871-1881 was "immigration—chiefly to Key West."

---

[34] *Bahama Herald*, November 30, 1849.

In 1885, Governor Henry Blake reported periodic migration to Key West by black Bahamians from Nassau. The black population had already begun to migrate periodically to Key West, which the expansion of cigar manufacturing businesses for the American market had raised from a village to a comparatively wealthy town.

Although the economic prosperity of Key West in the late nineteenth century attracted labourers from the Bahamas, the outward movement is largely explained by economic conditions in the various islands and by the way in which the sponging and pineapple industries (the main supports of their economies) were organized. By the mid-1880s, the pineapple industry, in some areas, was already showing signs of decline. One of the problems at this stage was that the land suitable for pineapple cultivation was becoming exhausted. Most cultivators worked the land for a few years, without using fertilizers and practicing rotation of crops, and then abandoned it for several years to regain its original fertility.

By 1884, the consequences of these agricultural practices were evident, and outward migration to Florida had already begun in the settlement of Rock Sound, Eleuthera, where the official report for that year noted: "Many are away on the Florida Coast. Quite a number have left altogether for Key West. No inducement for them to remain. The large Pine tracts were worn out". The collapse of the pineapple industry in the early years of the twentieth century led to further migration of the inhabitants of Rock Sound, who were not satisfied with mere subsistence farming. With the failure of cash-crop production, the cultivators in Rock Sound turned to wage labour in Key West.[35]

In Abaco and Harbour Island, outward migration was also directly related to the fluctuating fortunes of their major export sales. An unsuccessful season in pineapple cultivation was often enough to stimulate emigration. This was the experience of pineapple cultivators in Harbour Island in 1886, when the severity of the winter damaged their crop. Their problem was compounded by the failure of the agents who marketed the crop to pay them.

Labour migration to Florida in the late nineteenth century was also an expression of dissatisfaction by the labouring class of the colony with

---

[35] Appendix to *Votes of the House of Assembly*, February 24-August 22, 1885, pg. 10.

the way in which the sponging and pineapple industries were organized. Both industries were organized in such a way that the major part of the profits was appropriated by a white merchant class resident in Nassau, New Providence. These merchants controlled internal and external trade and credit, were owners of extensive "pineapple lands" in the Out Islands and the major investors in the pineapple and sponging industries. In both industries, the payment of labour was organized on a profit sharing, rather than a wage basis.

In the absence of regular wages, most Bahamians involved in the sponging and pineapple industries relied on credit to maintain themselves and their families until the proceeds of the sponging voyage were divided or the crop was sold. This credit, which most often took the form of goods rather than cash (in most cases the value of the goods had greater than normal markups), was usually advanced by merchants who were financially involved in these business ventures. It was a common occurrence for a sponger or cultivator to be caught up in a cycle of debt as a result of the credit system. In practice, spongers and cultivators were rarely remunerated in cash, but in provisions or "truck." Payment in truck and the credit system were generally referred to as the truck system in this period.

The evidence indicates that there was a direct connection between the operation of the truck system in the sponging and pineapple industries and the exodus to Key West. One of the attractions of Key West for the immigrant labourer seems to have been not merely higher wages, but wages paid in cash. As L.D. Powles observed in 1888: "The people of the Bahamas are daily coming more and more in contact with Key West on the Florida coast, and are gradually finding out that there are places in the world where not only a high rate of wages is paid, but the people get paid in cash."[36]

After 1905, South Florida became the most attractive destination for emigrating Bahamians. By 1896, the hotel and railroad magnate Henry Flagler had extended his railway system from Jacksonville to Miami and opened up that area to development. The accelerated economic activity created a demand for labour that sparsely populated southern Florida could

---

[36]   L.D. Powles, (1888) *Land of the Pink Pearl*, London, pg.88. Powles served as stipendiary and circuit magistrate for the Bahamas in the mid-1880s. In his book he exposed the workings of the truck system in the colony's major industries.

not supply. Labour requirements were thus largely provided from elsewhere. In the first two decades of the twentieth century, unskilled Bahamian labourers migrated to South Florida, principally for construction and agricultural work. Construction work was available not only in the rapidly growing city of Miami, which early on experienced a land and building boom, but also in the building of the Key West extension of Flagler's railroad between 1905 and 1912.

By 1905, the Florida East Coast Railroad had already reached Detroit (Florida City) and resulted in the establishment of large-scale capitalist farms in South Dade, which provided winter fruits and vegetables for northern markets. The development of this sub-tropical region required a large labour force to clear the pine lands for the planting of groves and for tending the vegetable fields. There was also a demand for women to perform domestic service. These labourers were paid higher wages than the Bahamas could offer. It is not, then, surprising that Miami, as one contemporary observer remarked, should have become "to the Bahamians seeking a livelihood, what Mecca is to the religious Muslim world." Bahamians who were attracted to South Florida included not only those who came directly from the islands, but also those who came via Key West, where the cigar industry was, after 1910, in decline.

The higher wages offered in Florida were an important inducement to Bahamians of the labouring classes to migrate in search of employment. In New Providence in 1911, the usual wage rate for an unskilled labourer varied between 1/6 [d] and 2/- per day, whereas in Florida the daily wage was from $1.25 to $1.50, or approximately 5/- to 6/- at the then existing exchange rate.[37] However, the Bahamians who earned a regular wage in the colony formed a small minority of the working population in the early years of the twentieth century. After emancipation, in the absence of opportunities for wage employment, most of the inhabitants of the Out Islands eked out a relatively independent existence by engaging in subsistence farming and sea-going activities. Up to the early years of the twentieth century, many Bahamians remained unproletarianized and essentially outside the market economy.

---

[37] *The Nassau Tribune*, January 19, 1911.

There is no doubt that lucrative wage employment in southern Florida represented an attractive alternative to independent production for many Bahamians in the Out Islands. Some of these independent cultivators were forced into wage labour in Florida because of the effects of droughts or hurricanes. In 1919, for example, many inhabitants of the islands of Long Cay, Acklins and Crooked Island migrated to Florida because the prolonged drought had resulted in the failure of food crops. Their situation had been worsened by the fact that the Bight of Acklins was closed to sponging.[38] These were the islands to which Sir William Allardyce, Governor of the colony, made reference to when he remarked in December 1919 that "both men and women have been obliged to migrate to Florida in order to obtain, not high wages alone but the means of subsistence and better conditions of living."[39]

In the first two decades of the twentieth century, those Bahamian cultivators who were linked more directly to the world economy by the production of two export staples—pineapple and sisal—experienced shrinking markets and usually unremunerative prices. Many cultivators responded to this deteriorating economic situation by moving to Florida to find means of employment. In the pineapple industry there were problems of productivity and of diminishing markets. The chief problems in pineapple cultivation by 1908 were exhausted soils and a failure to use suitable fertilizers. More important in explaining the decline of the pineapple industry was competition from other pineapple producing areas, especially from Hawaii and Florida, which dominated the American market with the help of a protective tariff. One result of the problems experienced by the industry was that the smaller cultivators gradually abandoned the cultivation of pineapples.

In a petition to the House of Assembly in January 1911, the residents of Tarpum Bay, Eleuthera one of the main islands cultivating pineapples, pointed out that within the previous five years the "deterioration of stock," the low prices paid for pineapples and the high tariff had forced most of the smaller cultivators to abandon the industry and devote their time to

---

[38] Report on Long Cay, Fortune Island for 1919. In Appendix to *Votes of the Legislative Council*, February 3- August 26, 1920, pg. 167.

[39] Speech of Sir W.L. Allardyce, December 18, 1919, *Votes of the Legislative Council*, February 18-December 18, 1919, pg. 140.

the cultivation of produce. By 1912, the cultivation of pineapples in the districts of Arthur's Town and San Salvador (previously two important centers of pineapple production) had "dwindled to [a] mere nothing."[40]

Developments in the sisal industry were equally frustrating for Bahamian cultivators. By the first decade of the twentieth century, sisal had become mainly a peasant crop, which provided cash for the cultivator during periods of drought when food crops were affected. However, for most of the period (with the exception of a few years during World War I), the price of Bahamian sisal on the American market remained low. This situation reflected the poor quality of Bahamian sisal and the competition from efficient producers like Mexico. Those years in which low prices for sisal coincided with a failure of food crops usually saw increased labour migration to Florida and elsewhere.

With the decline of the sisal and pineapple industries, labourers displaced from agriculture moved to Florida and other areas where there was a demand for their labour power. In the Out Islands, there were few alternative agricultural activities in which these labourers could become involved. Some major obstacles to agricultural development in the Out Islands were the lack of roads, poor and rocky soils, and regular and reliable transportation links with Nassau and external markets. Although this was a problem to which successive governors had called attention, the House of Assembly dominated by members resident in Nassau had shown little interest in improving the situation. In 1920, a commission of enquiry appointed to report on the general administration of the Out Islands attributed emigration mainly to the fact that there was, as yet, "no ready and reliable transportation to this [Nassau] or any other market for what is or might be produced."[41]

The main exception to the general pattern of economic decline in this period was the sponge industry. Its continued prosperity meant that labour was usually required for sponging crews. However, the widespread

40 *Votes of the House of Assembly*, January 10-July 13, 1911, pgs. 53–54/ *Report on Arthur's Town, San Salvador for 1912*, Bahamas Public Record Office.

41 "Second Interim Report of the Commission appointed to make Diligent and Full Enquiry into and Report on the General Administration of the Out Islands," June 22, 1920, *Votes of the Legislative Council*, February 15, 1921- January 16, 1922, pg. 238.

realization by spongers that they did not benefit from the prosperity of the sponge trade continued to stimulate migration to Florida. The principal source of their dissatisfaction was the advance system, which virtually guaranteed that they were always in debt to the Greek merchants.

It was never necessary to recruit Bahamian labourers for work in southern Florida, since news of employment opportunities circulated in the colony. Most migrants went to Nassau by the mailboats that travelled between the islands and then crossed the Gulf Stream by one of the several vessels engaged in the passenger traffic between Nassau and Miami. At $5 or £1, the fare was within reach for many members of the labouring classes. In Miami there were, until 1917, few immigration restrictions to bar the entry of male migrant labourers from the Bahamas. The evidence suggests, however, that immigration officials discriminated against unmarried women of the labouring classes who were usually suspected of being prostitutes.[42]

Initially, it was the young able-bodied men who migrated to Miami, leaving their families at home. The usual pattern was for these men to spend between six months or a year abroad and then return for a period of rest before migrating again. This movement back and forth was made possible by the proximity of Florida to the Bahamas and the relative ease of communication. The length of time spent abroad often depended on the type of work in which migrants were engaged. The agricultural labourers, for example, usually left in October and returned in March at the end of the harvest. Labourers from Bimini, who were primarily employed as fishermen in Miami, also returned home after the fishing season was over. On their visits home, the migrant labourers had an opportunity to display their new prosperity and material possessions.

---

[42] *"Florida—Impressions of a Visitor,"* The Nassau Tribune, December 2, 1911.

Wayne Neely

Table 1-Statistics of Migration between the Bahamas and Florida, 1911-1917

Year	Departures	Arrivals	Net Departures	Net Arrivals
1911	3,230	1,964	1,266	
1912	2,628	2,548	80	
1913	3,422	2,396	1,026	
1914	3,758	3,059	699	
1915	1,511	2,702		1,191
1916	2,734	1,895	839	
1917	1,750	2,090		340

The Annual Colonial Reports for the Bahamas, 1912-1917 (Courtesy of the Bahamas Department of Archives, Nassau, Bahamas).

As the Commissioner for Fresh Creek, Andros, noted of the returning migrants in 1911: "They bring some extraordinary clothes (and it is now *de rigeur* to change three times on Sunday)."[43] These migrants almost certainly acted as unofficial recruiters of labour for Miami. What government officials deplored as outlandish clothes were undoubtedly perceived by men and women, who had not yet migrated, as evidence of consumer items which the high wages available in Miami made affordable.

The outward movement of labour to Miami eventually included most of the able-bodied men in the Out-Island communities. In 1916, for example, the Commissioner of Long Cay, Fortune Island, noted that at the end of the year there were approximately 200 people on the island, but only twenty-four men willing or able to work. In his report for 1920, the Commissioner for Watling's Island reported a similar, if more extreme situation.[44]

"The island is almost denuded of young men. Throughout the whole of the year, both men and women have been going to Florida. I regret to report that at the time of writing there is not a single man on the whole

---

[43] Appendix to *Votes of the Legislative Council*, December 4, 1911-May 22, 1912, pg. 96A.

[44] *Report on Long Cay, Fortune Island for 1916*. Bahamas Public Record Office.

island. It seems incredible, but it is nevertheless true. If something out of the ordinary doesn't turn up soon, the district will be man less, because the married as well as the single are going."[45]

By 1911, yet another pattern had emerged in the migratory flow to Miami. Increasingly, wives and children joined husbands who had settled there. By 1910, there was already a large population of Bahamians who had settled permanently in Miami. The United States Census for that year indicated that in a Negro population of 5,000, there were 3,500 British subjects, most of whom would have been Bahamians. From Miami, Bahamians had distributed themselves in towns such as Coconut Grove, Dania, Fort Lauderdale, West Palm Beach and Daytona, which developed along the railway line. In 1915, it was estimated that at least 2,000 Bahamians lived in these communities.[46]

In Miami and the communities beyond it, Bahamians were employed as domestic servants, farmers, cooks, hotel waiters, bellmen, hackmen, draymen, carpenters, painters, masons, bakers and workers in laundries. On the railroads, Bahamians also held jobs as porters and firemen. The majority of the Bahamians who migrated to South Florida were poor and unskilled, but there were also immigrants from the middle classes, some of whom possessed skills and capital. Some Bahamians with capital established businesses in Coloured Town in Miami. These Bahamian businessmen were able to provide their fellow Bahamians in Miami with a wide range of services. The strict enforcement of a policy of residential segregation along racial lines in Miami ensured that coloured businessmen did not often come into direct competition with their white counterparts for the business of the Bahamian migrants.

Manuscript census schedules for 1900 and 1910 gave a more detailed picture of the black Bahamian immigrants in Miami. The McCloud family typified the early Bahamian presence in South Florida. Hiram McCloud, a forty-eight-year-old Bahamian, had come to the United States in 1878. The census described him as a "common labourer." His

---

[45] Appendix to *Votes of the Legislative Council*, February 15, 1921-January, 16, 1922, pg. 275.

[46] *"Bahamians in Florida, United States," Nassau Quarterly Mission Paper*, xxx, 1915, pg. 13/ *Petition from Bahamians in Florida, October 21, 1911*. Enclosure in Grey-Wilson to Lewis Harcourt, no. 188, November 17, 1911. C.O. 23/pg. 268.

thirty-nine-year-old wife, Clotilda, also came to the United States in 1878, as a "washerwoman." Clotilda gave birth to eight children, but only 5 survived, and most of them became farm labourers as well.

The McClouds came to Florida before the establishment of Miami in 1896. Many other Bahamians arrived during the 1890s, typically young, single males who worked as farm labourers or fruit pickers. Few were naturalized American citizens. They lived together in groups of four or five in rented premises or lodged with Bahamian families. Other occupations listed by the census enumerators for Bahamians included carpenter, fisherman, boatman, blacksmith's helper, deck hand, seamstress, dressmaker, dressmaker, cook, chambermaid, house servants, and 'odd jobs.'

By 1910, the Bahamian community in Miami had increased to well over 1,500. Indeed, a veritable wave of new Bahamian immigrants had arrived in Miami in 1908 and 1909—an early boatlift from the islands that captured the attention of the city's leading newspaper, the *Miami Metropolis*. According to the paper, more than 1,400 Bahamians arrived in Miami during the single year after July 1908, many of them temporary farm workers. They came fifty or sixty at a time on small schooners, often "so crowded with people that there was barely standing room on their decks." The new wave of Bahamians worked extensively in the citrus groves and vegetable fields. The surge of migration from the Bahamas intensified between 1910 and 1920. This mass movement of population is reflected in several sets of population statistics. Bahamian census reports, for instance, showed decennial increases in total population ranging from four to twenty-nine percent between 1851 and 1911. But the decade after 1911, the Bahamian population decreased by over five per cent, slipping from 55,944 in 1911 to 53,031. Most of the missing Bahamians went to South Florida.[47]

Throughout the early 1900s, the economic conditions of the Out Islands remained unchanged, and the flow of Bahamian migrants continued unabated. The year 1918 was described as the "darkest and hardest year ever experienced in the islands." The commissioner at Watlings Island in 1920 wrote that "The Island is almost denuded of young men. Throughout

---

[47]   Bahamas Government-Department of Archives, *Report on the Census of the Bahama Islands Taken on the 24ᵗʰ April, 1921.*

the whole year both men and women have been going to Florida." He further reported with regrets that at the time of his writing his report, there "is not a single man on the whole island." In 1921, the same Commissioner reported, a death occurred at one of the settlements, and "women had to be pall-bearers."[48]

The magnitude of labour migration from the colony in the first two decades of the twentieth century, especially to Florida, was reflected in the census figures for the colony between 1901 and 1921 (see Table 2). During that period, population growth was clearly affected by external migration. The intercensal rate of growth for the period 1891-1901 was 11.5 percent, but between 1901 and 1911 it had slowed to four percent. In the years 1911-1921, the population declined by 5.5 percent.

Table 2-Decennial Census Returns 1881-1921

Census Year	Population	Intercensal Change	Intercensal Change %
1881	43,521	+4,359	10.0
1891	47,565	+4,044	8.5
1901	53,735	+6,170	11.5
1911	55,944	+2,209	4.0
1921	53,031	-2,913	-5.5

The Decennial Census Returns 1881-1921 *Taken on the 24th April, 1921, 1911, 1901, 1891* (Courtesy of the Bahamas Department of Archives, Nassau, Bahamas).

Although the censuses do not, by themselves, provide us with emigration figures, it is possible to arrive at rough estimates of the outward movement by using them in conjunction with the data for natural increase. It is likely that, for the intercensal period 1901-1911, a net loss of 6,180 is too high a figure. Census takers would not have counted, for example, persons from the southern islands of the archipelago who were employed as stevedores on steamship lines or as labourers on one year contracts with

---

[48] *Annual Colonial Reports (CO-23-Governor's Dispatches) for the Bahamas, 1928-* The Bahamas Department of Archives-Nassau, Bahamas.

American companies in Central and Latin America. Such persons were usually only temporarily absent. These forms of migratory wage labour ceased after 1914 and therefore did not affect the results of the 1921 census.[49]

After 1920, the migration of Bahamian labourers to the United States was curtailed. Many Bahamians, who had worked as seasonal labourers on the farms in South Florida, were prevented from returning to the United States by a law that made passing a literacy test a requirement for entry. This legislation, aimed primarily at the immigrants from southern and eastern Europe, had been originally enacted in 1917, but was temporarily suspended as a wartime measure. However, it was strictly enforced after 1920.[50]

New federal immigration legislation in 1924 introduced the national-origins quota system and temporarily muddled the situation for Bahamians in Florida. Confusion over details of the law, and particularly how it might affect Bahamian labour migrants, created a panic in the South Florida labour market. One Miami labour agent, for instance, suggested that local agriculture would suffer "a serious labour shortage" and that wages would be driven up rapidly as a result. *The Miami Herald* noted that "since 75 percent of the labour used in and around Miami comes from the Bahamas, the sudden checking of this stream would injure Miami commerce." Local

[49] Patrice Williams, *"The Emigrant Labour Business: An Important Industry in the Late Nineteenth and Early Twentieth Centuries?"*, Journal of the Bahamas Historical Society, October 6, 1985, pgs. 9–14.
[50] *The Nassau Guardian*, January 14–24, 1920. The evidence which indicates that the introduction of the literacy test checked migration to Florida from the Bahamas is extensive. *See, for example,* letter from Dr. J.G. Long to Walter Long, March 6, 1918. C.O. 23/pg. 283; Report on Governor's Harbour, Eleuthera for 1917. In Appendix to *Votes of the Legislative Council*, November 26, 1917-July 4, 1918; Report on Watling's Island for 1923. In Appendix to *Votes of the House of Assembly*, February 19-May 15, 1924, pg.493; Report on Exuma for 1920. In Appendix to *Votes of the Legislative Council*, February 15, 1921-January 16, 1922, pg.206. Report on Exuma for 1921. In Appendix to *Votes of the Legislative Council*, March 23-May 23, 1922, pg.96.

businessmen believed that the Bahamian immigrants would come under the general quota of Great Britain and be limited to 100 per month.[51]

This was startling news to the South Florida business community, which had come to rely on the steady supply of cheap labour from the Bahamas. The Miami Chamber of Commerce and other local organizations led an effort to get the Bahamas excluded from the immigration law's restrictive provisions. Petition drives were organized, seeking particularly the help of Florida senators and congressmen. Amid the confusion, Bahamians crowded the steamers traveling between Nassau and Miami, trying to beat the deadline of July 1, 1924, when the immigration law became effective. "Boats in the Miami-Nassau passenger and freight service are laden to their capacity rushing the people into America," the *Herald* reported, causing a virtual evacuation of Nassau and the Bahamas."[52]

In Nassau, the news of the new immigration law came "like a bomb" to the islanders planning to work in Florida. The business community in Nassau was worried, too. Work in Miami and South Florida had provided a safety valve for Bahamians without jobs or prospects in the islands. The remittances sent back by labourers in Florida and the capital brought in by returning migrants helped keep the Bahamian economy afloat at a time when the local commercial elite had failed to invest in economic development. By the early twentieth century, the islanders had become heavily reliant on the economic connection with the United States. Thus, once the initial confusion was sorted out, the pattern of Bahamian movement to and from Florida continued uninterrupted. Only in 1926 was there any marked decline in Bahamian emigration—a drop in labour migration most likely due to the end of the Florida real estate boom, a severe economic decline, and a disastrous hurricane in September 1926.

With the passage of the Johnson-Reed Act in 1924, the exclusion of Bahamians from the Florida labour market was complete. Bahamians were no longer able to move freely from the Bahamas to Florida to work, but only by 6 months stay on a US-issued work permit. Labourers from the Out Islands who had worked in Florida sought jobs increasingly in Nassau,

---

51   *The Miami Herald,* June 24, 28, July 6, 1924; *Miami Daily News and Metropolis,* July 2, 8, 1924.

52   *The Miami Herald,* June 28, July 6, 1924; *Miami Daily News and Metropolis,* July 2, 8, 1924.

which had since the 1920s been experiencing economic prosperity based on bootlegging, tourism and the land and construction booms. As it turned out, however, the 1924 quota law had little impact on the Bahamian migration to Florida. According to the law, British West Indians, including Bahamians, were included under the quota of Great Britain. But since Britain's generous annual quota of 65,000 was never filled, Bahamians found little problem in obtaining permanent entry into the United States. By the 1920s, most of the Bahamas coming to Miami area were temporary labour migrants who were able to enter the United States with six-month work permits. Although there was a migration of Bahamian labourers to the United States between 1943 and 1966, it was different from the earlier migrations. In the latter period, Bahamian labourers went on short-term contracts on a scheme that was supervised by the British and American governments.

In the Bahamas, fears were frequently expressed in commercial circles that the migration of spongers would endanger the prosperity of the sponging industry-the number one industry in the Bahamas at the time-but little effort was made to halt this outward movement. The attitude of the white mercantile elite was reflected in the comments made by the commission of enquiry in 1920 on the question of emigration. They took the view that the loss of population (which meant the loss of a great number of producers) might be harmful in theory. However, they observed that emigration had not so far resulted in a financial loss to the colony and that until economic conditions improved at home, emigration must be expected. The commission of enquiry therefore recommended a policy of non-interference:

"We do not therefore think that any effort should be made to stem the outward tide by legislation or that obstacles should be placed in the would-be temporary emigrants' way. But permanent emigration should not be encouraged."[53]

This tolerance of emigration by the employer class is perhaps best explained by the fact that the demand for labour in agriculture had decreased. Merchants also benefited from the remittances sent by migrants

---

[53] "*Second Interim Report of the Commission Appointed ... to Report on the General Administration of the Out Islands*," June 22, 1920, *Votes of the Legislative Council*, February 15, 1921-January 16, 1922, pg. 284.

to their families in the Out Islands. Most colonial governors during this period saw emigration as evidence of the colony's economic decline. Although they deplored the depopulation of the Out Islands, they also recognized the importance of remittances to the economic well-being of the colony. In 1912, for example, William Hart Bennett, the officer administering the Government, while admitting that there might be a labour problem if large-scale business enterprises were established in the colony, commented: "There is however another side to the question that is the undoubted fact that large remittances are sent by most of the emigrants to their wives and families here."[54]

Colonial administrators reluctantly accepted the fact that emigration was one solution to the economic problems of a colony that could not support its population. It was for this reason that Sir William Allardyce endorsed the proposal by the Mason and Hanger Contracting Company of New York in July 1917 to recruit Bahamian labourers, on contract, for war emergency work in Charleston, South Carolina. Between July and October of that year, 2,573 labourers left for Charleston.[55]

Labour migration to the United States from the Bahamas in the first two decades of the twentieth century had far-reaching consequences for the sending area. An immediate consequence of the outward movement of men was that wives and children were increasingly relied on to maintain the provision grounds. In certain of the Out Islands, this was a continuation of an earlier practice. In Andros, for example, women and children usually tended the provision grounds while the men were away on sponging voyages. In many instances, the land deteriorated during the men's absence in Florida. It was not unusual for some men to remit funds to pay for the care of their subsistence plots while they were away. However, the absence of the male members of the household most often resulted in a cycle of neglect, which led to an even greater dependence on the wages that migration provided. This process described in the case of

[54] *"Second Interim Report of the Commission Appointed ... to Report on the General Administration of the Out Islands,"* June 22, 1920, Votes of the Legislative Council, February 15, 1921-January 16, 1922, pg. 284.
[55] *Speech of William Hart Bennett*, November 18, 1912, *Votes of the Legislative Council*, November 18, 1912-July 7, 1913.

the settlements of Rock Sound and Tarpum Bay, Eleuthera, in 1920 was fairly widespread in the Out Islands:

"The results of emigration to Florida vary; some are benefitted, while others suffer by leaving their fields and other properties with no one to care for them during their absence, and on their return find their fields in such conditions that to restore them would swallow up the little they bring back and the result is, that back to Florida they go, to earn more money and this is repeated over and over by many."[56]

The withdrawal of men from the rural economy, as a result of migration to Florida and to Nassau, contributed to the increased dependence on imported food. This trend was discernible in the 1920s, when the Bahamas began to import food items like eggs and fresh vegetables, in which it was previously self-sufficient and increased its importation of tropical fruits, which it had earlier exported. The increased demand for those food items, created mainly by an expanding tourist industry, was not met by local agriculture, as the Colonial Secretary pointed out in a memorandum on agriculture in the Bahamas in 1930:

"One might expect that tourist traffic would create a lively trade in farm and garden produce but in fact it results mainly in a larger importation of food stuffs."[57]

Remittances from migrants in Florida had important effects on the Bahamian economy. Many migrants were able to send money home because they earned enough to meet their subsistence needs and save. For Bahamians in Miami, the racial hostility directed at blacks also created a context which was conducive to saving. As the official report on Governor's Harbour, Eleuthera, for 1909 explained:

"In Miami the black man has to be extremely careful as to how he conducts himself, otherwise his liberty and even his life are endangered, and for this reason alone he abstains from liquor, saves his money and remits it to his people at home."[58]

---

[56] *Report on Rock Sound and Tarpum Bay, Eleuthera for 1920* in Appendix to *Votes of the Legislative Council,* February 15, 1921-January 16, 1922, pg. 194.

[57] *Memorandum by the Colonial Secretary, "Agriculture in the Bahamas, 1930,"* Nassau, 1938, pg.2; *See also,* editorial, *The Nassau Tribune,* June 29, 1929.

[58] *Appendix to* Votes *of the Legislative Council,* January 11-June 6, 1910, pg. 86.

The preferred method of remitting money to the Bahamas was in the form of U.S. currency in registered letters. Postal money orders were not, as in the case of Barbadians in Panama, widely used in the early twentieth century. Remittances seem to have been used primarily to satisfy consumption needs rather than for productive investment. The money was often used to build new houses and "in short time was dispatched to Nassau to procure clothing and articles of food not produced locally."[59] The Out Islands became "remittance societies." In the face of the declining importance of pineapple and sisal production (a situation made worse by the absence of adult males), remittances formed a major source of income. This dependence on remittances made the Out Islands vulnerable to changes in the demand for labour in Florida. Immigration restrictions in the United States therefore resulted in a further decline in the economy of the Out Islands by the late 1920s, as the editor of *the Nassau Tribune* pointed out in October 1929:

"It is well known that hundreds of Out Island people went back and forth between Florida and their homes and that thousands of dollars were brought or sent home by these people but the sum that found its way from Florida must have been much larger than was believed, to result in such a general collapse of the Out Islands when this source of invincible income is withdrawn."[60]

Labour migration had important consequences for the family. The prolonged absence of married men caused their wives to establish liaisons with other men. The existence of such relationships was repeatedly hinted at in official reports of this period. Some of the married men who went to Florida also formed other associations and abandoned their families. It was not unusual for both parents to migrate to Florida, leaving behind children who, without parental care and guidance, developed into juvenile delinquents.

Labour migration had important implications for the sending area. The withdrawal of adult males from the rural economy (often on a permanent basis) hastened the decline of agricultural production. The substantial inflow of cash from remittances became almost the sole source of income in many rural Out Island communities where export agriculture was in

59 *Letter by R.J. Bowe*, The Nassau Tribune, January 12, 1929.
60 *"Here and There,"* The Nassau Tribune, October 16, 1929.

marked decline. In fact it can be argued that, by the second decade of the twentieth century, the Bahamas had become more important as an exporter of labour than as an exporter of commodities. Finally, labour migration to Florida which partly had its origins in the underdeveloped economy of the Out Islands, resulted in the reinforcement of this underdevelopment—not least by its depopulation of those communities.

A second wave of Bahamian migrant workers arrived in Florida in 1943 and stayed until 1965 in a contractual agreement known as "The Contract", and the Duke of Windsor organized it. The Contract was the signing of an agreement between the War Food Department of the United States of America and the Bahamas Government to recruit Bahamian farm workers to help with nurturing, reaping and securing food mostly because of the great demand brought about by one of the most devastating wars in the history of mankind – World War II. The Contract also known as "The Project," was a farm labour agreement established on March 16, 1943.

A large number of Bahamians travelled to the United States in the capacity of contract workers. Many abled-bodied Bahamians decided to take advantage of this prime opportunity for economic advancement and joined many other Bahamians who sought work outside the Bahamas to support their families. In those days, there wasn't much work around, aside from subsistence farming and fishing on a minor scale mostly to feed the family, and there were no jobs or money whatsoever on the Family Islands. The agreement carried the name "The Contract" because each worker signed a contract with the Farm Security Administration of the US Government during the government-to-government era of the agreement. Each worker signed a tripartite contract with an employer and the government of the Bahamas during the government-committee phase of the agreement.

The Agreement between the United States and the Bahamas Governments stipulated conditions under which Bahamians could enter the United States. Not subject to military service, the labourers were mainly employed to produce food for the war effort. In order to qualify, one had to be 18 or over and be physically fit enough to pass a medical examination supervised by the American authorities. Transportation costs within the Bahamas and the entry point in the United States were borne by the home government. However, while in America, the travel expenses were taken care of by the US Government. Ensuring that wages would be no less than 30 cents an hour, the Agreement also vainly promised that the Bahamian workers would not be discriminated against because of their race, creed, colour or natural origin. A proportion of their wages were withheld and sent back to their families back at home in the Bahamas.

Because most of America's young men and women were actively involved on the battle field and in the war factories and most of America's allies were having a hard time, it was necessary and indeed helpful for America to recruit outsiders to help with preparations for a decisive victory. The unemployment conditions at the time forced Bahamian men and women to find new ways of being employed, so as to provide a better living for themselves and their loved ones, and at the same time shore up the economic foundation and reinforced the social fiber of the Bahamas.

Many of the workers were from the Family Islands, and most were black, unskilled workers. In the early years of The Contract, women were mostly excluded, but they eventually became accepted to perform menial tasks such as cooking and washing for the labourers. However, approximately ninety white Bahamians, mostly from the Family Islands, were recruited for dairy work. Finding the working and climatic conditions too severe, the majority of them returned to the Bahamas by 1946. The agreement continued, with changes in its organization, until 1966. It allowed thousands of Bahamian men and women from islands throughout the archipelago to carry out agricultural work in many North American States. Bahamians cultivated and harvested a variety of crops, from tobacco in Tennessee, peaches in Georgia, corn in Minnesota, citrus in Florida, and peanuts in North Carolina. Some workers returned to the Bahamas. Others settled in communities located around the United States, particularly in the states of Florida and New York. Bahamian society as a whole felt the impact of The Contract, including the social and economic effects. The wages earned on The Contract enabled a significant number of black Bahamians, for the first time in history, to leave industries in which they worked primarily for others and to start their own businesses.

They sent money home to their loved ones, made frequent visits, and bought land on their native islands. In the end, however, most settled in South Florida and made a life for them and their families. Unlike the rest of the Caribbean, working-class Bahamians migrated primarily for economic reasons, such as chronic unemployment and persistent poverty. For the most part, their main destination was Florida. The stream of Bahamian migrants to the United States and in particular Florida was relatively large compared with other states within the United States. There was a large wave of migration from the Bahamas and a smaller flow of black cigar-makers from Cuba. New York was the second most popular state for settlement, followed closely by Massachusetts. But Florida's preeminence was soon surmounted by that of New York, and the number headed for Massachusetts dropped sharply by 1920. During the peak years of migration, 1913 to 1924, the majority made their way to New York City, settling primarily in Manhattan and Brooklyn. By 1930, almost a quarter of black Harlem was of Caribbean origin.[61]

There were four main factors that contributed to increased Bahamian migration to Florida in the 1920s, and they were: the poor economic climate in the Bahamas; the lack of substantial employment opportunities in the Bahamas; more money being paid to migrant workers in Florida; and the short distance from the Bahamas to South Florida. South Florida developed Bahamian enclaves in certain cities, including Lemon City, Coconut Grove, and Cutler. In 1896, foreign-born blacks comprised 40 percent of the black population, making Miami the largest foreign-born black city in the US aside from New York. United States restrictive immigration policies of the 1917-1924 did not greatly affect the Bahamian migrant population; they continued to migrate in vast numbers to the US; however, many also participated in return migration back to the Bahamas during this time period. Those who chose to remain created institutions in the U.S. During this time in Florida, black Bahamians, too, faced state-enforced racism. Blacks could not vote, were persecuted by epithets in the Miami press, and were not allowed to stay in the hotels that employed them. Furthermore, in 1921 the Ku Klux Klan staged a large rally, attacking these black immigrants in Miami.

[61] http://www.inmotionaame.org/ US Government's Immigration Reports, 1899-1931.

**A Citrus grove in Clewiston, Florida in the 1920s
(Courtesy United States Department of Labour).**

Today, the majority of Bahamian Americans, about 21,000 in total, live in and around Miami, Florida, with the Bahamian community centered in Coconut Grove and the Lake Okeechobee region. Although the majority of Bahamian Americans live in the South Florida, large populations of these migrant workers in the 1920s were found in the farming belts of south and central Florida, from Clewiston to Canal Point, with the population particularly centered in Pahokee. Bahamian migrant workers in the South Florida area regularly provided manual labour for these new and burgeoning farms. Early on, the main crops were winter vegetables like beans, celery, carrots and tomatoes. However, in 1920 the federal government set up a research station at Canal Point. In 1922, farmers first tried planting sugarcane. The first mill started up the following year, in Canal Point. Soon others sprang up; however, by 1928, sugar was still a minor crop in the Glades and vegetables and fruits accounted for the largest agricultural investments in this region.

White Bahamian Americans were often referred to as "Conchs," and they also came to South Florida, but mostly stayed further south, and their communities in Key West and Riviera Beach were sometimes referred to as "Conch Towns." The name, from a shelled delicacy called conch, found in the Bahamas, refers to white immigrants from the Bahamas looking for a better life in the Florida Keys and on the South Florida mainland. The top US communities with the highest percentage of people claiming Bahamian ancestry are:

1. Bunche Park, Florida 3.80%
2. El Portal, Florida 2.20%
3. Goulds, Florida 2.00%
4. Golden Glades, Florida 1.80%
5. Richmond Heights, Florida 1.30%
6. West Little River, Florida and North Miami, Florida 1.20%
7. Munford, Alabama and North Miami, Florida 1.10%
8. Rincon, Georgia 1.00%

Florida was a popular state for workers from the Bahamas. It was becoming a very modern state, growing with amazing rapidity, and typically of the Southern States, "Colour Town," as they called it, was swamped with Bahamian labourers. The first wave of Bahamian migrant labourers on a large scale arrived in Florida in the late 1800s to early 1920s to work in the U.S. farm belts. The shortage of cheap male farm workers in the USA during this era made it necessary to import workers from the Bahamas. In the 1920s, the majority of Bahamian migrant workers worked in citrus and fruit groves and vegetable farms in Florida.

**A Citrus grove in Clewiston, Florida in the 1920s
(Courtesy United States Department of Labour).**

In both of these waves of migration in the 1920s and 1943 to 1965, the impact of this dislocation of the Bahamian migrant worker and his family back home in the Bahamas was great. Some men, having left behind a wife and children in the Bahamas when they went to Florida to work, came home to find the wife with more children than they had left. Some of them accepted it, while others did not. Some men had sent home large portions of their earnings to wives or other persons while they were away working, and when they returned home, they could find neither their wives nor their earnings. Some came home with money that they used to start a new life and are still benefitting from it today. Others came home with experience alone.

First of all, only the strongest and the fittest got to go. These farm owners and operators in Florida were only interested in strong black and able hands. The physical exam was most exhaustive; they were not taking any weaklings. Furthermore, for over 10 to 15 years out of the life of a country, the Bahamas was absent of the energy of a population who could have been contributing to the agricultural efforts of America. This was one of the negative effects of The Contract, and that was when they returned to the Bahamas there was no way they could or would engage in farming in the Bahamas as it was and still is practiced in the United States.

The immediate benefit of these waves of migration on the Bahamian economy was mainly economic, as they earned real, hard US currency, which circulated throughout the length and breadth of the Bahamas. When you signed up to go, if you were single, you could assign some of your earnings to a family member, but if single, it was compulsory to assign an amount to your mother. If married, then naturally assignments were made to wives, but the system ensured that some of your earnings were remitted to the Bahamas, and this was especially true of those who went to work on The Contract. That's not to say that it ran smoothly. Many men returned home to find girlfriends, wives and money gone, and themselves only richer for the experience. But by and large, good sums of money flowed to the Bahamas into small and large communities and villages, greatly enhancing the overall economy of the Bahamas.

For The Contract, relatives in Nassau had to collect the money from the Labour Office in Oakes Field, the Post Office Savings Bank and by registered mail. Excitement and great anticipation permeated the air as the family member's name was called to collect their money from the two disbursement centers. The money allowed family members to purchase the necessities of life in large quantities, like a case of lard, sacks of flour, grits or rice, a side of salt pork and a case of corned beef. Also, around Easter or Christmas time, if a son or husband was truly attentive to their wife or family member, they would go and pick up something that was ordered through the Sears Catalogue. In the Family Islands, they collected the money from the Commissioner's Office.

When the migrant worker came home, it wasn't uncommon for a hard working person to come home after a four or five-year' experience with three or four thousand dollars in the Post Office Bank, and in the 1920's that was a lot of money to have in one place. In fact, most of the housing for working class Bahamians south of Wulff Road, in the Englerston and Coconut Grove areas, was built by Bahamian migrant workers who had sent monies back home to their families. Many of them got a good head start and have not looked back yet. But as noted earlier, many of them were only richer for the experience.

After World War I, an unprecedented building boom began in Florida. The Roaring '20s was a time when a person's wealth and success were measured by what he or she owned. However, by the mid-1920s, people lost everything as the Land Boom went bust. Henry Flagler's death in 1913 did not diminish the popularity of the winter playground for the wealthy that he had created in Florida, nor did it slow the growth it precipitated in southeast Florida. An ever-growing flow of visitors and residents produced a need for businesses, fertile farmlands to feed this ever expanding population, entertainment facilities, and an expanded infrastructure of schools, houses of worship, services, and transportation routes. The resulting small building boom in the early teens paused during U. S. involvement in World War I from 1917 to 1918, when the government restricted the use of building materials. Following the end of World War I, growth in Florida exploded. The 1920s Land Boom was a period of extremes in wealth, development, and weather. By the end of the decade, it all came crashing down just as quickly as it had begun.

In the 1920s, Florida was the focus of one of the greatest economic and social phenomenon in American history, as hundreds of thousands of Americans of all types of financial strata poured into the Sunshine State and forever changed the global image of Florida. There were similar movements in the south of France during the 1920s, but the Florida story was so vast and complete, it changed the entire scope of the state. Two important elements played roles in the Florida Land Boom. For the first time, Americans had the time and money to travel to Florida to invest in real estate. For the educated and skilled working American, the 1920s meant paid vacations, pensions, and fringe benefits unheard of during the Victorian Era. The United States also had the automobile, which was that indispensable family transportation that allowed them to travel to Florida. This "welfare capitalism" of time and money contributed to the arrival in Florida of a new kind of tourist - middle class families.

It was also important that millions of Americans were captured by the materialism and prosperity of the times, which seemed to indicate that anyone could become rich by simply investing in the proper instrument of instant wealth. Florida land appeared to be in 1921 one of those instruments of future success. It didn't matter if you lacked the money; credit was easy to obtain with economic prosperity and a good job. These sudden winter migrations of vacationers and speculators had an enormous impact upon every aspect of public investment in Florida. Prior to 1920, the majority of Florida's Northern arrivals came to take advantage of Florida's warm climate, and they were mainly the elderly, the rich, and the ill, not necessarily in that order. The Florida Land Boom brought middle aged, middle class Americans, many with their families. The railroad hotels like the Tampa Bay Hotel, with its triple digit fares, was hardly the ideal vacation spot for this new tourist. With the rapid development of South Florida, so, too, came the Bahamians labourers in large numbers, seeking gainful employment in the agriculture, railway and tourism industries.

Just as the Republican administration of Warren G. Harding promoted lower taxes and greater business prosperity at the national level, the conservative state government of Florida in the 1920s acknowledged the need to improve the state's transportation and public services to accommodate this boom of visitors. The state of Florida and many cities borrowed considerable amounts of money at high interest rates to build facilities to attract the expected growth of new residents and tourists. Northern newsmen glamorized the early Land Boom in Florida with stories of how land investors had doubled their profits within months. Real estate firms soon realized that it was more profitable to sell land by auction than to set a listed price. As land prices rose, so, too, was the desire for profits to rise as well.

While not all land speculating met with success, most investors in the beginning stages of the Florida Land Boom made a profit selling the land to others. An elderly man in Pinellas County was committed to a sanitarium by his sons for spending his life savings of $1,700 on a piece of Pinellas property. When the value of the land reached $300,000 in 1925, the man's lawyer got him released to sue his children. In the 1920s in Florida, the difference between genius and idiot was never so narrow. The need for real estate salespersons was so great at the height of the boom that Florida relaxed its regulation of realtors. It didn't really matter, since two-thirds of all Florida real estate was sold by mail to speculators who never visited Florida. Those who came were gripped by the frenzy of land buying. In 1922, the *Miami Herald* was the heaviest newspaper in the nation due to its massive land advertisement sections.

The influx of people to Florida promoted an increase in farming, particularly of large scale agriculture along Lake Okeechobee, often called "the Muck Bowl" for its marshy terrain. In the 1920s, canals and dikes were built across the region, diverting much needed water from the Everglades. This development did not benefit Florida's Panhandle farmers, suffering from rising inflation and low farm prices. Most of these new farms grew winter fruits and vegetables and utilized a large migratory population. The Florida migrant population included workers from both the Deep South and the Bahamas, and to a lesser extent from the Caribbean. Working for nine to fifteen dollars per week in the tropical sun, they lived in crude company towns in sub-standard shacks or small homes, often just miles from the glamour of the coastal resorts. Large influxes of migrant workers were needed because of the lack of American labourers, and in the cases of quickly perishable crops such as tomatoes, which needed to be harvested and shipped to market in a relatively short period of time.

Many migrant areas lacked schools and health facilities. They usually did not lack a "jook joint." Jooks were usually the only recreational recluse for the migrant worker: a small tavern and frontier dance hall where music poured out of a coin-operated magazine phonograph. It was ironic to drive through the silent blackness of South Florida to discover a noisy, neon shack, blaring away music that at least temporarily lessened the agony of daily life. The small farmers of Florida did not benefit from the Florida Land Boom. Neither did most towns in North Florida, unless they were located along a major highway. The departure of many young Floridians into the urban work force also crippled Florida's small towns. The lifestyle and diet of rural Florida in 1928 was not greatly changed from 1898.

The Florida land boom of the 1920s was Florida's first real estate bubble, which burst in 1925, leaving behind entire new cities and the remains of failed development projects, such as Aladdin City in South Miami-Dade County and Isola di Lolando in north Biscayne Bay. The preceding land boom shaped Florida's future for decades and created entire new cities out of the Everglades land that remain today. The story includes many parallels to the modern real estate boom, including the forces of outside speculators, easy credit access for buyers, and rapidly appreciating property values. The news of the Florida Land Bust crippled the tourist market.

Despite the continued boom in the United States Stock Market, people no longer trusted buying Florida land. And yet, the land was merely overpriced. A triple take of disasters then followed in the shape of the September 1926 Great Miami Hurricane, which drove many developers into bankruptcy. The Great Okeechobee Hurricane and the Wall Street Crash of 1929 continued the catastrophic downward economic trend, and the Florida land boom was officially over as the Great Depression began. The depression and the devastating arrival of the Mediterranean fruit fly a year later destroyed both the tourist and citrus industries upon which Florida depended. In a few years, an idyllic tropical paradise had been transformed into a bleak, humid remote area with few economic prospects. Florida's economy would not recover until World War II.

As if the land collapse were not bad enough, a terrible hurricane hit South Florida in September of 1928, with winds in excess of 145 miles per hour and gusts to over 160 miles per hour. Initially briefly travelling parallel to the Atlantic Ocean, the storm suddenly turned northwest across Palm Beach County, into the heartland of the Muck Bowl. The migrant workers and small farmers of Lake Okeechobee were asleep. There were very little warnings given to these residents because very few had radios and they had no automobiles for a quick escape. As the winds of the hurricane moved counterclockwise across the lake, the south end of the lake was dried up. When the storm passed by, however, a huge tidal wave crashed down on the people of Belle Glade and Moore Haven.

The hurricane was an unwelcome coup de grace to the Florida's Land Bust and its agricultural sector. In South Florida, at least 2,500 persons were killed when the storm surge from Lake Okeechobee breached the dike surrounding the lake, flooding an area covering hundreds of square miles. In West Palm Beach, more than 1,711 homes were destroyed. The news of people drowning in the floodwaters from Lake Okeechobee amazed and shocked people from all across the world. The nameless migrants were piled up in masses and in some cases burnt to prevent diseases and contamination. The major developments were in ruins, many of them unable to recover.

It would take years to rebuild the confidence and spirit of Florida's Land Boom and agricultural sector. In fact, when the Great Depression hit Florida, it had a limited impact since so many Floridians were already in a weak financial state. A year later, the arrival of the Mediterranean fruit fly would hurt the citrus industry. Certainly, many Floridians wondered whether Florida would ever see again such wonderful, booming and confident times as they had before this hurricane struck South Florida.

CHAPTER FIVE

Impact of the Great Okeechobee Hurricane on the Bahamian migrant labourers in Florida

A black worker harvesting celery stalks on a farm in the Okeechobee region in the 1920s (Courtesy United States Department of Labour).

In September 1928, only about 50,000 persons lived in South Florida. The land and real estate boom was already beginning to fade, although many subdivisions and new communities were still being built. The devastating Great Miami Hurricane of September 1926 had already sounded a loud alarm to the new residents about the vulnerability of their new homes to tropical cyclones. However, most of the damage from that storm was in Dade and Broward counties. Even so, a bellwether of what was to come occurred with the Great Miami Hurricane of 1926 as flood waters from Lake Okeechobee were swept by that storm into Moore Haven, the county seat of Glades County, killing over 100 people.

The City of Palm Beach, founded only 34 years earlier by Henry Flagler, was incorporated in 1911 and had become a playground for the rich and famous, while West Palm Beach grew up on the opposite side of Lake Worth as a place where the support staff lived. The Atlantic breezes were balmy, and the climate was warm. On the opposite side of the county, a quite different situation was emerging. The rich, black muck soil near Lake Okeechobee was already being utilized for its tremendous agricultural productivity. The newly incorporated town of Belle Glade was growing steadily, fueled by the rapidly expanding agriculture in the fields nearby. A rural, agrarian society dependent on migrant labour was plowing and harvesting along the shores of the lake behind a hastily built muck levee.

Only two years after the Great Miami Hurricane of 1926, what would become the second Category 4 (Saffir-Simpson Hurricane Wind Scale) hurricane to strike South Florida in as many years formed just off the coast of Africa in early September of 1928. It churned across the Atlantic and devastated the island of Guadeloupe on September 12th, moved through the Virgin Islands, and struck a direct hit on Puerto Rico on the 13th, on the feast day of Saint Felipe. More than 312 persons were killed by this storm in Puerto Rico. To some extent, the devastation in Puerto Rico provided some warning to residents of Florida's east coast. It moved through the islands of the Bahamas on September 14th and 15th, and on Sunday evening, September 16th, the hurricane made landfall in the United States in Palm Beach County, between Jupiter and Boca Raton.

Damage in coastal Palm Beach County was severe, especially in the Jupiter area, where the eyewall of the hurricane persisted longer than at any other location because of where the storm crossed the coast. A storm surge around 10 feet, with waves likely as high as 20 feet, crashed into the barrier islands, including Palm Beach. However, the greatest loss of life was around Lake Okeechobee. As the Category 4 hurricane moved inland, the strong winds piled the water up at the south end of the lake, ultimately topping the levee and rushing out onto the fertile land. Thousands of people, mostly non-white migrant farm workers, drowned as water several feet deep spread over an area approximately 6 miles deep and 75 miles long around the south end of the lake.

It goes without saying that the effects of the flood were devastating, and the loss of life, both human and animal, was apocalyptic. Damages from this hurricane in Florida were estimated around 25 million dollars which, normalized for population, wealth, and inflation, would be around 16 billion dollars today.[62] The horrible flood in the towns of Pahokee, Canal Point, Chosen, Belle Glade, and South Bay resulted in the drowning of many people, probably three quarters or more of whom were non-white field workers. The flood waters lasted for several weeks, and survivors were found wandering as late as September 22nd.

Memorial services, one white, one non-white, were held at the same time, but at different locations, on Sunday, September 30, 1928, in West Palm Beach. The *Miami Herald* article (1928) on the memorial services reported nearly 1,000 victims of the hurricane disaster, 674 of whom were non-white. Additional *Miami Daily News* articles stated a death toll of 2,200 (September 24, 1928) and 2,300 (September 25, 1928), along with the observation that only the death toll in the Great Galveston Hurricane of 1900 was higher. The estimated death toll was at first set at 2,300, but later lowered to 1,770. The final Red Cross report in 1929 stated that 1,810 people were killed and 1,849 were injured in the 1928 hurricane. A news release from the Florida State Board of Health on December 7, 1928, estimated the deaths in Palm Beach County alone at 1,833.[63] The exact number of those who perished in the Okeechobee storm in Florida can never be ascertained. Probably three-fourths or more of the casualties were Negroes, many of whom had come from the Bahama Islands. Approximately 75% of the black victims were Bahamians migrant workers, and of that total it was estimated to be over 1,406 Bahamians workers who died in the storm over Florida. Accounting for members of this race was complicated by the migratory habits of their kind and the fact that most of them were known, even to their friends, only by a nickname.

At the end of World War I, all of Florida had undergone a spectacular real estate boom, but it finally collapsed under the burden of its own

---

[62]   http://www.srh.noaa.gov/okeechobee
[63]   http://www.srh.noaa.gov/okeechobee

weight. Fortunes were lost overnight, banks failed like falling dominos, and desperate, unemployed people tried to feed their families. It was a gloomy omen for the Roaring Twenties bull market that had one more year to run. In 1926, the fate of the doomed Florida real estate market was sealed by a vicious act of nature in the form of a devastating hurricane. This powerful Category 4 hurricane struck Miami head-on, killing 372 people and decimating three-fourths of the city—a crippling blow from which it would take the city twenty-five years to recover.

All of South Florida was thrown into a deep depression—except the Everglades. Unemployed people flocked to the modest settlements around Lake Okeechobee. In Belle Glade, Pahokee, Clewiston, and Moore Haven, they could buy a farm and live off the land and not starve. Houses and farms were sold and resold at a rapid pace. Belle Glade was changing so fast that it was incorporated in April 1928—making it a mere five months to the day in September when the storm hit Florida. Still, Belle Glade was a farming town, and in mid-September 1928, many of the farmers had their fields plowed and planted. A good year was anticipated because the price of vegetables was predicted to be high that winter—just in time for the harvest, if there was not a hard, long freeze like the one that had struck the previous New Year's Eve.

Migrant workers gathered at the International Labour Agency in Florida seeking employment in the 1920s (Picture Courtesy United States Department of Labour).

Not everyone, however, shared in the good times. Along with the farmers, the townspeople, the new people, and the speculators, the area was populated with black migrant farm workers, the majority of which were from the Bahamas, but were joined by a few Jamaicans and other Caribbean islanders. Some four thousand strong, they had come to help prepare the soil, plant, and then pick the crops. Many would stay through the harvest, living in shacks and shanty towns supplied by the farmers on the land where they worked. In the spring, a few would migrate northwards to follow the fruit and vegetable harvests. A few would even travel as far as New York State. In general, they stayed out of the way, unseen, uncounted, unwanted, except at planting and harvesting time. No one thought very much about them, though it was their labour that brought most of the prosperity to Belle Glade.

Once, the great Everglades flowed to the sea from Lake Okeechobee, the largest lake in the South. Then people decided that if they drained that useless swamp, the muck that was exposed would provide some of the richest and most fertile black farming soils in America. They were right; however, they didn't know or care to know about the environmental catastrophe they were helping set in motion. Farmers came in droves, seeking their fortunes in the black soil. They planted fruit and vegetable crops and, eventually, about 700,000 acres of sugarcane, supplying one-fourth of the nation's output. However, it didn't take long for these developers to realize that the soil was fertile only near the lake; one mile out, it's nutrient content plummeted, so anything grown beyond there would require lots and lots of fertilizer. Furthermore, it didn't take long to discover that when the muck was exposed to the elements, it would dry up and blow away.

Although northern capital financed the railroads, it was the labour of African-Americans and Bahamians that actually built them and kept the engines running. Bahamian blacks provided the heavy labour for clearing and grading of Henry Flagler's bold extension of the Florida East Coast Railway across the Florida Keys in the early 1900s (Courtesy of the United States Department of Labour).

These migrant workers worked hard for their money, and the work could be backbreaking and dangerous. Poisonous snakes were only one hazard. Workers had to be careful not to fall from ladders when picking. Migrant workers who toiled in the sugar beets and lettuce fields were forced to use a special tool. It was a short-handled hoe that they called *El Cortito*, "the short one." This special hoe had a handle that was only 12 or 18 inches (30.5 or 45.7 centimeters) long. A regular hoe has a long handle that allows a person to stand up while using it. El Cortito, however, forced workers to stay in the bent-over position, twisting their bodies to crawl along rows of lettuce or beets. After 10 to 12 hours of holding this position, many people were unable to stand straight. Because the children's bones were still forming, using El Cortito was especially harmful for them. It often resulted in horribly painful backaches for the rest of their lives. Even though the long-handled hoe could be used, the growers insisted that workers use El Cortito. These growers believed that the short-handled tool caused less damage to the growing vegetables.

Migrant workers, by their nature, had no vested interest in any one farm or area. The season was short, and most had to make what they could in a few short weeks. They went where the work was and the pay the best. There were no salaries; they were paid piecemeal. If they could make a cent or two more elsewhere, they simply left. Farmers were not above offering more to another farmer's field hands if he had a crop he had to harvest in a hurry. A farmer might find he had no hands to work the fields one morning and end up cursing his bad luck and what he saw as the disloyalties of the black race. In some cases a few farm owners built the labourers better living quarters—nothing elaborate, just enough to make them comfortable, dry, and warm, and some would say, "Don't want to spoil them." No farmer wanted to pay their workers any more than was necessary. They begrudgingly housed them in makeshift shacks constructed from leftover wood and tin. A farmer who did too much for his workers was resented by the other farmers and, worst of all, might be called a "nigger lover", and this was an epithet no true white southerner would tolerate.

But fortunately, the farms kept coming. Farmers and business leaders boasted about the rich muck soil, rich as manure, they said and they often referred to it as black gold. Truckloads of it were freighted north to Chicago during the early 1920s, put on display in store windows, and used to raise huge flowers and vegetables, all meant to attract people to Florida. Also, dreamy developers envisioned Clewiston, on the lake's southwest shore, growing into a metropolis of 100,000. The great Florida empire builder Henry Flagler turned to the lake's north shore and settled in the town of Okeechobee. He saw it as a great railroad crossroads, the Chicago of the South. Port Mayaca, a tiny settlement on the northeast corner, would be like the exotic Miami suburb of Coral Gables, with a sandy beach, yacht basin, and artificial lakes and inlets called Sapphire and Emerald. When Florida's real estate boom collapsed, a good two to three years before the stock-market crash, those lavish dreams also vanished as well.

**Workers washing Oranges in a Field in Florida in the 1920s
(Courtesy of the United States Department of Labour).**

In the hardscrabble towns of the Deep South and the desperately impoverished islands of the Bahamas and the rest of the Caribbean, people looked to Florida. They weren't investing in waterfront lots or homes or even mega shops because they were the poorest of the poor, struggling to meet their basic needs under the burden of grinding poverty and the constant fear that comes from oppression. So they came in droves, on airplanes or creaking ships, leaving their families behind for what they believed was their best chance to feed them. They lived in tent cities or shantytowns, and every day, in the blistering South Florida sun, they gathered the winter vegetables that brought colour to a gray winter's day or chopped the green cane that brought sweetness to households across the land. Many white farmers also toiled, and many of them also had little to their names. Towns and businesses sprang up to serve the farms. Canals and roads were built that moved produce to grocers and mills across the land.

In the 1920s, the long stretch of open land between the farmland and the coast made them into separate worlds. The coast was full of people who never got dirt under their fingernails. To them, the interior was an unknown place full of faceless blacks and poor, uneducated whites. Dreamers had envisioned a patchwork of small satellite farms managed and owned by white families. What was emerging was a collection of larger farms primarily owned by big businesses and worked by black migrants from the Deep South or the Bahamas and the rest of the Caribbean. However, the majority of these workers came from the Bahamas. The black man was the perfect answer to the labour intensive enterprise of farming the black gold. In the early twentieth century, blacks were the ideal candidates to work these farms. They were "in their place." They had been kept poor—and not just financially. They had been deprived of education, opportunity, or any kind of sense of rooted community. Many had come down to work on Henry Flagler's railroad and the communities that had been set up for them. In most cases, they were always planted on the west, inland or on the side of the tracks. But as many 5,000 migrant workers came from the impoverished islands of the Bahamas and the rest of the Caribbean.

Neither labour rights nor unions were part of the equation. In fact, if a worker was disgruntled or unhappy, there were many others who were more than happy to take his place. Workers lived in community houses, some of them provided by growers. Some lived in run-down rickety shacks or shanty towns thrown together with scrap wood. Some pitched tents, while others would lie down at the end of the day on the side of the road or under a stand of trees. Blacks were believed to account for at least half of the more 8,000 people living in the towns surrounding the lake. But it was impossible to get an exact number. Migrants from the South or the Bahamian Islands came in, worked, got paid in cash, and went back to their families. There was no paperwork, as payments were always in cash and many workers were known to their bosses only by a first name. If someone died, he might not be counted if no relative was looking for him.

An African-American worker standing in a corn field in Alachua County, Florida in the 1920s (Courtesy of the US Department of Labour).

At least 2,500 persons died in Florida from this storm, mainly due to the surge generated from the lake, but the unofficial count was much higher because more bodies and skeletons were discovered in later years. Of this total, about 75% were blacks, many of which were working on the railroads and as farm workers who were ill-served by the rudimentary emergency management of those segregated times. To this day, the number of people who lost their lives on the shores of Okeechobee is known only very roughly. Migrant workers especially from the Bahamas were not included in censuses, and at the time, State politics were dominated by northern Floridians, many of whom took a dim view of immigrants in the south.

In the words of Florida's attorney general, Fred Davis, "It is mighty hard to get people in other parts of the state interested in whether they [the workers of south central Florida] perish or not." This heartlessness toward the welfare of the migrant workers, most of whom were blacks from the Bahamas, contributed to the lack of an accurate death toll. The Red Cross at the outset estimated that 2,300 had died in the storm, but owing to intense pressure from officials who feared that such a large number would scare away tourists and investors, this figure was revised downward to the absurdly precise figure of 1,836, a number still repeated in contemporary literature.[64] An additional 312 people died in Puerto Rico, and 3 more were

---

[64]   Emanuel, K. (2005) *Divine Wind-The History and Science of Hurricanes*, New York, Oxford University Press, Pg. 120.

reported dead in the Bahamas and 18 in Grand Turk. Damage to property was estimated at $50,000,000 in Puerto Rico and $25,000,000 in Florida.

In 1928, the death toll in the United States was subdivided into two categories, *Whites* and *Negroes* or *Coloured*. The fact that racial distinction was made in classifying the death toll was very significant for the islands of the Bahamas. The non-white population suffered considerably more than the white population in most areas. In 1928, it can be speculated that the more affluent white population of South Florida may have been more at risk from hurricanes than the non-white population. This was because more rich white residents lived on or near the water in more expensive homes, thus being more susceptible to storm surge from the hurricane. In addition, whites were more at risk because of automobile ownership, because a number of fatalities occurred as residents of the area tried to drive back to the mainland during the lull in the eye of the hurricane. They were swept into the bay and drowned as the wind and seas returned on the opposite side of the eye. However, such speculation must be balanced by the known fact that non-whites of that era often lived in substandard housing, which would be very susceptible to hurricane-force winds.

This picture shows Bahamian migrant labourers on a vegetable farm in Florida, planting vegetable seedlings. The Bahamian economy was in the midst of a big squeeze, as new citrus and vegetable production in Florida competed with the output of the Bahamas (Courtesy of the US Department of Labour).

The extent of the Bahamian influx to Florida's new tourist town was revealed in the United States census reports. Miami had only a few hundred people when it was incorporated as a city in 1896. By 1900, the population had increased to 1,681, including a sizable number of black immigrants from the Bahamas. Over the next twenty years, the Bahamian influx helped to swell the population. By 1920, when Miami's population stood at 29,571, the foreign-born made up one-quarter of the total population. More than sixty-five percent of Miami's foreign-born residents were blacks from the West Indies. Black islanders, almost all from the Bahamas, totaled 4,815. They comprised fifty-two percent of all Miami's blacks and 16.3 percent of the city's entire population. By 1920, Miami had a larger population of black immigrants than any other city in the United States.[65]

The story of how Miami became a destination for black immigrants from the Bahamas begins early in Florida history. Bahamian Blacks had been familiar with Florida's lower east coast, and particularly the Florida Keys, long before the building up of the Miami area. In the early nineteenth century, when Florida was isolated and undeveloped, the area was commonly frequented by Bahamian fishermen, wreckers, and seamen, as well as traders who dealt with Seminole Indians. In fact, many black Bahamians first arrived in the islands from Florida as slaves of the 3,200 British Loyalists who fled after the American Revolution. Still later, in the early nineteenth century, numbers of Seminole blacks from Florida settled on Andros Island.

A reverse migration had also begun to take place by the mid-nineteenth century. Unlike the rest of the British West Indies, plantation agriculture was never successful or profitable in the Bahamas. Only about 2% of the total Bahamian land area of about 4,000 square miles was considered suitable for crops. Most nineteenth-century Bahamians earned a livelihood from the sea or from subsistence agriculture. By the 1830s, black and white Bahamians were beginning to migrate to the Florida Keys, especially Key West, where they worked in fishing, wreckage and salvaging, sponging, and turtling.

Facing meager economic prospects at home, free Bahamian blacks found better employment opportunities in Key West. By 1892, 8,000 of the 25,000 people in Key West were Bahamians, and sponging was their

---

[65] http://www.kislakfoundation.org/millennium

mainstay.[66] A large majority of Key West blacks can trace their ancestry to Bahamian origins. By the late nineteenth century, a second stream of Bahamian blacks had begun arriving on Florida's lower east coast for seasonal work in the region's emerging agricultural industry. As a result, after 1890 these newcomers from the Bahamas served as an early migrant labour force in Florida agriculture. The soil content, scanty pine and oolitic limestone topography of South Florida was similar to that of the Bahamas Islands. This made it very useful to the Bahamian farm workers because these Bahamians 'knew how to plant' on the Florida land and they brought in 'their own commonly used trees, vegetables, and fruits.' Thus, they demonstrated to Native American planters the rich agricultural potential of what seemed at first a desolate and forbidding land.

In Florida, the Bahamian newcomers found jobs in a variety of occupations and activities. The Bahamians were noted for their masonry skills. In particular, they were adept at building with oolitic limestone common to the Bahamas and South Florida. Thus, Bahamian blacks who came to Miami after its founding in 1896 found work in the burgeoning construction industry. As Flagler pushed his railroad south into the Keys, some clearing and grading work was assigned to Bahamians. The Bahamians also worked in local lumber yards and gravel pits, as stevedores on the docks, in the rail yards and terminals in the city, and more generally, as day labourers in whatever jobs could be found in Florida's growing economy.

Most of the Bahamian newcomers were men, but the emergence of Miami as a tourist resort provided special job opportunities for Bahamian women, especially as maids, cooks, and laundry and service workers in the city's new hotels and restaurants. In addition, Bahamians worked as domestic servants and caretakers for wealthy whites with permanent or winter residences in Miami. However, the majority of the Bahamian workers worked extensively in the citrus groves and vegetable fields. The census at the time suggested that these workers were mostly young, single Bahamian men living in boarding houses. The boom years of the 1920s brought tremendous population growth and urban development to South Florida from the Bahamas.

---

[66] http://gullahgeecheeconnection.wordpress.com/bahamas-folklore-gullahgeechee-connection/

The Lake Okeechobee region in Florida in the late 1920s was a new and lightly populated region. Only within 10 years or so had the Everglades region near Lake Okeechobee been drained to uncover the fertile black muck soil for agriculture. Many Bahamian blacks and other non-white persons had come to or were brought to the Lake Okeechobee region to live and provide field labour. The lake itself was partially surrounded by a levee from 5 to 9 feet above the ground. The hurricane moved ashore in Palm Beach County on the evening of 16 September 1928, only two years after the Great Miami Hurricane of 1926 had devastated Miami.

The hurricane passed over the eastern shore of Lake Okeechobee, causing terrible flooding in the towns of Pahokee, Canal Point, Chosen, Belle Glade, and South Bay. It was estimated that of the many persons lost in the flood waters, probably three-quarters or more were non-white field workers, and of that total, three-quarters or more were estimated to be Bahamian farm and railway workers. With this rough estimation, it would mean that in total approximately 1,406 Bahamians died in this storm in South Florida. This total is significant because this would make the Okeechobee Hurricane the deadliest hurricane to impact the Bahamas indirectly with such a massive death toll.

The exact number of those who perished in the Okeechobee storm can never be ascertained because the *Miami Daily News* on September 25th gave a total of 2,300 persons who died in the storm. The Red Cross gave an initial total of 1,810 persons and later revised it upwards to 1,836, and many other newspapers gave totals ranging from 1,800 to 2,350 persons; however, the official National Weather Service death toll was 1,836 persons for over 77 years, but in 2003 this total was revised to 'at least 2,500.' This revision made the Okeechobee Hurricane the second-deadliest natural disaster in United States history, thankfully, a record that still stands to this day.[67]

The exact number of those who perished in the Okeechobee Hurricane can never be determined because 75% of those blacks who perished were black Bahamian migrant workers, and it was complicated by the fact that most of them were known, even to their friends, only by a nickname. Going by the National Hurricane Center totals of 'at least 2,500', approximately

---

[67] http://www.srh.noaa.gov/mfl/?n=okeechobee

75% (which is 1,875), of that total were blacks, and approximately 75 % (which is 1,406) of the blacks total were black migrant workers from the Bahamas. This would mean that approximately 1,406 Bahamian migrant workers died in this storm in Florida. I must add here that this number is just an approximate amount, as no one really knows how many blacks or Bahamians in total died in this storm. Another reason the number cannot be established was the fact that many persons were carried by the flood waters far into the saw grass wastes.[68]

Furthermore, after the storm a considerable time and effort was made to return this region to some degree of normalcy and recover financially in the aftermath rather than making an effort in obtaining an 'official' death toll and obtaining their names. As a result, many of the bodies and skeletons were simply buried or burned on site without any form of documentation. This was mainly due to the fact that there were too many to count, too decomposed to identify, and rotting so quickly that they had to be burned or buried in mass graves so as to prevent the spreading of diseases and contamination. The majority of the blacks who died didn't even get a decent funeral. In addition, many bodies and skeletons were also discovered years later, thereby increasing the death toll even more.

Black immigrants from the Bahamas, in particular, gave Florida, but notably South Florida, a new jumpstart on life, and in particular its special character in the early years of the twentieth century. The Bahamians thought that South Florida was a young, magic area where money could be 'shaken from trees.' Although British officials preferred to keep Bahamians on the island to maintain population stability, it was not to be. The Bahamian economy was in the midst of a big squeeze, as new citrus and vegetable production in Florida competed with the output of the Bahamas. Rising American import duties on Bahamian agricultural production, as well as on sisal (hemp) and sponges, caused these industries to fall on hard times. New economic opportunities beckoned in Florida, and by the early twentieth century regular steamship service between Miami and Nassau made the trip to Florida cheap and convenient for Bahamians. It was a classic case of immigration prompted by the same kinds of economic forces that lay behind the massive European migration to the United

[68] http://www.srh.noaa.gov/mfl/?n=okeechobee

States during the same era. The changing economic pattern had a powerful impact on Bahamian migration trends.

In Florida, the Bahamian newcomers found jobs in a variety of occupations and activities. While most of the earlier Bahamians were men, soon the emergence of Miami as a resort provided special opportunities for Bahamian women, especially as maids, cooks, laundry and service workers in the city's new hotels and restaurants. In addition, Bahamians worked as domestic servants and caretakers for wealthy white families with permanent winter residences in Miami. Agriculture also prospered in the Miami area, along with tourism. Many Bahamians worked in the local citrus industry, particularly around Coconut Grove, a community where Bahamians lived since the 1880s. The Bahamian presence in West Coconut Grove gave the area's black community a distinctively island character that is still evident today. It was named 'Coconut Grove' after an area in the Bahamas of the same name.

The small community originally built by Bahamians became more segregated as the Grove expanded and prospered. The descendants of Bahamians lived on Charles Avenue, behind the Coconut Grove Playhouse. E.F.W. Stirrup built a large family home that stands today. Stirrup is also the builder of the shotgun houses on Charles Avenue. Most have survived over a seventy-year period, which is evidence of the sturdiness of the Florida pine. This wood is invincible against termites and strong enough to withstand major hurricanes.

By the late nineteenth century, a second stream of Bahamian blacks had begun arriving on Florida's lower east coast for seasonal work in the region's emerging agricultural industry. As a result, after 1890 these newcomers from the Bahamas served as an early migrant labour force in Florida agriculture. The scrubby pine and oolitic limestone topography of South Florida was similar to that of the Bahamas Islands. The Bahamians 'knew how to plant' on the Florida land, and they brought in with them 'their own commonly used trees, vegetables, and fruits.' Thus, they demonstrated to Native American planters the rich agricultural potential of what seemed at first like a desolate and forbidding land.

The Lake Okeechobee region in Florida in the late 1920s was a new and sparsely populated frontier. Only within 10 years or so had the Everglades region near Lake Okeechobee been drained to expose the fertile black muck soil for agriculture. Many Bahamian blacks and other non-white persons had come to or were brought to the Lake Okeechobee region to live and provide field labour. The lake itself, a large but very shallow lake on average less than 15 feet deep, was partially surrounded by a levee from 5 to 9 feet above the ground. The hurricane moved ashore in Palm Beach County on the evening of 16 September 1928, only two years after the 1926 hurricane had devastated Miami.

CHAPTER SIX

The Impact of the Great Okeechobee Hurricane of 1928 on the Caribbean and the United States

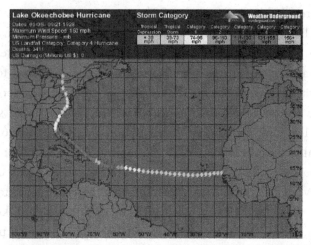

This map shows the track of the Hurricane of 1928 as it moved through the Leeward Islands, Puerto Rico, Dominican Republic, the Bahamas and the USA (Information courtesy of the Weather Underground Inc.).

The Saint (or sometimes referred to as 'San Felipe') Felipe-Great Okeechobee Hurricane, as it is commonly called, was a classic Cape Verde-type hurricane that was first detected over the tropical Atlantic on September 10, 1928, although it likely formed several days earlier. It moved westward through the Leeward Islands on September 12th. It then turned west-northwestward, making a direct hit on the island of Puerto Rico on September 13th (the feast day of Saint-Felipe hence the name Saint Felipe) as a Category 4 hurricane.

It was remembered as the Saint Felipe II Hurricane because the eye of the cyclone made landfall on the Christian feast day of Saint Phillip. The Latin American custom, since the Spanish colonial era began in 1492, was to name these storms upon their arrival after Catholic religious feast days. It was named "Segundo" (Spanish for "the Second") because of the eerie similarity in devastation with another hurricane that made landfall in Puerto Rico on that very same day 52 years earlier. The hurricane continued west-northwestward through the Bahamas and made landfall near Palm Beach, Florida on September 16th. It then made a north-northeastward track over the Florida Peninsula on September 17th, a motion that brought the remains of the storm to eastern North Carolina on September 19th. It then turned northward and merged with a non-tropical low over the eastern Great Lakes on September 20th.

No reliable wind readings were available from the near landfall area in Florida. However, Palm Beach reported a minimum pressure of 27.43 inches, making it one of the strongest hurricanes on record to hit the United States; it also remains the second deadliest hurricane on record to hit the United States. In Puerto Rico, San Juan reported sustained winds of 144 mph, while Guayama reported a pressure of 27.65 inches. Additionally, a ship just south of St. Croix, US Virgin Islands, reported a pressure reading of 27.76 inches. This hurricane caused heavy casualties and massive destruction along its path from the Leeward Islands to Florida.

The worst tragedy occurred mainly inland near Lake Okeechobee in Florida, where the hurricane caused lake surge of up to 9 to 15 feet that inundated the surrounding area. The hurricane tracked across Lake Okeechobee's northern shore, causing the shallow waters to reach heights of more than 15 feet. The surge was forced southward, causing significant flooding in the low-lands at the lake's south end, a region farmed primarily by migrant workers. To prevent future similar disasters, dikes were built around the lake by the U.S. Corps of Engineers. After this hurricane, the Florida State Legislature formed the "Okeechobee Flood Control District." The organization was authorized to cooperate with the U.S. Army Corps of Engineers in actions to prevent this disaster from happening again.

U.S. President Herbert Hoover visited the area personally, and afterward the Corps designed a new plan incorporating construction channels, gates, and levees. At least 2,500 persons died in Florida, mainly due to lake surge, but the unofficial count was much higher because more bodies and skeletons were discovered in later years. Of this total, about 75% were blacks, many of which were working on the railroads and as farm workers who were ill-served by the rudimentary emergency management of those segregated times. An additional 312 people died in Puerto Rico, and 18 more were reported dead in the Turks and Caicos Islands, and 3 here in the Bahamas. Damage to property was estimated at $50,000,000 in Puerto Rico and $25,000,000 in Florida.

The Okeechobee Hurricane, or Saint Felipe Segundo Hurricane, was a deadly hurricane that struck the Leeward Islands, Puerto Rico, the Bahamas, and Florida in September of the 1928 North Atlantic hurricane season. As of 2014, it is the only recorded hurricane to strike Puerto Rico at Category 5 intensity on the Saffir-Simpson Hurricane Wind Scale, and one of the ten most intense hurricanes on record to make landfall in the United States. Eighty-six years later, to say that the storm is still the deadliest weather event to strike Florida and the eastern United States does it a disservice. Nothing even comes close to the devastation and death brought about by this storm. Hurricane Andrew, the storm that defined hurricanes for most people living in Florida today, flattened much of one of America's largest metropolitan areas. But it killed only 44 people in Florida.

The destruction and flooding at the south shore of Lake Okeechobee after the Great Okeechobee Hurricane of 1928 (Courtesy of the Florida State Archives).

Prior to 2003, the 1928 storm's official US death toll was 1,836, and that number, assigned by the American Red Cross and state officials in the weeks following the disaster, is almost certainly too low. Too many people were hurriedly put into mass graves, stacked in piles and burned, or found as piles of bones years later in the fields. The volume of death was so staggering to the pioneer region that after a while, people just stopped counting. Historians suggest that 2,500 to 3,000 is a more realistic number, so in 2003 the National Hurricane Center upped the death toll to 'at 2,500.' This was not as a result of any new evidence, but reflecting a need to have a more accurate number in time for the storm's seventy-fifth anniversary. The storm would then be officially classified as the second deadliest disaster in American history, behind only the Great Galveston Hurricane of 1900, which killed between 6,000 and 12,000 people, surpassing the Johnstown Flood of 1889, which killed 2,209 persons.

The hurricane caused devastation throughout its path. As many as 1,200 people were killed in Guadeloupe. The storm directly struck Puerto Rico, an American possession or U.S. Territory, at peak strength, killing at least 312 persons and leaving hundreds of thousands homeless. The storm killed 3 persons in the Bahamas. In South Florida, at least 2,500 were killed when the storm surge from Lake Okeechobee breached the dike surrounding the lake, flooding an area covering hundreds of square miles. If you figure the higher death appraisals of the Okeechobee Hurricane and include those lost in Puerto Rico, the grim scoreboard of the dead on U.S. soil surpasses 2,812; add the deaths on other Caribbean islands, and it exceeds well over 6,800.

Image showing damaged buildings and debris-filled street in Belle Glade, Florida, after the Okeechobee Hurricane of 1928 (Courtesy of NOAA-National Hurricane Center).

The storm was first observed in the far eastern Atlantic, about 900 miles to the east of Guadeloupe, on September 10th by the *S.S. Commack*. It was the first time that sailors had encountered the Great Okeechobee Hurricane of 1928. It was located at Latitude 17° north and longitude 48.15° west. The crew reported the wind was blowing from the northeast at Force 7 on the Beaufort Wind Scale. They were measuring the speed of the wind on the old Beaufort Wind Speed Estimation Scale. Force 7 was equivalent to 32 to 38 mph. The crew took the measurements and radioed them back to the U.S. Weather Bureau. At the time, this was the most easterly report of a tropical cyclone ever received through a ship's radio.

A Cape Verde-type hurricane, hurricane re-analysis in the 1990s determined the strengthening storm likely formed four days prior, between Cape Verde and the west coast of Africa. While only 60 percent of any year's North Atlantic hurricanes are Cape Verde-type storms, they account for nearly 85 percent of the major hurricanes. The two greatest natural disasters to strike the United States—the Galveston and Okeechobee hurricanes—were in fact Cape Verde storms. Most Cape Verde hurricanes form later in the season, favoring late August and September, and the Okeechobee hurricane was right on schedule to fit into this mold. In the 1920s, the world had no satellites or hurricane-research jets or views from space. People judged storms only by what they could see of them on the horizon. Over the next eight days, weather officials would track the storm as it crossed more than 5,000 miles from the Caribbean to Canada.

At 2:00 pm, about 280 miles to the south, at latitude 14° north and longitude 51° west, the crew of the *Clearwater* measured winds of Force 5, which is equivalent to 19 to 24 mph and reported that their barometer had dropped 0.1 inch in just two hours. Later, the *Clarissa*, 70 miles to the south at 13° north and 51° west, recorded Force 6, which is equivalent to 25 to 31 mph. The three different merchant ships, almost lined up on a southwesterly line, provided all the evidence weather officials needed to conclude that a hurricane was 600 miles east-northeast of Barbados and heading due west. At the time, forecasting had improved dramatically but was still primitive compared to the advanced science it would evolve into today.

Early on September 11th, the U.S. Weather Bureau in Jacksonville issued the first advisory of the storm, announcing that at 8:00pm on

September 10ᵗʰ, a "tropical disturbance" was at about latitude 15° north, longitude 50°west, and moving west to west-northwest. That placed it 1,600 miles from Florida—as far as southeast Florida is from Denver. Even if it aimed straight at Florida, it was still some five days away. On the morning of September 11ᵗʰ, the merchant ship *Inanda*, at 17° north, 56° west, reported a northwest wind of Force 10, or 55 to 63 mph. the storm's sustained winds were now about 10 mph below official hurricane strength. The wind changed direction at Bridgetown, capital of the British colony of Barbados, a small island that sticks out into the ocean just east of the arc formed by the Windward Islands.

On the morning of Wednesday, September 12ᵗʰ, the center of the storm would pass just north of the largest of the Windward Islands: the French territory of Martinique. The first victim of the hurricane, however, was not Martinique, but its British neighbour, Dominica, about 30 miles away. At 290 square miles—Dominica is about four times the size of Washington, D.C., and less than half the size of Lake Okeechobee. Its highlight is a relatively small mountain range called Mount Diablatins, which stands at 440 feet. The storm struck about 8:00am on September 12ᵗʰ. The seawall was smashed, crops were destroyed, and at least one death was reported.

Most Intense US Landfalling Hurricanes

Rank	Hurricane	Season	Landfall Pressure
1	Great Labour Day Hurricane of 1935	1935	892 mbar(hPa)
2	Hurricane Camille	1969	909 mbar(hPa)
3	Hurricane Katrina	2005	920 mbar(hPa)
4	Hurricane Andrew	1992	922 mbar(hPa)
5	Indianola Hurricane of 1886	1886	925 mbar(hPa)
6	Florida Keys Hurricane of 1919	1919	927 mbar(hPa)
7	**Great Okeechobee Hurricane of 1928**	**1928**	**929 mbar(hPa)**
8	Great Miami Hurricane of 1926	1926	930 mbar(hPa)
9	Hurricane Donna	1960	930 mbar(hPa)
10	Hurricane Carla	1961	931 mbar(hPa)

Information Courtesy of: HURDAT, Hurricane Research Division-NOAA/ Wikipedia.

As the storm neared the Caribbean over the Leeward and Windward Islands, it was already a Category 3 hurricane. The Leeward Islands, fifteen large ones, arc away and down from Puerto Rico. Pronounced "LOO-word," with a maritime flair, their name is itself a bit of marketing; the lee side of a boat is the side sheltered from the wind. Just to the south, the Windward Islands form the lower arc, swinging back to the west and down almost to South America. They are comprised of five main islands, plus a chain of smaller ones. Because of their position, they are more exposed to the trade winds from the northeast; hence, their name. These fragile pearls are the easternmost chain of islands in the central Atlantic and the first stop for any storm crossing the vast bath tub of warm water between the continents of Africa and the Americas. Their small size makes them improbable targets. But it leaves their inhabitants with no place to run should a major storm like the Okeechobee Hurricane make its presence felt on these islands. Because of their geographical location, whereby they are orientated north to south, a large hurricane moving northwest toward Florida can rip these islands apart in a matter of hours.

On September 12th, the strengthening storm passed over Guadeloupe, with its eye centering over the capital city of Pointe-á-Pitre, which occurred between 1830–1930 UTC, with sustained winds of 140 mph. It then passed south of the other Leeward Islands while continuing to strengthen. Guadeloupe reported a pressure of 27.76 inHg (940 mbar), and the ship *SS Matura* just south of St. Croix in the United States Virgin Islands reported it as an even stronger storm, with a pressure of 27.50 inHg (931 mbar). On the 13th, the storm struck Puerto Rico directly as a Category 5 hurricane on the feast day of Saint Felipe, allegedly packing winds of 160 mph; reliable reports from San Juan placed the wind speed at 125 knots (145 mph), and a report from Guayama placed the pressure at 27.65 inHg (936 mbar). The 160 mph wind measurement from Puerto Rico was taken by a cup anemometer in San Juan, 30 miles north of the storm's center, which measured 160 mph sustained winds three hours before the peak wind speed was reached; however, the instrument was destroyed soon thereafter and could not be calibrated. This unverified reading was the strongest wind measurement ever reported for an Atlantic hurricane up until that time.

The hurricane was also extremely large as it crossed Puerto Rico. Hurricane-force winds were measured in Guyama for 18 hours; since the storm is estimated to have been moving at 13 mph, the diameter of the storm's hurricane winds was estimated very roughly to be 234 miles. At least 312 lives were lost, and many more died in the following weeks due to starvation and disease. Damages in Puerto Rico were estimated at $50 million, and over 200,000 were left homeless. Because of its horrible consequences, on this date in Puerto Rico the September hurricane is often referred to as "Saint Felipe."

In his book *Florida's Hurricane History*, Jay Barnes included this vivid description of the storm's terror in Puerto Rico: "Many deaths were caused by zinc roofs flying through the air like scythes. Sand was hurled from the beaches to homes a mile inland and came through the windows and blinded people's eyes. In the hilly country, water was pouring down in streams through the red sand, which was so brilliant, it '"looked like a river of blood."' Oxen ran wild through the country, some of them still yoked, fighting and snorting in an effort to gain freedom. Lightning flashed constantly, and there was the continual roar of thunder and the crash of falling debris. The waves, which swirled high in the air, contained sand and mud and fell heavily on the shore. Then another one would lead and bound, and a reflection of fire in the sky could be seen in the ocean."[69]

After leaving the Caribbean, the hurricane moved across the Bahamas as a strong Category 4 hurricane. It continued to the west-northwest and made landfall in southern Florida at 0000 UTC on September 17th (7:00 p.m. local time on September 16th). Initially, Richard Gray of the U.S. Weather Bureau was optimistic that the storm would spare the South Florida region. Atmospheric pressure at landfall was measured at 929 mbar (hPa), and maximum sustained winds were near 145 mph. The eye passed ashore in Palm Beach County near West Palm Beach, then moved directly over Lake Okeechobee. Peak gusts were estimated near 160 mph at Canal Point. The hurricane's path turned northeast as it crossed Florida, taking it across northern Florida, eastern Georgia, and the Carolinas on September 19th. It then moved inland and merged with a low-pressure system around Toronto on the 20th.

[69] Barnes, J. (2007) *Florida's Hurricane History*, Chapel Hill, The University of North Carolina Press, pg.128.

Impact and Death Toll of the Great Okeechobee Hurricane of 1928

Country/Island/State/City Affected:	Deaths:
Guadeloupe	1,200
Turks and Caicos Islands	18
Bahamas	3
Martinique	3
Puerto Rico	312+
St. Kitts	9
Nevis	13
St Croix	6
Montserrat	42
Dominica	1
Total Deaths in the Caribbean:	**1,607+**
Florida	**Official: 1,836 (Changed to 'at least 2,500' in 2003)**
Philadelphia Area	7
New Jersey Coast	3
Maryland	I
Total Americans Killed:	**2,511+**
Total Death Toll:	**4,118+**
Florida Health Department Death Totals:	
Belle Glade	611
South Bay	247
Pahokee	153
Miami Locks	99
Chosen	23
West Palm Beach	11
Prosperity Farms	5
Jupiter	4
Fort Lauderdale	2
Kelsey City(Lake Park)	2
Bartow	1
Boca Raton	1
Canal Point	1
Deerfield Beach	1
Pelican Lake	1
Orange City	1
Stuart Area	1
Unknown	669*(*Would include 25 reported dead at Okeechobee)
Total Deaths:	**2,500+**
Florida Damage and Red Cross Relief:	
Affected Area	112,200 People in 20 Counties
Buildings Destroyed or Damaged	32,400
Damage	$75 Million (In 1920s Dollars)
Livestock Killed	1,278
Poultry Lost	47,389
Families Given Aid	30,325
Volunteers Assisting	3,390

Information Courtesy of: National Weather Service/
HURDAT, Hurricane Research Division-NOAA/ Wikipedia/
American Red Cross/Individual Islands.

The hurricane moved directly over the Leeward Islands in the Caribbean, strengthening as it did so. On the island of Dominica, winds were clocked at 24 mph; there were no major reports of any significant damage, however, the seawall was smashed, some crops were destroyed, and at least one death was reported. In Martinique, even further south of the storm's path, there were three fatalities. All were apparently sailors who had tried to swim from small boats or help other people in the water. Most of the damage was among fruit trees; especially lime trees, cocoa trees, and sugarcane. However, there was enough sugarcane to allow a full complement of the island's precious export, which was rum. Newspapers reported as many as twenty boats foundered off the island.

Guadeloupe, a French colony of 230,000, had an especially grim history with hurricanes. For example, a powerful hurricane in September 1776 killed some 6,000 people in Pointe à Pitre Bay. It received a direct hit from this storm in 1928, apparently with little warning; the death toll there was 1,200, and damage reports relayed through Paris indicated "great destruction" on the island. Among those killed: Horace Descamp, editor of a local newspaper and correspondent for the Associated Press, and M. Bain, assistant administrator of the colony. Early on in the storm, at 7:00am on September 12th, about 16 miles east of the capital in the town of St. François, the *Albotros*, a small merchant vessel loaded with eighty cask of rum, had foundered. Five local men fought to save the ship, but drowned, as did her crew. The storm wrecked homes, trees, power lines, and sailboats. Only the city's police station, built of reinforced concrete, survived the merciless winds. According to news reports on September 19th, three-quarters of Guadeloupe's residents were rendered homeless by the storm. The storm destroyed the islands' coffee and banana crops and half the sugar cane crop and leveled most of the farm buildings and barracks. The distilleries that produced the island's liquor were damaged or destroyed.

Montserrat is a tiny, bean-shaped, British-controlled island of a mere 39 square miles. It was named by Christopher Columbus for a mountain in Spain. Montserrat, just north of the storm's center, was warned in advance of the storm, but still suffered £150,000 (1928 UKP) in damages, 42 deaths and 5,000 homeless, comprising half the population of the island. For ten hours, the storm ravaged the tiny island, with wind gusts reaching

140 miles per hour. All of the government and commercial buildings on the island were either damaged or totally destroyed. Well over 600 houses were destroyed. Plymouth (the capital on the island's south side) and Salem were devastated, and crop losses caused near-starvation conditions before relief could arrive.

Christopher Columbus had named the island of St. Christopher when he landed there in 1493; it was later shortened to St. Kitts. The storm passed to the south of the island of St. Kitts on Thursday, September 13th. Damage was less intense, but at least nine deaths were reported, six of them from the collapse of a schoolhouse. Ironically, the storm had a beneficial long term effect on the quality of housing, especially in slums. Most homes had been built on wooden foundations; following the storm, homes on the island had stronger foundations. Nevis did report thirteen deaths due to the storm.

The storm then passed to the south of St Croix, which suffered heavy damages to property and crops, but with only 6 reported fatalities. The Red Cross on St. Croix later determined that virtually everyone on the island of 11,000 had suffered some kind of loss. The agency reported that 143 buildings were flattened by the storm, including a sugar factory that was destroyed. Winds were reported to be as strong as 100 mph, and rain fell steadily for two days. The Red Cross sent by ship 125 square feet of galvanized corrugated iron sheets, 100,000 panels of roof sheeting, and 140,000 pieces of associated lumber. The agency decided food, clothing, and medical supplies weren't a concern for the residents on St. Croix. On the island of Antigua, northeast of Guadeloupe, a doctor's home and the "poor house" were among the buildings destroyed. Hundreds of homes were reported smashed. Government offices, schools and hospital were damaged. Damage reports from elsewhere in the Leeward Islands were not made available by the Red Cross. As many as 700,000 persons were reported homeless in the Virgin Islands after the storm.

In Puerto Rico, there is a very popular plena that goes like this:

> *"Temporal, temporal, allá viene el temporal.*
> *¿Que será de mi Borinken, cuando llegue el temporal?"*[70]

---

[70]   S.B. Schwartz-*The 1928 Hurricane and the Shaping of the Circum-Caribbean Region.*

(Hurricane, hurricane, here comes the storm)
(What will become of my Puerto Rico when the hurricane
arrives?)

Every Puerto Rican knows this plena and can sing its chorus, and on that island where from July to October everyone frequently checks the weather reports and looks to the sky, the song seems to describe a generic situation, a way of life, and a common reality. Few people today remember that the song was originally composed to commemorate a particular storm: the Great Hurricane of Saint Felipe II that traversed Puerto Rico on September 13, 1928.

When the Spanish-American War ended in 1898, the young United States was suddenly thrust into the international arena. The nation had succeeded in its primary objective of freeing Cuba from Spain. As a plus, the victor received the spoils of Puerto Rico, Guam, and the Philippines. With the acquisition of Spain's possessions in the Caribbean and the Pacific, America became a world power. Puerto Rico (Spanish for "rich port") encompasses an archipelago that includes the main island of Puerto Rico and a number of smaller islands, the largest of which are Vieques, Culebra, and Mona.

The main island of Puerto Rico is the smallest by land area of the Greater Antilles. It ranks third in population among that group of four islands, which include Cuba, Hispaniola (Dominican Republic and Haiti), and Jamaica. Due to its location, Puerto Rico enjoys a tropical climate and is subject to the Atlantic hurricane season and is almost dead center in the path of the typical route for the Cape Verde type hurricanes. Official languages of the island are Spanish and English, with Spanish being the primary language. Puerto Rico is a rectangular island roughly 100 miles by 35 miles, with a land area of about 3,300 square miles, making it about three fourths the size of Jamaica. When America took possession after the Spanish-American War in the spring and summer of 1898, it renamed it the island of Porto Rico. Congress would later change it back in 1932. In 1928, the island had only 2 million residents; Florida, sixteen times this size, had only about 1.3 million.[71]

---

[71] http://www.encyclopedia.com/topic/Puerto_Rico.

Puerto Rico was also home of the U.S. Weather Bureau's strategic island office, in the capital of San Juan. The office worked with colleges in Puerto Rico and the mainland, as well as forty different climate agencies, publishing daily rainfall data from 600 stations in the islands, Central America and parts of South America. Furthermore, for every place east of the Dominican Republic, it was responsible for tracking and forecasting hurricanes. During the storm, the bureau's office building lost its roof. That afternoon, the nearby shed that housed the weather balloons collapsed, and its roof was thrown 50 feet. The 50-foot tower on which weather instruments were mounted held up, but the anemometer cups and cross-arms were plucked off one at a time by the wind. Some pieces were later found at San Antonio docks one-third of a mile away.

In Ponce, on the central south coast, on the island's northwest corner, many buildings were demolished; ten were reported dead and 700 homeless. Initial reports said the Ponce area's coffee crop, the best in 10 years and much of it already pre-sold in Europe, was wiped out. It was valued at $15 million-$147 million today. In Coamo, northeast of Ponce and inland, switchboard operator Felicita Cartagena stayed at her post, relaying information until she was killed. She was one of nine who died in the town. In Guayama, east of Ponce along the coast, people ran into a church being built; the walls collapsed, killing fourteen. The storm destroyed many of the island's lighthouses and tore the roof off the headquarters of J.R. Monteiro, the lighthouse district superintendent.

The island received the worst of the storm's winds when the hurricane moved directly across the island at Category 5 strength. The island knew of the storm's approach well ahead of time; by about 36 hours in advance, all police districts were warned and radio broadcasts provided constant warnings to ships. Effective preparation is credited for the relatively low official death toll of 312; however, some estimate that the real death toll is more likely somewhere between 600 and 1,600. Had the storm dissipated after striking Puerto Rico, people would still be talking about the Great Puerto Rico Hurricane of 1928. Amazingly, not a single ship was lost at sea in the vicinity of Puerto Rico. By comparison, the weaker 1899 Hurricane Saint Ciriaco killed approximately 3,000 people.

On Thursday, just before the end of their noon siesta, the people of Ponce on the southern coast of Puerto Rico were awakened by the erratic ringing of church bells. It was the day of Saint Felipe, the Saint of the Hopeless. Rung by strong winds blowing through the centuries-old belfries, the bells toiled a sardonic melody. The storm was named the Saint Felipe II Hurricane because the eye of the cyclone made landfall on the Christian feast day of Saint Philip. It was named "Segundo", Spanish for "the Second", because of another destructive "Hurricane Saint Felipe", which struck Puerto Rico on that same day in 1876. Since European arrival in the Caribbean in 1492, all storms and hurricanes were named after the saint of the day the storm hit Puerto Rico and other Spanish lands. In 1953, the United States started naming hurricanes by female names until 1978, when both gender names began to be used alternately. Yet it was only in 1960 that hurricanes stopped being officially named after saints.

Saint Felipe II is officially classified as Puerto Rico's biggest, worst, and most devastating hurricane to ever have impacted the island. Even though it was the worst hurricane to hit the island, others such as the San Ciriaco Hurricane caused even more deaths. The first warning the island received was by the steamship *SS Commack,* under the captainship of Samuel Kruppe, at latitude 17° north and longitude 48° west, who had inadvertently sailed into the storm. Saint Felipe entered the island early in the morning of Thursday, September 13th, with its eye close to Guyama, and it traversed the island in a north-west direction, leaving between the towns of Aguadilla and Isabela. The eye of the hurricane made its Puerto Rico crossing in eight hours, moving at about 13 mph. In Guayama, located in south-eastern Puerto Rico, the lowest barometric pressure reading of the storm was 27.5 inHg (930 mbar) at 2:30 pm.

The rainfall recorded on September 13–14, 1928, are records for the maximum amount of rainfall associated with a hurricane in Puerto Rico within a period of forty-eight hours. Stations reported more than two feet of rain fell over the interior of the island-the most in three decades-with about 10 inches measured along the coast. In those regions where precipitation is more common-place, as in Adjuntas in the Cordillera Central and in the Sierra de Luquillo, the rain was over 25 inches, with 29.60 inches recorded in Adjuntas.

The anemometer located in Puerta de Tierra lost one of its cups at 11:44 am on September 13th, just when it had registered a maximum speed of 150 miles per hour, a speed that was sustained for five consecutive minutes. Previously, the same instrument had measured 160 miles per hour for one minute. The city of San Juan was 30 miles away from the eye of Saint Felipe when those measurements were recorded—because of which, at the time, it seemed possible that some estimates of 200 miles per hour near the center of the storm were not overdrawn. During the storm, many persons could be seen running about in the city, dodging the uprooted trees, lumber, stones and big pieces of metal that were being driven about over their heads. Ambulances and doctors were racing about, trying to gather up the dead and injured. The floodwaters washing the red soil from the hills looked like a river of blood.

There was general destruction through the island, with the towns where the eye passed being swept away. Property damage on the island from the wind and rain was catastrophic. The northeast portion of the island received winds in excess of Category 3 strength, with hurricane-force winds lasting as long as 18 hours. Official reports stated "several hundred thousand" people were left homeless, and property damage was estimated at $50 million ($669 million 2014 USD). Of those who died, many had been cut to pieces or lost limbs as sheets of zinc flew off roofs and cut through the air like machetes. In Cayey, a woman was found with a child in each arm; all three had been chopped up by the flying sheets of zinc.

Nearly 75 percent of San Juan's homes and 40 percent of its commercial buildings had been destroyed. On the island, there was no building that was not affected. Some sugar mills ("Centrales") that had cost millions of dollars to build were reduced to rubble. Reports say that 24,728 homes were completely destroyed and 192,444 were partially destroyed. Most of the sugarcane fields were flooded, thus losing the year's crops. Half of the coffee plants and half of the shade trees that covered these were destroyed; almost all of the coffee harvest was lost. The coffee industry would take years to recover since coffee needs shade trees to grow. The tobacco farms also had great losses. After this hurricane, Puerto Rico never regained its position as a coffee exporter.

Communications were impacted by fallen trees, landslides, and debilitated bridges. Of the school buildings, 770 were destroyed or debilitated. Governor Horace Towner wired President Calvin Coolidge that half the territory's homes were destroyed and 700,000 people were left homeless. He sent dispatches to the press, calling the disaster "the most serious the island has ever suffered." On Monday, September 17th, Coolidge ordered the military to divert two army transport ships, loaded with food, to the island. Plans were made to load a supply ship Tuesday morning in New York, with 1.5 million pounds of supplies for swift dispatch to the south by the afternoon. The cargo: one-third salt pork and salt codfish, one-third beans and rice, and one-third flour. The first army relief ship, the *St. Mihiel,* arrived in Puerto Rico on September 19th with 559 tons of supplies. The second ship arrived the next day. Colonel Henry M. Baker, national director of the American Red Cross, and four staffers arrived by ship as well.

After the storm, the Red Cross freed up $50,000 and rushed in two million pounds of flour, rice, beans, salt, pork, and equipment for two field hospitals, including 36,000 blankets, 5,000 cots, and nearly 1,000 tents. By the end of September, the agency would also distribute more than 24,000 pieces of clothing and a large supply of medicine. Cuba, Columbia, and the Dominican Republic sent money, and the Dominican president ordered that fresh fruits and vegetables be rushed to his American neighbour. On the island, mail service resumed, but carriers had a new problem. They kept returning to their post offices with mail addressed to buildings and homes that were no longer where they were supposed to be. The island's health commissioner reported on September 18th that bodies were being buried where they were found, sometimes without identification and with no report made to the authorities.

The newspaper also reported price gouging. Food was drastically marked up. For example, roofing and other construction materials tripled, and corrugated zinc went from $2.25 per sheet to $10, and in some cases $16. Candles that normally cost two cents rose to a nickel. Looting was rife at first, but diminished in two days after the storm "due to the use of revolvers and pistols…" There were 321 school buildings destroyed and 414 others badly damaged. Within three weeks, 90 percent of school operations were back up.[72]

Federal surveys concluded agricultural losses in Puerto Rico totaled about $85.3 million, $46.4 million of that to crops alone. The highs were:

---

[72] Kleinberg, E. (2003) *Black Cloud-The Deadly Hurricane of 1928*, New York, Carroll & Graf Publishers, pg. 55.

coffee industry, $21 million; sugar cane, $17.3 million; bananas, $5.7 million; citrus, $2.8 million; coconuts, $1.7 million; tobacco, $1.5 million. The surveys estimated rebuilding costs alone at $7.3 million. Congress approved $11.2 million in aid, $6 million of that in loans to farmers. These figures, in today's dollars, would be almost tenfold.[73]

Deadliest North Atlantic Hurricanes

Rank	Hurricane	Season	Fatalities
1	Great Hurricane of 1780	1780	22,000+
2	Mitch	1998	19,325+
3	Great Galveston Hurricane of 1900	1900	8,000 – 12,000
4	Fifi	1974	8,000 – 10,000
5	Dominican Republic Hurricane of 1930	1930	2,000 – 8,000
6	Flora	1963	7,186 – 8,000
7	Pointe-à-Pitre Hurricane of 1776	1776	6,000+
8	Newfoundland	1775	4,000 – 4,163
9	**Great Okeechobee Hurricane of 1928**	**1928**	**4,118+(4,118-5,000)**
10	Monterrey Hurricane	1909	4,000+

Information Courtesy of: National Weather Service/National Hurricane Center/HURDAT, Hurricane Research Division-NOAA/ Wikipedia/American Red Cross/Individual Islands.

The eye of the hurricane passed over much of the island chain as a strong Category 4 hurricane, again causing very heavy damage. Considering all the damage in Puerto Rico, the hurricane still hadn't done its worst. By Thursday afternoon, September 14th, the hurricane, had left Puerto Rico and moved north of Hispaniola, the giant, mountainous island that is home to Haiti and the Dominican Republic. In Porto Plata, on the Dominican Republic's northern coast, some homes lost roofs and ships were damaged. The freighter *Lillian* was driven ashore. Cap-Haitian, on Haiti's northwest coast, got only heavy rains. Over the centuries, Hispaniola has suffered for Florida's sake. Many powerful storms were ripped to shreds or shifted

---

[73]   Kleinberg, E. (2003) *Black Cloud-The Deadly Hurricane of 1928*, New York, Carroll & Graf Publishers, pg. 55.

harmlessly into the open Atlantic, or both, after slamming into the island's mountains. The mountains are the tallest in the West Indies, reaching as high as the Dominican Republic's Duarte Peak, which rises 10,417 feet, nearly two miles above sea level. They have the effect on the hurricane like a stick in a bicycle wheel's spokes, ripping apart the circulation of the giant hurricane and weakening it. But it moved too far to the north for Hispaniola to have any effect. A track of the storm's path reveals that it didn't make the large curve officials had confidently predicted for several days.

As in Puerto Rico, however, authorities in the Bahamas and Turks and Caicos Islands were aware of the hurricane's passage well ahead of time, and preparations minimized the loss of life in these islands. The only report of fatalities was from a sloop lost at sea in the vicinity of Ambergris Cay with 18 on board in Turks and Caicos Islands and 3 deaths in the Bahamas.

An image of destruction that occurred in West Palm Beach, Florida, during the Okeechobee Hurricane. In the background are houses that have been reduced to their most sturdy elements, while debris in the foreground is from other destroyed homes (Courtesy of NOAA-The National Hurricane Center).

Clearly, forecasters' technology in 1928 was downright primitive compared to that of their twenty-first-century counterparts. But today's forecasters have a certain degree of humility and pragmatism. Even with their best computer models, given the same track today, the best they can offer twenty-four hours before landfall would be a "cone of uncertainty or probability" extending from the Space Coast to the Keys. The difference is that while forecasters of today admit their limitations, the forecasters of

1928 believed—and were even convinced—that they knew where the storm was, and was not, headed. Unfortunately, they were dead wrong, and many persons died as a result of this wrong forecast of the storm over Florida. For example, at 8:00pm, the storm was placed in extreme North Florida, between Jacksonville and Tallahassee, and was arching toward the northeast, having begun that turn east and northeast at Tampa. The storm finally begun the "recurve" forecasters had so confidently said would occur long before it reached the Florida coast. It had come a little late, and that delay brought far different consequences than those the forecasters had predicted so boldly.

Coastal damage in Florida near the point of landfall was catastrophic. Miami, well south of the point of landfall, escaped with very little damage; Hollywood and Fort Lauderdale suffered only slight damages. In Fort Lauderdale, numerous power lines and telephone wires were blown down. Northward, from Pompano Beach to Jupiter, buildings suffered serious damage from the heavy winds and 10-foot storm surge, which was heaviest in the vicinity of Palm Beach; total coastal damages were estimated as "several million" dollars. In West Palm Beach, more than 1,711 homes were destroyed, while the Jupiter Inlet Lighthouse's mortar was reportedly "squeezed ...like toothpaste" between the bricks during the storm, swaying the tower 17 inches off its base. Because of well-issued hurricane warnings, residents were prepared for the storm, and the number of lives lost in the coastal Palm Beach area was only 26.

Inland, the hurricane wreaked much more widespread destruction along the more heavily populated coast of Lake Okeechobee. Residents had been warned to evacuate the low-lying areas earlier in the day, but after the hurricane did not arrive on schedule, many thought it had missed and returned to their homes. When the worst of the storm crossed the lake, the south-blowing wind caused a storm surge to overflow the small dike that had been built at the south end of the lake. The resulting flood covered an area of hundreds of square miles, with water that in some places was over 20 feet deep. Houses were floated off their foundations and dashed to pieces against any obstacle they encountered. Most survivors and bodies were washed out into the Everglades, where many of the bodies were never found. As the rear eyewall passed over the area, the flood reversed itself, breaking the dikes along the northern coast of the lake and causing a similar, but smaller flood.

The earth was already saturated from the prior rainfall, with the surrounding valley area and lakes full to their banks across South Florida. The tide was astronomically high at the autumnal equinox—when both the sun and the moon's gravity tug at the sea level. The stage was set for major impact from all aspects of the storm: wind, rain, and storm surge. In three days, well over 13.16 inches of rainfall flooded the Kissimmee River Valley. The Associated Press reported a sheet of water 25 miles across in places covering the swamp areas west of Fort Pierce and around the lake's eastern and northern shores. The report said many families were marooned, large areas of vegetable and citrus groves were under water, and bridges were washed out. Fish swam in the streets of Okeechobee, and many of the cattle drowned. Taylor Creek, one of the rivers that feed into the big lake, became a mighty, rushing river.

Floodwaters persisted for several weeks, greatly impeding attempts to clean up the devastation. Burial services were quickly overwhelmed, and many of the bodies were placed into mass graves. Around 75% of the fatalities were black migrant farm workers, making identification of both the dead and missing bodies very difficult; as a result of this, the count of the dead was not very accurate. The Red Cross estimated the number of fatalities as 1,836, which was taken as the official count by the National Weather Service for many years (and exactly equal to the official count for Hurricane Katrina). Older sources usually list 3,411 as the hurricane's total count of fatalities, including the Caribbean. However, in 2003 the U.S. death count was revised to "at least 2,500", making the Okeechobee Hurricane the second-deadliest natural disaster in United States history, falling only behind the Great Galveston Hurricane of 1900. A mass grave at the Port Mayaca Cemetery, east of Port Mayaca, contains the bodies of 1,600 victims of the hurricane. Thousands of people were left homeless in Florida; property damage was estimated at $25 million.

The cyclone remains one of three Atlantic hurricanes to strike the southern mainland of Florida, with a central pressure below 940 mbar (27.76 inHg), the two others being the Great Miami Hurricane of 1926 and Hurricane Andrew of 1992. As the hurricane approached the east coast of Florida, it gathered strength after the blow dealt by Puerto Rico, and the Bahamas, aided by deep waters of the Gulf Stream. But the U.S. Weather Bureau had mis-located the storm and failed to issue timely warnings, believing it would turn north and stay out at sea. By the time it hit an unprepared Palm Beach on the evening of September 16th, its central pressure had dropped even lower to an astonishing 929 mbar (27.44 inHg), the lowest central pressure ever recorded at the time in the United States.

a)Deerfield Baptist Church b)Stevenson Supply House, Deerfield c)Pioneer Hotel, Deerfield d)F.E.C.R.R. Station, Deerfield e)U.S. Post Office and Frazer's Store, Deerfield f)Club House in City Park, Lake Worth: This photo was taken at 4pm on Sunday during the peak of the storm g)Lake Worth Bridge (Courtesy of NOAA-The National Hurricane Center).

Limited damage reports are available for the United States outside of southern Florida. The storm was northwest of Charleston, South Carolina at about 2pm Tuesday, and that city also reported top winds of about 50 mph, a fraction of the storm's greatest power, but enough to damage piers, beach small boats, down trees and knock out telegraph service both there and back in Savannah. The storm caused flooding in North Carolina and brought near hurricane-force winds and a 7- foot storm surge to the Norfolk area. Nonetheless, most sources agree that the hurricane caused only minimal damage in these areas.

The storm had taken a turn to almost due north in southeastern North Carolina and was now passing through central Virginia, headed toward Pennsylvania. But as it did, the portion north and east of the eye was over the coast and was pounding it. Hundreds of families were moved out of coastal North Carolina as rivers rose. By the weekend, as many as 600,000 acres of farmland would be inundated, with losses approaching $5 million—about forty-five million in today's dollars—and Charleston,

South Carolina, to the south, would be isolated by washed-out roads. Soon, the storm became extra tropical (meaning it lost its tropical characteristics). But warnings were posted as far north as New England.

On Tuesday, officials aboard the train carrying presidential candidate Herbert Hoover from Trenton, New Jersey, back to Washington had been previously warned that they might have to roll through some of the storm's wind and rain. As the edge of the storm passed over Baltimore, a fifty-year-old man was crushed to death by a falling tree. On Wednesday night, the master of the lighthouse off Fenwick Island reported sustained winds of 90 mph, with gusts to over 120 mph. A critical baseball game between the New York Giants and Chicago Cubs had to be postponed due to inclement weather related to this storm. This meant that they had to play a 'make-up' game, and this game came to decide the National pennant. Three persons were reported dead on the New Jersey coast.

List of the Deadliest United States Hurricanes

Rank	Hurricane	Season	Fatalities
1	Great Galveston Hurricane of 1900	1900	8,000 – 12,000*
2	**Great Okeechobee Hurricane of 1928**	**1928**	**At least 2,500***
3	Hurricane Katrina	2005	1,836
4	Cheniera Caminada Hurricane	1893	1,100 – 1,400
5	Sea Islands Hurricane	1893	1,000 – 2,000*
6	Florida Keys Hurricane	1919	778
7	Georgia Hurricane	1881	700*
8	Hurricane Audrey	1957	416
9	Great Labour Day Hurricane of 1935	1935	408
10	Last Island Hurricane	1856	400*

Blake, Eric S; Landsea, Christopher W; Gibney, Ethan J; National Climatic Data Center; National Hurricane Center (August 10, 2011). The deadliest, costliest and most intense United States tropical cyclones from 1851 to 2010 (and other frequently requested hurricane facts), (NOAA Technical Memorandum NWS NHC-6). National Oceanic and Atmospheric Administration pg. 47.

*Estimated total

In Florida, although the hurricane destroyed everything in its path with impartiality, the death toll was by far highest in the economically poor areas in the low-lying grounds right around Lake Okeechobee. Black workers did most of the cleanup, and the few caskets available for burials were mostly used for the bodies of whites; other bodies were either burned or buried in mass graves. Burials were segregated, and the only mass grave site to receive a memorial contained only white bodies.

About 35 miles to the east, in West Palm Beach, is Tamarind Avenue. At the corner of Tamarind and 25th Street is a field enclosed by a chain-link fence. For three-fourths of a century, no marker noted the fact that over seven hundred people lay entombed under the street. Treated like second-class citizens in life, they became truly invisible in death when racial tensions forced them not to get a proper burial. They are the faceless dead of the Great Okeechobee Hurricane of 1928. The inequity has caused an ongoing racial friction that still exists. The effects of the hurricane on black migrant workers are dramatized in Zora Neale Hurston's world famous bestselling novel *Their Eyes Were Watching God*.

In the aftermath of the hurricane in coastal Florida, it became apparent that well-constructed buildings with shutters had suffered practically no damage from winds that caused serious structural problems to lesser buildings. Buildings with well-constructed frames, and those made of steel, concrete, brick, or stone were largely immune to winds, and the use of shutters prevented damage to windows and the interior of the buildings. Coming on the heels of the Great Miami Hurricane of 1926, where a similar pattern had been noticed, one lasting result of the 1928 storm was improved building codes.

To prevent a recurrence of disasters like this one and the Great Miami Hurricane of 1926, the Florida State Legislature created the Okeechobee Flood Control District, which was authorized to cooperate with the U.S. Army Corps of Engineers in flood control undertakings. After a personal inspection of the area by President Herbert Hoover, the Corps drafted a new plan that provided for the construction of floodway channels, control gates, and major levees along Lake Okeechobee's shores. A long- term system was designed for the purpose of flood control, water conservation, prevention of saltwater intrusion, and preservation of fish and wildlife populations. One of the solutions was the construction of the Herbert

Hoover Dike. Today, concerns related to the dike's stability have grown in response to studies indicating long-term problems with "piping" and erosion. Leaks have been reported after several heavy rain events. Proposed solutions to the dike's problems have included the construction of a seepage berm on the landward side of the dike, with the first stage costing approximately $67 million (US$).

CHAPTER SEVEN

The Great Okeechobee Hurricane of 1928 Impact on the Islands of the Bahamas and the Turks and Caicos Islands

M ajor damage was reported in both the Turks and Caicos Islands and the Bahamas. In the Turks and Caicos Islands, by midnight Friday and into Saturday, September 15th, the winds were up to 120 mph, but they dropped to only about 36 mph within half an hour. This was a sure indication that Grand Turk only suffered a partial blow from the storm. At about 3:00am, the winds increased again to 60 mph, however, by dawn they had already subsided. At 11:50am at Grand Turk on September 14th, a U.S. Weather Bureau advisory said the storm would pass near Turks Islands that night. As it approached, Weather Bureau workers, under the leadership of special observer Cleo Goodwin, wanted to keep their radio going for as long as possible, a strategy later credited with saving many lives, especially in the outer islands. This strategy meant waiting until the absolute last minute to take down the antenna. But when the radio equipment was finally shut down, no one wanted to go outside and climb the tower. Finally, Lance Corporal William A. Godet volunteered and scampered up the pole in the increasing winds.

Goodwin would later write, in his letter to weather officials in Washington, that his eyes were still sore days later from the constant barrage of blinding, sand, winds and water. Goodwin said one building rolled over twice and had to be torn apart to move it, and another house was carried over several walls and vacant lots and destroyed. Returning to his home after the storm, Goodwin was surprised to find his carriage house flattened and most of his poultry killed.

On the morning of September 15th, he reported that there was not a trace of green to be seen on the island of Grand Turk; which looked as if it had been swept by a forest fire. Thankfully, a month later, he wrote that rains had restored the island's lush foliage. Two ships the *C. Maud Gaskill* and *William A. Naugler*, belonging to a businessman from Grand Turk, Mr. George Frith, were loading salt for Canadian ports at Salt Cay and were washed ashore, but their crews were saved. On the island of Caicos, great damage was reported to the island's major crops, and residents were reported to be starving after the storm. It didn't help much, either, that 225,000 bushels of rock salt, the island's main economic industry, were lost.

The greatest tragedy had been at Ambergris Cay, about 12 miles south of South Caicos. Ambergris Cay is an island within the Turks and Caicos Islands. It was named for valuable deposits of ambergris, a waxy substance that migrating humpback whales secrete, found on the 8 miles of shoreline. The island is approximately four miles long, one mile wide, and 1,100 acres in area. It was uninhabited until 1997, but it has a small population today. In the late 18th and early 19th centuries, Loyalists settled on Ambergris Cay, raised cows, made pottery, and built houses, stables, and cisterns (ruins still exist of each of these). A sloop on its way to Grand Turk to be registered was lost, with 18 people drowned. Another version of this same event, reported that conch fishermen had anchored their boat in a small creek on the cay, but the entire island had become inundated and 18 of the crew of 21 were lost. Eight of the dead crew members left their wives at home, who became instant widows after the storm.

The storm had passed over the southern part of the Turks Islands and the northwest part of Caicos Island, and while the winds were stronger and more persistent than in the 1926 storm, the damage was actually less severe. Authorities again gave special praise to the U.S. Weather Bureau for its warnings. Many buildings that were repaired following the Great Nassau Hurricane of 1926 and were built better and sturdier received very little damage to their structures. A week later, on September 26th, a British Royal Navy ship, the *Durban*, would land at Grand Turk and offer relief.

It was politely declined by the island's commissioner. But the captain did turn over a ton of potatoes. The captain and some of his officers dined that night at the commissioner's home. Among the captain's party: his lieutenant, the future King George VI of England.

In the capital city of Nassau, 10-year-old Hilda May Sturrup died when she ventured outside just after the storm had passed. She fell into an open trench filled with water and drowned. Her parents reported her missing, but she wasn't spotted until Tuesday. Two additional persons were reportedly killed in this storm. Many persons were badly injured and had to be taken to the hospital for treatment. For example, one child had to have a leg amputated after it was broken during the storm. One of the male lunatics escaped from the city's hospital and hadn't been found. The storm also tossed debris through the streets of Nassau, knocked down power and utility lines, flooded homes, and terrorized residents, many of whom fled their homes for schools and church halls. A garage in the downtown area, where many residents had stored their cars for protection, lost its roof and was badly damaged; remarkably, most of the cars were undamaged. A golf tournament set to start Sunday morning was postponed for at least a week; the course was still under water.

Several ships sank or were tossed against the rocks on the seaside. A nearly completed pier built to handle passenger ships, the island's lifeblood, was swept away, leaving only its pilings. Major damage was done to shipping in the Nassau Harbour, and many schooners, such as *Carkum* and *Capt Charley,* and some other mailboats, were totally destroyed by the hurricane. Some of the mailboats that were destroyed were the San Salvador *Guanahani* and the Andros Island mailboat, *The William Carlos.* The Mayaguana mailboat *Non-Such* sank in the Nassau Harbour, opposite Malcom's Park. A small harbour dredger also sank in Nassau Harbour and turned over. The five-masted schooner *Abaco* was blown out of the harbour and sunk east of Athol Island. Several small boats sank opposite Malcolm's Park and over at Hog Island (now called Paradise Island).

The Bahamas, with its seven hundred islands and cays, lived primarily from the sea. Boats were its lifeline. Because of this storm—there were no boats. No fishing boats, no mailboats, and no rumrunners—all had been sunk, thrown miles inland, or crushed. The telephone poles and telegraph towers lay scattered and destroyed like broken toothpicks. After the storm,

Nassau and many of the other islands were isolated, cut off from each other and the rest of the world. There was no way they could warn residents in Florida of the massive hurricane that was headed their way.

At about 3:00pm, the German steamer *August Leonhardt* was about 250 miles east-southeast of Nassau at 23.10°N and 74.10°W, heading from New York to Porto Columbia, Venezuela. R. Sievers, the ship's second officer, watched as the barometer dropped to a frightening 27.80 inches and a northeast wind blew at Force 12 on the Beaufort Wind Scale, which was more than 75 mph. Then the center passed over the ship and was enveloped in a calm lasting ten minutes. Now the wind shifted to the south-southeast "with an indescribable force," Sievers wrote. "The force of the wind…could only be judged by the noise made by the storm, which reminded me of the New York subway going full speed passing switches." Rain and spray streamed horizontally across the deck, and the ship's whistle began to blow eerily in the violent winds. Sievers watched with fear and amazement as waves slammed against the 2,500-ton freighter and spray shot up to the masthead, about 130 feet above the ocean's surface, leaving salty residue that the crew later cleaned off the ship's antenna and insulators. Hatch tarps, boat ventilators, covers, and anything else that wasn't attached solidly flew off and disappeared in the vicious sea. "It is impossible to describe the sea and swell," Sievers wrote. "Spray, rain and foam was so dense that we could not see our forecastle head."[74]

Meteorologists guessed that the eye of the storm passed a 65-mile stretch of ocean between Nassau and Harbour Island, at the north end of Eleuthera, which was the birthplace of Isaac Miller, who was on this day on his farm near Belle Glade. At 10pm, D. Salter, who was the meteorological recorder for Nassau, measured a northeast wind at 40 mph "and freshing rapidly." It was 55 mph by midnight, 65 mph by 1:30am, and 75 mph at 2:00am. By 4:00am, it had crossed the 100 mph mark. But that was only a guess because at 3:30am Sunday, just after recording a speed of 96 mph, the cups on Salter's anemometer, or wind gauge, had blown away. By 5:00am, he estimated, winds were at 110 to 120 mph, with a driving rain. But by 6:00am, the winds had dropped dramatically. Salter measured a total of 9 inches of rain during the storm's passage. Salter's report to U.S.

---

[74] http://www.aoml.noaa.gov/hrd/hurdat/mwr_pdf/1928.pdf

weather officials concluded the storm had done 'considerable' damage to property in Nassau and lesser damage to crops, but had caused no deaths, 'probably owing to the precaution taken as a result of the numerous early warnings received by wireless telegraphy and made public.'[75]

Officials also credited the experiences of the Great Nassau Hurricane of 1926 and Great Miami Hurricane of 1926, saying they had blown away weaker buildings and surviving structures had been rebuilt to be much stronger. J. Frank Points, American Vice Consul in Nassau, called the storm the worst in the Bahamas since the historic and very destructive Great Bahamas Hurricane of 1866-even worse than the two 1926 hurricanes, which also went on to devastate Miami. He reported that this hurricane in 1928 had done considerable damage throughout the city and to both of his residences and that of two of his assistants, identified only as Miss Gyr and Miss Porter. Rain had rushed into their rooms at about 3:30am, drenching everything before it could be moved. The staff would spend the next few days in swimsuits and raincoats, "for any other clothing that was donned was wet through in five minutes time."[76]

Just across from Nassau's Harbour is Hog Island (now called Paradise Island-a tourist mecca for the Bahamas), once a place where farmers bred pigs to supplement their regular diet of fish, conch, turtle and other seafood. The storm had snapped the electric cable to Hog Island, and it shot out a shower of sparks, lighting up the night sky. Government agencies carried away some debris, and a contractor hauled away 1,709 truckloads of trash. In the hurricanes of 1926 hurricanes that impacted the Bahamas, there were so many downed trees that had been collected to make firewood that even in 1928, they were still being used two years later.

The heaviest sufferers in property damage were the churches. St Agnes in Grant's Town was completely unroofed and otherwise totally destroyed. St John's Baptist Church on Meeting Street and the Mission House were completely demolished after only being recently rebuilt after the Nassau Hurricane of 1926. Prior to the storm, the congregants had been

---

[75] *Extraordinary Hurricane Hits Bahamas- The Nassau Tribune,_Wednesday, September 19th 1928 pgs. 1 & 2.*

[76] *Extraordinary Hurricane Hits Bahamas- The Nassau Tribune,_Wednesday, September 19th 1928 pgs. 1 & 2.*

arguing over the fate of the current pastor. The hurricane, at least if only temporarily, made that argument moot when it destroyed the building.

The western portion of Trinity Wesleyan Methodist Church roof was torn away, and the interior badly damaged. A flying missile smashed into the western window of the church, causing the wind to rush into the building and tear away the roof. The Rev. and Mrs. W.H. Richards and their daughter barely escaped death. They had to take refuge on the back verandah for a few hours due to the fact that escaping from the building was virtually impossible, because they were blocked in from both the back and front sections of the church by massive piles of debris. This was quite a blow for them because the roof had only recently been repaired after the two major 1926 hurricanes had destroyed it. This Church was designed in England by Mr. Pockock and Mr. Walsh of the Royal Engineers Department, and Mr. H.J. McCartney was the builder. The architecture is gothic, and its roof, being very tall and sharp, was also destroyed in the 1866 hurricane. After the 1866 hurricane, it was rebuilt in 1868 or thereabouts. During the rebuilding process, the height of the roof was reduced by 10 feet. The original building and the rebuilding together cost £14,000, and £250 was granted by the legislature and £300 by the conference and a special collection in England made on their behalf.

The roof of St. Mary's Church, Virginia Street, and Wesley Church in Grant's Town also suffered some damage. Wesley Church in Grant's Town was completed in the year 1868, to replace a small wooden building that was destroyed along with many others by the Great Bahamas Hurricane of 1866. The roof and front verandah of Mr. R.B. Shepherd's home on West Hill Street was badly wrecked by a small porch that flew over from Mr. R.H. Curry's House on the opposite side of the street and smashed into it. The home of the Hon. Dr. G.H. Johnson, who was away with his family in New York, was blown away. The roof of Dr. Fisher's house was blown away. The roof of the Lucayan Garage on West Bay Street was swept away. Mr. J.E. Williamson a movie, studio executive, had a number of his movie studio equipment badly damaged or destroyed by the storm. The roof of the Aurora Hall, East Hill and Charlotte Streets, was blown away, and the building collapsed. Mr. P.A Huyler's Black Smith Shop and Mr.

C.E. Bethell's wharf were demolished, and Mr. P.C. Smith's sponge house was totally destroyed.[77]

Mrs. D. Sweeting's storeroom on Deveaux Street was totally destroyed. Mr. Morrison's sponge shed on Bay Street collapsed, and all of his sponges were lost. Another sponge shed owned by Mr. C.E. Bethell was also destroyed, and the sponges in the shed were washed away by the storm. The northern end of Mr. Chas L. Lofthouses' home on George Street was blown away. The southern roof of 'Blair' East Bay Street owned by Mr. R.H. Curry was blown over in Capt. Charley's yard. The roof of 'the Hermitage' was also destroyed. Government Hill was flooded to such an extent that the ball room looked like a swimming pool. A part of the roof of the warehouse of the Home Furniture Company was blown away, and some of the furniture was damaged by water. Mr. Barton's tailor shop on Blue Hill road collapsed. The two Government liquor bonded warehouses on the Southern Recreation Grounds, and the one at the rear of Mr. Edward Saunders's store on Bay Street, were unroofed and Mr. R.T. liquor warehouse on Bay Street was also unroofed. The windows, doors and the furniture of the Fort Montague Hotel were badly damaged. The roof of the Royal Victoria Hotel was badly damaged, and the furniture was seriously damaged, most beyond repair, while the British Colonial Hotel also suffered some damage. The gardens of all these hotels have been damaged almost beyond recognition, and the building where plants were stored at the British Colonial was blown onto the street.[78]

Mr. J.L. Lightbourn's home on the top of Blue Hill has been badly damaged. A portion of the southwestern section of the prison wall was blown down. The front verandah of Mr. Victor Saunders' home on Shirley Street was blown away. The roof of Dr. Albury's home on George Street was badly damaged. The home of Mr. Jonah Cox on Cunningham Lane was almost demolished. Several sheds on Knowles Dairy Farm were destroyed, and the roof of the home was lifted up a few inches. Mr. H.S. Black

---

[77] Wayne Neely (2006), *The Major Hurricanes to Affect the Bahamas: Personal Recollections of Some of the Greatest Storms to Affect the Bahamas*. Bloomington, Indiana: AuthorHouse. pgs. 84–88.

[78] Wayne Neely (2006). *The Major Hurricanes to Affect the Bahamas: Personal Recollections of Some of the Greatest Storms to Affect the Bahamas*. Bloomington, Indiana: AuthorHouse. pgs. 84–88.

and his family were forced to leave their home in Village Road during the hurricane because their house was badly damaged and the furniture destroyed. The band stand on Rawson Square was completely demolished.

The home of Mr. Thomas Murray was destroyed. Part of the roof was blown off the Church Hall, formally St. Hilda's High School. The Upper Piazza of the building situated overhead Mr. W.M. Hilton Store was blown away. The upper back verandah of the Law Courts Building was blown away and the building flooded. The upper verandah of Dr. Higgs' building, east of the Botanical Station on East Bay Street, was blown away. The back porch on the home of Mr. Rill Albury on West Bay Street, was blown away. Captain Allen Johnson's Garage and servant's quarters at the rear of Fort Charlotte was destroyed. The small house at the south of Mr. W.E. Fountain's old home on West Street, occupied by Mr. Jack Fountain, collapsed on a Buick car.

The northern half of the Higgs' sponge shed near the sponge exchange was blown away. The roof was blown away from the Munson Steamship Line building. The roof of the West India Oil Company on West Street was blown away. Mrs. Louis' O'Neil house in Mason's Addition was blown away. Several buildings in Rainbow Village and Chippingham were badly damaged. In Fox Hill, a number of houses were badly damaged, but most of the damage was done to fruit bearing trees. Some damage was done to the buildings in the Grove Development, West Bay Street, but nothing very extensive. The southern district of Nassau suffered very much, some homes being completely destroyed, while many more were badly damaged. A statue of Christopher Columbus was struck, and a piece of the explorer's hat broken off. A bandstand was demolished. Two outhouses at the hospital lost their roofs. No property owner on the island of Nassau had escaped entirely without suffering some loss.[79]

The Bahamas National Board of Agriculture would later rush shipments of corn seeds to the Out Islands and cabled elsewhere for tomato seeds. "No useful purpose can be served by Out Islanders coming to Nassau in search of work. There are enough unemployed people here to feed the labour market for some time to come," the *Nassau Guardian* reported in

[79] Wayne Neely (2006). *The Major Hurricanes to Affect the Bahamas: Personal Recollections of Some of the Greatest Storms to Affect the Bahamas*. Bloomington, Indiana: AuthorHouse.

a September 22nd editorial. It added that "It is no time for sitting down and bemoaning the sadness of one's lot. It is a time for action and when that action takes the form of rebuilding houses and churches it is to be hoped that they will be more securely and safely built than they were so that when the next hurricane strikes these islands, the toll of damage may not be so great."[80] At the end of the month, the Royal Navy ship *Durban*, which had already stopped at Grand Turk, would arrive in Nassau, again bringing its prominent crew member, the future King of England, George VI. It was the first visit by a member of the royal family in seven decades.

On Cat Island, major damage was reported as many roads, bridges and homes were destroyed. In Arthur's Town, the Public Wharf, the doctor's residence, churches and about one hundred homes were destroyed. In the Bight alone, about sixty houses were badly damaged or totally destroyed. Many roads were either washed away or rendered impassible after the storm. Meanwhile, on the island of Eleuthera, the winds were estimated at around 100 mph during the peak of the storm. The storm destroyed 128 homes, and 154 were badly damaged. At Harbour Island alone, it was reported that about 95 houses, including a few churches such as the Church of England, were badly damaged or totally destroyed. [81]

During the peak of the storm it was estimated that the island of Eleuthera had sustained winds of over 95 mph. The government buildings were badly damaged, but not destroyed. The Royal Bahamas Police Court, private warehouses and a wharf were all destroyed, and many government offices were badly damaged. Virtually every farm on the island was devastated. One loss of life occurred on this island when he was crushed under his house when it collapsed during the hurricane. "The years 1866 and 1926 will now be forgotten, and 1928 will hold first place as the year of the worst storm that has ever visited this part of the island of Eleuthera," a *Nassau Guardian* Reporter wrote on September 22nd from the settlement of Governor's Harbour. [82]

---

[80] *Here and There- The Nassau Guardian, Saturday, September 22nd 1928 pgs. 1 & 2.*
[81] Wayne Neely (2006). *The Major Hurricanes to Affect the Bahamas: Personal Recollections of Some of the Greatest Storms to Affect the Bahamas*. Bloomington, Indiana: AuthorHouse.
[82] *Here and There- The Nassau Guardian, Saturday, September 22nd 1928 pgs. 1 & 2.*

Things were different on the island of Exuma because the hurricane passed over this island, with only slight damage reported. On Long Cay, six houses were destroyed, and 200 people who were at Atwood's Cay to harvest tree bark lost their boats and were stranded for quite a while after the storm. In San Salvador, no lives were lost during the passage of the hurricane. However, serious damage to property was reported in the district, but not as bad as expected. Four buildings were destroyed including two Baptist churches, and many other buildings received slight damage. The sisal plantations and food crops were badly damaged. On Long Island, no major damage was reported. The island of Rum Cay reported sustained winds of over 80 mph, but fortunately no lives were lost. Minor damage was reported to some houses, and most of the food crops were totally destroyed.

On Inagua, about noon Saturday, government officials in Nassau lost communications with this island, some 400 miles to the southeast from Nassau. The island would suffer little damage, but it did experienced 110 mph winds, and the storm passed 50 miles to the southwest. However, things were different on the island of Acklins, as it was reported that forty boats and most of the crops were destroyed.

The island of Bimini reported sustained winds of 140 mph during the peak of the storm. Major damage was reported to several buildings, and nearly every home on the island was reportedly damaged or destroyed. Bimini's famed "rum row," the waterfront dock where smugglers picked up contraband rum and liquor for the short run across the Atlantic to the Prohibition-defiant United States, had been smashed by the 1926 hurricanes. Now it was reported to have sustained additional heavy losses in this hurricane. The wharf was badly damaged, and numerous small ships sunk.

In Grand Bahama, the schooner *Nellie B. Nora* was driven ashore by the hurricane, and the bow split off from the rest of the boat. Three other boats were total wrecks, and some other boats were badly damaged. The Docks belonging to Maury, Crawford, Ambrister, Bruce-Roberts, Claridge, and also the Government docks were all swept away. The dock belonging to DeGregory was the only one left standing. The roads were completely washed out, destroyed and rendered impassable. Most of the houses were totally destroyed or badly damaged.[83]

---

[83] *Here and There- The Nassau Guardian, Saturday, September 22nd 1928 pgs. 1 & 2.*

CHAPTER EIGHT

The Okeechobee Hurricane and the Hebert Hoover Dike

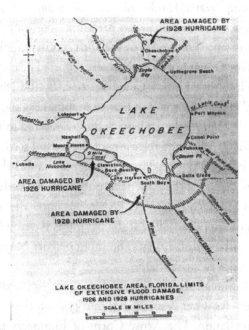

Map showing flood damage to the Lake Okeechobee area by the hurricanes of 1926 and 1928 (Courtesy of the Florida State Archives).

Before everything else there had always been the lake. Lake Okeechobee, locally referred to as "The Lake" or "The Big O", is the largest freshwater lake in the state of Florida. It is the seventh largest freshwater lake in the United States and the second largest freshwater lake (the largest is Lake Michigan with 22,300 square miles) contained entirely within the lower 48 states. However, it is the largest freshwater lake completely within a single one of the lower 48 states. It is so big that it stands out even on world maps and pictures from space as a giant gaping hole in the Florida peninsula, extending from North America towards the tropics. Lake Okeechobee covers 730 square miles, approximately half the size of the state of Rhode Island, and it is shaped like a saucer-shallow and round and is exceptionally shallow for a lake of its size, with an average depth of only 3 metres (9 feet). However, it holds enough water to give 300 gallons to every living person on Earth. The lake is divided between Glades, Okeechobee, Martin, Palm Beach, and Hendry counties. All five counties meet at one point near the center of the lake.

The name Okeechobee comes from the Hitchiti Seminole Indians words oki (meaning "water") and chubi (meaning "big"). The oldest known name for the lake was Mayaimi (also meaning "big water"), reported by Hernando de Escalante Fontaneda in the 16th century. Slightly later in the 16th century, René Gouaine de Laudonniére reported hearing about a large freshwater lake in South Florida called Serrope. By the 18th century, the largely mythical lake was known to British mapmakers and chroniclers by the Spanish name Laguna de Espiritu Santo (translated to mean "Lagoon of the Holy Spirit"). Early-nineteenth-century coastal settlers lived within 60 miles of the lake, yet doubted its existence. It was war that exposed the big lake to the romance of the American public. In the early 19th century, it was known as Mayacco Lake or Lake Mayaca, after the Mayaca people, originally from the upper reaches of the St. Johns River, who moved near the lake in the early 18th century. The modern Port Mayaca on the east side of the lake preserves that name.

The floor of the lake is a limestone basin, with a maximum depth of 4 metres (13 feet). Its water is somewhat murky from the runoffs from the surrounding farmlands. The Army Corps of Engineers targets keeping the surface of the lake between 3.8 and 4.7 metres (12 and 15 feet) above mean sea level. The lake is enclosed by the up to 9 metres (30 feet) high Herbert Hoover Dike, built by the U.S. Army Corps of Engineers after the Great Okeechobee Hurricane of 1928 breached the old dike, flooding surrounding towns and communities. Water flows into Lake Okeechobee from several sources, including the Kissimmee River, Fisheating Creek,

Lake Istokpoga, Taylor Creek, and smaller sources, such as Nubbin Slough and Nicodemus Slough.

The Kissimmee River is the largest source, providing more than 60% of the water flowing into Lake Okeechobee. Fisheating Creek is the second largest source for the lake, with about 9% of the total inflow. Prior to the 20th century, Lake Istokpoga was connected to the Kissimmee River by Istokpoga Creek, but during the rainy season Lake Istokpoga overflowed, with the water flowing in a 24.8 miles wide sheet across the Indian Prairie into Lake Okeechobee. Today, Lake Istokpoga drains into Lake Okeechobee through several canals that drain the Indian Prairie, and into the Kissimmee River through a canal that has replaced Istokpoga Creek. Historically, outflow from the lake was by sheet flow over the Everglades, but most of the outflow has been diverted to dredged canals connecting to coastal rivers, such as the Miami Canal to the Miami River, the New River on the east, and the Caloosahatchee River (via the Caloosahatchee Canal and Lake Hicpochee) on the southwest. On the southern rim of Lake Okeechobee, three islands—Kreamer, Ritta, and Torey—were once settled by early pioneers.

Herbert Clark Hoover (August 10, 1874 – October 20, 1964) was the 31st President of the United States (1929–1933). Hoover, born to a Quaker family, was a professional mining engineer. He achieved American and international prominence in humanitarian relief efforts in war-time Belgium and served as head of the U.S. Food Administration during World War I. As the United States Secretary of Commerce in the 1920s under Presidents Warren G. Harding and Calvin Coolidge, he promoted partnerships between government and business under the rubric "economic modernization". In the presidential election of 1928, Hoover easily won the Republican nomination, despite having no elected office experience. Hoover is the most recent Cabinet secretary to be elected President of the United States, as well as one of only two Presidents (along with William Howard Taft) elected without electoral experience or high military rank. America was at the height of an economic bubble at the time, facilitating a landslide victory for Hoover over Democrat Al Smith.

Hoover, a globally experienced engineer, believed strongly in the Efficiency Movement, which held that the government and the economy were riddled with inefficiency and waste and could be improved by experts who could identify the problems and solve them. He also believed in the importance of volunteerism and of the role of individuals in society and the economy. Hoover, who had made a small fortune in mining, was the first of two Presidents to redistribute their salary (President Kennedy was the other; he donated all his paychecks to charity).

On Wednesday, September 12, 1928, the top story in the *Palm Beach Post* concerned President Calvin Coolidge and his consideration of the budget and the Antiwar Treaty. No one in the Everglades was concerned about that, not from a lame duck president, especially when 1928 was an election year for choosing the new President of the United States. People were more interested in the race between Herbert Hoover and Al Smith. Democrats complained that "Hoover Democrats" were not supporting Al Smith. Yet he would find it very hard to vote for a Roman Catholic. One column in particular in the *Palm Beach Post* exposed the fabricated story that Democratic presidential candidate Al Smith had been seen drunk in public, which was part of the anti-Catholic and pro-Prohibition campaign that plagued Al Smith, the first Catholic to run for president. However, at the very bottom was the weather section. It predicted typical summertime weather, partly cloudy skies, with the possibility of afternoon thunderstorms. If you didn't pay close attention, you might have missed the inconspicuous story from the National Weather Bureau:

"Tropical disturbance of considerable intensity central near 18 North, 56 West, and moving west or west-northwestward. Its center will likely pass near Lesser Antilles North of Martinique, Wednesday."

Sadly, no Floridian paid this story any attention because, storms were always forming in the Atlantic, and besides, this was typical South Florida afternoon weather. No one needed a weatherman to predict that, it happened every afternoon. Sadly this inconspicuous disturbance would turn out to be one of the greatest storms that the United States had to endure. Furthermore, in its aftermath, it created one of the greatest engineering achievements that the US Army Corps of Engineers ever had to design and build, and that was the Herbert Hoover Dike.

The Herbert Hoover Dike (HHD), named after this president, is a 143-mile earthen dam that surrounds Lake Okeechobee, the heart of the Kissimmee-Okeechobee-Everglades system. The original dike was constructed with gravel, rock, limestone, sand, and shell. The project reduces impacts from flooding as a result of high lake levels for a large area of South Florida. Since 2007, the Corps has made a significant investment, over $300 million, in projects designed to reduce the risk of catastrophic failure of the aging structure. Actions taken include installing a cutoff wall, removing and replacing water control structures (culverts), and conducting a variety of studies and technical reviews to help ensure the safety of South Florida residents. Corps teams work daily on the dike, providing contractor oversight, quality assurance, inspections, and dike operations and maintenance. Much progress is also being made behind the scenes at the District, where a team of engineers, hydrologists, geologists, scientists, contract and real estate specialists, budget analysts, and many others, work to ensure the very best rehabilitation strategies are applied to the dike today and in the future.

The HHD Project team maintains close coordination and communication with other internal Jacksonville technical offices, such as Engineering, Planning, Contracting, Corporate Communication, Construction and Operations, while maintaining a presence (HHD Project Manager forward) in the local project area to communicate regularly with local communities and the construction field offices regarding project updates and problem solving.

The numerous hurricanes in 1926, especially the Great Miami Hurricane of 1926, had been a wake-up call for South Florida and the Everglades. The storms had exposed the stark inefficiencies of the dike in its present state. A new, larger dike was proposed, but money for the project was not rapidly forthcoming. Florida was in the middle of a major recession, and tax revenues were drastically down. For two years, the Everglades farmers lobbied the state for funds to strengthen the dike, and each year the Florida legislature, sitting securely in Tallahassee four hundred miles away, voted down money for a new dike. The latest reverse was a bond issue that failed to garner enough votes to pass. Once again, in 1928, Everglades farmers were assured that money would be approved next year. The memory of the 1926 hurricanes was, at least in Tallahassee, fading. After all, that was two years ago, and in politics, two years was an eternity, or as some might say, ancient history.

The first embankments around Lake Okeechobee were constructed by local interest from sand and muck, circa 1915. Hurricane tides overtopped the original embankments in 1926 and 1928. The River and Harbor Act of 1930 authorized the construction of 67.8 miles of levee along the south shore of the lake and 15.7 miles along the north shore. The U. S. Army Corps of Engineers constructed the levees between 1932 and 1938. A major hurricane in 1947 prompted the need for additional flood and storm damage reduction work. As a result, Congress passed the Flood Control Act of 1948, authorizing the first phase of the Central and South Florida (C&SF) Project, a comprehensive plan to provide flood and storm damage reduction and other water control benefits in central & south Florida. The new dike system was completed in the late 1960s and named the Herbert Hoover Dike. The dike system consists of 143 miles of levee with 19 culverts, hurricane gates and other water control structures.

Ever present and always there was the grand and expansive Lake Okeechobee, which gave those who resided around it a never-ending supply of water for their homes, crops, livestock, and fish for their tables and packinghouses. Shaped like a giant frying pan, only 10-16 feet deep at most, it appeared generous and benign. But then there was the water, which at first there wasn't anything to keep it from seeping out of the lake and into the countryside. So the government put together a berm of mud, dirt, and rock around it. In most places, it was about six feet high. It was just enough to protect the farms and villages—as long as it didn't rain too hard, too fast, and as long as the wind didn't slosh the water out of the shallow lake and up against that flimsy dike. In 1926, it did, and six hundred people died. But as was seen in Moore Haven in 1926, the dikes were never engineered to match the fury of a great hurricane. Even after this storm, no one changed anything about the dike. This was because the state legislators thought that not much damage from a hurricane could occur to a people or lake that was over forty miles inland from the sea. Oh, how wrong they were, because two years later, everyone would soon find out when a massive storm roared across Florida over the Lake Okeechobee region and devastated the area.

**The Herbert Hoover Dike surrounding Lake Okeechobee
(Courtesy of the Florida State Archives).**

By 1928, the state's plan to further drain and reclaim the Everglades for farming had collapsed. The Everglades Drainage District was deep in debt, work was halted, and landowners were refusing to pay the drainage taxes. Congress was being heavily lobbied to pay for flood control. But the federal government was reluctant to open that door. In 1928, the chief of the U.S. Army Corps of Engineers reported to Congress that until the state and local interests exhausted their money, Washington should not take that step.

Prior to the 1920s, water simply flowed unrestricted from the lake's south shore in a sheet, into the Everglades. From there, it gently flowed across that wide river of grass to the end of the peninsula and into the Florida Bay. For the early settlers and farmers, that simply would not suffice. So between 1923 and 1925, the state built a 47-mile long dike of earth. It was about five feet high and was considered inadequate because twice in the next three years, it would be shown as useless as a dike made of cardboard. Off in the distance of the dike was the reassuring hum of one of the massive irrigation pumps, which could be heard straining to empty the fields. They sucked up black, mucky water from the canals and deposited it over a five-feet-high mud dike that separated Lake Okeechobee from the flat plains of reclaimed South Florida farmland. Lately, due to the excessive amount of rainfall, the pumps had been working in overdrive. Late August was typically the peak of the rainy season in Florida, and summer rainfall was not only expected, but was outright necessary to balance or supplement the long, dry winter months. This was the Everglades, where muckland flourished and was said to be some of the richest, most fertile land in the world. This was the Everglades, America's winter breadbasket.

In the early 1920s, commissioners of the Everglades Drainage District, established in 1913, decided to build a more permanent dike around the lake. The plan was for work to commence on the dike in 1927. It was supposed to be 110 to 130 feet wide at the base and 20 feet wide at the crest and stand 27 feet above sea level. They concluded that such a levee would resist hurricane-driven surge from the lake. But the legislature didn't get around to approving the money for it. The $20 million bond issue was tied up by a lawsuit from Dade County, which claimed it would be contributing 80 percent of the money and only receiving a mere 20 percent of the benefits.

"It is indeed unfortunate that through almost trivial, and in some cases prejudiced legislation, plans or the construction of works essential to the safety of life and the protection of property can be thwarted or so long delayed,"[84] Fred Cotton Elliot would write bitterly in an October 1928 letter printed in the local newspapers. Elliot was a well-dressed fellow with a neat mustache who for more than half a century would be one of the ubiquitous figures in both the historic drainage of the interior and the battle to harness the great lake. The Glades and the lake would consume much of his life as well. He spent three years in his own engineering business. In 1911, he took a temporary job as an assistant engineer. A year later, when the state's chief engineer quit amid controversy, Elliot, then only thirty-four, started a job he would hold for more than four decades.

In many ways, Elliot was visionary. He designed and built the canals that led from the lake and helped drain the swamps. He foresaw a series of reservoirs around the drained Everglades, but unfortunately was abandoned due to the fact that it was deemed to be too expensive at the time, but thankfully today it is now in use. Two extremely wet rainy seasons in a row, 1926 and 1927, had raised the lake's water level at above normal levels. But more than 3,000 farmers flourished in ways that had not been seen in the decade or so since farming had started in earnest in the Glades. Most farmers were excited in 1928 because most of them foresaw a bumper year for their fruits and vegetables. It had drawn Carmen Salvatore to Pahokee

---

[84] Kleinberg, E. (2003) *Black Cloud-The Deadly Hurricane of 1928*, New York, Carroll & Graf Publishers, pg. 16.

and Clothilda Miller's family from the island of Eleuthera in the Bahamas to West Palm Beach.

There is no protection from a flood. That's why meteorologists and emergency planners use the simple mantra "hide from the wind, run from the water." The Great Okeechobee Hurricane of 1928 the second deadliest hurricane in US history, had killed so many, not from strong winds that destroyed buildings, not from buckets of rain that turned streets into waterways and creeks into raging rivers, not from ocean surging onto the land like a bulldozer. It had killed thousands in a way unlike any storm before it had, and probably none since. Its winds had pushed water from an inland lake and spread it across the land in a moving engine of death and destruction. Initially, it had been aided by the flimsy dike built in a foolish attempt to stop it. Had the water poured out of the lake gradually, it would not have killed as many persons as it did, but because the five-foot dike was compromised, the water washed people and houses away and killed thousands.

Just hours after the storm passed, the first complaint was made about doing something about the dike. Samuel L. Drake, president of the New River-Lake Okeechobee-Caloosahatchie Navigation Association, called for the state to turn over to its federal counterpart that job of making the big lake safe from future catastrophic floods. The flow into Lake Okeechobee in the three-month period before and after the 1928 storm was greater than for any other year on record, and had the outflow from the lake been greater, fewer might have died.

In November, the Everglades Drainage District board passed a resolution containing a scathing denunciation of the federal government. "It is alleged that maintenance of the said lake and water level specified by the United States Government presents a problem of hazard of life and property and citizens of the state of Florida who inhabit the territory adjacent to the said lake," the resolution said. It said the 1928 storm showed the need for cooperation between Tallahassee the capital of Florida and Washington about the setting of the lake level. It urged Congress, in its next session, to get to the business of protecting the Glades from another catastrophic hurricane or flood. On December 5th, the board sent out a telegram to Florida US Senator Duncan Fletcher that was even more specific: Build a big dike. Fletcher called the control of the lake "an urgent government problem" and said that as soon as the state engineers finished their studies they had started before the storm, he'd be pressing Congress for immediate action. So in January 1929, the House Committee on Flood Control wrestled with what to do about the big lake that kept trying to drown everyone.

US Representative Hamilton Fish, of New York State, even put in a good word for black people:

"We want to protect the lives of those people of African descent who sometimes have no way to flee and whose lives are just as dear to their families as those of the white man," Fish told the hearing. "Nobody knows how many coloured people have been drowned by these floods." At the hearings, some agreed with Jess Lee that the problem was insurmountable and that the best plan was to tear out the rest of the levee and let the lake return to its natural flow into the Everglades. Fred H. Davis, Florida's Attorney General only since 1927, went so far as to tell the committee, "I've heard it advocated in certain districts of Florida that what the people ought to do is build a wall there and keep the military there to keep the people from coming in there."[85]

How many people would die today? Probably very few, because today people would be warned and evacuations would be ordered. The lake now has a towering, presumably trustworthy dike. Like a twenty-car pileup, the perfect recipe for catastrophe at Lake Okeechobee, Florida, in 1928 required a shallow lake, an inadequate dike, lack of communications, few evacuation routes and a flawed forecast. Furthermore, a storm coming at such an angle like this storm did gets its surge not from the sea, the most populated area at the time, but from Lake Okeechobee.

During the hurricane, the winds drove the water toward Belle Glade and South Bay, the most populated area of the farming region around Lake Okeechobee. They pounded that water against the flimsy dike that protected those people from the giant body that brought both life and death to the Okeechobee region-then all hell broke loose as the dike broke over the region.

A pumping station near Pahokee, one of several installed along the lake to keep water from flooding the fields, had been operating around

---

[85] Kleinberg, E. (2003) *Black Cloud-The Deadly Hurricane of 1928*, New York, Carroll & Graf Publishers, pg. 194.

the clock since the August storm raised the lake level dramatically. Around noon, the pump operator, Edward Jensen's, supervisor told him a storm was coming and he should shut the pump down and go home. But Jensen's father and neighbours had just planted fall crops, and he was determined to keep the pump going, if only to protect the newly planted crops from flooding. Later, Jensen somehow took a brief nap amid the strong winds, and he was awakened by a crash as pieces of sheet metal flew off the pump house. He finally decided that keeping the pump operating might be as worthless as draining the fields with a thimble, so he shut it down.

Fearful of being cut to bits and pieces by the flying metal, he dove into a subfloor well beneath the pump. But the water down there was rising. Jensen abandoned the collapsing building and raced to a fuel tank, where he met another man, a black farm worker. The two held on until the wind and rain stopped. They discovered six or eight other black farm workers who had crawled along the levee. The other workers wanted to walk the levee back to Pahokee. Knowledge about the dynamics of a hurricane convinced Jensen that they were just in the eye of the storm and that it would return from the opposite direction with the same or even greater fury. Only the man who had waited out the storm with Jensen at the fuel pump opted to stay; the rest continued down the levee, now only a foot above the spreading water. Jensen watched their outlines grow smaller, and they were never seen or heard from after that. Then the strong winds suddenly resumed; the second half of the storm was bearing down.

State engineer F.C. Elliot later reported that trash and debris indicated water levels in Lake Okeechobee had reached 26.3 feet above sea level. This meant storm waters in the lake, already near the top, rose 10 feet above the lake level, 12 feet in South Bay. The rising water damaged the levee for a distance of 114,242 feet—more than 21½ miles—of the lake's southeast corner. In a few places, the dike was completely breached; in others, its top 2 to 3 feet washed away. The water flowed over and through the dikes and was unimpeded. A weather observer at Moore Haven said the winds were greater than in the 1926 storm, but the portion of the dike from that city along the lake's southwest corner to the Palm Beach County line did not fail. The storm surge was estimated at six inches at Moore Haven. At Canal Point and Port Mayaca, on the lake's northeast shore, the water level is believed to have risen only 1½ to 2½ feet. State engineer Elliot cited the storm's winds being nearly parallel to the east shoreline and noted that as close as 600 feet from shore, the lake fell to its deepest parts, and that depth diffused the water's energy.

The rise in the lake's level in the storm wasn't really the result of rain. Although gauges around the lake either didn't catch all the rain in the driving wind or were blown away, it was estimated at no more than about 9 inches. What weakened and destroyed the dike were the strong winds pushing the lake's water. A kitchen worker can't walk a cake pan full of water across the room without sloshing some. Likewise, water will rise and fall in a swimming pool, in even moderate winds. Okeechobee is a giant, shallow lake, not really much deeper than that of a swimming pool. It is never more than 21 feet deep, and usually 6 to 10 feet, and it's three-fourths the size of Rhode Island. On gusty days, there's considerable wave action. These were 150 mph winds, and with wind speed the power is exponential. The Great Okeechobee Hurricane was a Category 4 hurricane on the Saffir-Simpson Hurricane Wind Scale, and at 155 mph, it would have moved into the realm of the most catastrophic storms, but even 150 mph winds produce up to 250 times the damage of a minimal Category 1 hurricane.

The lake was already brimming. According to the Everglades Drainage District report, it stood at nearly 16½ feet above sea level during the week ending September 15th. The day after the storm, it stood at nearly 17½ feet. The land around the lake ranges between 17 to 19 feet above sea level. Along the lakeshore, the elevations of levee were 22 to 28 feet above sea level. Maximum winds probably reached the lake's eastern shore an hour before the eye reached Canal Point. As the storm crossed, at a slight diagonal, it passed over the lake's southeast corner. A hurricane's wind blows anti-clockwise, and what that basically means is that the strongest quadrant-the right front quadrant-passed over the southeast section of the lake-the most vulnerable and heavily populated portion of the lake. "While considerable water doubtless moved against the shore of Lake Okeechobee during the first half of the storm," R.V. Allison, researcher at the Belle Glade agriculture station, would write later, "it was during the latter half that the southeast and eastern sections received the heaviest damage and consequently greatest loss of life occurred during this period."

After President Herbert Hoover's tour of the Lake Okeechobee region in February of the following year, a plan was developed to rebuild the failed dikes on the lake's southern shores. On January 31, 1929, the Army Corps of Engineers submitted a new plan calling for a 31-foot dike around the lake, along with the deepening of key drainage canals, the Caloosahatchee and St. Lucie waterways. The Corps estimated the cost at $10.7 million, with the state and local interests paying about 62 percent. In most projects such as the proposed dike, regions had split with the federal government, paying one-third to Washington's two-thirds. In this plan, 62 percent would be more than $6 million. Florida hinted it would pay as much as half. But Florida State Representative Herbert Drane suggested the feds pay the larger share, since the money would be used to keep federally controlled water from drowning people who came to Florida from all over the country.

In February 1929, new Governor Doyle Carlton had invited the newly elected US President, Herbert Hoover, a month away from inauguration, to tour Florida's interior. Florida was one of only four southern states Hoover had carried, and Carlton knew the president, an engineer, had a special interest in flood control. Hoover left his vacation home in Miami Beach and traveled in a twenty-car motorcade around two-thirds of the lake. In his car: Carlton and the Ubiquitous F.C. Elliot.

Hoover attended a dinner in Clewiston and spent the night in the Glades. He had seen for himself the damage that prevailed some five months after the storm: houses standing twisted or half-destroyed, piles of wood that had been homes, highways still strewn with debris, fields still full of junk or simply too torn up to farm. The anniversary of the storm passed with no new threat on the horizon. But nine days later, on September 25, 1929, weather officials were saying a powerful hurricane was moving through the Bahamas, aiming at Miami. This storm would become one of the most devastating hurricanes to strike the Bahamas, killing 134 persons and lasting for three consecutive days over the Bahamas. The damage to its capital city of Nassau was catastrophic, wiping out many homes and businesses. That sick, uneasy and worrisome feeling started all over again. Coastal Palm Beach County battened up their homes and businesses and quickly moved out. Thousands of people called newspaper offices, tense and frightful, wanting to get news on this impending storm.

This time, the lake was low, some 4½ feet lower than it had been in the 1928 storm, but water was moving into it. Several hundred people left the Glades; some to the coast, others on free train rides to Central Florida. South Bay reported only eight people left in town. By the next day, the crisis appeared to have passed. The storm was weakening and seemed headed to the Keys. Hurricane warnings were dropped. But on September 27th, weather officials said the storm had strengthened again and was 100 miles southeast of Miami. Finally, on Friday, September 28th, the storm was moving through the Keys and out of the picture.

The plan to dike the lake went through more planning before finally, on July 3, 1930, Hoover signed it into law. Florida at the time had already been racked by the great real estate crash and two cataclysmic hurricanes, so finding that kind of money was out of the question. In May 1930, the state legislature, which held its first meeting in September 1929, created the Okeechobee Flood Control District, and soon a $5 million bond issue was approved to fund the necessary engineering. The first shovel for the new and improved dike was turned in November 1930, two years after its forerunner had washed away. Among those operating dredges was Belle Glade businessman Lawrence E. Will, who would later write a book on the history of the 1928 storm. A giant rock levee, eighty-five miles long and thirty-six feet high, was built along the lake's southeast, south, and southwest banks. This new dike was built eighteen to twenty feet higher than the lake's normal level.

The Hoover Dike was later put to the test during back-to-back hurricanes in 1947 and 1949, with only minor erosion occurring as a result of the storms' flooding associated with those two storms. The U.S. Army Corps of Engineers reported that the latter storm had "operated against the $24,000,000 levees for a period three times as long as any previous storm and with greater intensities."[86]

After the storm and the building of the new dike, the farms prospered. With Lake Okeechobee finally tamed by the new tall dike, the giant growing region between the lake and the growing metropolitan areas of the Atlantic coast began to switch to sugar. In the 1929-30 harvest seasons, the Glades had 17,000 acres of vegetables and less than 7,000 acres of

---

[86] Barnes J.,(2007) *Florida's Hurricane History*, Chapel Hill, The University of North Carolina Press. pg. 140.

sugar in cultivation. Sugar acreage doubled in four years, slowed down only by marketing quotas. World War II brought a temporary suspension of quotas, but a scarcity of manpower. By 1949, some 110,000 acres were in farming: 75,000 were in vegetables, 30,000 in sugar cane, and the rest in pasture and minor crops.

While most of the dike was in place by the late 1930s, it was not dedicated formally until January 12, 1961. It was named for Herbert Hoover, who had approved the project more than three decades earlier. Hoover was the keynote speaker at the dedication and official opening. At the ceremony were survivors and relatives of victims of the 1926 and 1928 storms. Before heading toward the lake, the eighty-six-year-old, then the oldest living ex-President, stopped in Palm Beach to visit President-elect John F. Kennedy, forty three, the youngest man ever elected to the White House.

An aerial view overlooking the Herbert Hoover Dike and the pumping station and hydraulic gate in the Central and Southern Florida Flood Control District at Lake Okeechobee (Courtesy of Florida State Archives).

CHAPTER NINE

Before the Storm

When Belle Glade was preparing to celebrate its fifth month of official existence, five thousand miles away, an easterly wave of superheated Sahara air slowly moved westward. It was not unusual because during any given year, an average of sixty waves form. Most meander across the Atlantic, changing air temperature but doing little else. But it was September, and the waters in the Atlantic were warm. In a swath from the coast of Africa to the Gulf of Mexico, the sea surface temperature was an unusually warm eighty-five degrees—as warm as it would ever be.

As the hot, dry wave passed off the African coast, it encountered water—lots of warm water. Evaporating the surface water, the clear air began to cloud. Puffy white cumulus clouds, fair weather clouds, billowed skyward. A warm-air updraft lifted more moisture into the air, carrying it higher and higher. The surface pressure fell, and by the time the wave passed the Cape Verde Islands, it had formed into a well-defined surface low pressure system. Though cloudy, it reluctantly refused to give up any moisture. It hoarded its water like a miser and passed over the island without leaving a drop of rain, much to the dismay of the people on the island. It then encountered the westerly trade winds blowing from the northeast. The low pressure drew winds slightly to the south, towards its center. The winds pushed the clouds together into a tighter circular pattern. The winds blew at a breezy twenty-five miles an hour. Cumulus clouds swelled into cumulonimbus clouds, with massive, anvil-like heads. High-altitude moisture condensed, releasing latent heat into the air. Droplets formed as it finally gave up its water. It had more than enough to spare because it had an entire ocean to obtain water from.

As the thunderstorms reached higher into the atmosphere, the low's surface air pressure dropped further. The westerly winds began to curve around them until they had formed a circle. More thunderstorms formed, and the low pressure area had morphed into a tropical depression. Four hundred miles west of the African coast, the depression's thunderstorms stretched their heads skyward until their tops brushed the troposphere. Encountering no contrary winds to disperse its upward movement, it rose further and further, creating downdrafts and heavy rains that warmed the air, further forcing its clouds to rise even higher still. Air pressure in its center dropped, and more air rushed in. The thunderstorms closed circle and spun around the depression. The wind speed jumped from forty-five to a gusty sixty miles per hour. The thunderstorms began to organize into a distinct circular form. A hole opened up in its center like a yawn, or more like a baby's cry at birth. It was the seventh of September, the first day of the storm's life.

However, about 48 hours later, the storm resumed strengthening and became a Category 1 hurricane on the modern-day Saffir-Simpson Hurricane Wind Scale. Still moving westward, the system reached Category 4 intensity before striking Guadeloupe on September 12th. There, the storm brought "great destruction" and 1,200 deaths. Martinique, Montserrat, and Nevis also reported damage and fatalities, but not nearly as severe as in Guadeloupe. The storm's forward motion was increasing on the morning of September 13th, and that gave the Weather Bureau little lead time to predict its course. Even with good communications, it would have made the Weather Bureau people extremely nervous. With communications down, there was no way to inform the world that the hurricane had shifted course. They reported: "The hurricane concerning which warning was issued last night is moving, according to reports, at a rate of approximately 450 miles a day. Its present course, if maintained, will carry it south of Cuba and thence into the Gulf of Mexico. No indications of an approaching storm were evident off the Florida coast last night. Local barometers were holding at normal, and no fear was voiced by weather-wise persons that this section would feel the effect of the storm." Oh, how wrong they were in their forecast track and strength of the storm.

Around noon on September 13th, the storm strengthened into a Category 5 hurricane and peaked with sustained winds of 160 mph. About six hours later, the system made landfall in Puerto Rico; it was the only recorded tropical cyclone to strike the island at Category 5 intensity. Very strong winds resulted in severe damage in Puerto Rico. The storm began crossing through the Turks and Caicos Islands and the Bahamas on September 15th & 16th. Due to preparations, minimal damage or little loss of life occurred, with 18 fatalities reported in Turks and Caicos, and 3 in the Bahamas.

As the storm was nearing South Florida, it never wavered from its parabolic path towards the coastline. Stories about the track had made front page of the *Palm Beach Post*. Advisory from Forecaster Mitchell's advisory from the forecast office in Jacksonville, from 9:00 P.M. on Friday, September 14th, as the storm was nearing the Bahamas, had said the storm was 75 miles southeast of "Turk's Island" and moving northwest about 300 miles a day. He told reporters, "The storm no longer threatens the lower East Coast of Florida." Furthermore, in Miami, forecaster Richard Gray also stuck to his prediction that the storm would continue to arc. "The recurving of the storm will take it east of the Bahamas unless it again changes its course," Gray said Friday. "Its present direction movement makes it improbable that it will affect the east coast of Florida."⁸⁷ Gray predicted that by Sunday morning, the storm would be 170 miles east of Miami, and no threat to South Florida. The experts of the Cuban Meteorological Service agreed with Gray. At the Jesuit observatory in Belan, Cuba, Father Mariano Gutierrez-Lanza said this storm posed no threat to Cuba or Florida and that they should not be concerned.

However, on Friday evening, the *Post* got a copy of a government weather report that had been picked up by the wireless station in Jupiter. Blaney T. Himes, a retired U.S. Navy hydrographic officer, looked it over. He told the paper that Florida's east coast was going to get some of or the entire storm. For the first time, the *Post* addressed the possibility that Palm Beach County would be struck. As a result, by Saturday morning, September 15th, the headline now read: "Florida May Feel the Storm's Path; Present Course Will Bring Hurricane to Lower Coast Sunday." A second

⁸⁷ Miami Daily News Vol. XXXIII No. 273 *Storm Curving East of the Bahamas*, Friday, September 14, 1928.

story said Saturday would be the critical day. "Tonight will be the longest (latest) it is considered advisable to delay preparations to forestall damage from the wind," the paper wrote. As it is in most cases, even to this day, the paper was still hedging its bets, trying to fall in line with other press reports, between giving adequate warnings and balancing that with one more "cry wolf" event.

"Giving ironclad forecasts upon the hurricane is practically impossible," trying to play it safe, the paper wrote. "There is the chance the hurricane might hover in its course, delaying the continuance of its march towards the Florida coast until Monday or Tuesday. Possibilities were apparent last night that the storm might veer to the right and travel northward, which would head it again to sea. Again, it may continue to the Florida coast and strike at a point which it is now too early to determine."

Another story arose with this dramatic description about what the storm had done so far: "Borne on a hurricane's back, desolation and death rode ruthlessly across the sunny, palm-decked islands of the Caribbean today, and it was believed that when the debris of the storm's fury settled, the specters of famine and disease would be found stalking in its wake."

Residents of the towns on the south shore of Lake Okeechobee had heard radio reports of a severe hurricane in the Caribbean and the Bahamas, but they paid no attention to it because most were assured by the forecasts that it would miss Florida. To add flame to the fire, that Saturday morning, weather official Richard Gray had still said the storm would miss South Florida, although it was now considered a threat to the coasts of northeast Florida and southeast Georgia. "The location of the tropical disturbance this morning shows it has followed the course indicated by yesterday's report," Gray said. "It will not cause high winds on the lower East Coast of Florida." He predicted maximum winds of only 35 mph.

Just to be on the safe side, Gray, for the first time in the life of the Great Lake Okeechobee Hurricane, issued storm warnings for the mainland of the United States. They stretched 200 miles, from Miami to Titusville, near Cape Canaveral. The advisory predicted winds at the southeast Florida coast would reach gale force during Sunday and by noon, hurricane force winds would be as far west as 79 degrees longitude, or 60 miles off Florida's southeast coast. The warnings disseminated directly to Miami and West Palm Beach said that "every precaution should be taken (Saturday) in case hurricane warnings should be found necessary on the east Florida coast." The advisory finished with a line that, for the first time, expressed some uncertainty that the storm would miss Florida, which the confident Gray had extended for several days. It said, "Recurve of hurricane's path not yet indicated."

In the black section of Palm Beach, fourteen-year-old Clothilda Miller, who was descended from Eleuthera and came to South Florida with her parents to work on the farms, had been hearing the neighbourhood gossip about the storm all weekend. She had heard it was big, and on the other hand, she had heard it was also little and that it would turn away from Florida and not impact the state. Clothilda's father, Isaac, and his brother-in-law, Ernest Rolle, were 40 miles away, on the small farm they had set up in Chosen, near Belle Glade. Her mother was also out there. She had gone out on Friday to help her sister pack for a planned move back to the coast. She had taken Clothilda's brother, Samuel, then about eleven. Ernest's wife, Anna Belle, had been put in charge of the Miller children while everyone was gone. A Mr. Ewell, who lived diagonally across the street, had offered them his home if the storm became too severe.

Every Sunday morning would typically find the Millers in church, but in a rare event, that Sunday morning, the Millers had not gone to church. The day had a holiday atmosphere. They had cooked a big dinner. Outside, it rained and rained. Lena, one of Clothilda's sisters, asked God to bless the food and keep them safe during the storm. They cleaned up the dishes and waited for the storm's arrival.

Beryl Lewis, a writer at the *Palm Beach Post*, had woken up early that morning and made plans to attend Sunday school, then play a game of tennis with Bill Matthews, a coworker at the paper. The wind was blowing fresh breezes of 25 mph, with gusts up to 40 which wasn't exactly weather conducive to playing tennis. But the sun was shining, and moreover, Lewis's own morning paper, which not only informed him during breakfast but paid his salary as well, had said the storm would miss Palm Beach County. Lewis and Matthews arrived at the church. They went from floor to floor. No one was there. Convinced Sunday School had been canceled, they returned to Matthew's apartment. Pretty soon, the rain began.

Early Saturday morning, Charles and Susan Thomas set off for West Palm Beach. Driving their Model T Ford along the Palm Beach Road

Highway, they crossed the new steel bridge at Six Mile Bend then drove due east to Belvedere Road, the entrance to West Palm Beach. With the new school year beginning that Monday, they needed to buy school supplies and clothes for the children. Charles had read in the previous day's newspaper that the Antilles hurricane would more than likely not hit Florida. The storm's track was thought to be to the south, affecting Santo Domingo, Haiti, and Cuba. While the headline asserted that the storm might hit Florida, it also stated it was still too far away to affect Florida. There was a good chance it would continue to the south or turn to the north, sparing Palm Beach County.

In West Palm Beach, he bought a copy of Saturday's paper. While the headline blared "Florida May Feel Storm's Wrath," the weather report at the bottom of the page was more reassuring, forecast "mostly fair Saturday and Sunday, increasing cloudiness, showers Sunday afternoon or night: gentle east and northeast winds Saturday increasing northeast Sunday: probably becoming strong off the northeast coast by Sunday night."

If he had read further, Charles would have seen a small, ominous box printed in the right-hand column that stated, "Wind reports indicate Hurricane likely to strike here." The Saturday *Palm Beach Post* covered so much contradictory information that it was hard to know what to believe. The editors were just as perplexed. They were inundated with conflicting reports and felt compelled to print them all. Radio station broadcasts were more optimistic. They reported that the storm would not hit Palm Beach. The last thing anyone wanted was to panic and scare off the tourists, investors and damage the winter season crops on which so many people in South Florida depended. Before returning to Belle Glade, Charles felt reassured that the hurricane would miss Florida because he was told by friends and associates that they were sure the storm would pass to the north and spare the county. By the time they headed back to Sebring Farms, Charles Thomas was convinced that there was no hurricane threat.

Meanwhile, the Red Cross' national headquarters in West Palm Beach issued a press release saying that money was flooding in to assist the wrecked islands and that ministers around the country were issuing pleas from their Sunday morning podiums. But, the agency said, it was now starting to gear up for a new threat: the state of Florida. "Indications that Florida might suffer another catastrophe of terrifying proportions became increasingly certain throughout the day," the agency announced. "With the hurricane moving steadily on a bee line for the east coast of Florida, gathering speed as it progressed and maintaining a wind velocity, but little less than it hurled itself across Porto Rico," the Red Cross was speeding disaster workers to Jacksonville. There, they made preparations to move into South Florida.

National Vice Chairman James L. Fieser was pulled out of a Red Cross conference in West Virginia. He immediately headed south to spearhead the effort. About noon, he said, "We pray this hurricane may be turned aside before it strikes our shores." But unfortunately, prayer did not deter the storm. Ruth Stewart, who was the wife of a well-known West Palm Beach dentist and mother of two, had phoned the *Palm Beach Post* newsroom and was told that the storm would strike some 20 miles north of West Palm Beach, in the early evening hours. Then the electricity and telephone went off at the Stewart home at 420 Independence Road. The Stewarts boarded up the openings in the porch and considered fleeing to Miami, but sadly, they decided it was too late for that, as winds were already starting to lift small pieces of debris into the air.

Ruth had stuffed some towels into window frames and doors, but wind-driven rain began to seep in. It gathered in the spaces between windows and screens and flowed down the walls. Approximately 3:00pm, a board, apparently from the roof, crashed down on the front porch. The family ran from window to window, trying to nail more boards, as they heard window frames cracking loudly and began to weaken. For the next three hours, they worked frantically to mop the growing flow of water furiously and continued to nail more boards into place. All the time, she wrote, the wind made a constant roar like a train on a track, which drowned out the crashes from both their home and adjacent ones, where chimneys were falling and roofs and walls were being ripped from their foundations. At this moment, the Stewarts debated making a run for it. They gathered their cash and sewed it into their clothes. But Ruth Stewart finally decided against fleeing, fearing she'd never be able to walk and hold on to her small son at the same time.

However, Dr. William J. Buck had not waited for the storm to arrive. Buck was believed to be the only doctor anywhere along the southern part of Lake Okeechobee, from Pahokee to Moore Haven. He was a major during World War I and had to run the base hospital for the U.S. 82nd Division in Le Mans, France. Buck was among the early settlers of Belle Glade when it incorporated in the spring of 1928. Not fully satisfied with his profession, he was also president of the Belle Glade town council and had founded the American Legion's Belle Glade post. Not satisfied with weather officials' continued reassurances that the storm would miss Florida, he relied on his gut feelings to take his own action on Saturday and Sunday. He dispatched fellow Legionnaires across the Glades to dispatch the warnings to prepare for a storm. Some four hundred people jammed into the town's two hotels. "White and negroes were brought in alike," Buck would say on September 21st. "It was a time of terror and there was no discrimination. Our effort was to save lives." Sadly, very few would share Buck's position.

In the afternoon, a rare and chilling symbol began appearing across coastal South Florida. It was a hurricane flag; a black square inside a larger red square. Now it is a pennant for the University of Miami Hurricanes football team. There was a time when it was virtually the sole method by which people were told a storm was coming. One flag signified a tropical storm, and two a hurricane. Flagpoles along the coast had already held a single square. On the afternoon of September 16th, two squares went up each staff.

At 5:00pm, the U.S. Weather Bureau began earnestly warning people in other parts of the state that were in the storm's path, specifically a section of the peninsula's west coast, along the Gulf of Mexico, from near Fort Myers to where the peninsula curves into the Panhandle. Their advisory read, "Change to hurricane warning 6pm Punta Rassa to Cedar Keys, Fla., and display northeast storm warnings west of Apalachicola to Mississippi Coast. Hurricane center 4:00pm near coast between Miami and Jupiter, still moving northwestward unless course changes. Hurricane center will reach west coast not far from Tampa Monday morning. Emergency… Advise all interests to take precautions. This hurricane is of great intensity and wide extent." There was an error with this advisory because it said that at 4:00pm, the storm was near the coast. The word 'near' was wrong. Because of the minimal technological weather advancements during the 1920s—primitive compared to today's technological era of advanced satellites and computers—there's a lot of uncertainty about "landfall," the term for the spot where the storm's center, or eye, came ashore. Of course, people began feeling the effects of the storm hours before landfall. And ironically, landfall was the time when the eye passed over and the winds subsided to nothing.

Any effort now, eighty-six years later, to pinpoint the exact landfall of the eye is almost a futile effort. This was a storm that spanned hundreds of miles, tore up 60 miles of coastline, and drowned thousands of people some 40 miles inland. But for this storm or any other, finding that center spot would give researchers then, and now, a starting point to help measure a storm's path and map its power and destruction as it moved across land.

Richard Gray, from the U.S. Weather Bureau in Miami, said on September 17, 1928, the day after the storm struck the Florida coast, that he believed landfall was at Delray Beach and hurricane-force winds were felt from just north of Jupiter, in other words, across two Florida counties covering about 75 miles of coast. Gray said that serious structural damage from the storm expanded from Gomez, a now-abandoned settlement just north of Jupiter in Martin County, to as far as Pompano Beach, a distance of 60 miles. Damage was reported as far north as Vero Beach and as far south as Miami. That means that tropical storm winds, of 39 to 73 mph, were present as much as 130 miles from the center. Gray said the storm extended as far out as 500 miles and brought strong winds to both Key West and Jacksonville. It was the first storm in history to trigger official Weather Bureau warnings to encompass the lengths of both Florida coasts. Eventually, Gray moved probable landfall about 11 miles north to Lake Worth, saying that the lull appeared longest there. He believed the storm's eye was about 25 miles across, nearly twice the estimated 13-mile width of the Great Miami Hurricane of 1926.

In Kelsey City, Charles Branch stopped by to see his mechanic, Robert White. He found White frantically stocking the storm shelter he'd built himself. He was planning to put thirty people in it. White had placed a map on his table and plotted the storm's progress. He placed a ruler on the paper, paralleling the track. It was heading straight to West Palm Beach. The two looked at each other. White told his supervisor that whatever he'd planned on doing, he better do right away. Branch was sufficiently frightened about the impact of this storm on his city. He immediately loaded one truck with lumber and the other with men and told them to begin boarding up and securing the company's properties. He called his wife and told her to take their son and head for Orlando. She, however, was defiant and refused the request because she said she wouldn't leave without him. After much arguing, he finally managed to convince her to leave, insisting he'd follow. Everyone was making plans to leave except Harry Kelsey's son, Ted. He didn't believe all of the hype over this storm hitting the area, and if it did, he was curious about what the impact of this storm would be like. Branch looked up; there wasn't a cloud in the sky.

Noah Kellum Williams, a dairy farmer and Palm Beach county commissioner from Jupiter, had driven the twenty miles down to West Palm Beach Saturday afternoon. He heard a report that the storm was coming. Men stood around in groups, discussing which buildings might survive and which might be destroyed. As the barometer started to fall and a brisk wind brought rains and squalls, people started battening down their windows and securing their boats and yachts. But the school year was scheduled to be open that Monday. West Palm Beach merchants were making preparations for Wednesday's "Dollar Day," when many stores were cutting prices to boost sales. For example, a car dealer's advertised the DeSoto Six, "brilliant and revolutionary in its field," for only $845. A meeting of American Legion posts from Key West to Titusville was still scheduled for Sunday afternoon in Fort Pierce. Thirty-nine Palm Beach County churches had advertised the times of their Sunday services. At First Baptist Church in downtown West Palm Beach, Reverend C.H. Bolton's 11:00am sermon was titled "God's Will for America" and at 8:00pm was "summer is ended and we are not saved." By 8:00pm Sunday, every person in West Palm Beach, of every religion, would be looking and praying to God for salvation.

In preparation for the storm, Bessie Mae had one of the black hands board up the lakefront windows. Then she placed her linens on top of the dresser, out of the high water level, she hoped. A heavy squall sent water roaring against the house. Then it suddenly stopped. During the lull, Bessie Mae and Raymond loaded the children into the car. Pools of water were forming around the house and in the fields. As the car drove away, a trio of black farmhands waved then disappeared behind the house. Bessie Mae looked back at the farmhouse standing like a lone sentinel in the water-soaked fields, wondering whether her linens would get soaked again.

She hoped that if it flooded, there would be little damage. Rounding the bend toward Belle Glade, she glanced back one more time. Hers would be one of the last pair of eyes to ever see the Martin farmhouse before it was destroyed in the storm.

Bessie Mae gathered up the children and the baby, threw a shawl over her head, and followed Raymond back to the store. Tempie and her children followed close behind. Tommy Wells, ever the doughboy, said he'd prefer to wait out the storm in his own house. But within two hours, he would be forced to change his mind and retreat with his wife, Willie, and little Eddie to the Glades Hotel. Henry and Arlin Martin were securing shutters and doors when Bessie Mae arrived. Chairs and tables were set up, and a pot of coffee was brewing in the side kitchen and the family settled down to wait out the storm. The few blankets were passed out. Annie Mae looked anxiously around the store, hoping they could return to the comfort of their own beds before it got too late. Tempie and Hattie with the other children settled on bags and boxes off to one side. Outside, the wind roared like a mad animal howling to get in. Tempie huddled closer to her children to comfort them.

Wooden coffins lined up on the side of the street at Canal Point, reserved strictly for the white storm victims (Courtesy of the Florida State Archives).

Henry was not so much worried about the storm itself, but about the floodwaters affecting his fields. He thought back of the more recent storms his farm had weathered in the last two years and came out unscathed. Early in the day, he sold out of candles, oil, and some canned goods at his farm store, but little else had moved. He would have returned the next day to make up business that he was going to lose. He thought about his saturated fields. They would probably flood, like in most storms. It should be over in a day, not like 1920 or 1922, when half the farmers were flooded out and left. Today, they had the dike. They had the large pumps that could pump a field dry in twelve hours; if it stopped raining, the crop should make it.

Martin also thought of his brother, Loney Martin, at the farm next to the dike. If the storm was as big as the reports indicated, then Loney and his family would be in danger. But it was too late to send anyone to check on or go out to get them. They would have to trust the sturdiness of their house to withstand the storm. He was hoping that it survived the storm, and he was offered some degree of solace knowing the farmhouse did make it through the two hurricanes in 1926. At least Raymond had taken Bessie Mae and the children to Belle Glade. They were just across the canal. If he looked out the window of the store, he could see Tommy's house. The rain rattled the windows as the winds howled and shook the store. Then the lights went out, and they were suddenly thrown into darkness. Henry and Arlin lit kerosene lamps and hung them from hooks in the ceiling. The lamps threw an eerie, yellowish sheen on the group of anxious faces, almost a deathly glow.

Leaving Arlin with the store, Henry went to Main Street. At Lawrence Will's gas station, he heard that the storm was likely to move north. People, mostly men, gathered around the stores trying to keep dry, but most of all to obtain news of the storm. The few radios were turned up full volume. They strained their ears to hear any news through the crackling static caused by the lightning of distant electrical storms. Lawrence E. Will, Everglades historian, had an active and varied part in the development of that colourful region at the time. He had experienced every hurricane that had visited the area and was in the center of the one described in this book.

There is some anecdotal evidence that people spread the word about the impending storm the old fashioned way by passing the message on about the storm by person to person. Several days after the storm, South Bay businessman Frank Schuster stopped by the Miami office of the U.S. Weather Bureau. He wanted to let Richard Gray know he'd received good advance warning of the storm, even out in the Glades; however, Gray's notes don't say how he knew. But Schuster said the alert had enabled him to save 211 people by making several car trips in that area, with the help of others, "for the purpose of collecting the white residents and moving them to a large barge." Apparently, Schuster didn't have time to save the black residents because there was no mention of him informing any of them.

A crowd of anxious people gathered in the Alston Drugstore on Main Street. At least one member of every family who had chosen to remain in Belle Glade milled about the crowded front room. The five-month-old town still had no town hall or meetinghouse. The drugstore crowd looked to their recently elected mayor for guidance. Mayor Walter Greer was a big man. A blacksmith by trade, he had a smith's imposing build. His six-foot frame, two-hundred-pound size, and round, stout face, framed by an imposing handlebar moustache, instilled confidence. The rain came down in drenching bursts, let up some, then poured again as sickle-shaped feeder bands swung their hundred-mile-long arms across Belle Glade and the lake's southern shore. It was gusting hard, at times very hard, but it was the rain and the water, and the frail muck dike, that stood between them and disaster.

What had anyone heard? Should they leave? Where should they go? Hoping to calm everyone's fears, Mayor Walter Greer took it upon himself to go out and examine the dike personally. Accompanied by two of the town's remaining officials, they drove to Chosen to examine the dike. They parked their car and walked up to the seven-foot-high, mud-slick bank. Along the top, they were buffeted by strong winds and soaked by drenching squalls. The lake was high; waves lapped less than two feet from the top of the dike. The dike looked to his untrained eye as sturdy as it had always been. As the wind blew against his face, causing him to squint hard, he knew it was a serious storm, but Walter Greer felt the dike would hold. It had to hold. The thought that it might not was beyond his imagination.

What the people needed at this time was a calming, reassuring leader, not an alarmist message that might cause mass panic. The three men returned to the drugstore. The mayor wouldn't lie. He told them that he wasn't going anywhere. He and his family were staying, and that would be that. Plus, the latest radio reports had the storm veering well to the north. In reality, the mayor knew they had no choice. Most of the people had no means of leaving at this late date. If they tried to leave by Palm Beach Road, they would be driving exposed in the flat open Everglades directly into the oncoming storm. The road north to Pahokee and Okeechobee was paved, but part of it was built along the lake dike. Anyone trying to take the risk of driving that route would risk being blown into the canal. Either way, they might be caught out in the open with a full-blown hurricane. Like the true pioneers they were, most would stay and tough it out. Though vaguely reassured, they all understood they had no choice. That morning there had been a chance to leave, but certainly not now.

Comforted or not, the meeting broke up and people returned to their homes, resigned to wait out the storm. There, some made basic preparations. Others went to one of the two hotels, which were larger and built of sturdier materials than most of the one story houses in Belle Glade. There was comfort in a crowd. A group of people could offer help and much needed company during the night that everyone knew was coming. Charlie Riedel crossed the street to the Glades Hotel, the hotel he had built and just sold. It was nearly dark, darker than it should be for 5:30pm. At least the hotel generator hummed above the occasional gale force gusts, giving a comforting, familiar sound. There, at least he would find light.

CHAPTER TEN

During the Storm

a) Ford Garage b) House tossed like a football c) American Laundry d) Long Distance Bottling Works e) Twin Trucking Company f) Presbyterian Church (Courtesy of NOAA-The National Hurricane Center).

B ack in West Palm Beach, the *Palm Beach Post*, in reporting the newest advisory on its September 13th front page, had reported there was every indication that the storm would move into the Gulf of Mexico, taking it away from Florida, and "no fear was voiced by weather-wise persons that this section would feel the effect of the storm." The story, now in its second day of coverage in the *Post*, was still receiving only modest play, at the bottom of the front page.[88]

At about 3pm, the power failed in West Palm Beach. Two hours later, the water stopped running. At 3:20pm, police officers fought their way to

---

[88]   *The Palm Beach Post*, September 13th 1928.

Okeechobee Boulevard near the waterfront, after receiving a report that a man was found dead in his car. The officers found only a dead drunk man and sent him to the county jail. Two miles up the road, Taylor's Auto Shop lost its roof. T.R. Gill, an Associated Press reporter, and J.P. Buchanan, a newsreel photographer for Paramount News, were driving in the storm in Kelsey City. They decided to get into a shed for cover. The moment the car stopped, the shed's roof came down; Gill dove under the car, and Buchanan under a nearby vehicle as the walls of the shed crashed down around them. Gill hid in a nearby hedge. He later broke into a home for cover, but its walls came down, too.

By six o'clock, dark, angry waves were already breaking over the dike. The storm had dropped six inches of rain directly on the lake, while the flooded Kissimmee River poured in more. Lake Okeechobee had risen three feet in twenty-four hours. By 6:30pm, water was streaming over the lower points of the dike. Lake water quickly filled the canals then overflowed their banks. The flat-lying fields flooded quickly. The water moved, inextricably joining large pools of rain water until a shallow lake was formed, leaving only trees, bushes, dikes, and houses standing out of the water like foreign objects. Then the lakes began to join together, forming one large body of water—a sea, really. The Everglades was reverting back to its primeval condition.

At 6:45pm, the storm-darkened sky threw a gloomy twilight over the Everglades, while a group of mostly men crowded around the radio at the Glades Hotel. The radio AM frequency crackled sharply with each lightning strike—a sure sign of a storm—but through the constant static, a voice announcing the news was loudly audible. The voice stated calmly that the people along the Palm Beach coast could rest assured because there was no danger from the approaching hurricane. Abruptly, the voice stopped and played on the emotions of the listeners, but then it excitedly blared out that at that very moment, a monstrous hurricane was battering West Palm Beach.

a) Central Market **b)** Richburg Building **c)** McClain's Garage
d) Florida Power & Light **e)** Service Garage **f)** Christian Science
Church (Courtesy of NOAA-The National Hurricane Center).

Shock and disbelief ran through the crowd. Relief was instantly replaced with anxiety and fear. They were caught in a trap. Memories of Moore Haven and hundreds of dead ran through their minds; their recently planted crops, their homes, their families were all in danger. Some ran through the rain back to their houses; others stayed where they were. They had no other place to go. Even as the residents of the mainland huddled against the grueling winds and cold, torrential rains, Lake Okeechobee was being battered into deadly submission. The wind that had been blowing for twenty-four hours from the north had begun to change direction, first from the northwest, then due west, directly off the lake.

As the eye of the storm approached the lake, the winds curved around in a tighter circle, shoveling the water into its center, fully securing it in its grip. Trapped, the water piled up on top of itself until it formed a dome of water twelve feet high, approaching some eight feet above the muck dike, which was rapidly softening and getting ready to give way. The watery mound was in an unnatural state. Any good engineer knows that water must seek its own level. It prodded and probed, searching for some area of weakness, seeking some way to escape. Then the winds changed, and it found a way out. The first to feel the effects of the massive storm surge were the lake island residents. The Belle Glade, Miami Locks and South Bay would have to wait their turn.

Dick Wilson, a bank director and lumber company executive, was one of those who fled to the Kelsey City town hall. The building's structure included a garage area that housed the fire truck. The people inside couldn't keep the giant doors closed against the wind. They rolled the fire truck against the doors and added their weight and strength. "I think we'd better pray," someone said. When it came Wilson's turn, he said, "Lord, I'm not much on offering prayers, and I don't do well with it. But I can promise you this: if you get us out of this, I'll know how to pray next time."

For the first time that day, Cliff Councilman could relax. Concerned about the rising lake water and the increasing strong winds, immediately after lunch he and his family had packed a few blankets and some food and left their Torry Island home. Most of the other island residents opted to stay in their homes. They wanted to be near their houses and farms to watch over them and care for their livestock. In their fourteen-foot boat, powered by a 5.5-horsepower outboard motor, the Councilman family had crossed the choppy waters strewn with thick clumps of windblown hyacinth and tree branches to the dock at Chosen. After securing the boat, they crossed over to Isaac West's store, which most people considered to be the sturdiest building in the area. Twenty people gathered around the store; some helped serve coffee; the rest made themselves as comfortable as possible. The telephone rang, and everyone looked up in surprise of the ringing sound it made because at the time, telephones were still novelties to most persons in South Florida. Isaac West answered the telephone, listened grimly, and then hung up. "It's a hurricane. And the edge has reached West Palm Beach," he said. "And it's definitely headed here." What about the others on the islands? Cliff wondered. Someone had to warn them. With his family secured, he decided to take the risk and return and alert the other residents about this new turn of events.[89]

Untying the boat, he cast off and motored along the south side causeway canal, fighting against the rain-driven north wind. The causeway afforded him some degree of protection from the breaking waves. The leeward north side of the causeway was heaped high with hundreds of acres worth of wind-blown weeds. Tying his boat up at John Aunapu's former storefront dock, he grabbed young Frede Aunapu, and together they ran

---

[89]   Mykle, R. (2006) *Killer 'cane: The Deadly Hurricane of 1928*, Taylor Trade Publishing pg. 150.

on foot to alert the other residents. Within half an hour, nearly all the residents on Bird and Torry Islands, except for the Lees, started for the mainland. They got as far as the causeway on the island. It was underwater and blocked by tons of wind-blown hyacinth. Wet and cold, they retreated to the only remaining safe place on the island, the Aunapus' big metal packing house. Cliff Councilman had left the group and returned to the dock for his boat, hoping to make it back to his family, but the water-soaked motor refused to start. He, along with the rest, was trapped. With the water slopping over the dock, he ran to the packing house.

Inside were twenty-two people mixed in-between a couple of trucks, tractors, plows, disks, crates, and tools. Of the twenty-two souls who had been in Aunapu's packing house, twelve survived. Those lost were BeaDer, his daughter, Gertrude Smith, with her son, Levon, Ralph Cherry's wife and all five children, and Capt. Ed King, who, when found, was clutching two of the children. Wind and rain battered the metal walls. As the water rose, they stood on top of crates, trucks, and tractors. How long could they stand like that? How much longer could the metal structure hold? Frede reached into each car and truck and turned on the headlights. The bright lights flickered as water lapped up against the bulbs. Still, they burned, and the water unavoidably rose higher. The men waded through waist-deep water, gathered up planks, logs, and boards, and placed them on the cross beams of the packinghouse roof. First helping the women and children, Frede climbed up on the rafters and waited. The walls of the packing house seemed to breathe with each gust. Below, the water covered the roofs of the cars. His father's new Buick was now ruined, Frede thought. The headlights still burned, but were slowly fading as they cast a ghostly figure over them as the water continued to slowly rise.

On Bird Island, the Aunapu party did their best to keep dry and out of the rising water from the approaching storm. Wind bowed the metal walls of the packing house with each gust. Rain pelted the metal roof with such force that a deafening roar precluded any conversation. Wet and cold, the packing house party suffered their fate silently. Sitting on the crossbeams, Ralph and Mary Cherry and their three young children had joined the group as they had waded across the water-swept island. In one corner, old blind Captain Ed King held the other two small Cherry children firmly in his arms, trying to console them.

Complete destruction of a house at Pahokee, Florida, after the Okeechobee Hurricane of 1928 (Courtesy of the Florida State Archives).

From the opposite side of Torry Island, the winds gathered a row of cut custard apple trees in a long chain of tangled trunks and branches and swept the hundred-yard mass rolling and tumbling toward Bird Island. With the trees acting as sails, the wind carried the mass like a schooner dashing across the rough lake waters. It slammed into the packing house with a heart-stopping thud. Wrapping around the metal building in a mortal embrace, it crashed against it again and again. The trees acted like a dam, piling up water and more debris behind it. The metal building groaned and strained against the additional weight. Then it began to bend. In slow motion one side, then the other doubled over and folded upon itself before collapsing into the canal.

Trapped in the twisted metal, Frede was pulled down then dragged under water. This is how it is to drown, he thought, as a strange sense of calm overpowered him. With his strained lungs burning, he took a gulp of water, welcoming death, but his body's survival reflex kicked in just as the building settled, and suddenly he was free. He kicked up and broke to the surface. Coughing up lungs full of water, he gasped for air and grabbed onto a wooden beam. Gathering his senses, he glanced around. Where was Elizabeth? Suddenly, something struck his leg. He reached down, felt a head full of hair, he grabbed it, and pulled. Green, one of the black hands, bobbed to the surface. Elizabeth was still down there! Quickly Frede took a deep breath and dove, groping blindly in the black water. He felt a dress tangled in the wreckage, tugging against the current.

It was Elizabeth, but she was stuck. A button on her jacket had caught in the tin roofing. He pulled with all the strength he could muster and then ripped the button from the jacket and, with Elizabeth in his arm, shot to the surface. Elizabeth, half-conscious, bobbed in the water. Fred grabbed onto a beam of the roof and held on, trying to orient himself.

They were still inside the packing plant wreckage. It moved and groaned in the wind-driven torrent. They had to get out before it completely fell apart. Barely making out a hole in the roof, they swam out just as the roof sunk under the waves. They grabbed at a floating tree and hung on. Frede's leg was caught in-between the trees, and he was repeatedly forced underwater as the tree bobbed and rolled. Elizabeth disappeared in the darkness. Finally, he freed himself then he found Elizabeth grasping onto another branch barely four yards away. They floated onto a barge, which they grabbed, and pulled themselves up onto its rain-slicked deck. Lying flat, they held on for dear life.

Jacob Porter stepped out of his shack and stared into wind-swept rain. The wind roared like a steam furnace. Water had risen over the small irrigation canal and had covered his yard. His wife, Jennie, complained that her herbs and vegetables would be destroyed in the flood waters. But Jacob was more worried about the dike. Water around the house was black, and it was lake water. Except for the occasional flash of lightning, it was pitch black. He stared through the blackness, but could not see where water was flowing over the dike. Then the water began to rise faster. They had to run! Jacob yelled to Jennie to get the children.

Jennie grabbed the baby, and Jacob took his boy and girl under his arms and dashed out into the angry storm. Other families joined them. The torrential rainfall blinded him as he leaned into the wind. Jennie and the baby clustered behind him. He wanted to get to one of the solidly built stores in Chosen. With the waves breaking over the rim of the dike, it was breached in several spots. Trees were blown down, and their roots were thrust into the air like grabbing multi-fingered hands. He was afraid he might step into an unseen canal. Then he was pushed from behind by a wave. At this point, he lost contact with Jennie and her baby as another wave pushed him under the water. However, it was the third wave, which was deeper than the rest, that toppled him over and kept him from the surface. He struggled to get to the surface with the children gripped tightly in his arms as he lost consciousness.

Soon after Councilman left Isaac West's store, a series of strong gusts shook the walls with such force that there was fear it would collapse. John Elliot decided to return to Max Morris' small, but sturdily built house. Within a few minutes, Bill and Lois Hunt and a North Carolinian named White, who were fleeing their own homes, joined them. They tried to make themselves comfortable in the sparsely furnished house, lit by only one kerosene lamp. Less than an hour later, water from the collapsing dike swept around the small house in increasing torrents. Water forced its way into the house, rising quickly to hip level. Elliot and the others barely had time to think of what to do when the house was swept off its foundation. Elliot sloshed to the back of the house when another surge of water displaced the house against the canal road embankment. The front reared up, driving the back of the house underwater. Without thinking, Elliot dove out through the screened window. The house plunged into the canal. He broke the surface with pieces of splintered wood near the roof. It was pitch black as he grappled for the roof, cutting his hands on the metal sheathing.

In the front, as the house reared up and pitched into the canal, Bill Hunt, his wife, and White had jumped through the windows. Grabbing onto the eaves, they made their way to the roof, where they rode the flood unknowingly a few feet from John Elliot. Forced by the surging lake water, the house began to move down the canal, where it crashed against the Belle Glade Bridge over a mile away and immediately broke up. John Elliot was thrown violently off the house into the very rough canal waters. Struggling to the surface, he swam desperately with his one good hand to the bridge. He held onto the structure, held tight, gathered his strength, and then pulled himself up. Once on top, he stood up and ran against the crosswind to the Glades Hotel. He could not believe that he had survived. The Hunts and their friend, he thought, must have drowned.

Clutching his bleeding hands, he ran into the hotel lobby. There, he found quite a number of confused and hysterical people on the first floor of the hotel. Seeing he was injured, he was led upstairs to have his hand bandaged. When he recounted his tale, the hotel refuges laughed. A house floating from Chosen; not likely, they thought. His assertion brought the only joking about the storm that night. Looking outside, the people could barely see a foot of water in the street. Everyone knew a barge might wash down from Chosen, but never a house. Before the night was through, fifty houses would have made the same journey.

At the courthouse, little Tommie Rickards found as many as 500 people crowding the halls, which were pitched into darkness when the power went out. Children screamed for water, of which there was none, and screamed with fear as the wind howled outside and plaster and glass crashed around them. Rickards collected water from a leak. But when he tasted some, he realized that it wasn't rain, but ocean water driven through the air all the way from the beach, more than a mile away.

In Jupiter, Bessie Wilson DuBois described hearing the bell at her home and realizing the wind had changed direction. She said nothing about a lull. People reported being in the eye of the storm all the way from Kelsey City-now Lake Park-to Delray Beach. Presuming a hurricane has a mostly symmetrical eye, Gray was correct in his assumption that the center of the storm was 25 miles wide. It must be noted that within the eye itself there is little or no wind; a hurricane's most powerful winds are in the eyewall of the storm. The eye is a region of mostly calm weather at the center of strong tropical cyclones. The eye of a storm is a roughly circular area, typically 20 to 40 miles in diameter. It is surrounded by the eyewall, a ring of towering thunderstorms where the most severe weather occurs. The cyclone's lowest barometric pressure occurs in the eye and can be as much as 15 percent lower than the pressure outside the storm. In the eyewall is the location within a hurricane where there are the most damaging winds and intense rainfall.

In a hurricane re-analysis project called 'HURDAT', by the National Hurricane Center, forecaster Brian Jarvinen estimated that landfall was near Lake Worth and the eye was 25 to 30 miles wide. Jarvinen said the most powerful winds would have been in the eyewall north of Lake Worth-in other words, downtown West Palm Beach. He believed the strongest winds extended 15 to 20 miles out from the center, from around Riviera Beach to around Boynton Beach, and weaker winds, but still hurricane force, were present much farther out. By comparison, Hurricane Andrew, which devastated an area of south Miami in 1992, would be a tight storm, with an eye only about 15 miles across and hurricane force winds extending outward only about 30 miles from the center.

If it had been daylight, the residents on the north shore would have seen the water receding away from the shoreline and the bottom exposed, with fish flipping around or trapped in small pockets of water. No doubt that had this happened during the day, this might have been noticed by the residents and they would have sought shelter and saved many lives. As the storm pushed all of the water to the southeast, it was as if the huge lake had been tipped and the north end drew down to the lakebed. As the storm continued its northwest track, over a two-hour period, winds shifted until they were coming from the south. The rest was elementary physics. The water came rushing back, then kept moving to the north end of the lake. Up there, there was no dike—not even a little one. Why would there be? The water, which under normal circumstances would have flowed towards the lake and not the opposite way around, came in torrents. So the water rushed northward into the town of Okeechobee.

Sitting in a wooden chair on the first floor, Lawrence Will's eyes kept focused on the ceiling. The wind on the outside roared like a freight train passing over their heads. The walls slowly started to give way as it slowly rocked from side to side; however, it was the unfinished roof he was more afraid of giving way. It rose and fell with each gust then began to flap until a monstrous gust of wind, sounding like two trains passing each other, lifted the roof and carried it away. He heard water crashing against the second floor, and then torrents spilled through the floorboards. For a brief second, Lawrence Will almost gave up. With his roof completely destroyed, Will and the carpenter, Whitehead Smith, and his young mechanic sat in the dark, ducking cascades of water streaming through the ceiling. The water had drowned the kerosene lanterns hanging from the rafters. It was getting a bit cool, so Will put on a sweater, and over that a raincoat to keep dry. The building creaked and moaned with each wind gust. Though they knew they had built the building sturdy, they each wondered whether it could withstand the might of the storm.

Suddenly, the building stopped shaking. The men looked at each other, having a fair idea of what would happen next, so with their flashlights in their hands, they immediately stepped out the front door. They swept the street with light beams and were met with an incredible scene. Main

Street was littered with boards, downed telephone poles, and building debris. The new Ford garage across the street was a flat pile of rubble. The three men cautiously walked along the street. A frantic mother yelled at them that she'd lost her child and asked that they please find her. They were still searching when the eye of the storm passed over them and the wind began with renewed fury, but from the opposite direction. Will was between the drugstore and the Glades Hotel when a blast of wind spun him around. He landed in front of the drugstore, which he was surprised to find empty. Just shortly before dark, there had been twenty people inside. He found the little girl huddling in the doorway and gave her back to her very appreciative mother, who then sought shelter in the Glades Hotel.

The young mechanic wanted to check on the safety of the bridge tender's family. The three men headed toward the canal. At each gust, they had to grab onto anything secure and hold on or be blown away. The bridge and the bank along the canal were the highest points in Belle Glade. Though the wind was blowing fiercely, the water was still only a foot deep, and it never occurred to any of them that the water would continue to rise much higher.

They made it to the canal as the back eyewall of the storm threw its strongest winds at them. The canal was clogged with debris: part of a houseboat, a barge on its side, walls and roofs of dozens of houses, and tangled messes of uprooted custard apple trees. Jam-packed up against the steel bridge was one of the Halloway brothers' barges. Hiding under the barge's roof from the storm's fury were Bill and Lois Hunt and White, who had made the harrowing rooftop journey from Chosen. Yet, the water in Belle Glade had only risen another foot. They tried to return to the hotel, but were forced back by repeated vicious wind gusts. Finally, they gave up and fled back to the safety of the canal and leaped onto the barge. With their flashlights, they examined the damp hold. The barge had a jagged hole just above the waterline. Rainwater streamed in through the floorboards. The barge was in danger of sinking. Knee-deep in the rancid, oily bilge water, the men took turns pumping out the water. The small pump moved just a little of the water, but the strenuous work helped keep the men warm. They could ride out the storm in relative safety if the cable held. Trapped on the barge in the middle of the canal, they could only listen powerlessly to the occasional desperate cries for help that drowned out in the dark, screaming winds.

Nancy Martin paused and ran to the window. The wind had suddenly died, almost stopping. By the light of a kerosene lamp, Nancy Martin looked outside the knee-deep water covering the entire yard and fields around their house. The only spot not underwater was the road bank. "If we don't want to get stuck here until tomorrow, I think we should leave," she said to the others, and they all agreed.[90] They got into the two cars and began to drive to West Palm Beach. Near the Experimental Station, the back winds of the eyewall caught them. Vicious cross winds cutting across the road threatened to blow their automobiles into the canal. Afraid to continue, they parked their cars in front of the main building to wait out the storm. Savage wind gusts so viciously rocked the cars that Nancy was sure the next gusts of wind would flip her car on its side. All she could do was hold on for life and pray.

Cold rain fell in wavelike sheets, flapping in the wind. The waterlogged muck could absorb no more water. The drainage pumps had stopped working, but even if they had continued to pump, there was no place to dump water. Lake Okeechobee was full. Strong, gusty winds started to send large, raging waves splashing over the lower sections of the dike. Dozens of little streams snaked their way down the dike's banks. They widened, carrying muck with them. Slowly at first, the water washed some mud here, cut a little gully there; the dike gradually at first started to give way, opening spaces for water to escape from the lake. Shortly after disk, the water-saturated dike began to melt. Rain converted soil into a liquid black slush. Waves churned up by the 150 miles-per-hour winds crashed onto and then over the dike, spilling more black water down its liquefying banks.

Two blocks away from the Pioneer Service Building, Mayor Walter Greer's small, gabled wooden house began to shake so violently that he feared the walls would give way. The group that had gathered there had to leave the house. He ordered everyone to pair up in groups of two, one man and one woman, and not to become separated. Then he and his wife grabbed what they could and fought their way to Tedder's Glades Hotel. In

---

[90]   Mykle, R. (2006) Killer 'cane: The Deadly Hurricane of 1928, *Taylor Trade Publishing pg. 156.*

the confusion, his daughter and her friend, Bonnie Parker, who somehow were paired up, were separated from the rest of the family. The girls were not missed until the Greers made it to the Glades Hotel. Someone said that the drugstore roof next door had just blown off into the street and that the girls were trapped underneath. Walter Greer rushed out into the street. Around the corner of the hotel, a gust blew him on his face, bruising his elbows and knees. The big man lifted himself up and struggled to the overturned roof. Looking underneath, he saw that the girls were not there. He retreated back to the hotel when again he was blown off his feet. Half-crawling on all fours like a wet bear, he made it back to the hotel, where he told his wife that the girls were not under the roof.

Frantic, Mrs. Greer insisted she had to know whether they were safe or not. The newly elected mayor fought his way through the rain and wind across the street to the Belle Glade Hotel. The water reached up to his knees. He knew the black, murky water was from the lake. He burst into the hotel and found Georgia and Bonnie safe. Knowing his wife would not rest easy until she knew the girls were safe, he once again fought his way across the street to the hotel and informed his wife that the girls were safe. Exhausted, he crawled up to the second floor and collapsed on the floor. He remained there, asleep, until the next morning. While Walter Greer slept upstairs in the Glades Hotel, Walter Peterson, with his family in tow, fought his way out of the coloured town. Blinded by stinging, wind-driven rain, he struggled through the rubble-strewn streets across 4th Street and up Avenue B. They remained in their house until one of the waves began to give way, threatening to carry the entire structure with it. There were only two places he deemed to be safe: two two-story hotels in the center of town.

Following his father, nine-year-old Ardie watched as tin roofs flew through the air like newspapers. In all of the confusion, the family inadvertently split up. Ardie and his father battled their way into the Glades Hotel. His sisters and their husbands were forced to seek refuge across the street at Belle Glade Hotel. It was the first time any of the Petersons had ever set foot in the "whites only" hotel. It was crowded; black and white families walked about nervously within the hotel itself. Anxious faces glanced out the front. The humid air was heavy with the stench of fear and anticipation of the storm's duration. When the water started to rise above the porch, all the children were ordered to the second floor. Ardie ran up the stairs and sat down on the hallway floor. "I couldn't lean up against the wall because it was moving in and out," he would later reply during his recollection after the storm.

To prevent any adult from going upstairs, a guard armed with a pistol was posted at the bottom of the stairs. When the water started to rise, one woman stormed past the guard, saying, "Go ahead and shoot me, but I'm going up." The rest pushed one another to get up the stairs. The lobby flooded so fast that the last two people almost drowned in the stairwell. The water rose until it finally stopped within a few inches of the ceiling as the winds howled on the outside. The crowd of people watched in silence as the building shook and the walls vibrated violently, threatening at any time to give way. Death, it seemed, was determined to carry them away. Yet against all odds, Tedder's Glades Hotel would hold out against all that the storm could give.

Across the street at the Belle Glade Hotel, nearly 150 people crammed into the dining room, sitting rooms, and hallways. Suddenly, during a powerful gust of wind, the purr of the hotel generator stopped and the lights went out. Kerosene lamps were lit, placed on tables, and hung from the rafters. The water was up to the first step of the hotel. The winds roared with unrelenting fierceness, so no one could see anything outside because the rain obscured the view. No one could tell if the water in the streets was rainwater or whether the dike had given away and it was lake water. The uncertainty raised everyone's anxiety up a notch. Charlie Riedel arrived with his family. After securing the family in one of the rooms upstairs, he walked around, reassuring the terrified townspeople that the storm would soon be over. The eye passed directly over Belle Glade. For the first time in two hours, many of the people allowed themselves to hope that the worst was over. But those who knew better mentally braced themselves for what they knew was to come—the back end of the storm, the storm's second act, the finale in which it would try to deliver the knockout punch, and for this they only had to wait another twenty minutes.

Craving a couple of cigarettes and moving away from the crowd, young Charlie Tryon and Tom Jackson went up the back stairs to the second floor to sneak a smoke when a strong gust of wind slammed into the hotel. With a mighty groan, and then a tremendous crash, the hotel shook and the roof flew off and sailed like a kite into darkness. A heavy downpour of water soaked the two boys. In total darkness, they carefully retreated back downstairs.

On the first floor, alarm set in as they noticed black water begin to rise up the front steps of the hotel. It covered the porch floor then leaked inside through the front doors. Main Street was a raging river. Swiftly, it covered the entire floor in crazed eddies. Women screamed in terror as some people ran about praying to God, while others panicked about the dilemma they were in. Fortunately, Charles Riedel stepped up and took command. He quickly got the women and children upstairs, followed by the men.

Behind the fleeing crowd, the water rapidly crept up the stairs at a rate of an inch a minute. Exposed to the furious wind, they cringed in corners against the relentless downpour. The women, wrapped in sweaters and blankets, huddled over their children to offer them some degree of comfort while trying to protect them from the cold, stinging rain. The lakeside wall threatened to collapse; Riedel got the men to brace themselves against it. The men gritted against the pelting, hail-like rain and leaned with all their strength, trying to keep the wall from collapsing onto their loved ones. Only a miracle would prevent the hotel from bucking into the water rampaging through the streets of Belle Glade. The building shook and, at times, seemed to rise up, only to settle back down. Once again, the entire building rose up off its foundation then squatted down hard on its cement pilings, which ripped through the floorboards like a pin cushion, anchoring the building.

Henry listened to the wind raking the side of the store. It scraped and scratched the roof. He thought he heard a piece of siding slapping in the wind. Then the wind slowly subsided. The air was ghostly still; the eye had passed over the store. "The worst of the storm has passed," Henry said, trying to reassure the rest. "The store will hold." With a flashlight in hand, Henry walked to the front of the store. Without opening the front door, he looked outside into the night. He could see the canal had flooded its banks. Dark lake water careened down Canal Street, carrying wood, tree branches, and pails. He watched as it rose slowly up the steps then began to seep under the doors into the store. Suddenly, the wind came roaring back with even greater fury. It screamed across the roof, sending blasts through every crack.

The water continued to rise, covering the floor. Henry ran back and helped Bessie Mae Martin put the children on top of the counter. He then grabbed Bessie Mae by her waist with his big hands and hoisted her onto the counter. She reached out and took baby Robert in her arms. Henry sloshed around in ankle-deep water to the front of the store, checking on the damage to his goods and trying to think of how to keep more water from coming in. Water was rising up at the door, pouring in around the jamb's sides. The Hillsboro Canal had been transformed into a three-mile-wide raging river. There was no way he could stop the water. Black lake water lashed against the front windows. Holding Bessie Mae's hand, he stood in knee-deep water.

Henry, noticing that the water was rising fast, put a table on the counter top and opened up the trap door into the attic. Into the black hole in the ceiling, he lifted Bessie Mae. Then he handed her each of the children, followed by Tempie, before he pulled himself up out of the water. The store went dark; the water had snuffed out the kerosene lights. It was pitch black, and the flashlight had gone out. By touch, Bessie Mae gathered the children around her as she cradled Robert in her arms. Ernestine was frightened, and just like Thelma, she was afraid of the water and couldn't swim. On the outside, Henry could hear floating boxes and wooden barrels thumping against the ceiling like a herd of angry trapped animals. Everything was ruined. The water splashed at his feet. "Hey Kid the water is up over my shoes," Henry said matter-of-factly to Bessie Mae as he lifted his feet from the trap door. In darkness, Henry crawled over to his wife and wrapped his long arms around her and three of the children.

Suddenly, the winds picked up and shook the entire store. The store swayed in the winds; water pounded its sides, then it groaned, slowly lifted up, and floated off its foundation. "Oh God, we're moving," someone cried out. Like a toy dollhouse, the surging waters carried the ill-fated store away from the lake. Two hundred yards away, the large Methodist church loomed like a white granite sentinel. The water pushed the house toward the church then struck it with an Earth-shattering crunch. The impact forced the two-story church off its foundation. The two buildings continued to wobble then the smaller store caught a corner of the church and rose up at an obtuse angle. Water rushed under the store and turned it on its side, then over on its roof.

The Martins were trapped under the store. Everyone was thrown up and over into the water. They were trapped inside a lightless coffin. Then the store broke apart. Pieces of the roof and wall crashed in on the family, forcing them underwater and then it bobbed to the surface.

Ernestine slid down the ceiling onto the roof. She was thrown and dragged along by the current underwater with broken pieces of the store. The onrush bounced her like a beach ball down Canal Street. She finally reached the surface, gasped for air, then suddenly stopped. She felt cold water rushing at her face and rain pelting her like rocks. Forcing her head above the waves, she spit out the water. She did not know where she was, but she knew she was not alone. Slowly turning her head, she saw Thelma. The two girls were lodged on an overturned root stand of a massive rubber tree on the northern bank of the Hillsboro Canal. Like fingers of the hands of God, Ernestine later thought, the roots had reached and grabbed them out of the torrent and held them tight.

When the store broke up against the church, twelve-year-old Thelma Martin was crouched beside Ernestine. The impact threw her headfirst deep into the water. Gasping for air, she felt something hold her under the water. She thought, "I can't swim well, and I'm going to drown," and lost consciousness. The current ripped her away from the house and tossed her up and over the canal, throwing her against the uprooted rubber tree. Thelma struggled, but her leg was caught in-between the roots, and she couldn't move higher up the roots. Water splashed around her neck, and she fought to keep her head above the black water. She felt something on her free leg and reached down to brush it away. She felt cloth, then she felt skin, and she pulled it up out of the water over her head. It was her baby brother, Robert. Two of Tempie's children, Hattie and Carl, were caught in the same tree. Like twining fingers, the roots grabbed the five children and held them against the onslaught of the wind and the raging black water. Ernestine scratched her way higher up the root stand as the waves broke over her. The wind slapped her face, and she could see nothing; she was blind.

Thelma, holding baby Robert in one hand, crawled against the wind and water as high up the roots as she could. She held Robert above her head as waves splashed over her head. With an iron grip on the baby and a deep desire to survive, she held on, refusing to give in to her aching arms or the force of nature. Her foot, still caught on one of the roots, stopped her from moving any higher. She was afraid that if the water rose any further, she would drown. But she refused to release her baby brother. She held him with her arms straight up over her head, out of the way of the breaking waves. A board with protruding spikes was lodged in her thigh just above the knee. Pain shot through her leg, but with a supernatural stubbornness, twelve-year-old Thelma refused to give in to either the pain or the freezing water. The two Martins girls hung on. When Thelma's arms tired, she passed the baby to Ernestine then took him back again. Back and forth they passed two-year-old Robert. Beside them, Hattie struggled to hold onto her own brother until a large wave carried the boy screaming off into the night.

With Robert weighing heavy in her hands, Thelma turned to Hattie and asked her to help hold the baby. "You hold him yourself," she screamed. Her own grip on the root was precarious, and she was scared. She felt her grip slipping and began to grab at anything, first at the slippery roots, and then desperately at Thelma holding Robert above her head. Thelma pushed her away; afraid she would grab onto Robert and drown him.[91]

When the Martin store crashed into the Methodist Church, Henry Martin was thrown onto his back. The shock spun the store around and upturned it onto its roof. For a moment, it stopped in that unnatural position, as if contemplating what to do. From behind, the water piled up and pushed the store around the corner of the church, tearing away the sides. Freed, the submerged roof shot to the surface. It caught Henry Martin from below, lifted him out of the water, and threw him to one side. He bobbed in a cauldron of boiling water and broken lumber. He immediately grabbed onto part of the roof with one hand, and with the other felt around in the water for Bessie Mae. Sadly, she was not there, so he took a deep breath to dive around, looking for her, but a wave broke over his head, pelting him with pieces of water-tossed broken lumber. A beam hit his head above his eye, almost knocking him unconscious. He breathed deeply and regained his senses. He felt something struggling around his legs. It was Sonny, and he grabbed him and lifted him up and

---

[91]   Mykle, R. (2006) <u>Killer 'cane: The Deadly Hurricane of 1928</u>, *Taylor Trade Publishing pg. 161.*

onto the piece of broken roof. Suddenly, Raymond bobbed to the surface beside Henry and Sonny.

"Daddy, I'm here, too," Raymond said, grabbing onto the roof. "Hold on, Son," Henry yelled at Raymond.[92] He instinctively tightened his grip on Sonny as their makeshift raft began to spin. His eyes desperately tried to see through the night and into the angry black waves. He yelled out for Bessie Mae, but was answered only by the screeching wind. It was pitch black. Flashes of lightning glowed across the sky, and with the strobe-like light gave microsecond glimpses of a scene from the blackest reaches of hell. What had been a quiet street in small country town was now a raging torrent of black-water vomit.

The makeshift raft was tossed up and over the breaking waves. Lumber shot like missiles over their heads. The water was filled with nail-studded, jagged wood, and one board hit Sonny in the chest, implanting a nail close to his heart. Henry pulled the board away and wrapped his arm completely around Sonny. The floodwaters carried them swiftly over the Hillsboro Canal. Five-foot waves flowed over their raft. The spinning raft narrowly missed smashing into another house. Over weighted with three people on one side, it kept tipping on one end, threatening to flip over.

"I'll get on the other side so it won't sink," Raymond shouted at Henry, and before he could respond, his son swam to the other side of the roof. At that moment, a massive wave broke over them, flipping the roof up and over. In a flash of lightning, Henry saw Raymond struggling to hold on as a board violently struck his son's head, and then he saw nothing after that. Henry bobbed to the surface with Sonny still in his grip and grabbed onto another floating object, and as that was ripped from his grasped, he desperately grabbed onto another.[93] It seemed like hours that he and Sonny floated. The constant fight against the waves, current and wreckage had weakened Henry. He knew Raymond had been killed, and he was afraid he'd let Sonny slip away.

"Oh, Lord, please save my only son," Henry murmured as he felt his strength give way. Then something hit his back, and they stopped moving.

---

[92] Mykle, R. (2006) Killer 'cane: The Deadly Hurricane of 1928, *Taylor Trade Publishing pg. 172.*

[93] Mykle, R. (2006) Killer 'cane: The Deadly Hurricane of 1928, *Taylor Trade Publishing pg. 172.*

"Daddy, I've got hold of a telephone pole," Sonny cried out. Henry let go of the post and grabbed onto the top of the supports of a telephone pole. The water was fifteen feet deep. Exhausted, Henry wrapped his arms around Sonny and locked his legs in the cross bars and held on for the rest of the night.[94]

As the water receded, Henry and Sonny climbed down from atop their precarious telephone perch. The water was three-feet deep in all directions. When Henry hit the ground, he almost doubled over. His foot was badly sprained. He felt his face and the cut above his eye. Sonny was naked, because the water had completely stripped him of his clothes. He had two nail punctures in his chest, one just above the heart and another below it. His chin had a severe gash, but was no longer bleeding. He stared at his son, who stoically stared back without even so much as a whimper. Henry reached down and hugged Sonny, something he rarely did. Keeping on top of the dike road, father and son started off toward Belle Glade, and it was during this time that they truly witnessed the true scope of this disaster. There were entangled and toppled over trees, downed power lines and dead bodies scattered everywhere. So many dead that Henry tried to shield his son from these gruesome images of dead corpses. There were so many dead bodies that they were almost impossible to even count.

By seven o'clock, Bill and Mattie Mae Boots had to make a quick decision. Outside, it was pitch black. Water reached their knees, and wind gusts blew them sideways. It took them fifteen minutes fighting the wind and stinging rain to make the hundred yards. Finally, they reached the Thirsk house. Three of the four steps of the cement stoop leading up into the house were underwater. Inside the Thirsk house, two gas lanterns burned brightly, casting a yellow pallor through the gloom. When the Bootses arrived, nearly everyone left in Sebring Farms milled about the Thirsk house. In the front room, most black families huddled around the few chairs and sat on the floor. In the kitchen and back rooms, the white families had bunched up—a total of sixty-three people. Most of the people huddling in the Thirsk house had experienced the Great Miami and Nassau Hurricanes of 1926. Thirsk and his wife and eleven neighbours had weathered the Moore Haven storm in the house. It had been bad. The

---

[94]   Mykle, R. (2006) <u>Killer 'cane: The Deadly Hurricane of 1928</u>, *Taylor Trade Publishing pg. 172.*

house shook just like now. The winds howled just like now. But this wind was different. It had a different tone, more guttural, more monstrous. In 1926, they had not experienced the center of the storm; the force of an eyewall never passed directly over them, so in these regards, both storms were significantly different than this one.

In the Thirsk house, after the dike gave way and water in the house rose to over four feet, the men went into the bedroom, moved the double bed aside, and placed a large wooden trunk that held all of Mrs. Thirsk's valuables and heirloom clothes under the trapdoor to the attic. Charles Thomas pulled himself up then reached down to help the women and children up into the attic. Vernie Boots was, at fourteen, a man, and one of the last to go up. As they were handing people up through the attic, a gust of wind hit the house and in shook, breaking a window. Wind and water stormed in. Vernie lost his balance, slipped, and fell on top of the broken glass, gashing his right hand to the bone near his fingers. Blood spurted out, and he wrapped a piece of shirt around it to stem the flow. The water was rushing at his chest and rising. He could taste the muddy water, and it tasted like death.

The white families were on one side, not wanting to mix with the blacks, and they huddled together quietly, listening to the freight train roar of the wind and the rain whipping at the roof. During the lulls, the cries and lamenting wails of the black families were heard as they prayed out loud and bemoaned their plight. It was dark, and sixty-three people were trapped in a coffin-like air pocket in the cramped attic, one on top of the other. A flashlight would come on, then quickly be turned off to conserve the batteries. Except for two vents at each end of the attic, there was no other opening but the trap door down to the raging waters. The house trembled as the water tried to lift it off its foundation. They had to make ready to escape. There was only one way out—through the roof.

Taking the axe he had grabbed from the kitchen, Charles Thomas began to chip away at the roof. Thomas swung up with all his might at the roof, as wood splinters sprayed on everyone. He with all of his might swung again, and eventually he hit with a crunch the thick metal roof, which had been nailed tightly over the wood. Swinging the heavy axe upward, pieces of thick wooden plank and metal sheeting grudgingly gave way. Desperately, he swung again and again until the axe finally broke through.

Thomas had managed to cut open a small hole. Wet, cold wind blasted through the opening. The winds howled in like a screaming banshee, with low moans and ghostly whistles. He squeezed through the hole. Sleet-like wind and rain pelted his face, stinging his eyes and his cheeks, forcing him to turn away from the wind. He squeezed through the opening, grabbed the metal ribs of the roof, and held on. A gust of wind caught him and flung his legs out from under him. He fell, slamming onto the rain-slick metal roof. He held on and began to peel back the metal roofing. The hole was bigger. Thirsk shoved himself up through. Charles Thomas tried to move out of the way when the now floating house violently hit the new Clewiston Road bank. The entire house shook. Jarred, Thomas lost his grip just as a gust caught him, and he tumbled backward. Thirsk watched helplessly as the wind flung him off the roof into the black, whirling waters.

Thirsk squeezed through the hole, gained a hold on the roof, and then pulled his wife up after him. Grasping at whatever piece of roof she could get a hold on, Mrs. Thirsk crawled to the peak of the roof, where she could get a better grip. The house crushed violently a second time against the road and sent a violent shudder through the structure that nearly shook Thirsk off the roof. He reached down through the hole and grabbed a boy. In his strong right hand, he pulled Mutt Thomas out through the hole. Thirsk pushed him up toward the top of the roof, where his wife was. He reached down for another person when the house lifted up and crashed onto the roadbed one last time, and it then collapsed. The three people on the roof were thrown off into the night.

The house shifted again and slammed against the raised roadbed and shook, then settled. Again every beam and two-by-four of hard Florida pine moaned as it strained against the force of the water and the wind. Once more, the house shifted and smashed against the roadbed. People screamed inside as the house turned and tilted, and one last time a wave lifted it up and it came down on the raised roadbed and broke apart. The sides buckled as the studs and slats broke like toothpicks, with a series of sickening snaps; the roof suddenly collapsed, trapping the sixty people left inside, dragging them down into a water-filled mass coffin. Desperately, they scrambled for the openings, holding their breaths, grabbing their children and loved ones. The roof strained then separated from the house.

Vernie Boots shot a glance at his mother. Flashlights went on. The precious batteries were needed to show the way out—and for that matter, any way out.

"Whatever happens, stay together," he heard his mother cry out in the dark. It was the last thing he ever heard her say.[95] With a blood-chilling moan, the roof broke up. Vernie, fighting the drowning waters, instinctively grabbed at anything to keep from being pulled under. His hand reached a piece of the ceiling that bobbed up under him, and he wrapped his arms around it and held on for dear life. He felt the water rush over him, pulling him down. But the buoyant wood broke the surface, and he gasped at rain-soaked air. Below, he could see the eerie glow of flashlights briefly lighting up the escape hole of the roof six feet underwater and sinking. There were people still inside. Then the lights went out.

It was pitch black, and there were no lights whatsoever-no moon, or even stars; but simply just pure darkness. The rain was black; the water was black; the waves were black; the air was black. He might as well have been blind as well as dead. But he hung on. Vernie Boots grasped that precious piece of wood and nails as he hung on to his life. He screamed out for his mother, his father, his brothers, but sadly was only answered by the howling roar of the strong, gusty winds. It screamed in his face—the howls of the dead, the dead that he might soon be joining. He fought to keep afloat, fought to keep his head into the wind. He fought with all his might to keep from turning over into the black, merciless waters. Soaked, cold, and pelted by wind-driven rain, Vernie Boots hung onto his precarious life raft, not knowing whether he was the last person alive on the face of the Earth.

Blown off the Thirsk house roof, Charles Thomas came up bobbing. With all his full strength, he struggled to swim toward the house. This was a great challenge in itself, because with each stroke the current carried him farther away from the house. In the flashes of lightning, he saw the house, saw it stopped and saw it shook. A wave broke over him, plunging him underwater, and he lost sight of the house. Caught in the current, he was dragged under. Desperately, he grabbed at floating pieces of wood and trees, but could not get a firm grip. He struggled to keep his head above

[95] Mykle, R. (2006) Killer 'cane: The Deadly Hurricane of 1928, *Taylor Trade Publishing pg. 166.*

water. In front of him he saw a white wave, then a fountain of dirty white water. There were the top crossbars of a telephone pole, and he lunged at the arm and pulled himself up. He hung there all night, wondering whether he could go on living considering he had lost his entire family.

Holding his head down against the stinging cold rain, Mutt Thomas held onto the peak of the roof. In front of him was Mrs. Thirsk, her dress blowing like a storm flag. Mutt looked back at where he had just crawled up. He saw Mr. Thirsk reaching into the hole. Who would come out next? Was it his mother or one of his sisters who would emerge? He glanced back at Mrs. Thirsk, and he saw absolute terror on his facial features as she opened her mouth in a scream muffled by the roaring wind. He looked back down when the house jolted suddenly, wobbled, and then tilted up on its side for one long, agonizing second before breaking apart. He tumbled from his perch and fell into the raging black waters. Almost immediately, a corner post shot out of the water like a missile and splashed down near him. With a couple of hard strokes, he made it to the post and wrapped both arms around it. He was not sure where the water was carrying him. For a while, he thought he was out in the middle of the lake since the waves were so high and kept breaking over him one after another. All he could wonder now was if these waves would ever stop.

The Hughes family huddled in their houseboat. The wind viciously buffeted the houseboat, and it began to sway like a rocking horse, first side to side, and then from stern to bow. Edna was afraid. Although she had taught hundreds of young children to read and write, no one had taught her how to swim. She was afraid of water; she was afraid of drowning. The rising water in the canal pulled at the mooring lines, and the boat strained. One of the mooring lines broke, and the boat was violently flipped around, and then shook hard. The boat listed on its side and began to sink. John grabbed Edna and Paul and fought his way to the deck. The boat heaved up; he grabbed his wife in his right arm and Paul in his left just as a wave of black water threw them overboard into the raging canal waters. They bobbed up to the surface, John desperately holding his family. Edna Hughes threw her arms around John's shoulder, grasping him tightly while trying to help him hold their son. A wave broke over their heads. She spit out mud-flavored water and gasped. Her hands were raw and tired, and she felt them numbing in the cold water. Brush and boards, tossed by the water, knocked her hands back until she could no longer hold on.

The three people were thrown over and under the water. John held his family tightly against him until they were caught on some debris. The suction of the undertow quickly ripped his wife and son from his arms. At this time, Edna felt her husband grab at her then she felt the strength of his large hands disappear and she gagged on another wave and slipped away. Trying to grab the two, he felt them break from his clutch, and then he was alone. He wanted to scream, but no sound came out of his mouth. His throat was clogged with water, mud, and agony.

As the eye of the storm passed over the Padgett house in Pahokee, the family members looked at each other, wondering if the storm was finally over. The silence, after such a constant wind roar, was very eerie as they listened for sounds, but heard none. They were in the center, the core, the very heart of the storm. "Suddenly, we all felt funny. We had to grasp for air. We couldn't breathe," Lillian said.[96] As the eye passed directly over their house, the atmospheric pressure dropped so low that the Padgetts experienced oxygen deprivation and nearly fainted. The barometric pressure had fallen dramatically, a sure indication that they were in the heart of the storm and that the worst was not over. Outside, two of the black farm hands walked up to the house to report the storm damage. Calvin told them to return quickly to their homes, as this was the eye of the storm and the worst winds were coming right behind it. Not realizing the urgency of the matter, the two men left the Padgett house in a slow and unassuming walk, obviously not believing that the storm was not over. Sadly, they were never seen or heard from again and were presumed dead.

The lull lasted one hour and fifteen minutes. The hurricane's eye looked directly down on Pahokee, examined its handiwork, and then, unsatisfied, gathered up more strength. Taking one last breath, it aimed its total fury at Pahokee. The storm had saved its worst for Pahokee. Behind the Padgett house, the water rose in rapid increments, carrying trees and large sections of houses, barns and fences. Flashes of lightning gave a strobe-light glance through the driving rain to anyone staring out of the house. The Pelican River had returned to its own. Surging waters angrily

---

[96] Mykle, R. (2006) Killer 'cane: The Deadly Hurricane of 1928, *Taylor Trade Publishing pg. 168.*

reclaimed its old banks and victoriously charged over them. The town of Pahokee perched on its sand ridge and became an island, a frail refuge in an angry sea of black lake water.

The folks inside heard a sharp, cracking sound coming from the roof over the roar of the wind. The eastern ceiling of the house came crashing down. Rainwater flooded the top floors, and water oozed through the ceilings. Another soaking wet family who had lost their home stumbled into the Padgett house. Even the houses on the sand ridge, thought to be flood-proof, were being swept away. Water was crashing at the backdoor steps. Lillian wondered at that moment whether the house would hold. Calvin Shive gathered the families together, and they prayed, as a long lost people prayed thousands of years before. Over the roaring wind scouring the Padgett's Pahokee house, Calvin Shive heard a vague pounding noise coming from behind the kitchen. "Listen," he said, and they heard it again. "Look out back. There's a house floating by!" Dan called out.[97]

In the glow of lightning flashes and flashlight beams, Calvin and Dan watched in horrific fascination as a one-story house with two desperate people holding onto the roof slowly floated by the back yard. Suddenly, it turned and lodged up on their back yard, settling at an obtuse angle. The two men ran out and helped the couple off the roof and brought them into the house. Lillian, in the bedroom with Duncan, was not aware of the new arrivals. Duncan had trouble breathing, and she was trying to comfort him when she noticed the wall breathing. It moved in and out. She yelled for her father. The bedroom wall had begun to tear away from the house. Outside, Calvin and Dan gathered up some long planks, nailed them to the wall, and secured it to the floor. As a carpenter, it was all Calvin could do, but as an ordained minister, he could pray, and yes indeed-pray he did. For now, they were all in the hands of God.

At 8:18pm, the anemometer at the University of Florida's Agricultural Experiment Station, near Belle Glade, was destroyed; its last wind speed reading was 92 mph. At almost that exact moment, a similar instrument was destroyed at the U.S. Agriculture Department's Cane Breeding Station at Canal Point, about 15 miles north along the lakeshore. Its last reading was 75 mph. As had happened at the telephone company at West Palm

---

[97]   Mykle, R. (2006) <u>Killer 'cane: The Deadly Hurricane of 1928</u>, *Taylor Trade Publishing pg. 177.*

Beach, the Everglades Experimental Station showed a dramatic drop in air pressure. At about 9:15pm, the winds died down at the Everglades Experimental Station. Researcher R.V. Allison timed the lull—apparently, the passage of the eye of the storm occurred at 9:25pm, with the winds returning at 9:40pm. The Canal Point station timed it at 9:30pm to 10:05pm. Right in the middle of the eerie lull, Allison saw a remarkable sight. A Ford automobile emerged from the darkness. Inside it were four adults and eight children. They had somehow kept the car on the road at the height of the storm. Allison said later the station's rain gauge measured 11.35 inches, but he wondered about the credibility of that number because the top of the rain gauge blew off, and that could have affected the readings.

"During the height of the storm in this section there is little doubt that the wind reached speeds of over 140 to 150 miles per hour," Allison would write later from Belle Glade. If those were sustained winds, then after having crossed 40 miles of land, the storm was still a strong Category 4, and perhaps as little as 5 miles per hour below the threshold for a Category 5 storm. It must be noted that storms usually lose strength rapidly as they pass over land area because first, they are denied their rich, moist supply of energy in the form of warm ocean water; and second, because friction with the land surface impacts the storm's winds and weakens the system. So the next question is, how was it that the Great Okeechobee Hurricane was powerful when it crossed the Lake Okeechobee as when it first plowed through Puerto Rico and the other small islands of the Atlantic Ocean? The answer, once again, is in the eye, the quiet center around which the storm rotates like a massive wheel on an axle. The eye is where the storm sucks up warm ocean water to feed its winds.

When the eye passes over land, it weakens. But that center had to cross only 40 miles; much of it was swampland, from Palm Beach to Lake Okeechobee. The eye was 25 miles in diameter. As the western eyewall was almost upon Belle Glade, the eastern eyewall had just crossed the coast. The eye had been continuing to draw warm water—and energy—from the ocean. It hadn't had much time to weaken. However, it must be noted that if the storm had hit anywhere in Florida, or even southern Louisiana, the hurricane would have weakened at a faster rate. Friction with the ground causes the storm to weaken, or outright kills it, especially when it passes over trees, buildings, hills, and other obstructions. But this hurricane, once it got through the thin strip of development along the coast, was crossing flat terrain consisting of fields and swampland. Added to that, it could have fed on the waters of the lake itself. The storm weakens very little between the coast and Lake Okeechobee, only by about 10 mph.

By late afternoon, as the full force of the storm began to arrive in West Palm Beach, auto repairman Milburn A. Bishop left his home at 722 Sunset Road and took refuge in a nearby house. "The sky turned that peculiar colour," he later wrote, "and then, 'Oh Boy'!"

The wind was coming out of the northeast, and "the rain just came down by the bucketful. The ladies then set the table and had plenty of hot coffee, so we sat down at the table and were eating when it started in again, as we thought, 'full blast.' In about five minutes, we felt the house quiver all over and heard a great crash to the rear. It was the roof of the adjacent apartment, which came sailing into the house. Of course, that scared Mama half to death."[98]

Five minutes later, a garage at a nearby home smashed into the other corner of the house. Each time, Bishop wrote, he expected the house to collapse. "Somehow, through the grace of God it held on, and the wind continued to blow for another two hours." Bishop watched, like a spectator in a gruesome flying parade of homes, as the structures on the street lost their roofs one by one. At the county courthouse, skylights in the Criminal Court of Records broke, and water poured in.

Up the coast at Jupiter, many residents, both black and white, took refuge in the schoolhouse, which weathered the storm much better than did their homes. One cement-block house collapsed during the storm, crushing several members of a family-the only reported deaths in Jupiter. The Jupiter Lighthouse, the red brick sentinel that had witnessed many storms, was said to have swayed a remarkable seventeen inches "as mortar squeezed from between bricks like toothpaste." Prior to the hurricane, the light had been converted from oil burners to electricity. As the storm reached the coast, all power lines were downed, and the lighthouse auxiliary generator failed to work. Captain Seabrook, the keeper, refused to let the light go out and scrambled to reinstall the old oil burners. Without electricity, the light's mantle had to be turned by hand, and Seabrook, who was suffering

---

[98]   Kleinberg, E. (2003) *Black Cloud-The Deadly Hurricane of 1928*, Carroll & Graf Publishers, pg. 77.

from blood poisoning at the time, was prepared to push the apparatus around all night. His son Franklin, noticing the bright red streaks on his father's arm, stepped in to work the mantle, continuing to near exhaustion. As a result, the light shone through one of the century's most dreadful storms, and later the younger Seabrook was officially commended for his heroism.[99]

Various reports gave different times for the lull in West Palm Beach. Ruth Stewart, the dentist's wife, said it started at 5:40pm. Another West Palm Beach report, by Charles H. Ruggles, a consulting engineer who had his own barometer, puts it between 6:30pm and 7:30pm. Even then, weather savvy South Floridians knew that this was not the end of the storm, and it would soon come back and strike from the opposite direction, with the same or greater fury. Tommie Rickards, only fourteen at the time, felt the lull, as it was dead calm. A candle on a sill didn't even flicker. His father, Tom, stepped outside the courthouse and saw a sky he would describe as "an inverted funnel, with stars shining through the opening overhead." Meanwhile, Ruth Stewart drank cold coffee while her husband and sons had some bread and milk. She knew the horrors of the last few hours were about to be repeated, perhaps even more viciously.

Milburn A. Bishop guessed he had about thirty to forty minutes to spare before the storm struck, so he raced back to his home to secure it by nailing up any and everything he could—provided there was anything left. Arriving home, he found one off its hinges; two men helped him nail it back. He also nailed up other openings, added some braces, and raced back to the home where he'd waited out the storm's first half. He looked at a clock. He had been out about thirty minutes. Then the wind returned even stronger—this time from the opposite direction. Bishop watched as part of another home smashed into the house he was in, and then its own chimney crashed in; finally, a bedroom window blew in. Men huddled with nearly hysterical women in the center of the home as water poured in from the hole made when the chimney tore away. Bishop and the other men dashed around the home, taking the closet doors from their hinges and nailing them over the windows. It took all four of them to hold a closet door over a window long enough to nail it.

---

[99]   Barnes, J. (2007) *Florida's Hurricane History*, Chapel Hill, The University of North Carolina Press, pg. 129.

As Bishop checked in the bathroom, he heard the wind screeching over his head. He climbed up and shone a light up into the attic and saw the sides of the house moving in and out like lungs expanding and contracting during a breath. "The hair still rises on my back every time I think of the tremendous, blood-curdling shrieks it would let out." He knew the roof could not last long and feared its inevitable separation would kill not only him and his companions, but probably his neighbours as well. So he gathered with the other men, and they agreed to try to get into the attic to brace its walls. Some passed shelves from closets up into the attic for two men to nail to the wall. Bishop thought to himself that if the roof gave way, he could ride one of the shelves down the street.

At Ruth Stewart's home, within fifteen minutes of the storm's return, the wind tore apart the porch and the rain flooded in. However, just down the road in Lake Worth, J. Luther "Bo" Wright, the *Palm Beach Post's* composing room superintendent, had worried that his home at Fifth Avenue and K Street would not survive the return of the hurricane winds. During the lull, he had grabbed his wife and small son and some blankets and food and raced down an alley to a nearby building. It was the two-story parsonage of the First Congregational Church at 10th Avenue and N Street. Wright quickly helped cover two blown-out windows, and everyone waited out the second half. It came with such ferocity, "we all just thought it was the end of everything. I held the baby in my arms for hours and kept Vera close to me. There were nineteen people crowded into the dining room, and just a candle burning." Parson Lillian B. Fulton took a Bible from a shelf. "All the women were on their knees, praying," Bishop would recall, "while the men snatched doors from the closets upstairs and nailed them to the windows. No lying. This was a horrible night." Sadly, an Episcopal church was demolished, and Lake Worth City Hall lost three of its walls.[100]

Charles Ruggles, the West Palm Beach engineer, placed the height of the storm's second half at about 8:40pm. The walls of his home vibrated violently, and he could see them bowing out at the bottom. Fearing that the roof would collapse any minute, he grabbed his wife and the two threw open the door, which disintegrated almost immediately, as they

---

[100] Kleinberg, E. (2003) *Black Cloud-The Deadly Hurricane of 1928*, Carroll & Graf Publishers, pg. 80.

crawled about 30 feet from their home, lying in the open in about five inches of water for the next two hours. About 11:00pm, the two developed the shakes from the chill. They decided they could get into their car and dashed the 75 feet to it in wind that bent them over. Ruggles found a pack of cigarettes and lit one with the car's cigarette lighter. The two spent the night in the car.

Charles Sears, Jr., and Effie Sears Ransom had been born in the South Bay with a big tree in the yard. It was less than a mile from the dike. Their parents had come, like so many other migrant workers from the Bahamas. They came from the island of Exuma. Charles Rufus Sears, Sr., one of seventeen children, had come from Forbes Hill around 1917, and Lucinda from Mosstown around 1920; they were married in Miami in 1921. They found no jobs in Miami and heard there were some positions available to work in the farms fields around the lake, picking tomatoes and beans. Lucinda had had two boys and a daughter and was ready to deliver her fourth child when the storm came. An aunt and her two sons decided to leave. They went down the road and were never seen again, dead or alive.

As the wind grew, the roof came off, and rising water approached the porch. Lucinda grabbed little Effie, not yet 2, and Charles reached Cleo, 5, and Charles Jr., 3. They looked for a high spot, but saw only an old tree in their front yard. They ran to it and climbed high into the branches. The mother went first, and the father passed the boys up. As the wind howled, Charles was losing hope. He kept saying, "We're going to die." His wife didn't want to hear it. He began to sing: "Jesus, Lover of my soul, let me to Thy bosom fly. While the nearer waters roll, while the tempest still is high. Hide me, O my savior, hide, 'til the storm of life is past." Lucinda saw three bolts of lightning and took that as a sign from God. But sometime in the long night, three-year-old Charles, Jr., slid from his father's arms. He was gone.

Post employees Beryl Lewis and Bill Matthews stood in the lobby of Matthews' apartment house, 325 Gruber Place. They watched out a window, in amazement, as a service station across the street, built from strong concrete block, collapsed piece by piece until all that was left were the pumps and the plumbing. With the eye passing, Lewis, now separated from Matthews, sped in the lull to the offices of the *Post*. With no electric power, everything had stopped, except the wind. Outside the newspaper building, a man was clinging to a fence. As fearful as he was of the winds, he was just as worried that he wouldn't get to his post as a night watchman across the Intracoastal Waterway in Palm Beach. Lewis and another man dragged the watchman into the *Post* building. Lewis and others then took the barometer from the wall and began taking pressure readings every fifteen minutes, and the pressure got so low that they started to feel it aching in their eardrums.

In West Palm Beach's black section, at the Miller home, young Clothilda felt the winds grow stronger and the walls shake. Suddenly, the porch of the home across Henrietta Avenue came apart, flew through the air, and crashed through her bedroom window. "We got out of the house and ran across the street," she recalled later. "You could see things flying. Afterward, I wasn't looking for anything flying. I was flying myself." They ran to the home of their neighbour, Mr. Ewell, who had offered his place in emergency. Clothilda would recall that for several minutes, no one said anything. If they were praying, she said later, they were keeping it to themselves. Someone made coffee, while the men tried to calm the women. In the meantime, Clothilda snoozed off in a chair, but no one else slept.

There was little concern about Palm Beach, the famed island of the rich. Fortunately, most of its wealthy residents were part-timers and were up north, not to return until winter drove them to Florida's warm, tropical climate. The Palm Beach Yacht Club lost its pier. The Northwood warehouse district was heavily damaged. St. Ann's Church lost the roof of its school. Palm Beach High's brick clock tower came crashing down. Two 75' feet Coast Guard cutters, from a base at Fernandina Beach in Florida's extreme northeast corner, had become caught in the worst of it just off the Palm Beach coast. The skippers, Morris Anderson on the "230" and Richard Abernathy on the "188," wrestled their ships during the storm through an inlet and into Lake Worth, the body of water located between Palm Beach and the mainland that is part of the Intracoastal Waterway. The seas dragged their anchors, and ocean water poured into the engine rooms. The "230" lost its steering gear and the "188" its rudder, and both slammed into the land. About 150 feet offshore, the eight men on each ship had thrown on life vests and dived into the rolling water. All sixteen climbed, exhausted onto land and slept where they landed. At first light, they found the "230" missing 40 feet of keel and the "188" punctured by holes at several places. They figured the ships were totally destroyed. The crew members insisted on working street patrols and were still there at midnight late on Monday, September 17th.

The barograph reading at the AT&T office in West Palm Beach showed a steep drop in pressure-that might mean nothing to a layperson, but to a professional meteorologist that would mean the storm was either getting stronger or getting closer to that location. Overall, it showed air pressure readings remaining steady through most of Saturday, September 15th. Then, just after midnight, the line started to slowly drop, but then just after midnight, the readings started to show a steep drop in pressure until noon. The reading bottomed out at 27.43 inches, with normal at 30 inches and a change of even a tenth of an inch lower than the 27.61-inch level reached by the furious hurricane, which had leveled boomtown Miami and inundated Moore Haven in 1926. And it is the lowest pressure ever recorded in the United States to that time, lower even than the 27.49 for the Great Galveston Hurricane of 1900. Weather officials said at the time that, while the Great Lake Okeechobee Hurricane of 1928 had a lower barometric pressure than the Great Miami Hurricane of 1926, they believed the 1926 storm had stronger winds. Their evidence: trees in Palm Beach County had some leaves left, while those in the Miami area were completely stripped, even those in dense groves.

The low pressure reading measured at West Palm Beach in the 1928 storm was so low that most meteorologists at the time surmised that this record would never be broken. But it was—and only nine years later—when it reached a low of 26.35 inches, more than one inch lower, on September 3, 1935. That storm, called "The Great Labour Day Hurricane of 1935", tore through the Florida Keys with maximum sustained winds of 160 mph. The storm's barometric pressure set an all-time low record that still stands today. Because a hurricane's strength is measured solely by barometric pressure, the 1935 storm is listed as the most powerful ever recorded in the United States; stronger even than Camille, which flattened Mississippi in 1969 with top winds at landfall of an unbelievable 190 mph, but a barometric pressure low of 26.84 inches. Interestingly, the Great Labour Day Storm of 1935, Camille, and Andrew are the only storms ever to strike the U.S. mainland at Category 5 intensity on the Saffir-Simpson Hurricane Wind Scale. Category 5 storms have winds of at least 157 mph.

All along the coast, piers, docks, and waterfront structures were lifted by the tide and carried for hundreds of yards. In some instances, houses were raised from their foundations and spun ninety degrees, their porches and stairs twisted into tangled arrangements. Trees were knocked down on virtually every street, wrapped in webs of electric cables. Throughout the area, the problems faced by the storm survivors were similar to those endured by survivors of the Great Miami Hurricane of 1926-they lacked food and water, thousands of homeless were in need of shelter, and they suffered the emotional wounds of having to cope with disaster. At least twenty-six lives were lost on the coast.

By noon on that day of the storm, many of the people around the lake had heard of the approaching hurricane. In South Bay, several men took the initiative to drive the maze of roads around the lake to spread the news and warn people to seek safe shelter. Many women and children gathered on a large barge anchored in the lake. But as the afternoon progressed and the great storm grew nearer, hundreds of families, landowners, and labourers went about their work on the broad, flat terrain with no idea of what was about to occur.

Normally, the water level in the lake was maintained slightly above the level of the land so that the water could be drained off as needed. In the weeks before the storm, heavy rains had kept the lake level high and filled the ditches and canals around the glades to accommodate the requests by fishermen and residents along the drainage canals to keep water levels up. By September 10th, the lake level had risen three feet in thirty days, and the ten or more inches of rain that fell during the storm added to the burden. But it was the intense hurricane winds, estimated at over 140 mph at Canal Point that lifted the waters of Lake Okeechobee and tossed them southward, completely washing away entire communities and the dikes that were supposed to protect them. According to some reports, the waters rose from four to six feet in the first hour of the storm, and still-water marks in some buildings were almost eight feet above the ground. Few were able to survive this incredible wall of water. In the darkness of the next few hours, Florida experienced its greatest recorded tragedy.

Kreamer Island was one of the first areas to feel the effects of the rushing floodwaters. Here, as in most of the communities around the lake, the majority of the people chased by the rising waters were black

Bahamian migrant labourers, brought to the fertile Okeechobee region to work the fields. As news of the storm first spread on the island, labourers and land owners, women and children, both black and white, gathered together in any shelter they could find. In some homes, twenty to thirty people took refuge and were forced to stand on tables and chairs above the rising waters. Many of these homes were lifted off their foundations and bashed into rows of pines, and others were swept more than half a mile away from their original locations. Amazingly, only one drowning occurred on the island.

On Torry Island, residents tried their best to escape to the mainland when word spread of the hurricane, but by this time the causeway was already under water. In a period of desperation, twenty-three people returned to John Aunapu's packing house, where they stood on tractors, trucks, and sacks of field crates or anything else they could find to keep themselves above the flood waters. The sturdy structure rocked and swayed in the ferocious winds and driving rain on the tin roof. Floodwaters soon covered the structure's dirt floor and forced them upward into the rafters. After the structure was battered by uprooted custard apple trees, it heaved then folded into the dark waters of a nearby canal.

One man kicked out a gable near the roof of the structure just before it sank and escaped into the branches of a tree, pulling his fiancée from the building as well. They soon were swimming in the pitch-black torrent and, after several minutes, were fortunate to grab onto the frame of a large floating dredge. Several others from the packing house miraculously found safety on this same dredge. Others were swept far beyond the dredge. Margaret Beader was swept into Belle Glade Bridge, where she badly injured her knee, and then onto a dike, a total distance of some three and a half miles. Unclothed by the wringing waters, and unable to walk because of her injury, she was not found for two days after the storm had passed. Some of the Torry Island survivors were swept into treetops, and one woman successfully tied herself to a stationary telegraph pole. A teenage boy outdistanced everyone when he was carried some eight miles to the Experiment Station by the floodwaters. Ten of the twenty-three people in the packing house were drowned, and they were some of the first victims of the Okeechobee flood.

Burning the bodies of the drowned storm victims near Canal Point, after the Okeechobee Hurricane of 1928 (Courtesy of the Florida State Archives).

A coloured family of two men and a woman on Jess' farm, after the roof had left their house, took refuge in a pop ash tree. The tree bent before the gusts, nearly drowning them in waves, but rebounding long enough to give them a breath of fresh air before immersing them again. Nearly all the trees on the island were uprooted, but by good fortune theirs remained, and all three survived. At Chosen, the small frame house owned by Pat Burke provided shelter for nineteen persons. Realizing that the rising water was soon to flood the structure, they all rushed into the attic, where the men worked frantically to break a hole through the roof. Ripping through the corrugated iron and sheathing was no easy task, but they managed to create an opening through which most of the group crawled out into the stinging rain and wind. Just as they had gathered on the roof, the lake broke through the dike and sent a huge wave that rolled the structure over on its side. Sadly, only two of the nineteen survived.

Twenty Chosen residents took refuge in Isaac West's store, which lost its roof during the storm. They managed to survive by cramming into a bathroom. Another house full of people was floated by wind and flood for half a mile. Its journey was apparently so gentle that those inside were unaware of its movement until it crashed into a railroad embankment. Those caught in the storm without shelter were fortunate to find any high ground. Chosen's Indian mound was one of the few elevated sites, and it provided escape for thirty-one residents and labourers. Throughout the night, this group clung onto the grasses on the lee side of the mound to avoid being blown or washed off into the dark waters below. Surprisingly, this entire group survived the wrath of this storm. The mound was reported to have been eight feet, ten inches above the surrounding ground, and at the peak of the flood, water was two feet above the surrounding land and the crest of the mound.

At Belle Glade, the largest community affected on the lakeshore, the destruction and loss of life was of staggering proportions. Many of the town residents took refuge in two hotels. In houses throughout the area, residents fought the storm by working feverishly to chop through the ceilings with axes to provide an escape route into their attics. In many cases, families survived by clinging onto the attic rafters with their faces just above water.

Frede Aunapu was a dragline operator in Belle Glade. He and twenty-one others, including his girlfriend, Elizabeth Beader, had gone to a packing house made of corrugated tin. Wind and waves battered the place, and floating trees banged against it. Strong men broke into tears and prayed for rescue. A ceiling joist broke and snaked its way down Aunapu's back and through his pants leg. He was carried underwater as his belt wrapped around the wood. Aunapu struggled desperately underwater for what might have been as long as five minutes. He ran out of air and began breathing water and began to sense what it was like to drown. But somehow he got free and made a dash to the surface, his throat burning as he spit up water from his lungs. He grabbed his girlfriend, and the two crawled through a hole in the roof. They worked their way to a floating tree. A wave knocked Elizabeth off. She stayed under, and Aunapu dove for her. He searched through black water 10 feet below, felt a body, brought it up, and placed it in a tree. He ran his hand through the person's hair. It was kinky. Aunapu had pulled up a black man. Elizabeth was still down there. He searched again, and this time he found her. He pulled her up and pounded her back to get the water out of her lungs. The two climbed aboard a floating clump of trees. Aunapu left Elizabeth on the edge and moved to the middle, figuring it was safest. But as his girlfriend watched, the cluster of trees rolled inward, squeezing Aunapu like a wringer.

The 1928 Mass Burial of Black Hurricane Victims at Tamarind Avenue & 25ᵗʰ Street (Courtesy of the Florida State Archives).

Eleven people took refuge in the 'storm proof' home of Mahlon Eggleston. As floodwaters lifted the structure off the ground, it soon crashed into another wayward home. It was discovered that two women and a man were holding onto a windowsill on the outside of the Eggleston house, having been dashed into the waters after their house collapsed. The occupants broke a windowpane and brought the three people inside the drifting home. The house soon crashed with a thud into some unknown object, pitched to one side, and came to a sudden stop. The two rooms on one side of the house rolled under the water, and the pressure broke out half the windows. In one of these rooms was Mrs. Eggleston, her six-year-old daughter, and her infant son. Their quarters submerged in the flooded darkness, they could only survive by breathing the air trapped near the ceiling of the room.

Immediately after the house came to a sudden stop, Ray Browne, Mrs. Eggleston's nephew, struggled through the house to their door. Without hesitation, he dove through the submerged doorway and swam up to the air pocket where the threesome was trapped. He then proceeded to rescue the two children, one at a time, by swimming back through the doorway while clutching them under his arm. But when he returned for his aunt, she finally allowed Ray to rescue her after Ray's father agreed to swim before them with a flashlight. Similar rescues followed in another submerged room of the house, and soon all were gathered in the attic, the only remaining refuge. Because they feared the house might collapse and

215

sink in the howling storm, they decided to cut a hole through the roof to allow their escape. Once again, Ray swam down into the house in search of tools for the job, but none could be found. Instead, the men proceeded to cut through the gable end of the house with a pocket knife, a job that took them three hours to complete. As they peered out the opening, they saw that the house was stuck on the opposite bank of the canal, over a quarter of a mile from where it had originally stood.

At South Bay, news of the storm's quick arrival forced many to take refuge on Huffman's barge. Nearly 200 people survived the storm aboard this vessel, working through the night on a bucket brigade to bail out the vessel's hold. Some residents unwisely abandoned their homes when the waters first approached and sought shelter in their automobiles. Most were soon thrown from the vehicles into the raging waters, where they struggled to hold onto any passing floating debris.

Stories abound, as in many other hurricanes, of survivors sharing rafts of debris or treetop branches with water moccasins. One account was by historian Lawrence E. Will about his encounter with one of these snakes, who said, "I could hear the pitiful mewing of a kitten. Between the hulls of my barge and another adjacent one, huddled on a bit of floating trash, and almost touching one another, were a kitten, a rabbit and a good sized moccasin. By lying flat on the deck, I could rescue the kitten while the venomous serpent looked on with apathy, too concerned with his own worries to have any enmity for anyone. That snake was like the wildcat in the Moore Haven storm. He was crouched on one limb of a tree while a badly frightened Negro clung to another. The Negro later stated, "Dat wildcat wasn't a studyin' me, and Ah wasn't a-studyin' him!"[101]

At Sebring Farm, one house became a refuge for sixty-three residents and labourers-21 whites and 42 blacks, who were squatting down in the pitch-black darkness of the attic, the white people in one end waiting in tense silence, while in the other end the negroes screamed, prayed and wept. Soon they chopped a hole through the metal roof with an ax, but the first man through the hole was swept away by the wind. However, before the others could attempt to escape, a surging wave hit the house and the roof collapsed on the crowd. A few managed to free themselves

---

[101] Will, L. (1961) *Okeechobee Hurricane and the Hoover Dike 3rd Edition*, The Glades Historical Society, pg. 91.

from the wreckage and were washed three miles into the sawgrass, while others perished amidst the wreckage of the house. Of the 63 persons, only six whites and no blacks survived.

Charles Aston "Mutt" Thomas' father had borrowed $100 in 1921 to move from North Florida to Ritta Island, at Lake Okeechobee, to grow vegetables, mainly green beans and onions. On Sunday afternoon, Mutt's family had spent the early afternoon boiling peanuts. The wind was beginning to blow, and Mutt could see the wave action over the little muck dike that protected the mainland. Around dark, having thoroughly enjoyed the peanuts, the Thomas family decided it might be a good idea to go inside. Mutt's father, Charles E. Thomas, tried to decide which action might mean salvation, and which death. He decided to abandon the home and took his wife, three sons, and three daughters to the nearby home of V.F. Thirsk, caretaker of Thomas' farm. Charles Thomas believed that this would be the safest option. They waded through waist-deep water in strong winds; as they entered the house through a back door, the water followed them over the doorpost. The Boots family went there as well, and in total, 60 people—about 20 whites and about 40 blacks—sought refuge there. Mutt's Uncle Minor stayed in the Thomas home. As Mutt looked down at the floor, to his amazement he noticed that water was flowing up through the cracks in the floorboards. In minutes, the water already reached up to his knees. Women pulled their children onto the tabletops. At one end of the home, men began chopping holes into the ceiling. By the time people began crawling into the attic, the water was up to the windowsills.

Swiftly, there was a huge surge of water into the house, and the house started to move. Mutt's father had gotten a hole in the ceiling big enough for another man to crawl into the attic and started ripping away the panels of corrugated sheet iron covering the roof. Unexpectedly, the man vanished, tossed by the high winds through an opening in the roof and out into the black night. As the house broke apart, Mutt scrambled toward the hole in the roof, deciding his chances were better in the open wind than the collapsing structure. Suddenly, a strong hand grabbed his wrist and lifted him through the hole. He said later he believed it to be Mr. Thirsk's. He then grabbed onto the roof for a few moments before he was tossed into the water. He grabbed a piece of floating wreckage and held on, but his father had vanished.

At the south, at the Boots place in Sebring Farms, the dike and the high land of U.S. 27 formed a basin, with the home in the low-lying middle. Inside the house, water rose through the floorboards. Everyone moved to the attic. Neighbour Charles Thomas, Mutt's father, brought an ax and started chopping at the roof to make an opening to the outside. Many had flashlights. The water followed, and by the time they got into the attic, they could hang their feet down and touch water. Boots noticed the whites sitting quietly and the blacks praying loudly and crying. They impatiently waited for the storm to pass, but during the wait the house actually lifted off its foundation, with them in it. The home moved 75 to 100 yards at a speed a building had no business traveling, then it struck the raised roadbed of the unfinished U.S. 27. It slammed into it three times, and it was during the third time that building came apart like a cardboard house crushed by a giant's foot. Everybody tumbled into and under the water.

One man named Vernie Boots grabbed a piece of ceiling and floated. He was on its smooth side and had to keep struggling for a handhold and to prevent it from flipping over. The wind formed five-foot black waves, some cresting as high as four feet as the waves pounded over him. Boots had to turn his head into the wind constantly, or it would have thrown him from the board. He held tight to the rafter boards still nailed to the chunk of ceiling. The wind blew violently without ceasing. Feeling his strength drain away, Vernie wanted to cry out for his mother, but he knew she was probably dead. That thought haunted him through the night as he fought for his life. As he drifted in the storm, he imagined that his mother, father, and brothers were all dead. How could they be alive? How could anyone have survived? How could he survive? He felt lonely, abandoned, and scared. But he was not about to give up without a fight. He would survive; he had to. If there were any chance he might find his parents or brothers, he had to live. Alone on his tiny raft, that one burning thought kept Vernie Boots alive.

The hell-hound roar of the storm had stopped. The wind sounded like a sad, pitiful whimper, but then it sounded like a moan. Then he heard it again—another moan. The darkness was all-enveloping, except when the bright white bolts of lightning stretched and glowed across the sky. Vernie Boots saw none of his three brothers as they floated all night during the storm, at that time he never did hear Willie and Ray. They had been floating nearby, and they were able to call to him in the dark until he finally was able to have contact with them and hear them. Daring for the first time to raise his head above the piece of ceiling, Vernie glanced around his life raft. Off to his right, he saw that a larger part of the ceiling he had been clinging onto all night was connected to his piece. The joists had twisted around. He heard the moan again, and in the ghostly glow of dawn's light he saw his brother, Willie.

"Willie!" he screamed at the top of his lungs. "My hand—I can't move my hand," Willie cried out. Throughout the night, Willie had ridden less than ten feet away from Vernie on the same piece of ceiling, and neither brother had seen the other. Willie cried out again. Clambering over splintered boards and protruding nails, Vernie reached his younger brother. An iron spike from the split ceiling had completely pierced through Willie's hand, in essence nailing him to the ceiling, saving his life. Vernie pulled his brother's hand from the nail. Willie never made a sound. It barely bled; the cold water had sealed the wound.

"Where's Mama?" Willie asked. Vernie just shook his head. As the light shone dimly on the two brothers, Vernie realized they were in the Everglades, and not the lake. A couple of uprooted custard apple trees on their sides stood out of the water. It can't be too deep, Vernie thought. He slid slowly off his life raft. His feet touched bottom. Soft, mucky bottom, but it was land, the first land he had touched in nine hours. The water reached up to his navel. Water three feet deep spread out in all directions— to the eastern horizon, to the west, to the north, and to the south it was all water, one vast ocean of black water. "We got to go, Willie," Vernie said.

Willie nodded in agreement. Wrapping his hand in a piece of his shirt, Willie started off behind Vernie. The two brothers began to trek to the north to the edge of the lake and, Vernie hoped, home. Before they had gone far, they heard a distant shout. "Over here." It sounded like it came out of the sky.

They stopped and saw a figure sloshing through the water a half-mile behind them. He shouted again, and then they saw that it was their brother Roy. When Roy caught up, they started off again, blindly at first until they spotted the tops of the four royal palm trees of Bolles Hotel in Miami Locks. Now they had a target.

"Hey, wait!" they heard someone yelling off to their left. Behind them, about a half-mile farther out into the sawgrass, they saw someone splashing through the water. The three Boots boys slowed their march. "It's Virgil!" Roy exclaimed.

The splashing figure got bigger and bigger until they finally recognized Mutt Thomas. Gasping the corner post all night, he had been carried nearly a mile farther out into the Everglades, where the water was only a foot deep. As he trekked toward the lake, the water deepened up to his waist, and then his belly. Thinking he was going in the wrong direction, he had stopped until he spotted the three Boots boys. There was no place to rest and wait for Mutt, so the Boots boys kept on wading slowly until Mutt caught up to them. The four stunned boys waded in waist-high water all morning. "Are we the only ones alive?" Mutt asked.

No one spoke. The answer was too much for any of them to think about. Vernie, though, believed his parents were dead. Near noon, they arrived at Sebring Farms. There was nothing—no houses, no barns, only a couple of piles of rubble, rows of custard apple trees, tangled rubbish, and broken lumber. The dike was gone. Nothing stood in the distance except the four tall royal palm trees, their fronds bent and bowed low. The boys spotted the steel tower of the turn bridge at Miami Locks and began to make their way there. They saw the keeper's house and the Bolles Hotel, and beyond, barges tied up at the docks and boats cruising the canals. Boats meant people. Just outside the Sebring Farms, they found the Lees' house stuck on a canal bank. The floods had swept it off its foundation and carried it a quarter of a mile with the Lee family inside, all of whom survived. The Lees gave the boys pieces of sugar cane the chew on, and it was certainly a welcome treat.

The boys waded on until they came to a canal where people were being ferried across by boat. While waiting their turn, Mutt heard someone yelling out his name. "Mutt! My God, Mutt. Over here!" Mutt glanced across the flooded canal, and there was his father. "Daddy, Daddy!" Mutt cried out. Jumping into the canal, he swam across to his father. Embracing, father and son broke into tears. Charles Thomas had searched all morning and believed he had lost his entire family. He thought it was a miracle his son had been saved.

Finally, after ferrying across the canal, the Boots brothers were led to the Bolles Hotel—the only structure that remained standing in Miami Locks. People too tired and still in shock rested anywhere they found a dry spot. The former luxury hotel in the swamp, the famed resting spot for thousands of Everglades land buyers had sustained damage, but it was still standing. When the first survivors arrived to seek refuge at the hotel, the caretaker had refused to let anyone inside. An angry crowd gathered in front of the hotel, threatening the caretaker. He was led away and was never seen in that area again.

At the hotel, dazed and confused people were walking about with no sign of urgency or purpose; others had gone inside to rest or be treated as best they could without medical aid. Any news of survivors or dead was eagerly awaited. People desperately asked each person they encountered whether they had seen relatives or friends. Most of the survivors had lost everything they owned in the world; many had lost their entire families.

At Eagle Bay and East Street, the new two story high school building was thrown open, and a large number of people remained there in safety. Only six or eight white people of Pahokee were drowned. These lived in the south part of town and off the ridge, or as was said, "out in the muck." Among these were Rony Levins, Arlin Woodham, crippled Horace Reddick, one of Joe Carver's twin boys, and Andy Smith's wife, who had taken shelter from the wind behind an unfinished brick wall at the Gulf warehouse. Here at the power and ice plants, the angle in Belle Glade Road was a catch-all for all debris and carcasses, human and animal, which were washed up from a wide area. Near this bend also, on Padgett Island, was Hansen's dairy. In its barn, 34 blacks took refuge from the storm.

When the wind changed and the lake came surging up Pelican River, they were trapped. Two of them helped all the others out of the windows, as they believed, was a path to safety, but was actually a path to destruction. The tide rose so fast, these two could not get out, so they climbed to the highest part of the barn and survived. All the other 32 persons were lost. Just south of where Pelican River entered the bay, Cowhorn Slough ran back through Section 30. It, too, was dammed off by the dike in which returning waters now made a clean breach three or four hundred feet wide, and swept on across the farm of Charlie Moran, destroyed his barn and quarters. He states that nearly sixty of the blacks drowned. Only one, Calhoun, in fact, survived.

Robert Hazard, a resident of West Palm Beach and a man of deep personal commitment and profound love for all African people, lobbied government officials, business leaders, clergy and private citizens endlessly and tirelessly in the late 1990s and early 2000s to have a memorial built to remember the Black victims of this storm in Florida. He did this along with the help of his non-profit group, 'Storm of '28 Memorial Park Coalition,' which he founded. With a group of others, Robert sought to create a lasting memorial to the storm victims. In 1975, while attending a Kwanzaa celebration one night, Robert met an elderly Black woman who told him her story of surviving the Great Okeechobee Hurricane of 1928. In his book, *The Storm, God, The Gator and Me*, he wrote about her amazing story of how she survived the storm with the help of an alligator.

"As it got dark from the clouds, my friends went home and I went into the house to eat. I was eating oatmeal and bread along with my three brothers and baby sister when the wind started to blow harder and the rains came. The candles on the table went out, and only two lanterns in the living room gave off light. Our house shook in the wind. The living room windows crashed in, and in came the rain, carried on the wind. My father turned the table on its side, with the top between us and the broken windows. We had the kitchen wall at our backs, and it shook like a wet dog. My mother and father, each having a lantern, told us to hold hands, and my father led us in prayer. After the prayer, my father told all of us children, 'We must leave the house. We must find a safer place to ride out the storm, and we must do it now.'"

"My father took the lead as we continued to hold hands going out the door. 'Don't let go!' he yelled over the storm. My mother was in the back of my father, carrying my baby sister. My two brothers were on either side of me, and my oldest brother, who was about 12, was at the rear. We walked single file, out into the storm. The rain poured in my face, and the wind blew my wet clothes. I had a difficult time walking with my face down and my eyes closed against the wind and rain. If I had let go of my brothers' hands, I would have been blown away. We left what used to be our front porch and pushed through the storm. I remember seeing a big tree lying on its side. Large pieces of wood and furniture, including a couch and chairs, along with clothes and parts of buildings, were all over the place. They were scattered in trees, on the ground, and flying in the air. Trash was blowing all over the place. I saw several wagons and cars on their side. We used one wagon for shelter and prayed, until we could go on. When the wind died down, my father pulled us away from the wagon. We struggled out into the hurricane again.

"By now, I was very scared, wet, tired, and crying. My mother said to me, 'Ya gotta be a good, strong girl, so God would take care of us all, ya hear!' The storm slowed some more. I found out later it must have been the eye of the hurricane passing over us. My father said very loudly, 'We have to find shelter before the storm comes back!' He pointed toward the buildings in the direction he wanted us to go. We grabbed hands and started off into the darkness of the night. It became easier to walk this time, but I could not see where I was walking because of the puddles. Sometimes, I was stepping in water knee deep on me. I struggled to keep up with my family. Sometimes one brother would carry me through the deep water, and then he handed me off to the other brother, who pulled me over fallen objects. My father would help my mother with the baby as best as he could because it was his job to find high ground and get shelter for us.

"I remember us going into a government building of some kind. I don't know if it was a school, courthouse, or post office. It was still standing and a lot more secure than the house we just left. I know it was a government building because my brother told me. 'We are safe now,' he said. 'God blesses America, and we are in a building owned by America. So God will bless us, too.' Then he pointed to a government seal on the wall. We followed a light we saw through some doorways toward the rear of the building. As we entered the lit room, trying to stay dry, both white people and coloured people were sobbing and whispering. I think there were more coloured people than white, but I can't be certain. The children were sitting on the floor with their backs against the walls, while the adults were in the corner of the room, talking very low.

"The white children were on one wall, the coloured folks on the other walls. Some children were screaming, some were praying, and some were just staring off into the night. Even the storm couldn't mix us in those days. It was a scene you would see in a newspaper, magazine, or scary book. I had just gotten used to being in that room when the wind and rain started up again. This time, it was worse than before. Rain, pushed by the wind, came in through the broken windows and holes in the walls. The walls of the building made noise, and more water started to cover the floor. As the storm raged on, the water got deeper. The small children had to get off the floor and stand. The children smaller than me were put on the shoulders of the taller ones. The babies went with their mothers into another room.

"Water started to flow down the walls and drop from the ceiling above us. It came through the doors and from under the floor. The water rose faster and faster. The adults scrambled around to find boxes, tables, chairs, anything for us children to stand on. I was given a box crate of some kind and stood on it. As the storm carried on outside, the water inside began to rise higher and faster. It rose very fast. It was around my ankles. Then it was around my waist. Soon it was up to my chin. There I was, standing on a crate, on my toes, talking to God, asking for help from the storm. The water was dark, dingy, and it smelled. It was very dirty, full of garbage and debris. Paper, books, and other things floated around the room before disappearing under the water.

"While I was standing on the crate, the water rose to my mouth. Every time I opened my mouth to breathe, I could taste the muck in the water. I had to keep my mouth shut and my chin up as I stood in the dark. As the night went on, I got tired. I tried to rest a while, standing still on the crate, but I fell off several times. I think I fell asleep standing up. I was already wet and falling into the water for a third time, and it woke me up. I was six at the time and didn't know how to swim. I liked playing in the water at the beach, but girls simply didn't learn how to swim back then. I still don't know how to swim today, but I am not afraid of the water anymore.

"I, too, began to cry. I was sobbing and shaking so much, I fell off the crate again. But before my head went under water, something grabbed ahold of my arm. I was held by the arm by something I could not see in the dark. This arm here," she said, grabbing her right arm midway between her elbow and shoulder. "I was so afraid of going underwater that I didn't move. I knew that if I moved again, I would die in the dark, dusky water. I couldn't find that crate with my feet or keep my head above water. So, I stayed that way for the rest of the storm. The wind and rain was still howling through the building. The storm gusts were slapping at its sides. The room was dark, and there was nobody close enough for me to see or hold on to. I guess it was too noisy for anyone to hear me call for help. I didn't know where my father was, and I was too exhausted to scream over the sounds of the storm for my brothers. So, I made up my mind to just stay as I was, hanging there, praying.

"I don't know how long it was, but it seemed like forever before the wind and the rain eased up. Soon, I could see the light of dusk. It was a welcome relief that dawn was breaking. My head was still above water, even if the rest of me wasn't. When it was light enough for me to see, I looked around the room. I saw children standing on things, anything to keep their heads out of the water. Some children were still sitting on the heads and shoulders of adults and taller children. Everyone was soaking wet and looked scared, like me. It seemed to me like I stayed in that position for an eternity. I looked for my mother, father, and brothers for help. They were on another wall, out of reach. Then I looked to see what it was holding me up by my arm. What I saw was more frightening than the storm. It was more than a six-year-old could imagine. No one in the room could believe what they saw. My arm was in the mouth of an alligator. Yes, an alligator! It had grabbed my arm right here, above my elbow, and held my head above water.

"My prayers were answered that night. I didn't want to die. I had prayed that my parents, brothers, and baby sister would be all right, too, and God heard me. Yes, sirree, God is good!" Someone else in the room responded, "All the time!" This elderly, kind, genteel, regal woman said, "I believe that God put the fear of dying in both that gator and me. He heard my prayers that night and sent that gator to save me. That gator held onto my arm and saved my life. Both the gator and I were at God's mercy that night. My fear of dying and the gator's desire to live saved both of us from that storm. To this day, I pray and give thanks for all of God's creatures, big and small, and I count my blessings every time it rains."[102]

Robert Hazard, immediately following his interview with this unnamed elderly lady, stated that he felt confident in the feeling that he had grown spiritually that night after listening to her recollecting her experiences in the storm, and was convinced that she was a saint protected by God.

---

[102] Hazard, R.(2006) *The Storm, God, The Gator and Me-An inspiring story honoring the African-American survivors of the Storm of '28.* Self-Published by Robert Hazard.

Damaged home at Belle Glade, Florida after the Great Okeechobee
Hurricane of 1928 (Courtesy of the Florida State Archives).

CHAPTER ELEVEN

The Victims

Dead bodies covered up at Clewiston after the Great Okeechobee
Hurricane of 1928 (Courtesy of the Florida State Archives).

In life, black migrant workers helped turn a South Florida swamp into
a booming tropical mecca and one of the major agricultural areas of
the United States. In death, they were pitched into a trench and left to
be ignored for three-quarters of a century, neglected and nearly forgotten
for this time period. A sewer-treatment plant and a slaughter house were
built adjacent to the site, and a road was built over a section of the mass
grave. For decades, this mass gravesite was an empty field where the dead
lay unseen and buried under a mound of dirt. Then the people of the area
demanded action and by 2003, on the 75th anniversary of this great storm,
a fence was installed and trees were planted. Furthermore, 674 white lilies

one for each storm victim, were planted on the mass grave in honor of the 674 victims buried there. A marker and pillars told the world: We do not forget. The Memorial was so necessary because it deservingly honored the victims whose physical lives were taken away in the Great Okeechobee Hurricane of 1928, but most importantly it will keep their spirits alive as they are remembered and honored by their descendants.

In September 1928, in the steaming hot South Florida sun, some 2,500 bodies lay decomposing, along with uncountable carcasses of snakes, chickens, cows, pigs, and every other animal, not to mention rotting vegetation. Most of the corpses were in standing water. The result was a medical crisis. That's what faced health managers in September 1928. While it's easy to condemn institutional racism for the less-than-decent way they solved the problem, the immediate health emergency was real and had to be handled promptly. Some bodies had to be fished out of the standing water with boat hooks. Sometimes they were so deteriorated that there was nothing strong enough to grab onto, or the bodies simply fell apart. Often workers had to use nets.

At first, the dead were laid out face up for easy identification in the first floor of the Bolles Hotel. But soon more room was needed, and simply burying the dead was out of the question. There was no place to dig a grave. The rescue workers realized that with the heat and humidity, a corpse would rot in a couple of days. They had to be buried, and that meant taking the bodies to West Palm Beach, Clewiston, or north to the high ground around Port Mayaca.

Sewage from the town's cesspools overflowed into back yards and side alleys, and gasoline from underground tanks oozed out, leaving a multi-coloured rainbow blotch that rippled eerily over the black water. There were no dry clothes, and few places dry enough to even rest, and in a land of abundance, there was no food. Knee-deep water covered the entire town. What little produce and meat remained had been contaminated by water from the lake. In a brisk walk through the clutter on Main Street, Dr. William Buck, the only doctor on the south end of the lake between Pahokee and Moore Haven, saw that with no fresh water, little food, and hundreds, if not thousands of decaying corpses floating in stagnant water, Belle Glade was ripe for an epidemic outbreak. He laced up his campaign boots left over from his Army service and made his rounds, stopping to take care of injured persons or offer comfort to the dying. Quite a few people needed to have broken arms or legs set, and he did that as well. He worked under horrific conditions and without sleep for over 82 hours— just like in a battlefield—with no anesthesia or drugs, and little antiseptic except bootleg whiskey.

He felt he and his patients could hold on until help arrived. What he did not know was that no one outside Lake Okeechobee knew the serious predicament they were going through in Belle Glade, or anywhere else stricken by the storm. There were no telephones—the lines and the poles were down. No one had a ham radio. The roads were flooded, the bridges were out, and the canals were clogged with debris and sunken vessels. Their closest help, West Palm Beach, was undergoing its own recovery from the damage the hurricane had left and gave little thought to what might have happened in the distant Everglades.

Bewildered people filtered in from Chosen with stories of entire families lost. At first people talked of dozens dead, then hundreds, and finally over a thousand persons. The rural roadbeds and dikes were littered with bodies—mostly black migrant farmhands. Of all the Everglades towns and rural communities, Chosen had been chosen to suffer the most. Moving along what was the Belle Glade-Chosen Road, one would reach the Hector Supply House, and it was one of the few buildings still standing between Chosen and Belle Glade. In West Palm Beach, there wasn't a building or house that had not been damaged.

Once the wind had died down and the water receded, Fred Aunapu and Elizabeth BeaDer slipped off their barge and headed for Chosen. Most of the town's houses had been swept away, leaving a few stilts jutting through the surface like late afternoon beard stubble. Already people were stacking the dead bodies along the road in improvised body dumps. Elizabeth was shocked that most of the bodies were black. She wondered, "Couldn't they swim?" Later she was told that most, but not all of them, were actually black victims. Many drowned people turned black from oxygen starvation.

The first news out of the Everglades arrived from Pahokee. Dr. John Hall, bringing in the injured from Pahokee, informed the officials that there were at least ten confirmed white dead, and probably fifty to

229

seventy-five Negroes killed. He also stated that they needed immediate assistance around the lake.

Initially, rescue workers—some loosely organized, some under the official supervision of the National Guard or local law enforcement—tried to bury people in a prompt, but still-dignified manner. Soon, sheer numbers of the dead made that plan unworkable. Compounding that problem was the fact that the Glades were still water-logged with standing water, and would be for weeks. Where there was high ground, the muck was so saturated that bodies would just pop out of it after being buried. As a result, rescue workers resorted to using barges to float bodies toward the coast. Once the barges were at high ground, near land, the bodies could be transferred to trucks to drive them the rest of the way to burial sites. Some bodies, on the other hand, when identification was impossible, were taken to body dumps in the middle of the fields and doused with coal oil. Black plumes of heavy smoke scarred the Everglades sky as piles of bodies were burned.

Considering the segregated times when this storm occurred, it goes without saying that the blacks and whites had to be separated. The whites would go to the city's Woodlawn Cemetery. The blacks would go to a lot beside the city incinerator near Tamarind Street. Some corpses were too deteriorated to determine race, leaving workers with the terrible possibility that a Negro would go into a white grave, but they toiled on nonetheless. At Woodlawn, a backhoe dug a deep trench for the white dead. Inside were placed 69 people, most of them laid in coffins. Where possible, the names of the deceased white persons were then scratched in chalk on the outside and the coffins piled up beside the canals for burial. Over on Tamarind Avenue, at the informal black cemetery, backhoes dug a much longer trench, 75 feet long and 20 feet deep. Inside were placed 674 bodies, and none were buried in coffins. However, not all burial grounds accepted the Everglades dead. One truckload of bodies was taken to be buried in Miami, but was turned away because they were in an advanced state of decomposition. The truck returned to Belle Glade, where the corpses were burned.

Bodies of the white dead were placed on display for twelve to twenty-four hours to give loved ones a chance to identify them before they went into the grave at Woodlawn Cemetery. Black bodies pretty much went from the trucks to the trench at Tamarind Avenue, with no time for their relatives to view or identify the bodies. If a worker had been able to identify a black victim in the field or en-route to Tamarind, it was tagged. Sometimes relatives got a chance to view, and possibly identify, the black bodies just before they went into the hole, and a name was quickly written on a foot tag. The rest went in unidentified and unclaimed. Lime was sprinkled over the pile of bodies. Clothilda Miller wasn't even allowed to come near the mass grave on Tamarind to try to look for her relatives. While she believes some or all of them are in that hole, she never found out which, if any, they were buried in. She said that very few others ever got the opportunity to identify their relatives either.

The inscription over Woodlawn Cemetery read, "That which is so universal as death must be a blessing" and had stood there for decades. However, no such marker pointed to where Clothilda Miller Orange believes her loved ones lay buried. Over the years, on the tract along Tamarind Avenue that held the 1.5 acre mass grave in its northeast corner, a slaughter house was built on top of this grave. A dump, an incinerator and a sewage plant were also built on top of this cemetery. In 1964, 25th Street was moved, and part of it was built over the grave and neighbouring graves from a paupers' cemetery. Workers pulled out bones to make way for the road and reburied them at Woodlawn. After many complaints from the black community, who said that area was sacred ground, in 1991 the city of West Palm Beach repurchased the lot and erected an historical plaque commemorating the dead black hurricane victims.

At 3pm on Sunday, September 30th, recovery workers at the two West Palm Beach mass graves stopped their labour. For one hour, by the proclamation of Major Vincent Oaksmith, everyone was to stop their labour in honor of the dead. Two separate ceremonies were held. Long before they began, people had begun gathering at the giant trenches about three miles and a world apart. At the Tamarind grave for the black victims, 2,000 to 3,000 people came for the service. Clothilda Miller Orange said decades later she may have gone, but with her fading memory she wasn't sure. She did say, however, that her family held no formal service for their dead relatives, although they may have done something at their church.

Mary McCleod Bethune, the black education pioneer who also founded what is now Bethune-Cookman College in Daytona Beach, did attend.

"Our hearts were torn at the sight of the one large mound encompassing the hundreds of bodies of men, women and children," Bethune would later write about that moment in black history. She further noted, "Those who had been spared stood with tear-stained cheeks, wringing their hands, because many of them had lost entire families, or a large part of their family members had been taken. The sadness of this scene fell upon us like a pall."[103]

It's important to note that no official sat behind his desk and said, "Let's embark on a conscious and conspiratorial effort to treat blacks separately and without dignity." Local cops, weekend National Guardsmen, and everyday citizens who'd volunteered or been drafted into positions of leadership suddenly found themselves in charge of an unprecedented crisis. So they simply followed the critical needs of the moment and the behaviors of the era. Considering the segregated times, Floridians in the 1920s would never have imagined any other response than to draft blacks for the menial or dirty work. They'd never have imagined any plan other than to bury white bodies in the white cemetery and the much larger volume of black corpses in the larger trench in the black cemetery.

In the 1920s, race infused every aspect of life, and while plenty of the usual discrimination followed the storm, complaints of exaggerated or nonexistent slight complicated matters. On October 30, 1928, Colin Herrle, the Red Cross' storm recovery coordinator for the Glades, wrote A.L. Schafer, the agency's West Palm Beach-based head of overall storm recovery. He reported on a meeting held that morning with A.L. Isbell, "field organizer" for the obscure Negro Workers Relief Committee, headquartered in New York.

"We had a very agreeable meeting, and I believe he left satisfied with the idea that we are doing everything possible to eliminate any discrimination in the handling of the white and coloured cases." Herrle said Isbell mentioned a black woman who was sick; Herrle got to pick through donated clothing, but blacks were handed clothes. Herrle said this might have been the case early on, but not now. Still, he promised to look into it. Herrle admitted that most of the rationing was indeed going to the white families, but said that was because blacks were able to find

---

[103] Kleinberg, E. (2003) *Black Cloud-The Deadly Hurricane of 1928*, Carroll & Graf Publishers, pgs. 229-230.

work, presumably in the cleanup or collection of bodies. "Personally, I rather feel that the whites are getting a little bit better of the argument on this point, but very little," Herrle conceded. He said he hoped to iron out the discrepancy.

Most black victims had received little or no aid from relief groups, including the Red Cross, and blacks had to depend on their own ranks for survival after the storm. For example, a black Fort Lauderdale woman who had lost everything was given $4 for food for a family of five. When she returned a third time, "They drove her away from the station." A family of nine got only $3, another only $5. A Delray Beach woman said her home was totally destroyed, and all the Red Cross gave her was "a few old pieces of clothes and a few cans of tomatoes and potted meat and a small can of milk for me and my kids."

The Chicago Defender, in a story published November 3rd, quoted Grace Campbell, their chair of the workers committee, as claiming the relief was running 80 percent for whites and 20 percent for blacks. Campbell recounted some of the earlier anecdotes from South Florida and added some: black families with four children got relief cards for $2 in groceries, while white families, some childless, got vouchers for $6 and $7. A pregnant woman who had been ordered hospitalized waited for a bed for a very long period of time when the whites were served immediately. If that weren't bad enough, the Red Cross had hired no black staffers even though the majority of the victims were black. They sent white staffers, into black homes to strong-arm families into requesting only the bare minimum aid. Campbell said the workers' agent—presumably Isbell—actually joined a body-fishing crew, and he and the other blacks had to eat at the rear of the kitchen "among the garbage and flies." Of course, the Red Cross would later deny most of the alleged cases of mishandling, except for those that carried no name, and therefore could not be investigated.

Schafer wrote to his bosses in Washington that his agency was employing blacks, although he admitted he had no black caseworkers, but his staff was "entirely sympathetic" to blacks. He said any delays in rebuilding black homes were attributed to the fact that labour agreements between white and black carpenters' unions prevented white carpenters from working in black neighbourhoods. Schafer said the state health department—not the Red Cross—was the governing body assigned to collecting the dead bodies, so he couldn't respond to any of Isbell's allegations about that. Furthermore, he said that most of the difficult conditions under which blacks lived were the same ones with which whites were contending.

Around the same time, the Red Cross debunked one damning anecdote. It was about a black man named Levi Brown—the same Levi Brown whose heartbreaking story had moved Governor John Martin himself. The Negroe Workers Committee had said that Brown, after an exhausting day of helping collect bodies, had gone into a Red Cross mess tent and was eating a piece of ham given by a relief worker, when the director of relief work in the Glades "grabbed an 18-inch ax and made a ferocious assault on Brown, uttering the vilest oaths and telling him that 'ham was not for Niggers.'" The report said Brown was struck in the head and shoulder. However, on November 29th, Herrle, the Glades Director, telegrammed Schafer in West Palm Beach to say he'd met with Brown. The man said he had been struck with a meat cleaver, but not by the director, for whom Levi reportedly said he has "never had anything but kind words" all his life, or any other Red Cross representative.

Herrle followed that with a longer note that same day, with the story he says Brown told him: Brown had gone to a restaurant and requested a meal ticket for himself and his daughter. Three white people, peeved at the celebrity Brown was getting as a result of his harrowing tale of rescue and tragedy, began to give him a hard time, and when he tried to leave, one of them grabbed him and struck him in the face and in the back of his head with the flat side of the meat cleaver.

The three finally let Brown go. Brown had said the director hadn't even been there during the attack, and he would sign a statement about the whole affair as long as the Red Cross checked out his story with others involved. Herrle went on to say that Fleming Ruttledge, the man who apparently assaulted Brown, would glad to himself sign a statement. Ruttledge later did, on November 28th, saying he struck Brown "following an argument in which he became impudent and called me a liar." Ruttledge also said the director wasn't even there. "Brown, I imagine, would like to prosecute Ruttledge, but I doubt whether he would have any chance before a white jury, and I should imagine that the best thing for Brown would be to have the matter quieted down as much as possible," Herrle wrote.

After the hurricane, even though the request for 'able-bodied persons' in the region was being ordered to work, the bulk of the labour fell on the usual group, which was the "negro labourers." Official reports, correspondence and news accounts all refer not to the dray-load of workers of all colours, but to the "negro workers," "negro labourers," and "moving negroes to the scene." Some were paid a small stipend, but most were not. Some went willingly, and others did not. During the cleanup phase, many blacks were ordered or forced to load bodies at Pahokee and other Everglade towns at the point of a gun.

At the corner of Eighth and Division Streets, a black man named Coot Simpson was on his way to work when a guardsman on duty, Knolton Crosby, a member of Company 'C', 124th Infantry Florida National Guard, ordered him to "Get on that truck, nigger." Coot told them that he needed to ask his boss for permission to go and started to walk across the street, but was forced to get on the truck without informing his boss. As guardsmen went through the city, rounding up blacks to help clean up and bury the dead, Coot was drafted. He worked for a few days, and after he was finished one evening, he said, "Now, I'm going to go home," and started to find the foreman to let him know. Crosby told him he couldn't leave, and he lifted his rifle and fired, striking Coot in the lower back and blowing out his abdomen, killing him instantly. He was charged in the coroner's court, but later the jury determined that it was 'justifiable homicide' and cleared him of all charges.

By Wednesday night, only a few blacks showed up to volunteer for the cleanup. About sixty were rounded up and ordered to dig graves. Coroner Tom Rickards and his family, including his young son Tommie, had a lot of work to do, and they got help as well. "Well, a nigger here is tearing away the debris so we can move our piano out," Tom's wife, Helen, wrote matter-of-factly to her sister-in-law, Kate Rickards, in North Carolina, on September 23rd. In another case, Willie Rawls, fourteen, of West Palm Beach, and another fifty men, presumably all of them black, went to work in teams of two with crosscut saws, cutting down damaged palm trees. He would later say that he worked from 7:00am to 6:30pm.

All kinds of condescending, self-righteous, pseudo-benevolent racism was prevalent at the time. A page full of commentaries in the paper that day included a call that only proper authorities, not just private businessmen, had the right to recruit area blacks for cleanup work. It added, of course, that the blacks deserved to be properly paid for their labour. The paper raised this issue because its very own janitor, a likable man named A.O. Arnold, had been commandeered by two men; at least one of them had a gun. The villains ignored the pass West Palm Beach officials had given Mr. Arnold, identifying him as an employee of the newspaper and exempting him from recruitment. They took him and another black man to their private property on the south side of town, where they worked the two of them all day without feeding them or paying them a cent. The column said the two men were later too afraid to identify their kidnappers and that Arnold returned to work too sunburned and worn out to be any good to himself or the paper and was sent home. "This damnable outrage was the act of a two legged skunk, pirate, and enemy of the public welfare and a coward," the columnist gnashed. "If such things are permitted, they will demoralize negro labour."

Shortly after the storm, a writer named Don Morris published and sold a booklet filled with details and pictures. He claimed to be the first reporter on the scene, even though the region had several newspapers whose staffers had lived through the storm, including those from the *Palm Beach Post*. And he said of the dead, "nearly two thirds were Negroes, and the death panic among the simple and superstitious black folk must have been terrible to witness." By Friday morning, September 21st, most people had been moved out of the Glades. Buzzards had returned, and their lazy circling was an indication of a dead body in the vicinity, and this was one of the ways many of the cleanup crews found the bodies.

On Saturday, a group of blacks arrived with a new baby, born on a barge in the floodwaters on Tuesday. Also that day, a haggard man walked into the Salvation Army headquarters at the West Palm Beach Chamber of Commerce building. He had a pile of baby clothes he wanted to donate. The attendant asked him if he was sure he wouldn't need them, and he told her no because his baby was blown out of his hands during the storm and died.

The Florida Children's Home Society, in Jacksonville, arranged for the placement of orphans—only the white ones. Placement of the black orphans was left to the Richmond, Virginia-based Commission of Interracial Cooperation. On Friday, the number of blacks housed at a Pompano Beach horse track had swelled to 1,000 persons. Thirteen white survivors were taken to the Broward County Courthouse in Fort Lauderdale.

Of course, the effects of the flood from the hurricane were devastating, and the loss of life, both human and animal, was apocalyptic. Damages from this hurricane were estimated around 25 million dollars, which, normalized for population, wealth, and inflation, would be around 16 billion dollars today (Landsea, 2002).[104] The horrible flood in the towns of Pahokee, Canal Point, Chosen, Belle Glade, and South Bay resulted in the drowning of many people, probably three-quarters or more of whom were non-white field workers. The flood waters lasted for several weeks, and survivors were found wandering as late as September 22nd. In Pahokee, only a few whites were killed. Most of the farm owners had houses in town on the ridge or near to it. The migrant farmhands had no place to retreat to when the reverse surge broke over the Pelican River dike, sending a wall of water up the old Pelican River and killing hundreds.

How many persons died in the hurricane on September 16, 1928? The exact number of storm victims will never, ever be known. Prior to 2003, the National Hurricane Center and the almanac and encyclopedia people use place the storm's official death toll at 1,836. Few historians and scholars believe it. Even as government and relief leaders were issuing their final figures soon after the storm, they were already conceding that the numbers were too low.

The precise number of deaths in and around Lake Okeechobee caused by this hurricane will never be known, reported Stewart G. Thompson, director of Florida's Bureau of Vital Statistics, in October 28, 1928 *Health Notes*, the newsletter of Florida State Board of Health. Most of the deaths were among Negro labourers who moved into the Everglades for planting season, which had opened a short time previously. Since a large percentage of these Negroes were from Nassau in the Bahamas, which is outside of the state, it was not possible in a great many instances to identify the bodies, he reported.

Most of these migrant workers were from the Bahamas, and many were only known by a 'nickname' or on a first-name basis, making documenting

---

[104]   http://www.srh.noaa.gov/okeechobee

and identifying the bodies very difficult. The exact number of those who perished in the Okeechobee storm can never be determined. Probably three-fourths or more of the casualties were Negroes, many of whom had come from the islands of the Bahamas. Accounting for members of this race was complicated by the migratory habits of their kind and the fact that most of them were known, even to their friends, only by a nickname. Another reason the number cannot be determined was that many were carried by the flood far into the sawgrass wastes. For example, not one of the blacks that took refuge in the Thirst house attic at Sebring Farms survived. There was no one to miss them, no one to look for them, and no one who cared whether they were found or not because most of those migrant workers were from the Bahamas.

Palm Beach County Red Cross chairman Howard Selby, in a September 26th radio address broadcast in Washington and New York, placed the estimate at 2,300. He said 1,500 were confirmed dead and buried, and many others had been buried in fields and outlying areas. Lawrence E. Will, author of *Okeechobee Hurricane and the Hoover Dike*, wrote the State Board of Health and the Red Cross in 1958, saying he had always accepted a figure of 2,500. Will said that the mayor of Belle Glade at the time had told him 1,850 bodies had been taken from Belle Glade alone. There is nothing in Will's files to indicate a response.

If you just add up the number in the graves, the number is already past 1,836. The mass graves for the blacks on Tamarind Avenue: 674. Woodlawn: 69. In a trench dug into a canal bank at Miami Locks: 22 to 800. Ortona: 28. Sebring: 22. And that mass grave at Port Mayaca, on the northeast shore; a marker says 1,600 are buried there.[105] News reports suggested that there might be additional burials of blacks at Loxahatchee, at western edge of the coastal communities. If such a cemetery was established, historical contacts would say in 2002 that they never heard of it, although it may be there, back in the bush somewhere. It's not hard to imagine a small burial site for dead black migrant workers in a rural area being established, and then forgotten as quickly. In 1991, after many complaints from the black community, a formal funeral service was conducted for the 624 black storm victims of 1928 buried there.

---

[105] Kleinberg, E. (2003) *Black Cloud-The Deadly Hurricane of 1928*, Carroll & Graf Publishers, pg. 214.

As winds howled in the Glades on September 16, 1928, black migrant workers huddled, wept and prayed, and while they stared into darkness, "their eyes were watching God," Zora Neale Hurston wrote. One of Florida's bestselling authors, Zora Neale Hurston described the mass burial in her 1937 classic novel *Their Eyes Were Watching God:* "Don't let me ketch none uh y'all dumpin' white folks, and don't be wastin' no boxes on colored," a guard in the book says. "They's too hard tuh git ahold of right now." In this book, Hurston also describes how a character in the book, Tea Cake, and other black workers laboured to bury the hurricane dead in two giant pits. White supervisors made sure the labourers checked each of the swollen, discolored bodies as carefully as possible to make sure whites went in the correct pit and blacks in the other.

Zora Neale Hurston (January 7, 1891 – January 28, 1960) was an American folklorist, anthropologist, and author. Of Hurston's four novels and more than 50 published short stories, plays, and essays, she is best known for her 1937 novel *Their Eyes Were Watching God*. In addition to new editions of her work being published after a revival of interest in her in 1975, her manuscript *Every Tongue Got to Confess* (2001), a collection of folktales gathered in the 1920s, was published posthumously after being discovered in the Smithsonian Archives.

Hurston wasn't at Lake Okeechobee, or even in Florida, when the winds and surge took the lives of so many black men, women, and children. Much of her narrative of that night is based on her actual experience with a powerful hurricane in the Bahamas called, the 'Great Bahamas Hurricane of 1929' or the 'Great Andros Island Hurricane of 1929.' This storm lasted over the Bahamas for three consecutive days and resulted in the deaths of 134 persons and destroyed hundreds of homes. Many of the people she spoke with are also described in this work. But she immortalized the hurricane just as she captured the lives and humanity of mid-twentieth-century black Americans. This book was made into a movie starring Halle Berry, who starred as the main character, Janie. It was a made-for-TV movie, which aired for the first time on March 6, 2005, and was produced and developed by Quincy Jones and Oprah Winfrey. The TV movie was watched by an estimated 24.6 million viewers, further entrenching the novel in the public consciousness and in the American literary canon. Zora

Neale Hurston encountered this hurricane in the Bahamas while she did research for this book.

From New Orleans she travelled to South Florida and on to the Bahamas. Her stay in the Bahamas was devoted mostly to the collection of native songs and learning about the Jumping Dance. Hurston called on the memory a few years later to develop and duplicate the terror in her Everglades hurricane in *Their Eyes Were Watching God,* which is actually based on the Great Okeechobee Hurricane, which struck Florida in 1928 and caused severe flooding. She repeated her trips to the Bahamas during the latter part of the 1920s and early 1930s. Today, *Their Eyes Were Watching God* is widely regarded as a literary masterpiece.

During her life, Huston had limited success in the literary world. She died in obscurity, but there has been a resurgence of interest in her writing after her death in 1960, and she has finally taken her place among America's influential black writers. She had been in the Caribbean in the summer of 1928 and arrived in New Orleans that August, and she probably was there when the hurricane struck South Florida. She stayed in New Orleans through the winter, returned to South Florida, and then, in October 1929, she went to the Bahamas. She was there when a powerful hurricane struck the islands. Inspired partly by that experience and partly by the end of a romantic relationship, she later wrote *Their Eyes Were Watching God* in Haiti. In her autobiography, *Dust Tracks on the Road,* she said *Their Eyes Were Watching God* "was dammed up in me." She wrote it in seven weeks. It was published in 1937. The story takes some liberties. For example, it described winds of an unrealistic 200 mph, and it perpetuates the legend of the Seminoles fleeing the storm before everyone else because they saw the sawgrass blooming. Otherwise, Hurston does give an accurate account of the storm's slow, but steady assault and its aftermath.

Their Eyes Were Watching God did not draw great attention to the legacy of the 1928 hurricane. Perhaps this is because it came out nearly a decade later, after the Great Labour Day Hurricane of 1935 and others had created all new stories of horror, or on the other hand, perhaps because, as with many news events, people move on to the next one. And perhaps because, while the storm was the mechanism that formed the climax of the book, it was the characters, not the weather, that people remembered.

Coffins being transported to West Palm Beach, Florida for Mass Burial in Woodlawn City Cemetery (Courtesy of the Florida State Archives).

Vera Farrington and Mary Alfred are sisters, and their parents met while working the fields in the Glades. They said their mother left their family members, living in a house at South Bay, to ride out the storm with her husband and his family in Clewiston. Their house was not very well constructed, so around 3 o'clock in the afternoon, was when she last saw her mother, father and four brothers and sisters. It was near nightfall when the hurricane finally moved from the coast to the inland area. First the storm forced the water to the north end of the lake, and the back side of the storm drove that water to the south, they recalled, and that was when all hell broke loose and the disaster as they knew it began to take form and claim its victims.

A coloured family of two men and a woman on Jesse D. Lee's farm, after the roof had left their house, took refuge in a pop ash tree. The tree bent before the gusts, nearly drowning them in the waves, but rebounding long enough to give them a breath of air before submerging them again. Nearly all the trees on the island were uprooted, but by good fortune, theirs remained and all three survived.

Mahlon C. Eggleston's house had been built to be storm proof. Constructed of that pitchy lumber known as "Dade County pine", as hard as teak, it was double sheathed and double nailed. The house was so tight that it started to rise with the flood, though in a peculiar jerky way, as though the pilings were still attached. Then another drifting house struck it with a resounding blow, which sent it careening off in the darkness. It was discovered that clinging to a window sill on the windward side were two Negro women and one man. Wind pressure prevented raising the sash, so the pane was kicked out and the half-drowned people were pulled inside. One woman said she had lost her husband and four children. The other couple had lost three.

One large group had assembled in the home of Oliver Wilder, near the dike. Besides Wilder and his wife were their sons, Melvin, Floyd and Raymond, and daughters, Laura and Hilda, with Hilda's husband, Clarence Lee, from Sebring Farm, and three small children. A neighbour and old settler, Mrs. Thigpen, whose first house here had been constructed of pine poles thatched with palmetto leaves, arrived with her daughters, Pearl and Lillian, and boy, Philip. When, in the darkness, the water began to rise in the house, a hole was chopped in the ceiling and all fourteen huddled in the attic. Then the dike burst, and the house simply disintegrated.

Floundering blindly, the human debris was carried by the rolling flood and shrieking gale toward the southeast. Raymond caught and hung onto the truss of the bridge. Floyd missed the bridge and lodged in a guava tree across the canal. Melvin found temporary refuge on the roof of the shack of D.F. Hutchinson, a hunter, back of Franz's store, just in time to reach down and catch his sister Hilda as she was carried past. The first body found after the storm was that of Oliver Wilder, his head crushed, lying only a few feet from the bridge where his boy Raymond had perched. Of the fourteen in his house, eight were lost, Oliver Wilder, his wife, his daughter's three children, Mrs. Thigpen and her children Pearl and Philip.

In Bean City, the Rashley brothers, usually most apprehensive of any storm, refused to leave or even go to their new house, a deadly mistake. This was the only house in Bean City that was not demolished. Besides Mr. Lyons and the carpenter, it sheltered 30 Negroes. Arthur Wells lost six of his Negroes and every one of his houses. The entire Rashley family was wiped out. After the storm, both of the dead Rashley brothers were placed in wooden coffins, and their names were scribbled on both ends and loaded onto a truck bound for West Palm Beach.

It took several days for the water to recede, before the survivors dared to come down from the trees, rafters, rooftops and buildings where they sought refuge. When it was safe, Vera and Mary's mother left Clewiston to check on her family members in South Bay, but when she got there, she found the house was gone. She desperately wanted to see someone from her family that resided in that house. Next to the location of her house was a stream of water, and in the water floated a body. Her husband, who was with her at the time, took a stick and turned the body over, and that was when she saw the face of her oldest brother, and then she passed out. She never saw or heard from any other family member that rode out the storm in South Bay.

Mary Rolle Alford lost her family members in the storm as well. She recalled that the water started rising in the house and they didn't know what to do then, but then the men said, "Let's take the doors off the house" which they did and put them on top of the rafters and put the women on top of the doors for safety. The water was so high that their feet were dangling in the water below. They were quite fearful because everything was in this water trying to survive, including the water moccasins, rattlesnakes and any other wild animals trying to get up on the same doors with them. My aunt was pregnant at the time, and during this ordeal she lost the baby. It was such an impactful storm that they really had a hard time during and after the storm.

Robert Hazard, an organizer for the Florida 1928 Hurricane Memorial for the victims of the storm, reflected on the impact of the migrant farm workers on the cleanup efforts in Florida after the storm. He said that these black migrant farm workers were in such a tight-knit community that everyone in the family or in the household was a migrant farm worker. This hampered the identification of the bodies because the only people who could identify these bodies were also killed in the storm as well.

Storm victim Bessie Wilson DuBois had come to the very beautiful Jupiter Inlet at the very young age of 11 in 1914. She would later recall hearing, on the day of her arrival, what sounded like people applauding politely. It was thousands of mullet boiling the water of the Loxahatchee River as it emptied into the Atlantic Ocean. It's a sound long since washed away by commercial fishing and development along the river and inlet. DuBois would later become the Jupiter area's unofficial historian, writing several small books about the region. Back in 1928, her home was situated right on the inlet, across from the historic Jupiter Lighthouse. Bessie was one of the three sisters. On that day in 1928, she was also just recently married three years earlier and the mother of three kids, Susie, 3, Doris, 2, and Louise, 7 months. The family had read the increasingly alarming newspaper reports of the approaching storm. Bessie's father, brothers Bob and Jack, and sister Grace gathered in the home Bessie shared with her husband John. Giving her recollection of the storm, she said, "Papa wanted to take refuge in a reinforced concrete building" but John refused.[106] He had built the home and was pretty sure it would withstand the strong winds of a hurricane. So they made the decision to stay put.

Bessie spent the morning baking bread and a ham, boiling potatoes, and fixing pudding for the kids. With no electric refrigerator, the food she had prepared was placed in an icebox to keep it from spoiling. The family took up rugs and took down pictures, John DuBois tied up the boats and pumped full a large water tank attached to a tower, hoping the weight would keep it from blowing over. Some of the men decided to drive to the nearby U.S. Navy station for the latest weather report. Just as their car had passed under the water tower, the tank slid off its perch and crashed down onto the road, narrowly missing them.

"The winds galloped over us like a thousand freight trains, accompanied by that high-pitched whine that beggars description," Bessie wrote. "Huddled on the lee side of the back porch, it was still light enough for us to see the great breakers coming straight across the ocean as if the beach no longer existed." The water surged into the inlet and up the Loxahatchee River and into the DuBois' front yard. "The tremendous surges were breaking among the palm trees in our yard. As every new crest swept in, a few more cabbage palms went down. The tide was higher than any of the family could remember, as the foam from the waves crashed against the windows. Papa made a macabre joke by shaving and dressing so that he would make a 'handsome corpse'… but soon the strain had overcome even gallows of humor. About all that held the house together was the chimney and the concrete back porch…I found myself praying over and over again that the tide would change and that the center of the storm would pass."[107]

The men gathered by the coffeepot while the women stayed in the bedroom with the children. The old house up on the hill, where John DuBois had been born, was vacant at the time, and Bessie had packed

106 Kleinberg, E. (2003) *Black Cloud-The Deadly Hurricane of 1928*, Carroll & Graf Publishers, pg. 88.
107 DuBois, B. (1968) *Memories of the '28 Hurricane* published by *Bessie* DuBois, pg. 51.

food and clothes in a basket for a hasty retreat should the water continue to rise. Susie saw her and asked her mother repeatedly, "When are we going up the hill?" As the winds blew violently, Susie danced on the porch, her eyes showing the excitement of innocence. Bessie had assigned one child to each man. But as she saw them watching the water swirling around the falling trees, she realized even a grown man alone could never get up the hill, let alone one carrying a child.

The tide had risen so high that seawater ran several inches deep over the home's floorboards. The winds pushed on the uncovered windows, turning the clear glass at their center white with pressure; fortunately, they held together. The family heard a loud crash, and when they went to investigate it, they discovered the front porch had lost its roof and was separating from the rest of the house. They feared the home would come off its foundation and begin floating off. The children, oblivious to their danger, played happily with crayons and paper.

According to South Florida resident Jeanne Griffin, her husband's great grandfather, Willie Williams, was killed in this hurricane. He lived in West Palm Beach and went to play cards at a tavern on the lake. His body was not recovered, but his watch was later found and returned to the family. In another case, dairy farmer Noah Kellum Williams had driven south on Sunday morning to the plant in Kelsey City that bottled his milk. Owners of buildings in the town were preparing for the storm by boarding up the windows and doors. He returned to his farm in Jupiter, around where Florida's Turnpike now crosses Jupiter's main east-west road. Normally, Sunday morning would find him in church; however, he stayed home to board up his home, and then went to shelter at the schoolhouse. After arriving there, Noah Kellum Williams was finally able to stretch out on the floor to try to get some sleep. Less than an hour later, he was awakened.

An older couple lived in a second-story garage apartment nearby. It turned out they had stayed as long as they dared, then they tried to make it to the schoolhouse, but the winds had knocked them down. They were crouching under a stairway on the side of the building away from the wind. But the second floor had blown off, and the garage had wobbled, trapping the couple. The man had been able to crawl to the school for help. It took several men to remove the stairway off the woman, who was badly hurt, and bring her to the schoolhouse.

At about 3pm, a neighbour came by. A large fruit company had built a high-powered radio station nearby to communicate with its farms in Central America. Someone at the station had sent word around to the neighbours to get out as quickly as possible before the storm hit the region. The neighbour had no doubt exaggerated his story just a bit at each doorway; so, by the time he got to Williams, the storm had sustained winds of 200 mph and was accompanied by a 50-foot storm surge. Williams knew the ridge on which his home sat was only 25 feet above sea level, but it was five miles inland. The house wasn't very strong, but the barn was new and sturdy. A tenant said the people who were calling for escape must have known what they were talking about. Williams stepped into his barn and gave his employees the bad news. The men had just milked and fed the first group of cows. He told them to fasten the big barn door open so it wouldn't blow shut and to unyoke the cattle.

Williams finally decided the safest place was the area's new $160,000 schoolhouse. He piled everyone into two trucks, along with bedding and pillows. At the schoolhouse, the winds reached their peak at 5:30pm, Williams recalled. He watched from a giant window as lumber and tree limbs flew and trees snapped. A dog sheltered from the wind against a building suddenly decided to make a dash to safety. When the animal got into the wind, it rolled him over; he crawled back to the wall and was still there when darkness hid him from Williams' view. Windows and doors were smashed in by flying debris. The group grabbed lumber left by workers on the newly finished building; two men would force a door shut, while others hammered the lumber across the door and frame to brace it. "Strong men prayed who had never prayed before," Williams would later recall. "Strange to say, those who were not in the habit of praying, prayed the loudest."

When the storm arrived, Walter Lewerenz decided his home wasn't safe. The obvious alternative was the brand new high school. They went first to the room used for manual training, now called shop class. It was on the west side, and they believed it would be safer than the home economics room on the east side. Other families had also come there. Soon, plaster started to fall. Suddenly, the entire ceiling started to come down. The second floor auditorium came with it. Walter and his family were in a corner of the room and weren't hurt, but one boy was seriously injured. During the lull of the eye, Walter ran to his home. The yard was full of dead chickens, so he gathered them up and returned to the Shepard home. He had been gone less than a half-hour. The winds picked up again. When it was finally gone, the problems of freshly dead chickens and hungry refugees solved each other quickly. The high school survived and was repaired, but the storm had destroyed the Town Hall, the Hotel Cassandra and the First Methodist Church. Florida East Coast Railway freight train "130" had gone into a ditch, and railroad crews later furiously cleared tracks of debris for both regular and relief train traffic.

Soon after Lee and Maribell Rawls fled from the Grimes' house, the Grimeses and the McAllisters, believing the house was ready to collapse, left for their car. The surge drowned everyone except Mrs. McAllister and Grimes. Out of the fourteen people who remained in the house, eight drowned. Grimes, though he survived, later died of his injuries. Half of the South Bay dead were never recovered.

At the inlet, the U.S. Navy radio compass station wired a report that winds were at 90 mph and the tide was five feet above normal and its tower had blown over. The station was in the middle of advising that the wind was increasing when the dispatch stopped in mid-sentence. A boxcar on a siding in Lake Worth had broken loose and gone hurtling down the track, pushed by winds to speeds approaching 75 mph; it finally derailed 11 miles down the track in Delray Beach. In Boca Raton, just south of Delray Beach, ten boxcars were overturned. Two cars had come right off their wheels, leaving the framework and wheels standing naked on the tracks. South of that, across the Palm Beach-Broward county line in Deerfield Beach, another freight train was blown off the track. Many buildings in Delray lost their roofs or came down altogether. A lumber company, an ice plant and a grocery store were completely destroyed. Even houses of God were not spared from destruction because two churches were leveled, a third left irretrievable and two were slightly damaged. Firefighters had set up a first aid station at the Chamber of Commerce building. When it was smashed, they moved to City Hall. Delray Beach officials later reported 227 homes destroyed and 730 badly damaged, with a total of 1,268 buildings suffering some form of damage.

On Monday morning, one Glades resident began helping with collecting the dead bodies. "Ugly death was simply everywhere," he would later recall. Arriving at one site, he was handed an ax and told to start chopping at debris while another man dug. "Within minutes, I caught sight of what he was after. A human hand appeared above the mud beneath the treetop. I felt a little sick at the gruesome sight, but I knew that would not work. I steeled myself and tried not to look." The hand was that of a woman about twenty. The crew found four more bodies, of an older man and woman and a young man holding a small child. All of them were washed off in a water hole—perhaps for dignity's sake, perhaps just to help with identification—placed beside the road, where they lay mute until another crew in a truck came and took them away. Just who got buried in coffins and who in a funeral pyre, basically depended on the availability of a coffin, a passable road, and a vehicle, but it must be noted that coffins were not 'wasted' on black victims because of the segregated times they were living in.

About noon, Young's crew found an older woman who was alive but had a foot caught in the branches of a downed tree. She said her name was Aunt Hattie, and she was waiting for her son and grandson to come and free her. Young's crew had to cut the limb that trapped her foot and set out to find her family. First they found the bodies of a young woman still holding a two-year-old child in her arms. Aunt Hattie identified them as the wife and child of her grandson. The next body was that of Aunt's Hattie's daughter-in-law. Then two boys, of about six and nine, and two girls, of about twelve and fourteen, were uncovered. Soon Aunt Hattie's son and grandson were found, also dead. The crew loaded a dazed and confused Aunt Hattie on a truck with the bodies of her family. Young's team worked until it was too dark to see. Later in the week, C.L. Reddick, an old settler, was found dead, his dog still standing by him and barking at rescuers. The animal had stood faithfully by his master's body amid the carnage for five days.

a) Damage at Cromer Block b) Damage at Delray Motor Co-Ford Agency c) Damage at Delray Laundry d) Damage at Casa Del Rey Hotel (Courtesy of NOAA-The National Hurricane Center).

Six bodies were brought in Monday morning to a hotel in Belle Glades and laid out on pool tables. At the lake's north end, in the town of Okeechobee, twenty-five were reported dead. In Clewiston, west of Belle Glade, along the lake's south shore, five people were reported dead and twelve homes were destroyed, but there had been no flooding. At the Southern Sugar Company in Clewiston, later to become the industry giant US Sugar, damage was minimal to both crops and buildings, including a new sugar factory not even finished. At the county cemetery in Ortona, 25 miles west of Clewiston, burials were underway. By Thursday afternoon, twenty-eight people, presumably identified, had been interred. To the north, Moore Haven—swamped almost exactly two years earlier the first time a hurricane toppled the Lake Okeechobee dike—reported no deaths or damage.

By Tuesday, people were already coming to West Palm Beach from the Glades, dead and alive. The living arrived for help covered in scratches and cuts; the storm had torn their clothes away, leaving them helpless against the razor-sharp sawgrass that grows waist-high or higher in much of the Glades and had slashed victims as they struggled through the floodwaters. Three Seminoles, who had apparently not seen the blooming sawgrass (according to these Indians, it was a sure sign of an approaching hurricane), were rescued in high water Monday night. They said they'd been separated from others in the storm and feared many were lost.

On Monday, West Palm Beach migrant workers and other blacks, desperate for information and support, had begun to gather at their unofficial town hall, Industrial High School. There, people were starting to come in from the glades. The first to come in had been survivors, many of them badly hurt. They came with many stories to tell. Later the dead began to arrive in trickles, and later on in droves. They, too, told a tale, at least by their sheer numbers. There were shouts of joy as families separated in the storm were reunited and shouts of utter despair as others learned that their loved ones were among the dead. One man walked an astounding 12 miles from the Glades with his wife and several children and was looking for his twelve-year-old-daughter, who had become separated from the family while they were fleeing from the storm. Suddenly, the girl was brought in, alive. Rescuers in a car had found her alive, walking in the road. By Tuesday night, survivors at the black school numbered more than 1,200.

For the first time, Eleuthera descendent Clothilda Miller learned the storm had been even worse in the interior. That's where her parents had been. Clothilda and her siblings went to the local school, hoping her mother would be there, but she wasn't. "After all, a mother will try to get to her children," she would recall decades later. On Tuesday, after two long, excruciating days with no news of her parents and brother, Clothilda was finally reunited with a relative from the Glades; however, it wasn't her mother. It was Ernest Rolle, the brother-in-law, roommate and business partner of her father, Isaac Miller. Ernest had found the children at the wreckage of their home. He had told them what they did not want to hear. He said he and Isaac had sat down in their shack and watched as the water came up until they were floating out the door. They got separated. Isaac was a good swimmer. The two kept calling out to each other, trying to determine each other's location. Soon, Isaac did not answer. By the end of the week, Clothilda and the other children had made up their minds that their relatives and parents were dead and would not be coming to the Glades to reunite with them.

On Monday night, a relief worker and *Palm Beach Post* employee, R.N. Jones, had joined a caravan out of the Glades. He came back with a truck carrying the bodies of thirteen black people—and a grim pronouncement hinting at the carnage in the interior: he said this was "a small percentage of the corpses found floating in the hyacinth-choked and muck-filled canals," and added, "the loss of life was terrifying." Relief workers fed the survivors and took with them able-bodied blacks, putting them to the grim task of collecting rotting and dead bodies.

In Clewiston on Saturday, September 22nd, American Legion officials requested airplanes to survey the damage done by the hurricane by air. The same day, at South Bay, some forty-one bodies still remained in the field within 200 yards of the main part of the town. There weren't enough people to handle them, and relief coordinator V.C. Denton said they would stay there, covered with lime, "until we can get enough men to pile them up and burn them." As individual corpses were discovered, they would sprinkle them with lime to lessen the stench by searchers, and a pole with a white flag would be placed on the side of the body to guide the collectors to the body. Hundreds of remains, so bloated they could not fit in caskets, were stacked like cordwood on flatbed trucks.

Considering the general unsanitary conditions present in the 1920s, the fear that the storm's death and destruction and standing water would open the door for diseases was a valid one. After the storm, health officials reported some cases of typhoid, tetanus, and influenza. But a report of a flu epidemic in Clewiston was later debunked. The Board of Health workers treated drinking water wherever they could with sodium hypochlorite and started administering typhoid shots at once; more than 8,000 people started the series of shots, and the Board reported 6,490 completed the treatments. The group reported no great outbreaks, crediting its extensive vaccination program over previous years. By September 28th, the state Board of Health declared the area health conditions as "excellent," saying the anticipated outbreaks hadn't happened. Crews began putting screens on the barracks for blacks, to keep out mosquitoes, and building toilets on the canal bank.

Ellsworth L. Filby, chief engineer for the state's bureau of sanitary engineer, kept a diary of what he saw:

On September 20: rescue of a man who'd been clinging to a telephone pole since the storm. That day: intermittent rain. The wet stuff just added to the misery of those looking for survivors, collecting the dead, cleaning up debris, and trying to rebuild. Saturday, September 22: Bergan discussing plans for disposing of bodies. They agreed on cremation, using driftwood and oil. The gathering of bodies into piles was almost impossible, probably due to their state of decomposition. "Water 2½ feet deep. Work very tiring and depressing," Filby wrote.[108]

Sanitary situation western part of Palm Beach County became increasingly serious, reported disaster relief director A.L. Schafer as he reported to Washington on September 20th. He told them that bodies kept coming to surface after being buried, so it became necessary to bury bodies without identification. He also wrote that a new "negro cemetery" was being established at "Loxahatchie," which was situated sixteen miles west of Palm Beach, to accommodate the black storm victims. In the town of Okeechobee, where twenty-five persons were reported dead, managers reported that the bodies could not be buried there because the ground was too saturated and they would simply float back to the surface after being buried, so they were being buried in Sebring, which was located on much higher ground.

Coffins reserved for whites only are stacked high along the bank of a canal, after the Great Lake Okeechobee Hurricane of 1928 in Belle Glade, Florida (Florida Photographic Collection, Courtesy of the Florida State Archives).

On the lake's northeast shore, a small, informal cemetery stood on high ground in a settlement called Port Mayaca. Soon bodies were being sent there. Eventually, a mass grave would be established at Port Mayaca. Located a few miles east of this intersection is the Port Mayaca Cemetery, which was chosen in 1928 as the site for the mass burial of over 1,600 unidentified people who lost their lives in West Palm Beach County as the result of the Great Okeechobee Hurricane. Originally operated by a trust set up by the cities of Belle Glade, Pahokee and South Bay, the cemetery has been operated since 1992 by the city of Pahokee alone.

---

[108]   Kleinberg, E. (2003) *Black Cloud-The Deadly Hurricane of 1928*, Carroll & Graf Publishers, pg. 147.

On Wednesday afternoon, in Belle Glade, people started constructing caskets. Palm Beach County Sheriff Robert C. Baker came in about 4pm and said he was short of caskets. He told officials to load them on trucks. They would be driven to a collection area at the airfield in West Palm Beach to await burial. In West Palm Beach, at the black cemetery along Tamarind Avenue, a large hole had been dug. By Wednesday night, 250 black corpses had already been laid into it. Orel J. Myers, the assistant medical director for the Red Cross, told the newspaper, "All white bodies will be held for 12 hours at Woodlawn," the official—that is, white—cemetery. "Colored bodies are being buried immediately."[109]

It wasn't uncommon for the newspaper to carry lists of name after name: "Marvin Lee and entire family. Three grandchildren of Oliver Wilder. Mrs. Raus and four children, newcomers to the community." Then: "Six negroes. Two negroes. There are from 100 to 150 negroes dead and missing in the South Bay section." The newspaper said 34 blacks had been buried in Pahokee and Belle Glade. No names. Brief announcements on the front page served as a bulletin board.[110] James Felton of Lake Worth, feared dead, was safe. H.L. Douglas of Chosen, near Belle Glade, was looking for his wife and children and could be reached at the courthouse. Thursday's newspaper carried a list of names of people for whom Western Union had undelivered telegrams. It contained at least three columns, and most of them were assumed to be dead.

Among the dead listed in the newspaper; five from the Schlecter family of Belle Glade. There was E.E. Schlecter, 50, and four children: 18, 11, 4, and 3 respectively. The four were Erma, Emma, Johnnie, and Kathleen, a neighbour wrote to a cousin in Indiana on September 20th. Only Clara Schlecter had survived. She floated on a log, holding little Johnnie, until a wave swept him away. Walter Schlecter had been out of town when the storm killed his parents, three sisters, a brother, and a niece. Shortly after the storm, Schlecter reported that he couldn't realize his predicament he was in because almost all of his family members were lost in the storm and he would never see them again on this Earth. He said that it felt like

109 Kleinberg, E. (2003) *Black Cloud-The Deadly Hurricane of 1928*, Carroll & Graf Publishers, pg. 148.
110 Kleinberg, E. (2003) *Black Cloud-The Deadly Hurricane of 1928*, Carroll & Graf Publishers, pg. 148.

it was all a dream and he would wake up with them by his side. He was comforted with the fact that our lives on this Earth are pleasing in His sight and that we would meet again in Heaven; this sure helps to bear the burden we have to bear, he said.

During the storm, Charles Green had held onto the crossbar of a light pole outside the icehouse in Belle Glade. Separated from his wife and children, he held a memorial service for them, but he didn't stop working. Three and a half weeks later, he would enter a refugee camp in West Palm Beach and find his family, alive. At mid-morning on Wednesday, 1,000 storm refugees in West Palm Beach, some of whom had been brought to the coast from the Glades, climbed aboard fourteen rail coaches—half-white, half-black—for relief centers farther south. The whites went down to Miami, the blacks to Pompano Beach. "As we walked through the destitute places," famed black educator Mary McLeod Bethune wrote in an article carried by several black newspapers, "our souls cried out to God for help, because He alone could sustain us under such conditions as these."[111]

Labourers had already been at work with axes and saws, cutting away at trees and buildings. The debris was piled along the road for some 20 miles. Frank Stallings and his father Festus, driving from Georgia, came to Florida to help with the grim job of helping pull bodies from the canals. Workers would tie them behind boats and drag them to where they could be collected. Eventually, local health officials stepped in and said the crews would have to burn the bodies where they had piled them. Because the ground was so wet, they used driftwood and crude oil as fuel. For example, on September 26th alone, apparently following the commands of health officials, workers burned 267 bodies, 87 of them in a single pyre.

A National Guard unit from the Tampa area had been sent to the town of Okeechobee, and unit leaders left by car from Tampa late Monday night. On September 17th, they arrived in Okeechobee about 4:30am Tuesday. By noon Wednesday, the Guard had helped recover nine bodies there. Eventually, twenty-five people would be found dead or declared missing and presumed dead. A scan of the list reveals grim groupings of surnames that tell a story of families destroyed. Five Lees: one 78, one 39, one 22, one 3, one 4 months. Five Frasers; one 40, the others 7, 4, 3 and

---

[111]   Kleinberg, E. (2003) *Black Cloud-The Deadly Hurricane of 1928*, Carroll & Graf Publishers, pg. 149.

14 months. Two adult Stevenses, plus two toddlers, one 5-month old. Four Lightsey children. Three children of the Upthegrove family. The list also includes Old Man Hamlet and Old Man Yeats, hermits, both unaccounted for. Some bodies came in with skin and hair gone, their eyes swollen until they burst, their tongues protruding "longer than your hand." Many of the dead were buried in the Ortona Cemetery.

Thomas Richard Brown, a National Guard colonel, described housing materials and dead livestock were scattered everywhere, adding that he wouldn't know what he would do when he smelled fresh air again, because the pungent odor of the decaying corpses was quite over-powering. He said Lake Okeechobee reeked from the dead things in it, including dead bodies. In fact, workers were banned from even bathing in it and fresh water for drinking and cooking was not obtained from the lake, but was brought in by boats from elsewhere. They also brought medical supplies, including antibiotics and perhaps penicillin, which was only discovered that year. Guardsmen were even forbidden to shave for fear of cutting themselves and the cut becoming infected. As Brown watched, a man who hadn't slept since Friday and was searching for his family came to a pile of bodies and found his father, mother, and wife, their clothes tattered, and their bodies were in the advanced stage of decomposition and in pretty bad shape. Another man had also just identified his fifth dead child, and at the time his wife was still missing.

Thursday morning's *Palm Beach Post* carried new estimates that were moving into the level of the unthinkable. They said the death toll could pass 1,000. On Saturday, September 22nd, the Associated Press reporter in the Glades was quoting National Guard Captain G.G. South's estimate that the toll would triple to 1,500; that was a minimum figure, he guessed. The day before, Coral Gables Health Chief Dr. A.F. Allen had said from Pennsylvania Hotel in West Palm Beach that they had gone over the death toll situation pretty closely. When the final report is written, the general agreement among the doctors is that the dead will not be far from 2,500.

On Friday, Governor John Martin finally toured the area after having driven down from Tallahassee. Blaming the technology of the time, he said he would have come sooner had he realized the damage was so severe. He called it "appalling." A total of 357 had already been confirmed dead. Martin had spent a half-hour talking to Levi Brown, a black farmer from the Bahamas in the region since 1921. Brown had brought his wife, four daughters, and three sons to the roof to escape the rising flood, but his home had been smashed and everyone thrown into the water. He heard cries in the darkness and recognized one as that of his twelve-year-old daughter. A water moccasin that had climbed aboard the same log showed its gratitude by biting Brown; the man's right hand swelled enormously, but Brown said he had found the pain bearable if he slipped it underwater.

Brown had worked his way to his skiff and set out to find more survivors. The first three he found were two white men and his twelve-year-old daughter. Brown later received a shot of antivenom for his hand and spent the next several hours helping rescue dozens of people and identifying the dead. On Thursday, September 20th, he found the body of his eight-year-old daughter. He later found another child, his eldest, dead on a heap of twenty-five corpses. His wife and six of his children, all except his twelve-year-old, had died in the storm. When Brown had finished his story, the governor did something very unusual at the time when segregation between blacks and white was at an all-time high, and that was to shake a black man's hand. "Brown, I am glad to shake your hand, and I wish Florida had many more citizens of your caliber, for you are a credit to your country," Martin said. He gave the devastated man $25, and another official gave him $5.

Railroads offered free passage for bodies, and for refugees who wanted to leave South Florida. By the first weekend after the storm, some 800 survivors had accepted the offer of a free ride. The total reached 1,427 through 6:00pm, September 28th. The railroads finally stopped the practice amid complaints that the not-so-needy were exploiting their generosity. After that, the Red Cross paid the fares, either full or half. The organization also guaranteed the return fare of refugees likely to find themselves welfare cases at the end.

Monday, September 24th, eight days after the storm, had been the first day that no bodies came in from the Glades. Workers were still finding bodies, but they were too decomposed to transport. They would still be finding bodies in late October—ten in one day on October 19th. In 1930, two years after the storm, workers clearing a large pile of debris and parts of the failed dike from a railroad embankment at the state prison farm would find the remains of Glades resident Dave Burnett. He was the last storm victim to be positively identified.

On October 1ˢᵗ, schools finally opened and life's 'new normal' was starting to set in and people were starting to pick up the pieces and getting on with their lives. Helen Sherouse, later Helen McCormick, the thirteen-year-old who had lost eighteen of her nineteen relatives, told the story many times in her life. She would say that for the rest of her life, each approaching hurricane filled her with trepidation. "It leaves you with the feeling that anything can happen at once," she said in 1988, still tearing up and feeling deep emotions some sixty years later. "I live with it every day." But, she said, "It wasn't me that saved me. A thirteen-year-old kid couldn't have saved themselves. It just wasn't my time, I guess."

In high school, in a fit of cleansing encouraged by her teachers, she wrote her memories of the storm. She later gave them to a friend. But years later, when she wanted to give the notes to the local historical society, the friend could not find them. Helen died at eighty-four in February 2000. In 1988, in an anniversary article, she had said ominously of Palm Beach County, "We haven't had a hurricane here in years. And the next one's going to be terrible." Then along came Hurricane Andrew in 1992 and devastated Florida and became one of the North Atlantic's most enduring hurricanes.

Carmen Salvatore rebuilt the home he had lost and returned to farming. He would say later that, every once in a while, as he worked the land, he'd run across a collection of bones in the muck. Whether these skeletons were new or prehistoric or were, in fact, the remains of 1928 storm victims perhaps will never be known. Carmen retired from farming in the 1960s, because it was becoming unprofitable to continue.

The 1928 hurricane and the dramatic real estate crash that followed decimated Harry Kelsey's finances, so in 1931 he left the city he had founded and which bore his name. Eight years later, it changed its name to Lake Park. The arch that greeted visitors turning into the town near Old Dixie Highway was torn down. Kelsey died in 1957. Meanwhile, Kelsey's former business partner, Sir Harry Oakes, an American-born British Canadian gold mine owner, entrepreneur, investor and philanthropist, had moved to the Bahamas for tax evasion purposes, where he was bludgeoned to death in 1943 in one of the area's most sensational society murders. His son-in-law, Count Alfred de Marigny, was charged with the slaying, but later acquitted, and the case remains officially unsolved to this day. In 1997, some Lake Park residents floated an idea to restore the name "Kelsey City," but the plan never materialized.

After the hurricane of 1928, a cousin had taken in Clothilda Miller and the rest of her family until the Red Cross rebuilt their home. For the rest of her life, she donated to the organization in gratitude to what this organization had done to help them during their time of need. She said that she could not remember the exact time that things returned to normal, but she had to go back to work very shortly after the storm. As a result, she didn't have time to grieve because their house was destroyed and she had to work to provide for their siblings with the meager resources she gained from working.

Soon after the storm, Clothilda dropped out of school and found employment washing clothes in the afternoons for several West Palm Beach families. She was paid a mere $3 per week, and so she never had to look for work because of the small fee she charged to these families. Work was plentiful, and she got many references. Five years later, on October 4, 1933, Clothilda Miller, then nineteen, was married to clothes salesman Willie Orange at Palm Beach County Courthouse by County Judge Richard Robbins. The couple later divorced about fifty years later, in July 1982, and Willie Orange died at seventy-six on October 31, 1982.

Over the years, many ceremonies were held to honor these victims of the storm. In the 1970s, Ruth Wedgworth, whose husband owned a large Glades produce business, got the idea of a memorial to hurricane victims and survivors. It would go in front of the Palm Beach County Library branch in Belle Glade. Hungarian-born sculptor Ferenc, of Delray Beach, got a $30,000 commission to design and create it. Bert Roemer, a local contractor, donated a big chunk of concrete, and Varga made a relief that was mounted on it on April 13, 1976. It showed farmers, animals, homes, and telephone poles caught up in waves. On Memorial Day in 1976, the town held a festival for the US Bicentennial. The parade grand marshal was Lawrence Will, the Glades' "cracker historian." A section of the county library was dedicated as the Lawrence Will Museum, and a bronze statue was also dedicated at the same time. It depicts a man, a woman and a boy running. The woman carries an infant in her arms. As they look over their shoulders, they raise their arms in a feeble attempt to ward off an unseen wall of water.

The memorial sculpture of a family fleeing the killer storm of 1928 was commissioned by the Belle Glade Bicentennial Committee and created by Ferenc Varga "to honor the early Glades pioneers and the more than 2,000 persons who lost their lives in the disastrous 1928 Hurricane" (Florida Photographic Collection, Courtesy of the Florida State Archives).

In West Palm Beach, the Okeechobee Hurricane Memorial Garden Coalition and several historical and cultural societies in Palm Beach County held commemorative events for the hurricane's seventy-fifth anniversary, in September 2003. Banners were hung at buildings that had survived the storm. Lectures were held to educate Florida residents about the impact of this storm. Furthermore, a symbolic motorcade of pinwheels started at the Glades into West Palm Beach, and then ended at the mass grave. The pinwheels represented the faceless dead of the hurricane of 1928.

CHAPTER TWELVE

After the Storm

How to stop hurricanes, and how to stop them from killing people? These were two top priorities after the 1928 hurricane. Its black victims were not. In West Palm Beach, in the black neighbourhood along Tamarind Avenue, a large hole was dug, filled and covered up. The grass grew over it, and soon things returned to normal. After a while, people outside the neighbourhood forgot that anything dramatic lay beneath the street. Memorial services, one white, one non-white, were held at the same time, but at different locations on Sunday, September 30, 1928, in West Palm Beach. The *Miami Herald* article (1928) on the memorial services reported nearly 1,000 victims of the hurricane disaster, 674 of whom were non-white. Additional *Miami Daily News* articles stated a death toll of 2,200 (September 24, 1928) and 2,300 (September 25, 1928), along with the observation that only the death toll in the Galveston hurricane of 1900 was higher.

In Lawrence E. Will's book *The Okeechobee Hurricane and The Hoover Dike,* which seems to have the best details on the 1928 hurricane of any source available, the estimated death toll was at first set at 2,300, but later lowered to 1,770. Will quotes the final Red Cross report in 1929 as stating that 1,810 people were killed and 1,849 were injured in the 1928 hurricane. But Will also quoted a news release from the Florida State Board of Health on December 7, 1928, which estimated the deaths in Palm Beach County alone at 1,833. From Will's book:

> The exact number of those who perished in the Okeechobee
> storm can never be ascertained. Probably three-fourths

or more of the casualties were Negroes (sic), many of whom had come from the Bahama Islands. Accounting for members of this race was complicated by the migratory habits of their kind and the fact that most of them were known, even to their friends, only by a nickname. Another reason the number cannot be ascertained was that many were carried by the flood far into the sawgrass wastes.[112]

The National Weather Service (NWS), using the Red Cross number, had long listed the Okeechobee Hurricane of 1928 official death toll as 1,836, making it the second worst hurricane death toll since the Galveston Hurricane of 1900. Initially, with this count there were no rounded numbers, as this was a time of science.[113] Exact numbers were required, since they gave any report more exactitude and believability. Only bodies physically recovered and counted were included in the total. The number of the dead, however, was underestimated. The report failed to take into account the many persons listed as missing and presumed dead, many of whom were black migrant farm workers from the Bahamas who had worked in the Okeechobee region. Many of them were only known by just a nickname, and many of the bodies of these migrant workers were buried with no documentation because they were rotting so quickly and had to be buried right away, making it difficult to get an accurate count. Furthermore, many of these victims were from the Bahamas, and as a result, no one came to look for them or reported them missing or dead to the Red Cross officials, thereby further complicating the documentation of the dead or missing bodies.

No doubt, the use of this figure by the NWS dates to Mitchell (1928), who quoted a Red Cross official casualty estimate dated October 28, 1928. Dunn and Miller (1960) also quote the Red Cross figure. Pfost (2003) called for a revision of the death toll to 2,500 with an asterisk, denoting that the exact number of people killed will never be known. Blake et al. in the latest (2005) update to the National Hurricane Center publication "The Deadliest, Costliest, and Most Intense United States Tropical Cyclones", lists the death toll from the Okeechobee Hurricane of

112 http://www.srh.noaa.gov/mfl/?n=okeechobee
113 http://www.srh.noaa.gov/okeechobee

1928 as "at least 2,500", establishing the Okeechobee Hurricane of 1928 as the second worst natural disaster as far as number of people killed in U.S. history.[114]

The hurricane continued northwest across the lake, and then turned north through Highlands and Polk counties, passing near Gainesville and west of Jacksonville before paralleling the Atlantic coasts of Georgia and the Carolinas. It finally moved inland over Virginia and became extra-tropical over Pennsylvania and the Great Lakes.

The State Marker at a Mass Burial Site for the victims of the Okeechobee Hurricane at Port Mayaca Cemetery in Martin County (Courtesy of the Florida State Archives).

There is still tangible evidence of this historical tragedy. In West Palm Beach's Woodlawn Cemetery, a stone marker stands today in memory of 69 victims of the storm, of which 61 were white. Also in West Palm Beach, at the corner of Tamarind Avenue and 25th Street, a new state of Florida historical marker stands in sentinel over the place where 674 victims of the storm were buried after being transported from the Belle Glade area. At the Port Mayaca Cemetery in Martin County, another stone marker was placed over a mass grave of about 1,600 victims. Near the Belle Glade Public Library in downtown Belle Glade, a beautiful memorial stands as a remembrance of the deadly storm and its devastation. As part of the 75th anniversary of the devastating hurricane, the dead at 25th Street and Tamarind Avenue got the respect they were so unjustly denied in 1928.

---

[114] http://www.srh.noaa.gov/okeechobee

"We're here to recognize an incredible demonstration of the power of nature, a reminder that Mother Nature is the boss, and we're here to right the wrongs of the past," said Lois Frankel, West Palm Beach's mayor who spoke at the dedication ceremony.

While today's Hoover Dike, with a grade elevation approaching 30 feet, is reassuring, it has not yet been tested with a direct hit by a Category 4 or 5 hurricane, and it needs continuing maintenance. The only sure thing is that South Florida will have future encounters with hurricanes, perhaps even a Category 4 or 5, in years to come. It is important that South Florida residents know their hurricane history in order to better prepare for tomorrow's hurricane threats.

On Tuesday morning, September 18th, thirty-six hours after the hurricane's arrival, headlines around the nation summarized the calamity: "Florida Destroyed! Florida Destroyed!" The initial news of the disaster at West Palm Beach was just beginning to emerge when a far more ominous catastrophe was discovered-the mind-boggling massacre on the edges of Lake Okeechobee.[115]

This disaster happened within a few miles of a large city and a world famous resort, yet so isolated was the location that it was not until three days later that Florida's own governor learned of its enormity. So extended and so difficult was the terrain that after six weeks, the search for bodies was discontinued, with many still unrecovered.

Perhaps one of the greatest tragedies and loss of lives of the storm took place at Pelican Bay, where hundreds of bodies were later recovered. Most were black labourers who had ventured out from their camp at Tishomingo during the eye of the storm. Believing that the worst of the storm was over, they began to walk the dike toward Pahokee when the hurricane conditions resumed from the opposite direction. The lake quickly became engulfed in the surge from the hurricane, and it spilled over the dike and drowned many of them.

As the storm moved on and the sun emerged the following day, few relief agencies rushed to the give support to the survivors at Okeechobee. In fact, most attention was first placed on the destruction along the coast. Soon, however, word spread of a great disaster inland, the scope of which

---

[115] Barnes, J. (2007) *Florida's Hurricane History*, Chapel Hill, The University of North Carolina Press, pgs.129-130.

would take many days to realize. Dead bodies were scattered everywhere, decomposing in the hot Florida sun with each passing day, and there were fears of diseases, such as typhoid fever, dysentery, and cholera being spread throughout the area. This was because, by some accounts, the contaminated floodwaters remained waist deep for over five days. Many of those who had managed to survive had been swept for miles into the sawgrass and were forced to walk or wade back to whatever recognizable roadway they could find. Some, too weak or injured to stand or walk, sat for days in hopes of being spotted by passersby. Some who survived the storm were believed to have perished later as they wandered the vast Everglades.

Loading Bodies of those who perished in the Everglades into a Truck at Belle Glade (Courtesy of NOAA-The National Hurricane Center).

Five days after the storm, Governor John W. Martin toured the region and reported:

> "In six miles between Pahokee and Belle Glade, I counted twenty-seven corpses in the water or on the roadside, but not taken from the water. Total dead on the roadside and not buried and counted but not in plank coffins was one hundred and twenty-six. In six additional miles over five hundred and thirty-seven bodies were already interred. Fifty-seven additional bodies were hauled out of this area today in trucks and tonight for truckloads of bodies were brought from adjoining areas by boat, loaded and sent to West Palm Beach for burial. One military officer reported to me that while in Belle Glade today for thirty minutes,

ten bodies were brought in and added to the piles of bodies, thirty-seven in one pile and sixty in the other."[116]

Looting became a problem almost immediately. For example, resident Helen Buchanan called to say her garage had been blown down and people were "carting off everything," a West Palm Beach police clerk wrote in the blotter. "Watch out." But few incidents were officially reported. That didn't prevent Police Chief F.H. Matthews from ordering a sundown-to-dawn curfew, saying everyone must be off the streets "unless an extreme emergency demands it, and then must have a pass or permit signed by the chief of police or his assistant." At the island town of Palm Beach, mansions had been reported open and being looted. One wealthy family reported priceless paintings had been removed from their frames by the winds and were lost. Officials declared 'martial law' for the island on Wednesday, but rescinded it the next day. Officials also worked quickly to quash rumors that bodies had been found in the lakes that were used as the city's water supply.

West Palm Beach Chief F.H. Matthews decreed no one except authorities could carry a gun. All Girl Scouts and Boy Scouts were expected to report to the Red Cross headquarters Saturday morning. Furthermore, on Wednesday, Mayor Vincent Oaksmith issued a "no work, no food" order, saying all able-bodied men and those unemployed men must offer themselves for work within twenty-four hours or face being drafted. "All able-bodied persons in West Palm Beach are ordered to work," the *Palm Beach Post* said in an editorial on Thursday, September 20th. Praising the quick restoration of utilities, the paper added, "Let us all take our lesson from these examples. They have started rebuilding, they have taken care of the emergency, and they are planning for the future. Face the situation soberly, for it is grave, but remember that while we have people of courage, we have hope."[117]

After the storm, on Monday the head of the Florida National Guard had contacted John Wellborn Martin, the governor of Florida, for permission to activate the troops. He told him no because he said that the

---

[116] Mykle, R. (2006) *Killer 'cane: The Deadly Hurricane of 1928*, Taylor Trade Publishing pg. 205.

[117] *The Palm Beach Post*, Thursday, September 20th 1928.

storm didn't do that much damage to require the use of them, a decision he would later come to regret after the death toll and damages from the storm came in to the command center. Fortunately, the National Guard didn't wait for permission from Martin because he activated some troops from Tampa to assist with rebuilding efforts in the Okeechobee region. From Pensacola, as far away from Palm Beach County as you can get and still be in Florida, a legislature wired Martin to call for a special session of the legislature, so that money could be moved from the state treasury for relief. Martin, who had also rejected a special session after the Great Miami Hurricane of 1926, would later deny one for this storm as well.

On Wednesday, September 19th, Martin had finally activated the Florida National Guard, including two regiments in West Palm Beach area. But as early as the day after the storm, a local lieutenant, J.A. McIntosh, had already taken it upon himself to activate Company C, 124th Infantry. By Thursday, four days after the storm, the number of militia patrolling the streets was up to 161 guardsmen and 11 officers. Martin was back in Belle Glade on Monday, September 24th. It had now been eight days since the hurricane struck. He toured the Glades by car and boat and issued a statement that "the destruction of property is enormous." He said that while driving the six miles from Belle Glade to Pahokee, he counted six corpses floating in the water or lying in the road. Martin called on all cities in Florida to send whatever cash they could.

The President of the United States, Calvin Coolidge, also had not waited either. As early as Sunday night, with hard reports of devastation already back from Puerto Rico and the news from Florida growing worse by the hour, he had already been in touch with the Red Cross and told the War, Commerce, and Labour departments to make themselves available to relief agencies. On Monday afternoon, he issued a statement that "an overwhelming disaster has overtaken our fellow citizens." He was asking the Red Cross to lead the effort and urged people to give quickly and generously. After this appeal, the Red Cross headquarters in New York and around the country soon were reporting a flood of donations. Millionaire J.P. Morgan gave $10,000. People of more modest means came in to give what they could. By Friday, September 21st, the Red Cross was estimating that relief in the islands and Florida would require $5 million. Leaders called on each chapter, suggested a quota, and urged the chapter to exceed it. Help came from benefactors large and small from all over the country.

At dawn, Tom Rickards and his family stepped out of the Palm Beach County Courthouse shelter in downtown West Palm Beach. It was the only building standing for blocks, stark against the rolling hills of scattered lumber. Debris on the street came almost to the shoulder of his young son, Tommie. A piece of a tall flagpole was tossed several feet into the ground. Buildings were totally destroyed across the horizon, as far as the eyes could see. Three weeks later, on October 3rd, he would describe the carnage experienced: "The suffering throughout is beyond words. Individual tales of horror, suffering and loss are numberless."[118]

In the aftermath of the storm, the exhausted survivors, many of whom were very injured and hungry, needed food and medicine as a first priority. Transportation of any kind was totally paralyzed. The roads and canal embankments used as secondary roads were washed out and rendered impassable. Most of the canals were totally clogged with debris and broken boats. The boats and barges lodged in the canals had sunk and were damaged or immobilized by the wreckage. Splintered wood, crumpled custard apple trees, and twisted metal roofing piled high at the bridges, and the locks dammed the outflowing water. From the lakeshore, a three-mile inland sea covered the entire area. The only form of transportation was small, shallow draft boats that could maneuver across the watery wasteland with impunity. The fishermen whose boats had survived the storm siphoned the water from the gas, dried the carburetors of their outboard motors, and got them to run.

The boats, their outboard motors rudely disturbing the quiet after the storm, went first to family farms to search for relatives and friends. They passed near the lake dike banks covered with dead fish and birds. At prosperous farms, there were no houses, no animals grazing in fields—only dead and bloated cows with their legs stiffly in the air, headless horses, and denuded chickens. A few found family and friends; the rest were corpses floating in black water. Stunned and confused survivors were taken aboard and transported back to the relative havens of South Bay and Miami Locks. The tops of the dikes were the only land above water.

---

[118] Barnes J.,(2007) *Florida's Hurricane History*, Chapel Hill, The University of North Carolina Press, pg. 129.

Along the broken dikes, survivors picked their way through the mulch and over the rubble. The injured waited on soggy banks, nursing their wounds, too numb and confused to move or do anything else. There was no food or fresh water. A boat was sent to Clewiston in the hope that they might find food or water there. Clewiston had not escaped unscathed either. Its streets were underwater, and the railroad track, ripped from its bed, was a twisted ribbon of steel. Houses were blown off their foundations, while others simply collapsed or were strewn to bits and pieces.

Clothilda Miller and her siblings looked out of Mr. Ewell's home, back to their own. All that remained was a pile of wreckage and a few clothes the family would salvage. Clothilda sat down on a piece of lumber that had come off the house. She said sadly to herself, "What must we do?" Despondently, she saw no way out of the sad and depressed situation they were unexpectedly placed in because of the storm.

In Belle Glade, Lawrence Will crept out of the barge's holding area. The Hillsboro Canal looked like a construction dump, completely jammed with broken houses, trees and sunken boats. Crawling over the extensive amount of rubble that clogged Main Street, he finally made his way to his building. The roof had blown off, and there was extensive rain and flood damage, but the Pioneer Building was one of the few structures in Belle Glade that remained standing. The once-prosperous little town was now in shambles. Ten-foot piles of rubble, twisted metal, and broken wood blockaded the streets. There were telephone poles, house beams, and dead pets. There were automobiles crushed under intact roofs. Ragged, ripped clothes fluttered in the trash. Main Street was covered with soaked debris.

Stepping over and around piles of splintered wood and twisted rubble, Will sloshed his way in knee-deep water back toward the canal. There, he found the distorted body of Raymond Martin. Nearby, dumped like a broken doll, was the corpse of his little sister Lucy, who, because of her short-cropped red hair, was assumed to be a young boy. The two bodies were gently taken to the pool hall in Tedder's Hotel and laid on the pool table. He thought about his own family and what might have happened to them. He realized if he wanted to find out their plight, he had to travel to Fort Lauderdale.

After depositing the bodies of Raymond and Lucy in the makeshift morgue in the poolroom at the hotel, Lawrence Will returned to the canal.

Across the debris-clogged canal, he saw a huge uprooted rubber tree lying on its side. At its base the roots fanned out, and he saw movement. Rushing over, he found Thelma Martin, still holding baby Robert above her head. Beside her, there was Ernestine, who stood there emotionless in the tree roots, too exhausted to move. Thelma's foot was still solidly lodged in the roots. She had a nail in her knee. Will took the children back to the hotel. The baby, limp and discolored, seemed dead, and the two young girls were cold and in a state of shock. At the hotel, Dr. Buck quickly examined baby Robert and shouted out loud that he was alive. They took the baby upstairs and rubbed him in whiskey and gave him a few drops as well to help him with his recovery. Lawrence Will, worried about the safety of his family, hiked a ride to Fort Lauderdale on a truck. Once assured that his family was safe, he reported the conditions in Belle Glade to the Red Cross and the Coast Guard.

After the storm, little Thelma Martin became an instant celebrity for her bravery during the storm. Her heroic exploits were recounted in a hastily printed booklet with pictures and personal recollections of the storm, published three weeks later for $1 a copy. The image of a little girl saving her baby brother made exceptionally good press when everyone was focused on the devastation caused by the storm. The media and the Red Cross recognized that people needed a hero. The outside world needed someone they could identify with, and that would help collect funds, clothes, and food for the victims. Thelma, however, was too injured and shocked to appreciate it, and the shock never wore off. Considering everything she went through, after her wounds healed, she refused to discuss the night of the storm, preferring to keep the traumatic events of that night buried deeply in her subconscious.

Considerable amount of debris on the road from Pahokee began to change from trees and branches to wood and twisted metal roofing. Henry Martin knew they were near town. He had only one objective: he had to get Sonny to Dr. Buck. The boy was injured and shivering in his wet shirt, and Henry was afraid he, too, might die. He was sure that, except for Sonny, he had lost his entire family. If Sonny died, too, he would lose the will to live. They crossed over the Hillsboro Canal Bridge and saw that Tommy Well's house was gone. Were Tommy and Willie Emma also dead? he wondered to himself. On Main Street, people walked around in a daze—some nodding recognition, while others moved along silently, like zombies.

"Where's Dr. Buck?" he asked. "At the Glades Hotel. That's where they're taking everybody." He reached the hotel and helped Sonny up the stairs. Dr. Buck was in the lobby, attending to a patient. "Do everything you can for him. He's the only one I have left." Henry said. "Henry, I have three of your children upstairs in bed, and they are going to be all right."

A disbelieving and surprised Henry Martin stared silently at the doctor. "I even have your baby up there." One of the women escorted Sonny and Henry upstairs, where Henry found Thelma, Ernestine, and baby Robert. He hugged his three children as he fought back tears. "I'm sorry, Henry. Your oldest son is in the pool hall with the rest of the dead," Dr. Buck said. Downstairs, as Henry passed along the rows of bodies, he saw Minnie Lucy's head.

"That's my youngest girl," Henry said. "No, that's a boy," Dr. Buck said.

Henry just shook his head. He knew it was his girl. She had been infested with red bugs in the summer and had her hair cut short like a boy's. He reached down and held her head in his hands. On the next table over was Raymond; his head gash was quite visible. But Henry had no time to grieve. He had to find Bessie Mae and the other children. Leaving the hotel, Henry headed to go out and look for them. At every stop where the dead had been gathered, Henry walked to rows of corpses, forcing himself to stare into each vacant face and at every broken body—one might be Annie or Bessie Mae. They were the faces of the drowned, some grimaced in agony, and others posed in serene tranquility. There were battered bodies with freshly scarred limbs; others lay peacefully, as if they had just fallen off to sleep. There were white bodies and black bodies dumped together; all sharing in death the equality that had so eluded them in life. At first Henry could not believe that all these people were from Chosen and Belle Glade. Did the storm blow the bodies from across the lake? There were so many dead, but Annie Mae wasn't one of them. Instead of Annie Mae, he found another girl's corpse. She was Annie Mae's size and her colouring, but her eyes—still staring out in awe at an unexpected death—were dark. Exhausted and suffering from the effects of hypothermia and injuries, a dejected Henry Martin walked back to the Glades Hotel.

This photo shows the damage done to a cluster of Everglades
scientific work stations in Belle Glade after the Great Okeechobee
Hurricane (Courtesy of the Florida State Archives).

Annie Mae was not in Chosen, when the Martin store had broken
against the church, she grabbed at the floorboards in a panic. She watched
the vent window in the gable go past as the store flipped over. It collapsed,
and she was thrown into the water and dragged under. Desperately kicking
with her dress tangled in the rubble, she struggled to reach the surface.
After what seemed like eternal minutes, she finally broke through. A piece
of the store rolled over her, breaking her left shoulder blade. She fought
to remain conscious. With her good arm, she grabbed onto a part of the
house and held on for the next four hours until the water stopped moving,
and it didn't help either that it was pitch black, and she had no idea where
she was located at the time. Gingerly, she stepped off her piece of wood
onto a canal bank and collapsed. Nearby, a houseboat with its keel up had
been thrown up on the bank; she crawled under it to get out of the cold
and stinging rain. Cold and confused, with twenty-nine puncture wounds
and badly bruised, she huddled, doubled over in pain. Her broken shoulder
throbbed as she waited for rescue, or morning, or even death.

Annie Mae lay there for two days in a dazed and confused state,
wondering if she had the strength to survive. She huddled under the
houseboat unable to even stand. All of her clothes were ripped off her
during the ordeal, with the exception of her slip. Downpours of stinging
and ice cold rain pelted her body, further weakening her. Night came and
went as she drifted in and out of consciousness. Tuesday morning, two
black men found her shivering. One took off his sweater and covered her
before walking her to Belle Glade. For the entire two-mile walk, Annie

Mae said nothing because the shock of her experience kept replaying over and over in the back of her mind.

The trio reached the bridge over Hillsboro Canal, and Annie Mae remembered, "I was walking across the Pahokee Bridge and saw a man coming towards me. I thought, 'He looks familiar,' but I didn't recognized him initially, but then he spoke to me, called me by name, and I realized it was my daddy." Henry put his arms around his daughter and gave her a great big hug. After seeing that she was taken care of, Henry once again set out for Bessie Mae by going back to the farm. When he got there, he found out his entire black farm workers were all dead by drowning and all of the buildings destroyed. Henry slogged around in two feet of water that covered the entire Everglades, searching until his battered body could take no more. By the time he returned to Belle Glade, he was suffering from hypothermia and had contracted a lung infection. He did something he had never done in his life—he gave up. Henry Martin was a man dejected and defeated. Bessie Mae Martin was never found.[119]

Cecil Warner searched the wreckage for his friend Arlin Martin. He found Henry Martin's cousin under a pile of broken wood, two hundred yards north of the Hillsboro Canal. He turned over the body and reached down around his bloated stomach and removed an alligator money belt. Inside was the $1,140 he had made while working in the automobile factories. Just two days before the storm, Cecil had helped him count the money—his farm money. Across the street, a Red Cross official spotted him removing the money belt. All the authorities had strict orders to prevent looting of corpses. Wedding rings and bracelets were targets of opportunity. The Red Cross official demanded the belt. Cecil explained that the corpse was Aaron Martin, Henry Martin's cousin, and that the belt and money should go to the family. The Red Cross man insisted it be given to him. "I'll see that they get it," he said. Not wanting to be accused of looting, Cecil reluctantly gave him the money belt. "You can retrieve this at the Red Cross," he said and left. That was the last the Martins heard of that money.

Henry knew they could not remain in Belle Glade. There was no place for them to live. He was suffering from a lung ailment. Sonny, Thelma,

[119] Kleinberg, E. (2003) *Black Cloud-The Deadly Hurricane of 1928*, Carroll & Graf Publishers, pg. 145.

and Annie Mae had lesions, and Robert had pneumonia. After the canals and roads were cleared of debris, the Martins were loaded onto a boat and sent to a hospital in Miami. Within a few days, they had recovered enough to be released from the hospital and sent to a crowded refugee house ten miles north in Hollywood.

Nancy and Josh searched for two weeks until finally they found Henry and the children in the Hollywood refugee camp. In the tearful reunion, Henry Martin thought only of returning to the Everglades. He had a family to support. He had to feed them; he had to build a house. It was September, and there was still time to find Bessie Mae, but sadly he never did.

In Jupiter, a bleary-eyed and disheveled Bessie DuBois and her family surveyed the damage to her home, the lighthouse, and the area around the inlet. Everyone and everything was all wet and stayed wet for a long time. The house hung from the chimney and porch. The dock was standing out of the water and was covered with debris. Boats were scattered or smashed. The DuBois men had to cut away trees just to get out of the house. They later learned that John DuBois' sister's home had been destroyed and the woman's infant son, less than a year old, had been killed when the strong winds had pulled her from her father's arms and slammed her into a building, and her father was badly injured. The baby was never found. Her empty casket had no flowers; after the storm, there were simply none to be found. Bessie DuBois' father and siblings returned to their home, about two miles away, and found it twisted around the chimney; stairs were at angles, dishes lay scattered everywhere and broken in bits and pieces, and the house was off the blocks. Considering everything about their circumstances, Bessie recalled that they did not know how well they fared until the reports began to come in.

The U.S. Weather Bureau Building south of the lighthouse along the inlet was totally destroyed. In the nearby vicinity, a cement-block home belonging to a black family had collapsed, and several people were dead; another report placed the deaths at six. Six persons were killed just west of Jupiter when a school building where they had sought refuge during the storm collapsed. The only survivors had found sanctuary huddled under oak and metal desks.

The three Boots boys immediately after the storm had decided to leave their wooden floats and soon found themselves in chest-deep water. They had floated 2½ miles to the southeast when they heard another boy screaming at the top of his lungs, and as they got near to him, they were desperately hoping it was their brother Virgil. But it was the neighbor, Mutt Thomas. Mutt had also floated in the darkness until the water receded, then sat on a large piece of wood floating and remained there until daylight. He had waded three miles before finding the Bootses. The group began wading back to their home. With the land covered in water, they had to use palm trees, the Bolles Hotel, and draglines as landmarks. Mutt heard someone shout out his name from across the canal and was surprised to see that this person was his father. He immediately jumped into the canal and swam to his dad for an emotional and tearful reunion. Charles Thomas had held on to the cross-arm of a telephone pole all night.

a) Damage at North End Pharm, N. Poinsettia b) Damage at Riviera c) Damage on Third Street across from Barcos d) Damage at Lytal Pratt Furniture e) Damage at Church of Christ, Rosemary f) Damage at Hibiscus (Courtesy of NOAA-The National Hurricane Center).

The very tired Thomases took refuge on the floor of the Bolles Hotel. The Bootses later linked up with their half-brother, who later took them back to Sebring Farms. Later, the Boots' father and brother would be found dead. They were later buried in Ortona Cemetery, along the Caloosahatchee. Sadly, Vernie's mother was never found. Victor Thirsk searched among the rubble for his wife, but didn't find her. No one, either dead or alive, was found at the farms. Thirsk, the three Boots boys, along with Charles and Mutt Thomas, were the only Sebring Farms survivors.

Everything they owned—every piece of furniture, every family memento, all memories of the dead—were all gone. It was as if they had never existed. Only their bodies would be final proof that they had lived and died.

Mutt and his father went back to Sebring Farms. There, they saw Mutt's Uncle Minor, his father's brother, who remained with the family home. Minor said he'd held on to the flat roof for dear life when it came off the house. On Tuesday, the Thomases found the bodies of Mutt's mother and all five of his siblings, along with Charles' brother Richard and his wife. Richard's two children, aged five and seven, were never found. The bodies of the Thomas family were taken on Wednesday to high ground, and then trucked to Ortona Cemetery, where thirteen-year-old Mutt helped his family buried the dead at midnight. It was only much later that he learned his teacher, Edna Denniston, had clung to her husband, John, and son, Paul, in a cypress tree in the rising water. Edna and little Paul had drowned in John's arms. The impact of the storm was so great on the life of Mutt's father, who died in 1947, that he worked the farm furiously non-stop. Sometimes, some of his workers came up to him for instructions, but he would not answer and simply stare at them in a daze. It was as if he were a zombie or somewhere else. He never truly recovered from this tragedy.

In the days following the disaster, help was slow to come into the Okeechobee region. To make matters worse, only one route to West Palm Beach was open, and most roads were impassable and clogged with huge piles of debris. No cars in the area could operate, and food and fresh drinking water were virtually non-existent, and it was difficult next to impossible to get them into the area shortly after the storm. William J. Buck, the only physician on the south end of the lake, took command of the immediate cleanup effort by issuing a radical order. He sent all of the surviving women and children away from the area on foot. Even though West Palm Beach was forty-two miles away, walking there was seen as their only chance of survival. Over 100 women, carrying their babies and necessary belongings, set out on the difficult journey. Most made it only as far as the Experiment Station, and some went on to Six Mile Bridge, where they were later greeted by the Red Cross. The remaining men, fatigued and emotionally drained, slowly began sifting through mounds of wreckage in search of loved ones. Another doctor volunteered to go to

Belle Glade to render assistance to the storm victims, but when he got there, he was shocked at the significant death toll and destruction and immediately changed his mind and quickly caught the first truck back to Fort Lauderdale.

A few days after the storm, more dumbfounded survivors from Chosen and South Bay filtered into the Red Cross shelters with horrifying stories of their experiences with the storm and the report of hundreds of dead that lay unclaimed as yet. Little by little, the scope and magnitude of the disaster became quite obvious, and Belle Glade was the center of a world-class catastrophe.

By the first weekend after the storm, relief workers had a new problem. To the north, rain-swollen waterways from the swollen Kissimmee River valley were emptying into the big lake. To make matters worse, the canals that spread like spider webs south of the lake, draining water to the coast, were jammed with debris or broken locks. As a result, instead of the water level finally receding, the level was rising and the swollen lake lapped over what was left of the dike that had failed so miserably on September 16th. Areas of standing water extended to the western neighbourhoods of West Palm Beach. Many of the few passable roads were flooding again. Officials issued an urgent call for motorboats to help with the recovery of the dead and the cleanup efforts.

The Coast Guard's Fort Lauderdale base, normally active at sea, found itself in unfamiliar territory of working inland. Several Coast Guard boats, a cutter and four dinghies, worked their way towards the Glades, rescuing distressed storm victims and recovering dead bodies. Along the way, it picked up, on Thursday, 18 more men and four boats. They met up with 27 men from the West Palm Beach Station and 56 men and seven boats from the Palm Beach station and a mobile reserve based at Fort Lauderdale. Over the next several days, the Coast Guard found 14 survivors and recovered 475 bodies.

When the Coast Guard had arrived in West Palm Beach, the National Guard had not yet arrived. At Belle Glade, the Coast Guardsmen found people in private boats haphazardly trying to round up survivors and the dead and took charge, with the permission of Governor Martin. Later, the Coast Guardsmen commandeered a group of labourers and, over three days, cleared the 13-mile road between Belle Glade and Pahokee, thick with three trunks, muck, and "debris of all kinds of depth from two to five feet," reported R.L. Jack, commander of the Florida East Coast Patrol Area. In fact, Jack reported, Coast Guardsmen found themselves playing "police, courier, mechanic, road building, burying the dead, butchering live animals, milking cattle." Along with its other supplies, the Coast Guard had brought 25 gallons of a special supply of Prohibition contraband. It was grain alcohol and strictly for the volunteers, to give them strength for their awful work. This was one of the only ways some of them were able to work under such wretched conditions.

Shortly after the storm, in the West Palm Beach area, a significant amount of emergency trucks drove into the affected area to gather and remove the dead bodies. It seems as if there were too many dead for anyone to care. The trucks carrying the Everglades dead came day and night with unidentified bodies stacked like sardines in the back. By the fifth day, the trucks were recognized from far away by their smell and the long trail of opaque body fluids dripping from the back. For the blacks, there were no coffins, no name tags, only a tarpaulin unceremoniously thrown over them.

The difficult task of recovering the dead went on for days. Efforts to identify loved ones, however, were quickly abandoned. Because of the rapid deterioration of the corpses, it soon became virtually impossible to even determine their race. A carpenter at South Bay spent his days making caskets called "rough boxes" from the planks of what used to be the homes of the region. As the news of the disaster finally reached the coast, truckloads of cheap pine boxes were soon delivered.

Lake Okeechobee was brown with mud, torn vegetation, and debris. Dead snakes, turtles and rabbits were found everywhere around and near to the lake, along with swarms of fish that had suffocated in the stagnant water. The horrible odor was overwhelming, not only from the decay of human flesh, but also from the scattered carcasses of fish, alligators, and other animals. In the first few days, the cleanup moved along very slowly because of the lack of boats and the limited amount of able-bodied workers. Eventually, groups of Legionnaires and black workers were brought in to give a hand to the cleanup effort. Workers wore cotton gloves that were regularly cleaned and applied with a massive dose of disinfectant. Even though Prohibition was the order of the day at the time, law enforcement officials bent the rules a bit to allow the workers to consume massive amounts of bootleg whiskey to get over the horrible task ahead of them. The whiskey was donated by local rumrunner Jack Mansley, who became an unlikely hero.

Frede Aunapu, crushed inside of a pile of swirling trees, somehow survived. When he pulled off his clothes later, his body was a crazy quilt of bruises. Half of the twenty-two people who had been with him in the packing house didn't survive. Frede and Elizabeth were married the next May and eventually had three sons.

Lawrence Will, in his book *The Great Lake Okeechobee Hurricane and the Herbert Hoover Dike* commented about the horrible task at hand:

"It would be impossible for anyone who has never been so engaged, to realize the utter repulsiveness of the task of searching for and recovering those reeking corpses in all stages of decomposition. Add to this the heartbreak experienced by those who identified and brought in remains of their own wives, children and friends. Without the stimulated effect of the whiskey ration, it is doubtful if many would have the stamina to continue. It was customary when a boat returned with its string of bodies for the crew to be given a stiff drink. The Negroes, also, who loaded them on trucks, were given periodic doses. Nobody got drunk (with the possible exception of sightseers), but all could look forward to their bit of refreshment."[120]

All the shallow draft boats were pressed into service to search the flooded farms and communities for survivors and to recover the dead. Young and old men were sent to look for friends and relatives. When they found bodies, they would tie the rope around their ankles. After gathering up half a dozen or more, they returned with their dismal cargo floating behind them.

Every town had its own outdoor morgue. Soon the stacks of bodies grew so large that corpses could no longer be put into boxes; instead, they were "loaded like cordwood" into large trucks and driven away for burial. Most were buried at the new Port Mayaca Cemetery, where a stone marker was later placed that reads: "In Memoriam: To the 1600 pioneers in this mass burial who gave their lives in the 1928 hurricane so that Glades might be as we know it today." Some were buried at Ortona Cemetery, where the

---

[120] Will, L. (1961) *Okeechobee Hurricane and the Hoover Dike 3ʳᵈ Edition*, The Glades Historical Society, pg. 160.

dead from the 1926 storm at Moore Haven were buried, and some were even shipped for burial in other states. Steam shovels dug trenches for mass graves in two locations in West Palm Beach, one for blacks and one for whites. In the common grave dug between Twenty-third and Twenty-fifth Streets and Tamarind Avenue, at least 300 black labourers were buried. Recent campaigning efforts have brought recognition to the site, and in 1991 the state of Florida finally ceded to the wishes of the campaigner's requests to formally recognize the site as hallowed grounds for the dead black migrant workers and other black victims of the storm. They also held an official funeral where the direct descendants of the dead were in attendance.[121]

Throughout the coloured town, neighbours helped neighbours. Houses and churches became homes to hundreds of families. As in most tragedies that strike the black community, the residents did not expect any help from the white-controlled city, or Palm Beach County. Years of neglect and Jim Crow postures had made them self-sufficient. They would take care of their own themselves.

The search for the corpses was a long and tedious task, and it continued through October, until finally on November 1st it was called off due to the lack of funding. Most of the dead had been found. Sadly, many of the bodies were never buried, but were torched in makeshift funeral pyres. Furthermore, some of the dead were reportedly eaten by alligators that infested the canals. Since not all of the bodies were recovered, farmers through the years have often reported digging up the bones of storm victims in the fields that surround the lake region.

Several unusual storm events were reported in the aftermath of the storm. One involved the murder trial of a man named Arthur Stokes, who was on trial for the murder of another man named Gilbert Gibson. Fortunately, luck was on his side when the only witnesses to the case were drowned in the storm and the state was forced to dismiss the case due to the lack of witnesses. In another similar turn of events, a black resident of Belle Glade named Freeman Smith had been put on a $500 bond for assaulting a black woman. He had to be acquitted, since no witnesses could be found. Another case involved the whereabouts of Deputy State Hotel

---

[121] Barnes J.,(2007) *Florida's Hurricane History*, Chapel Hill, The University of North Carolina Press. pgs. 137-138.

Commissioner Pat Houston, who was believed to have absconded with a considerable sum of the state's money because of his long absence. It was reported that Houston's good name was returned when his body was found near the town of Pahokee. Governor Martin said that the body of one of the storm victims, C.L. Reddick, was found five days after the flood, still guarded by the man's trusted dog. One local man, emotionally numbed by the calamity, worked long hours in search of bodies, even though he himself had twice been bitten by a poisonous water moccasin.

The next event involved a lone two-story house situated like a solitary sentinel near the roadway. Even before the storm, the old house had a very dilapidated look. Its owner was an elderly, partly deaf man named Callahan. Alone and without any information, the old man rode out the storm. That morning, as he did every morning, he dressed, had breakfast, and set out on foot for the South Bay Post Office. He saw people searching through the water, but couldn't hear them when they talked to them. Finally, curiosity got the better of him, and he stopped, cupped his hand around his ear, and asked, "What the hell is going on?"

"We had a hurricane. Where are you going?" one of the men shouted.

"I'm going down to the post office to see if I got some mail," he replied.

"There ain't no post office—it's gone!"

"Gone! Gone where?"

The post office, run by Maude Wingfield out of her store, had been built out into the lake on pilings. The storm surge had carried it off without a trace. Perhaps most amazing of all, an eighty-three-year-old woman from Belle Glade was found alive in a steel washtub on September 20th, four days after the storm.

Unfortunately, due to the negative publicity the state of Florida received after the 1926 storm and the economic bust that followed, some officials at first downplayed the disaster at Okeechobee. But word of the tragedy soon spread, and more relief poured in. The Red Cross was well prepared for the storm's aftermath, having gained valuable prior experience during the Great Miami Hurricane of 1926 and the flood at Moore Haven. Local volunteer chapters went to work as soon as the news of the storm's impact in Puerto Rico was known. Well before the hurricane struck Florida, the Red Cross had dispatched six experienced relief workers to the state. After the storm hit, while the American Legion was busy with the rescue efforts and the search for bodies, the Red Cross set up twenty-two emergency feeding centers. Shortly afterwards, thousands of refugees had access to food, clothing, and shelter. The people of the glades were in particular need of clothing, as the swirling floodwaters had left many of the survivors nearly naked.

The black St. Patrick's Catholic Church in West Palm Beach had suffered $40,000 damage and the white Holy Trinity Catholic Church $17,000, with lesser damage reported at Catholic churches from Micco, in southern Brevard County, to Deerfield Beach, in far northern Broward County. Two months after the storm, on Sunday, November 18th, every Catholic Church in America would devote its offering to hurricane relief; $202,800 was collected, with $84,200 of it going to South Florida and the rest to Puerto Rico. Within an hour of hearing the grave reports from West Palm Beach, residents in Miami sprang into action. About 7:30pm, Red Cross workers from Miami began working their way up the coast highway, pushing away debris that grew thicker by the mile, in winds still gusting almost to hurricane strength. Miami city officials later authorized donations of 20 barrels of disinfectant, 24 lanterns, 2 tanks of chlorine, and 5,000 paper cups.

"When Miami suffered its hurricane disaster in 1926, it was the recipient of much needed outside assistance," Monday afternoon's *Miami Daily News* said in a front-page editorial. "Sunday's hurricane found Miami prepared to meet such an emergency, and it regarded it as a privilege to lend assistance to its suffering neighbours." An accompanying cartoon showed a nurse leading a procession of ambulances into the "stricken area" and carrying a box reading "Miami Relief." The headline read, "Miami Does Not Forget." The next day's editorial was just as forceful. In 1926, it said, "Miami, weak and helpless, following its saddest visitation, raised its hands in supplication. And quickly the cry was answered. Other cities and states answered that cry of distress from Miami. And in its saddest hour, the stricken area to the north and west of Miami may be sure that this community does not forget."

**A badly damaged home in Palm Beach after the hurricane
(Courtesy of the Florida State Archives).**

Telephone officials were quite busy after the storm, reporting 32,000 accounts out of service, 400 poles broken and another 2,500 poles leaning. Telephone linemen got the word out about the damage, and soon Southern Bell and AT&T workers were rushing south with equipment from centers in Atlanta and in Jacksonville, where employees worked in inches-deep water left by the hurricane as it left Florida. The phone company shipped down 150 tons of copper wire from inventory and another 75 tons from factories, as well as 20 railcars full of poles and a railcar full of switchboards. The phone company's office in Delray Beach was almost destroyed when the roof had caved in.[122]

Workers set up operations in a nearby building while a team, in a 48-hour turnaround, quickly went 150 miles to Titusville and took over the equipment there to get Delray Beach's service up and running. In February 1929, the phone company would hang a bronze marker at its West Palm station, at 326 Fern Street, "in grateful appreciation and to hold in remembrance the men and women of the Bell system who so faithfully and courageously exemplified the spirit of services during the Florida hurricane, September 1928." The marker remained on the wall of the building until Southern Bell was sold to BellSouth and moved out of the building in 1998. It sat in a closet for about three years until the company placed it outside its central switching center at 120 North K Street, in downtown Lake Worth.

---

[122] Kleinberg, E. (2003) *Black Cloud-The Deadly Hurricane of 1928*, Carroll & Graf Publishers, pg. 134.

On September 25th, the city of West Palm Beach had declared that 2,881 homes were damaged beyond repair and 700 were destroyed. Some 8,200 whites and 4,000 blacks were homeless. The Red Cross would eventually pay $471,770 to victims or vendors and help 12,707 families in the storm area. The agency set up twenty-two feeding centers, where workers dispersed prepared food packages. Shipping and railroad lines shipped used clothing to the region for free. At the height of its deployment, the Red Cross had 93 cars of volunteers averaging more than 500 trips a day and some 50 trucks making about 200 regular trips from the supply centers to the needy, plus 38 boats and 4 airplanes were placed in operation.[123]

On Thursday, September 20th, the West Palm Beach city commission, in a special session of the legislature, approved an anti-gouging ordinance. It basically said that anyone found jacking or hiking up the prices on goods and services more than its pre-September price could pay a fine of $500 and go to jail for up to 30 days. Within hours, a merchant who had hiked up the price on ground beef and a gas-station operator who had hiked up his price on kerosene from 20 cents to 25 cents a gallon, were each charged and were found guilty and sentenced to 30 days in jail. The merchant was also fined $250, and the kerosene gouger $100. The jail sentences were later suspended, however the disgraced and embarrassed merchants still had to pay the fines.

By early October, the basic needs of the storm victims were being met, and the Red Cross announced that its part in the recovery would soon end since rebuilding the devastated towns was "not the job of the Red Cross." Controversy erupted as a result of this announcement, and the organization was denounced as a fraud. The little money and materials the Red Cross had for rebuilding were cautiously rationed to the people of Belle Glade and the surrounding community. But within a matter of weeks, the Red Cross' policies were dramatically changed. By mid-November, with the help of the Red Cross, many new home constructions were underway, most of which were built to a much higher and rigorous standards than they had been before, thanks to newly implemented Florida building codes. This storm led to the introduction of new and strictly enforced building

---

[123]   The American Red Cross Society official 1928 Okeechobee Hurricane Records.

codes in the state of Florida. Soon the Red Cross was even supplying seeds, fertilizer, and fuel for the replanting that was destined to rebuild the economy of the Okeechobee region. When all was said and done, the hurricane victims expressed their deep gratitude to the Red Cross and the many other relief organizations that had eased their burden and gave them a new start on life.

The newspapers began offering free ads for those seeking work or workers. It also cautioned the outsiders from coming in to profit heavily from rebuilding storm-damaged buildings. Stores ran advertisements saying, "moved temporarily," "temporary quarters," "our merchandise is not damaged," "ready for you: a clean, fresh stock of groceries." By September 28th, newspapers were full of advertisements assuring residents that things were returning to normal. Everyone's gas service station was also back to normal selling gas. The water was uncontaminated and safe to drink. As soon as Frost Hardware's insurance adjuster released the stock, the place was reopened "with some very attractive sacrifices."

On September 25th, in New York, the Giants split with the Chicago Cubs in a double header. They had to make up the September 19th game that was rained out when the hurricane passed through the Northeast after devastating Florida. The Giants would eventually lose three of the four games to the Cubbies and lose the National League pennant to the St. Louis Cardinals.

The hurricane did a favor for the Port of Palm Beach, and that was it washed away a sandbar that had blocked the inlet to the ocean, deepening the channel from 14 feet to 17 feet and saving the inlet commission as much as $40,000 it had planned to spend to clear the inlet before the storm did it naturally for them.

The Red Cross had spent more than $1 million, an astounding amount in 1928, for building materials and labour to help rebuild 3,624 homes. It was four times what the agency had spent in any other category. In 81 cases, houses were shoved back onto their foundation. Another 704 were anchored to concrete foundation piers. The already-collapsing real estate market had left many people "property poor": their homes were destroyed, while the owner still held mortgages now on the brink of foreclosure. The Red Cross policy was to help the homeowner, not the creditor.

The farm losses had also been astounding. C.W. Warburton, Director of Extension for the U.S. Department of Agriculture (USDA), which at the time also supervised the U.S. Weather Bureau, was asked by the Red Cross to go to Florida. He arrived in the Glades on September 30th. He reported back to the USDA that the storm had destroyed virtually all the crops. But Warburton also reported farmers were in excellent spirits and quite anxious to continue farming. Unfortunately, the planting season had just recently started when the storm struck, and the land stood in water for weeks. The Red Cross provided seed, fertilizer, feed for labour animals, and fuel and oil for the tractors. The Ford Motor Company sent two truckloads of parts and two mechanics to fix up more than 150 damaged and soaked tractors. The Palm Beach County Loan Farm Fund spent $100,000 giving out loans of up to $300 at 5-percent interest. Congress approved $15 million in crop aid to the southeast farmers, much of it in loans to buy seeds and fertilizer. Most of the attention was concentrated on the Glades. "Those people are very energetic and enterprising and are trying to return to their little farms," Florida's US Senator Park Trammell told the Senate Committee on Agriculture and Forestry on December 19th. "It is all they possess: the land."

Statewide, the storm ruined what would have been the best citrus crop in the history of the industry, the Florida Citrus Exchange reported on September 26th. The exchange stated that the storm's winds scratched much of the fruit, reducing the quality. It also reported 6 percent of the oranges and 18 percent of the grapefruits were lost. Especially hard hit was Polk County, east of Tampa, which lost 12 percent of its oranges and more than 33 percent of the grapefruit. In the Indian River region, between Palm Beach County and what is now the Space Coast, 20 percent of the oranges and 40 percent of the grapefruits were lost. Managers said harvesting would be delayed until mid-October because the groves were flooded.

The storm would have been even more devastating had it hit the area at the height of financial health in the early 1920s. But it came at the time when the great 1920s Real Estate Boom had collapsed and South Florida was already heading into the Great Depression. For Florida, the one-two punch of the storm and its 1926 Miami predecessor had hastened what had already been a steep slide. In Palm Beach County alone, fourteen banks had failed in the year preceding the storm, and banks, which two years before had $50 million in deposits, now reported totals of $10 million to $12 million. B.D. Cole, founder of the West Palm Beach-based insurance company of the same name, established in 1919, said later that, at least for West Palm Beach, the storm was a blessing in disguise. Cole, noting that the collapse had started in 1926 or even before, argued the flush of insurance money into the area helped start its recovery, or at least soften its slide.

About a month after the storm, on October 12th, Richard W. Gray, assistant meteorologist for the U.S. Weather Bureau's Miami office, made the difficult journey into the still-ravaged interior to make a first-person's account to his bosses in Washington. It was like a descent into hell. Miami, the town Gray had watched the 1926 storm tear to pieces, was about 70 miles from downtown West Palm Beach, but even it had provided hints of this storm's power, in the form of some torn awnings and broken windows. Next stop: Hollywood and Fort Lauderdale, up the road in Broward County. Gray saw only slight structural damage, along with some broken windows and leaking roofs. Most of the losses were from water damage, and Gray figured a few thousand dollars would cover everything in those two towns. North of Fort Lauderdale was Pompano Beach, and it was there that Gray first started to see what the storm had done. He estimated that the losses were in the millions of dollars.

Then he moved inland. At the settlements along the lake's southeast shore, "The small houses in these localities were washed away or inundated," he wrote on October 23rd. "Practically the entire Everglades region south of Lake Okeechobee has been flooded, making it impossible for the growers to prepare the land for the usual early winter crops." Gray reported crops in the Glades were still flooded a month after the hurricane. He wanted to emphasize the lack of major damage to major buildings, something he noted in the 1926 storm as well. He said that proved that well-constructed buildings can even withstand the most powerful of storms that Mother Nature can throw their way.

a)Total devastation near Palm Beach b) Boat blown up on the Wharf c) Damage on First Street d) Damage on Third Street looking West from Railroad e) Damage at McClain's Garage f) Damage at City Auditorium at North Bridge (Courtesy of NOAA-The National Hurricane Center).

On October 23rd, Florida National Guard Major B.M. Atkinson reported roads were dry and in good condition from Belle Glade east to West Palm Beach, north to Okeechobee and west to South Bay. On the side of the roads, two feet of water still stood. Most of downtown Belle Glade was still under standing water; Atkinson said it probably would be for at least another week. Only 150 people were in the town. No one was doing repairs; it was impractical until the land was dry. Atkinson reported some minor scuffles, blaming them on lazy and unhappy residents of the smashed city. Atkinson reported spotting one diligent man. It was Levi Brown, who had lost almost his entire family, whose story had touched the heart of the Governor of Florida, and whose assault had been wrongly blamed on a Red Cross official. Atkinson said he watched as Brown strode through the flooded fields, strenuously, but progressively planting peas.

Christmas brought a few prospects of happiness to those still recovering from the storm. Junior Red Cross chapters across the country sent care packages, including, books, candy, and handmade cards done by art classes in schools around the country, and thousands of dollars to the children stricken by the storm. The Salvation Army provided toys. The Red Cross also spent about $5,000 on new playground equipment, books, and other supplies for schools devastated by the storm. At the end of the year, the Red Cross pulled its recovery team out of South Florida, but the Palm Beach chapter remained and continued to provide services and collect money from donors nationwide for another two years to finish the job of rehabilitation and rebuilding South Florida.

In its recovery efforts after the hurricane, the Red Cross would spend nearly $6 million, $50,000 directly from its funds and another $5.88 million in contributions. State-by-state totals for donations from people and institutions ranged from $1,038 from South Dakota to $1.12 million from New York. The agency spent $3.23 million in Puerto Rico and the Virgin Islands, and $2.7 million in Florida. The Red Cross pointed out two key differences between the relief efforts in South Florida and Puerto Rico, and that was the fact that the island was mostly rural and Florida was more urban, and relief in Puerto Rico was on a "mass" basis, while in Florida "the wide divergence in economic status imperative a case-by-case determination of need." Once again, these totals would be tenfold in current dollars.[124]

As for the Martin family, when they were finally allowed to by the authorities, they moved back to Belle Glade, living first in a tent near Chosen before moving into a newly built house. Henry Martin never recovered financially. The storm and the loss of Bessie Mae, the store, and the farm had drained the entrepreneurial spirit away from him. He began to farm again, but the dream of being the largest landowner in the Everglades and having a chain of stores throughout South Florida drowned in the black waters of Lake Okeechobee on September 16, 1928. Henry Martin never remarried. As he'd drive by the old store site along Canal Street, or across the sawgrass plains, he'd stare, out as if still looking for Bessie Mae.

The Business Section of Belle Glade Florida after the Great Okeechobee Hurricane-The Tedder Hotel, Darden block, Badger's two story store and post office (Courtesy of NOAA-The National Hurricane Center).

---

[124]   The American Red Cross Society official 1928 Okeechobee Hurricane Records.

Many survivors found it too painful to remember the impact of this storm. Ernestine and Thelma never spoke about their long, terrifying night on the tree stump, not even between themselves. Nancy Martin developed a serious hurricane phobia. At the very mention of a hurricane that stood a chance of hitting Florida, she demanded someone drive her further north to West Palm Beach or Frostproof, out of harm's way. Some found solace in God. Agonizing over the loss of his sister, Tommy Wells went through a spiritual conversion. The wild boy and war hero from northern Florida became a preacher. He eventually moved his family to Everglades' city and established a church there. Vernie Boots studied in Fort Lauderdale, leaving high school just before acquiring his diploma. With his intuitive mind and active imagination, he developed a number of grassroots inventions, but memories of the storm never left him. Charles Thomas was continually haunted by that September night. Except for his son Mutt, he had lost his entire family. With the terrible memory of the storm never leaving him, he applied that sorrow and applied it to his farm and became one of the largest landowners in the Everglades.

Duncan Padgett recovered from his attack of heartworm. The same humour that had carried him through life, had won the heart of Lillian Shive, and had helped him overcome his illness now also helped him become mayor of Pahokee. Lawrence Will, the sociable service station owner, stayed in Belle Glade, becoming one of the leading citizens. Self-styled "cracker historian," he recorded the oral histories of many of the Everglades' early settlers and went on to write six history books about the 1928 hurricane and early life in the Everglades, including his most popular one to date, *Okeechobee Hurricane-Killer Storms in the Everglades*. The Lawrence Will Museum, located on Main Street in Belle Glade, is dedicated to preserving the Glades history.

The storm forever changed not only the lives of the survivors but also the Everglades themselves. Today, Lake Okeechobee is completely surrounded by the massive, forty-foot-high Hoover Dike. Constantly monitored by the United States Corps of Engineers, the levee has served its purpose. It has never broken. It has protected the farmers and fertile Everglades farmlands from a repeat of the 1926 and 1928 hurricanes. However, gone are the dead rivers. Gone are the massive sweeps of grass beds—the lake's fish hatcheries. Gone are steamship lines. Boats still use the lake, and the intercoastal waterway's Okeechobee Canal, one of Disston's dreams, cuts through central Florida to the lake, connecting the Atlantic Ocean with the Gulf of Mexico.

A building damaged in Palm Beach County after the Great Okeechobee Hurricane (Courtesy of NOAA-The National Hurricane Center).

The Everglades farm area has expanded over fivefold since the hurricane. It continues to be the American winter breadbasket. After years of trying to make a profit planting and refining sugar, the Southern Sugar Company went into receivership. United States Sugar Corporation bought the remains of Southern Sugar, and through better management and science finally was able to produce profitable sugar in the Everglades. Today, miles upon miles of dark green sugarcane grow to the horizon, strangely reminiscent of the old sawgrass plains. But to see the old sawgrass plains as they once were, a casual tourist only has to cross Route 75, Alligator Alley, as it crosses the Everglades from Fort Lauderdale to Naples. Secure in their cars, tourists can conjure up images of the sights that greeted the first Calusa Indians in their search for wild game. Meanwhile, a generation of Everglades farming families would carry the psychological scars of the 1928 hurricane for the rest of their lives. And, for better or for worse, the Everglades was forever changed.

CONCLUSION

The Earth emerged over 4.5 billion years ago and has been evolving ever since. Natural forces millions of miles beyond its atmosphere are forever affecting life on our planet. Changes in climate are constant. Our daily weather is ruled by the sun, and every sublime summer morning and devastating hurricanes are products of the sun's energy impacting our atmosphere from 93 million miles away. The weather shapes the Earth's landscape, in turn, but it's not the only element at play in this regard. Yes, there is vigorous debate about mankind's influence—or lack thereof—on global warming and climate change. But whether violent weather becomes more intense or frequent is not the point we are addressing here. What we are concerned with is not the effect man may be having on the planet, but the historical record of what Mother Nature has meted out to it, and the reality is that nature has raged all about this little sphere of ours for billions of years.

At the end of the long, long day, nature has delivered us these gifts: our precious planet and life itself. Even as we bewail tragedies of hurricanes that occasionally afflict us with their killer winds, surges or even torrential rainfall—we should remember that the forces behind these catastrophes are also responsible for why we are here in the first place. This is because a hurricane is one of the most destructive forces of nature the Earth experiences. Besides the great devastation they create, they on the other hand have some great benefits as well, such as the transfer of heat from the equator to the poles and providing the tropical regions of the Earth with over 60% of their annual rainfall. We can call it nature's fury, but it is really just nature's way.

The Okeechobee Hurricane (also known as Hurricane Saint Felipe Segundo), occurred in September of 1928. The hurricane made landfall in the Leeward Islands, Guadeloupe, Puerto Rico, the Bahamas and the state of Florida and was at different times of its life a Category 3, 4 and 5 hurricane. The damage caused by this hurricane was, at the time, estimated to be over one hundred million dollars. By today's standards, that would be equal to over $1.34 billion 2014 US dollars. The Great Okeechobee Hurricane of 1928 was one of the most devastating natural disasters in U.S. history. In its wake, cities and towns were demolished. Communities on the eastern edge of Lake Okeechobee were washed away in a matter of minutes, and whole families were lost that terrible night. When the storm was over, at least 2,500 people had lost their lives in the Okeechobee region in the state of Florida alone.

The Great Okeechobee Hurricane was first spotted 900 miles east of Guadeloupe on September 10th, 1928. Two days later, on September 12th, the hurricane struck the island chain as a Category 3. The storm caused around 1,200 deaths in Guadeloupe and major property damage. The hurricane then hit the Leeward Islands, causing a significant number of deaths. The damage to crops and property was extensive.

The very next day, the storm was a Category 5 hurricane when it made landfall in Puerto Rico. Winds were reported around 160 miles an hour on the island. Around 36 hours before the storm hit, the residents had been forewarned of the impending danger. They were able to prepare, so loss of life was comparably low, with only 312 fatalities. Hurricane Okeechobee was responsible for over 50 million dollars ($500 million today) worth of damage in Puerto Rico. Several hundred thousand people on the island lost their homes. The hurricane then moved across the Bahamas as a Category 4. In the Bahamas, the residents were also prepared due to well-executed warnings being given ahead of time. There were only 3 fatalities on the island of Nassau; however, in the Turks and Caicos Islands, 18 people went missing when their sailboat was lost at sea and were later declared dead.

On September 16th, the hurricane made landfall in the state of Florida as a Category 4 storm. The deaths and damage to the state of Florida were astronomical. The eye of the storm passed over Palm Beach County and went straight for Lake Okeechobee. Most of the deaths and the damage sustained on the Florida mainland were in the Lake Okeechobee region. When the hurricane finally hit Lake Okeechobee, the sustained winds were around 140 miles per hour. As the winds blew southward across the lake, a storm surge overflowed a dike on the southern edge of the lake. This resulted in floods covering hundreds of square miles of farming land and lakeside communities. A smaller flood on the northern part of the lake occurred a little later, when the dikes there were breached.

Many of the bodies of the deceased were lost as flood waters poured into the Everglades. The flood waters remained for some weeks, so it was very difficult for relief workers to recover and bury the dead. Eventually, mass graves were dug for the bodies, but after a few days even that was not enough. The bodies had begun to decay in the Florida sun, so survivors were forced to burn the dead. All told, 2,500 people or more were killed in Florida on that fateful day. Around 1,600 of them were buried in one grave in the Port Mayaca Cemetery. After leaving Lake Okeechobee, the hurricane moved northeast over Florida and into Georgia and the Carolinas, causing only minimal damage in these places. In the aftermath of the hurricane, it became apparent to the authorities that flood control on Lake Okeechobee needed to be brought up to par, and building codes were also changed in the hopes that future hurricanes would not cause such extensive damage.

Among the many beautiful aspects of life on our planet, nature's resiliency is primary. After inflicting great damage, nature seems to begin to repair itself almost instantly. And if nature's progress sometimes appear slow by our clock, it is in fact quite fast when viewed in the context of the millennia of evolution. Nature, which can sometimes terrify us, reminds us constantly that tomorrow is another day. Empires, nations, and people in the Caribbean and the Americas have created historical realities and cultural differences that have served as the basic markers for our understanding and interpreting the region. However, the Great Okeechobee Hurricane of 1928, like others of its type, demonstrated an underlying environmental unity that also provides a central thread or means to understand hurricanes of this region, and that is too often viewed in terms of its insularity and cultural differences.

These storms marked the importance of the region in a historiography of places. As much as slavery, race, immigration, or imperialism, the hurricanes have defined the region. The same storm produces a differential impact on the societies that it crosses, and within those societies, its effects are suffered differentially by different groups and interests. Recently,

293

Hurricanes Katrina, Gilbert, Mitch and Sandy have made that all too clear. It is by looking both comparatively across imperial and national frontiers and internally across social and ethnic boundaries that the impact of the hurricanes are best understood. The Great Okeechobee Hurricane of 1928 can serve as an example of the commonly shared threat of natural disasters and the differential effects caused by the social, cultural, economic, and political contexts of the storms.

Hurricanes present a variety of opportunities for historians. They are natural phenomena, but they are not necessarily natural disasters, for only when a storm encounters dense concentrations of people or property does it become a catastrophe. The location of populations, the development of beachfront homes, hotels and businesses, and the failure to impose proper building codes all have contributed to increasing the destructiveness of these storms. We confront a seeming anomaly. Despite technological and scientific advances in prediction, the destructive effects of natural disasters have increased considerably since 1928. With the advancement of modern technology, the death toll from hurricanes has decreased dramatically, but sadly, the property damage has increased even more.

The writing of the history of hurricanes, like that of much environmental history begins with a problem. For all their power and destructive potential, the history of the hurricanes is, because of their frequency, almost inherently boring. Unlike volcanoes or earthquakes, the great storms are somewhat dependable. Almost every year, some island or coast is inundated or devastated by these mighty forces of nature called hurricanes. While for individual islands or cities or stretches of shoreline, hurricanes may be spaced decades apart, in a regional sense, the phenomenon is repetitious and the results expected.

The scenes of destruction are all too common and all too similar: shattered homes and shattered lives, flooded coastlines and interiors, boats piled up on the beaches or carried far inland, destruction in all directions, and later on, scenes of relief and aid amidst a backdrop of ruin. The individual stories may be poignant, but their repetition is numbing. Accounts seem to vary only in the level of destruction, the amount of loss, or the level of the force of the winds. If the story to be told is only that of the storms themselves, then the repetitiveness is inherent. The variations from one storm to the next may be interesting from a meteorological perspective, but have less significance from a historical one.

Moreover, as acts of nature or the handiwork of God, the hurricanes are beyond human control and are therefore outside of history; this explains why they have been ignored as a theme in themselves. Storms are the classic deus ex machina that we as historians, social scientists and meteorologists are admonished to avoid like the plague. But at the same time, because of their ubiquity and regularity, we can also fall into the opposite error of seeing them as the explanation of everything. Almost every event, battle, revolt, revolution or election in the Americas and the Caribbean region has been preceded by one or several hurricanes. To find the balance between explaining too much and too little in the history of the hurricanes is a tricky business, at best.

The 1928 Saint Felipe II or Okeechobee Hurricane is a particularly interesting example because the storm's differential impact in Florida and the rest of the Caribbean allowed us to see the ways in which local conditions contextualized the same natural threat. Leadership in both societies had a vision of an ideal future and was willing to use the disaster as a tool to implement that vision. In Florida, too, there was a desire to rebuild for the future. The power of the storm had not been shared equally. Bahamian and other West Indian workers at Belle Glade and other small communities near Lake Okeechobee had borne the brunt of the storm. In the racially differentiated world of 1920s Florida, it was to be expected that in the effort to relieve and rebuild, differences of colour played a critical role as well. Attention went to property losses in Delray and Palm Beach, not to the unnamed bodies swept away by the waters or burned in communal pyres. The Red Cross, in fact, created a Coloured Advisory Committee that had among its tasks the refutation of "rumors" about aid not being apportioned equally among blacks and whites.

From the time of Columbus, hurricanes shaped the patterns of settlement in the region and the structures of maritime commerce. Their effects challenged governments to respond, and those that failed revealed their weakness and lost their legitimacy. Revolts and upheavals have sometimes followed the storms. The storms determined or contributed to the outcome of individual military engagements and imperial struggles, as well as the competition for markets. Devastating hurricanes caused populations to rethink the role of God and Nature in human affairs and to seek in the technology of communications and prediction finding ways to answer the threat. And above all, the hurricanes and their effects have served as prisms through which societies can be seen. Here in the Caribbean and South Florida, and in fact the entire region, more people are flocking to the hurricane-prone places, most notably the vulnerable coastlines in droves. Understanding how climate change and humans influence the weather is quite essential to unlocking the mysteries of these severe storms. Whether it's Hurricane Sandy in 2012, Hurricane Katrina in 2005, Hurricane Andrew in 1992 or this one in 1928, you can bet there are more severe hurricanes in the making. Knowing and understanding some of the most severe storms around the region in days gone by and today will show you what tomorrow could bring and how scientists are working to better understand our world.

Hurricanes present a variety of opportunities for historians. They are natural phenomena, but they are not necessarily natural disasters, for only when a storm encounters dense concentrations of people or property does it become a catastrophe. The location of populations, the development of beachfront homes and hotels, and the failure to impose proper building codes all have contributed to increasing the destructiveness of these storms. We confront a seeming anomaly. Despite technological and scientific advances in prediction, the destructive effects of natural disasters have increased considerably since the 1960s, when meteorologists started monitoring them by satellites. The average annual mortality rate due to disasters decreased significantly after that period, but on the other hand, property damage has increased even more. But property values aside, Hurricane Mitch of 1998 and the New Orleans Hurricane Katrina of 2005 underline the fact that in human terms, by far the worst sufferers of the effects of "climatic" disasters have been poor people and poor countries. In the contemporary world, "natural disasters" like hurricanes have been socially selective, and they have probably been so in the past and will perhaps be so in the future.

REFERENCES

❖ *"HURRICANE!"A Familiarization Booklet by NOAA, April, 1993.*
❖ Chris Landsea, et al. (2003). *"Documentation of Atlantic Tropical Cyclones Changes in HURDAT: 1900-1930"*. NHC-Hurricane Research Division. http://www.aoml.noaa.gov/hrd/hurdat/metadata_1928-30.htm#1928_3.
❖ Chris Landsea, et al. (2011). *"Documentation of Atlantic Tropical Cyclones Changes in HURDAT: 1928 Hurricane Season"*. NHC-Hurricane Research Division.
❖ *Votes of the House of Assembly-1917-1930*-The Department of Archives-Nassau, Bahamas.
❖ *The Sponging Industry Booklet-Department of Archives Exhibition 18-22 February, 1974. Pgs. 1-31.*
❖ Wxeltv-Heritage, Episode 10: *Hurricane of 1928.*
❖ *A Columbus Casebook-A Supplement to "Where Columbus Found the New World"* National Geographic Magazine, November 1986.
❖ *Annual Colonial Reports (CO-23-Governor's Dispatches) for the Bahamas, 1917-1929*-The Bahamas Department of Archives-Nassau, Bahamas.
❖ *Censuses of the Bahama Islands, 1891, 1901, 1911, 1921.Department of Archives-Nassau, Bahamas.*
❖ *"Hurricanes and the Shaping of Caribbean Societies,"* Florida Historical Quarterly, 83:4 (2005), pgs. 381-409.
❖ *Miami Daily News,* Monday, September 24, 1928, *Miami Public Library*
❖ *Miami Daily News,* Monday, September 25, 1928, *Miami Public Library*

❖ *Miami Herald*, Monday, October 1, 1928, University of Miami, Fla. Otto G. Richter Library.

❖ *The Palm Beach Post*, September 13th 1928.

❖ *The Palm Beach Post*, September 20th 1928.

❖ *The Tribune*, Wednesday, September 19th 1928 pgs.1 & 2 'Extraordinary Hurricane Hits Bahamas.'

❖ National Weather Service, *Weather Forecast Office, Miami Florida, Memorial Web Page for the 1928 Okeechobee Hurricane.*

❖ *The Florida Historical Quarterly*, January 1987. Published by the Florida Historical Society.

❖ Mitchell, Charles L. *"The West Indian Hurricane of September 10-20, 1928."* Monthly Weather Review Vol. 56, No. 9. Weather Bureau. 1928. pgs. 347-350.

❖ Saunders, Gail (1985) *The Social History of the Bahamas 1890-1953*, A thesis presented to the University of Waterloo in fulfillment of the thesis requirement for the degree of Doctor of Philosophy in History.

❖ *The Nassau Daily Tribune, Saturday, September 28, 1929 pgs. 1&2-'Courage.'*

❖ Blake, Eric S., E. N. Rappaport, J. D. Jarrell, and C.W. Landsea, 2005: The Deadliest, Costliest, and Most Intense United States Tropical Cyclones from 1851 to 2004 (And Other Frequently Requested Hurricane Facts). NOAA Technical Memorandum NWS TPC-4, Tropical Prediction Center, Miami, FL.

❖ Landsea, Christopher W., 2002: personal communication.

❖ Gross, Eric L., 1995: *Somebody Got Drowned, Lord: Florida and the Great Okeechobee Hurricane Disaster of 1928*, Vol. I and II, Dissertation submitted to the Department of History in partial fulfillment of the requirements for a doctoral degree, College of Arts and Sciences, Florida State University, Tallahassee, FL.

❖ *Miami Daily News*, Friday, September 14, 1928, Miami Public Library.

❖ *Miami Daily News*, Monday, September 24, 1928, Miami Public Library.

❖ *Miami Daily News*, Tuesday, September 25, 1928, Miami Public Library.

❖ *Miami Herald*, Monday, October 1, 1928, University of Miami, Fla. Otto G. Richter Library.

❖ *"1928 Okeechobee Hurricane."* Wikipedia. 2014. Web.

❖ Mykle, Robert, (2002), *Killer 'Cane-The Deadly Hurricane of 1928*. Cooper Square Press, New York, NY.

❖ *Palm Beach Hurricane 92 Views*, American Autochrome Company, Chicago, IL, 1928

❖ Pfost, Russell, 2003: Reassessing the Impact of Two Historical Florida Hurricanes. *Bulletin of the American Meteorological Society*, 84, Issue 10 (October 2003) pgs. 1367–1372

❖ Pielke, Roger A., and C. W. Landsea, 1998: *Normalized Hurricane Damages in the United States: 1925-95*. Weather Forecasting, pgs. 13, 621-631.

❖ Ahrens, D. (2000) *Meteorology Today, An Introduction to Weather, Climate, and The Environment*, USA, Brooks/Cole Publishing.

❖ Albury, P. (1975) *The Story of The Bahamas*, London, Macmillan Education Ltd. Pgs. 163-169.

❖ Barnes, J. (2007) *Florida's Hurricane History*, Chapel Hill, The University of North Carolina Press.

❖ Barratt, P. (2003) *Bahama Saga-The Epic Story of the Bahama Islands*, Indiana, Authorhouse Publishers.

❖ Burroughs, Crowder, Robertson, et al. (1996) *The Nature Company Guides to Weather*, Singapore, Time-Life Publishing Inc.

❖ Butler, K. *The History of Bahamian Boat Builders from 1800-2000*, Unpublished.

❖ Butler, E. (1980) *Natural Disasters*, Australia, Heinemann Educational Books Ltd.

❖ Challoner, J. (2000) *Hurricane and Tornado*, Great Britain, Dorling Kindersley.

❖ Clarke, P., Smith, A. (2001) *Usborne Spotter's Guide To Weather*, England, Usborne Publishing Ltd.

❖ Craton, M. (1986) *A History of The Bahamas*, Canada, San Salvador Press. Pgs. 236-238, 250-254.

❖ Davis, K. (2005) *Don't Know Much About World Myths*, HarperCollins Publishers.

❖ Domenici, D. (2008) *The Aztecs-History and Treasures of an Ancient Civilization*, White Star Publishing.

❖ Douglas.S.M. (1958) *Hurricane*, USA, Rinehart and Company Inc.

❖ DuBois, B. (1968) *Memories of the '28 Hurricane*, published by *Bessie* DuBois.

❖ Duedall, I., Williams, J. (2002) *Florida Hurricanes and Tropical Storms 1871-2001*,USA, University Press Of Florida, pgs. 1, 6 & 17.

❖ Durschmied, E. (2001) *The Weather Factor-How Nature has changed History*, New York, Arcade Publishing, Inc.

❖ Emanuel, K. (2005) *Divine Wind-The History and Science of Hurricanes*, New York, Oxford University Press.

❖ Fitzpatrick, J.P. (1999) *Natural Disasters-Hurricanes*, USA, ABC-CLIO, Inc.

❖ Green, J., MacDonald, F., Steele, P. & Stotter, M. (2001) *The Encyclopedia of the Americas*, London, South Water Publishing.

❖ Hairr, J. (2008) *The Great Hurricanes of North Carolina*, United Kingdom, The History Press. Pgs. 81–104.

❖ Hazard, R.(2006) *The Storm, God, The Gator and Me-An inspiring story honoring the African-American survivors of the Storm of '28.* Self-Published by Robert Hazard.

❖ Horvitz, A.L. (2007) *The Essential Book of Weather Lore*, New York, The Reader's Digest Association, Inc.

❖ J.D. Jarrell, Max Mayfield, Edward Rappaport, & Chris Landsea *NOAA Technical Memorandum NWS TPC-1 The Deadliest, Costliest, and Most Intense United States Hurricanes from 1900 to 2000 (And Other Frequently Requested Hurricane Facts).*

❖ Johnson, H. (1998) *Bahamian Labour Migration to Florida in the Late Nineteenth and Early Twentieth Centuries" from International Migration Review, vol. 22, no.1* (Spring 1998) pgs. 84-102.

❖ Johnson, H. (1991) *The Bahamas in Slavery and Freedom*, Jamaica, Ian Randle Publishers Limited, pgs. 163-176.

❖ Jones W. (2005) *Hurricane-A Force of Nature*, Bahamas, Jones Communications Intl Ltd. Publication.

❖ Kahl, J. (1998) *National Audubon Society First Field Guide To Weather*, Hong Kong, Scholastic Inc.

❖ Keegan, W., (1992) *The People Who Discovered Columbus-The Prehistory of the Bahamas*, Tallahassee, University Press of Florida.

❖ Kindersley, D., (2002) *Eyewitness Weather*, London, Dorling Kindersley Ltd.

❖ Lauber, P. (1996) *Hurricanes: Earth's Mightiest Storms*, Singapore, Scholastic Press.

❖ Lawlor, J & A., (2008) *The Harbour Island Story*, Oxford, Macmillan Caribbean Publishers Ltd, pgs. 154-177, 203-226.

❖ Lightbourn, G. R. (2005) *Reminiscing I & II-Photographs of Old Nassau*, Nassau, Ronald Lightbourn Publisher.

❖ Lloyd, J. (2007) *Weather-The Forces of Nature that Shape Our World.* United Kingdom, Parragon Publishing.

❖ Ludlum, D. M., (1989) *Early American Hurricanes 1492-1870*. Boston, MA: American Meteorological Society.

❖ Lyons, A.W. (1997) *The Handy Science Weather Answer Book,* Detroit, Visible Ink Press.

❖ MacPherson, J. (1967) *Caribbean Lands-A Geography Of The West Indies,* 2nd Edition, London, Longmans, Green and Co Ltd.

❖ Millas C.J. (1968) *Hurricanes of The Caribbean and Adjacent Regions 1492-1800*, Edward Brothers Inc/ Academy of the Arts and Sciences of the Americas Miami, Florida.

❖ Mykle, R. (2002) *Killer 'Cane-The Deadly Hurricane of 1928*, Maryland, Taylor Trade Publishing. Pgs. 65-217.

❖ Pearce, A.E., Smith G.C. (1998) *The Hutchinson World Weather Guide,* Great Britain, Helicon Publishing Ltd.

❖ Phillips, C. (2007) *The illustrated Encyclopedia of the Aztec & Maya,* London, Lorenz Books.

❖ Redfield; W.C., 1846, *On Three Several Hurricanes of the Atlantic and their relations to the Northers of Mexico and Central America*, New Haven.

❖ Reynolds, R., (2000) *Philip's Guide To Weather*, London, Octopus Publishing Group Ltd.

❖ Robinson, J. (2009) *Historic Osceola County: An Illustrated History*, Historical Publishing Network, pg. 40.

❖ Rouse, I., (1992) *The Tainos-The rise and decline of the people who greeted Columbus*, New Haven, Yale University Press.

301

❖ Saunders, A. (2006) *History of Bimini Volume 2*, Bahamas, New World Press.

❖ Saunders, G. (1983) *Bahamian Loyalists and Their Slaves*, London, MacMillan Education Ltd, pg. 2.

❖ Saunders, G. (2010) *Historic Bahamas*, Bahamas, D. Gail Saunders. Pgs. 85-87.

❖ Saunders, G, and Craton, M. (1998*) Islanders in the Stream: A History of the Bahamian People Volume 2*, USA, University of Georgia Press. Pgs. 43-44, 79 & 237.

❖ Sharer, C. (1955) The Population Growth of the Bahamas Islands, USA, University of Michigan. Pgs 2-118.

❖ Thompson, C. (1990) *Home from The Contract-The 50th Anniversary of The Contract.*

❖ Triana, P.(1987) *San Salvador-The Forgotten Island*, Spain, Ediciones Beramar.

❖ Will, L. (1961) *Okeechobee Hurricane and the Hoover Dike 3rd Edition*, The Glades Historical Society.

❖ Williams, P.,(1999) *Chronological Highlights in the History of the Bahamas 600 to 1900*, Nassau, Bahamas Historical Society. Pgs. 1, 54.

❖ Wood, D. (1987) *Bahamian Migration to Florida 1898 to 1940*, Florida International University.

❖ www.wunderground.com

❖ www.noaa.gov

❖ www.nasa.gov

❖ www.weather.unisys.com

❖ www.wikipedia.org

❖ www.hurricanecity.com

❖ www.nationalgeographic.com

❖ www.weathersavvy.com

❖ http://www.pbchistoryonline.org

❖ http://www.historicalsocietypbc.org/images/file/Storm_of_28_Teachers_Guide.pdf

❖ http://agora.ex.nii.ac.jp/digital-typhoon/help/world.html.en

The writing of this book has been a highly satisfying project, made so not only by the subject itself but also by the people who have helped and assisted me in some way or the other, so here are the persons I wish to thank: -

My Father and Mother Lofton and Francita Neely
My Aunt and Uncle Coleman and Diana Andrews and family
My Grandmother the late Mrs. Joanna Gibson
Ms. Inger Simms
Mr. Wendall Jones
Mr. Kerry Emanuel
Mr. Christopher Landsea
Mrs. Stephanie Hanna
Mrs. Angela Rahming
Mr. Kevin Hudson
Mr. Dwayne Swaby
Mr. Ray Duncombe
Mr. Ethric Bowe
Mr. Rupert Roberts
Mr. Peter Graham
Mr. Leroy Lowe
The late Mr. William Holowesko
The Hon. Glenys Hanna-Martin
Mr. Murrio Ducille
Mr. Charles and Eddie Carter
Dr. Gail Saunders
Mr. Joshua Taylor and family
Mrs. Patrice Wells
Professor William Gray
Mr. Bryan Norcross
Dr. Steve Lyons
Mr. Phil Klotzbach
Mrs. Betty Thompson-Moss
Mrs. Jan Roberts
Mrs. Nancy Saunders
Ms. Jeffarah Gibson

Ms. Carole Balla
Mrs. Shavaughn Moss
The late Mrs. Macushla Hazelwood
Mr. Rodger Demeritte
Mr. Michael and Phillip Stubbs
Mr. Robert and Dorothy Hazard
Mrs. Debi Murray
Mr. Orson Nixon
Mr. Neil Sealey
Dr. Myles Munroe
Dr. Timothy Barrett
Rev. Theo and Blooming Neely and family
Staff and Management of Logos Bookstore
Staff and Management of The Nassau Guardian Newspaper
Staff and Management of Media Enterprises
Staff and Management of The Tribune Newspaper
Staff and Management of Island 102.9fm
Staff and Management of Star 106.5fm
Staff and Management of Jones Communications Network-JCN &
97.5fm
Staff and Management of Guardian Radio 96.9fm
Staff and Management of the Broadcasting Corporation of the
Bahamas (ZNS)
Staff and Management of the NB12 News
Staff of the Department of Archives
Staff of the Department of Meteorology
Staff of NOAA and National Hurricane Center in Miami
Mr. Jack and Karen Andrews
Mrs. Margaret Jeffers

The good people of the Bahamas and South Florida who opened their
doors, hearts and minds to assist me with this project and provided me
with overwhelming research materials, and many others too numerous to
mention who gave me their take on this devastating hurricane. But most
of all, I would like to thank the many sponsors below who made this book
possible.

J.S. JOHNSON
PEACE OF MIND
INSURANCE AGENTS & BROKERS

34 Collins Ave.
P.O. Box N-8337
Nassau, Bahamas
Phone: 242-322-2341
Fax: 242-323-3720
E-Mail: info@jsjohnson.com
Website: www.jsjohnson.com

Branch Office
Thompson Blvd
P.O. Box N-8337
Nassau, Bahamas
Phone: 242-676-6300
Fax: 242-325-3979
E-Mail: info@jsjohnson.com
Website: www.jsjohnson.com

Branch Office
Soldier Road
P.O. Box N-8337
Nassau, Bahamas
Phone: 242-676-6301
Fax: 242-394-5376
E-Mail: info@jsjohnson.com
Website: www.jsjohnson.com

Sunshine
insurance
(Agents & Brokers) Ltd MARSH
Correspondent

Sunshine House
East Shirley Street
P.O. Box N-3180
Nassau, Bahamas
Phone: 242-502-6500
Fax: 242-394-3101
E-Mail: info@sunshine-insurance.com
Website: www.sunshine-insurance.com

Branch Office
Sunshine Plaza, Blue Hill Road
Nassau, Bahamas
Phone: 242-322-3511
Fax: 242-322-3518
E-Mail: info@sunshine-insurance.com
Website: www.sunshine-insurance.com

BAHAMAS FIRST
FIRST IN INSURANCE. TODAY. TOMORROW.

32 Collins Avenue
P.O. Box SS-6238
Nassau, Bahamas
Telephone: 242-302-3900
Fax: 242-302-3901
Email: info@bahamasfirst.com
Website: www.bahamasfirst.com

Insurance Company of the Bahamas Ltd.
33 Collins Ave.
Nassau, Bahamas
Tel: 242-326-3100/3130/3144 Fax: 326-3132
E-Mail: arahming@icbbahamas.com or
       dosborne@icbbahamas.com
Website: www.icbbahamas.com

SUPER VALUE FOOD STORES LTD.

P.O. Box N-3039
Nassau, Bahamas
Phone: 242-361-5220-4
Fax: 242-361-5583
E-Mail: svfsltd@batelnet.bs

Branch Store-Cable Beach Shopping Center
P.O. Box N-3039
Nassau, Bahamas
Phone: 242-327-8879
Fax: 242-327-3494
E-Mail: svfsltd@batelnet.bs

Branch Store-Mackey Street (Top of the Hill)
P.O. Box N-3039
Nassau, Bahamas
Phone: 242-393-4533
Fax: 242-394-2991
E-Mail: svfsltd@batelnet.bs

Quality Markets Store-Sea Grapes
P.O. Box N-3039
Nassau, Bahamas
Phone: 242-364-0979
Fax: 242-364-0709
E-Mail: svfsltd@batelnet.bs